I0883123

Freedom's Distant Shores

Freedom's Distant Shores

American Protestants and Post-Colonial Alliances with Africa

edited by

R. Drew Smith

Baylor University Press
Waco, Texas USA

©2006 Baylor University Press
Waco, Texas 76798

All Rights Reserved. No part of this publication may be reproduced, stored in a retrieval system, or transmitted, in any form or by any means, electronic, mechanical, photocopying, recording or otherwise, without the prior permission in writing of Baylor University Press.

Cover Design: Pamela Poll

Library of Congress Cataloging-in-Publication Data

Freedom's distant shores : American Protestants and post-colonial alliances with Africa / R. Drew Smith, editor.
p. cm.
Includes index.
ISBN-13: 978-1-932792-37-9 (pbk. : alk. paper)
1. Africa--Church history--20th century. 2. Africa--Church history--21st century. 3. Protestantism--Africa. 4. Christianity and politics--Africa. 5. Church and state--Africa. I. Smith, R. Drew, 1956-

BR1360.F74 2006
276'.0825--dc22

2006019271

Printed in the United States of America on acid-free paper with a minimum of 30% pcw recycled content.

Contents

Preface

Although this project was initiated a few years ago, fortunately most of the writing and editing for this volume took place while I was in South Africa earlier this year as a visiting professor at the University of Pretoria. Being in South Africa at that time was like locating at a major intersection where ecclesiastical and social forces from across Africa and from places further away were actively converging and giving shape to new forms of global religious and social life. In South Africa I interacted with many Christians who represented this diversity—in classrooms, worship venues, and informal settings—and I received important confirmation and critiques of previously formed perceptions, especially about relationships between American and African religious and social life. I am grateful for this opportunity and offer special thanks to the Fulbright Program and to the School of Theology at the University of Pretoria for facilitating my visit. I also extend my gratitude to each of my colleagues who contributed chapters to this volume. Each of them cast significant light on the important issues they addressed. I would also like to thank Carey Newman, director, Baylor University Press, for his strong interest in this project and for the valuable feedback given along the way. My primary conversation partner in all of my scholarly projects has been my wife Angelique. I will always be grateful to her for her support and encouragement.

R. Drew Smith
Autumn 2005

Introduction

R. Drew Smith

American Religious Outreach to Contemporary Africa

A volume focusing on western ecclesiastical involvements in the contemporary affairs of developing nations could seem anachronistic if one accepts the presumed obsolescence of foreign missions as a point of contact between these two worlds. In 1964, an eminent missiologist declared that "the age of missions is at an end," at least in the traditional sense of western and developing nations relating as "sending" and "receiving" countries.[1] One task the present volume sets for itself—against the backdrop of Africa's rapid Christian expansion and evolution into a leading numerical and cultural center of worldwide Christianity[2]—is to show that American Protestant mission involvement in Africa is hardly at an end. The volume also intends to make a case for ways American Protestants might appropriately position themselves within the "coming global Christianity"—in which Africa seems destined to occupy a leading place.[3]

Certainly, predictions of the end to traditional missions voiced in the 1960s and 1970s were based upon real declines in the mission involvements of U.S. mainline denominations. Episcopal missionaries overseas decreased from approximately 500 in the 1930s to fewer than seventy by the mid-1970s;[4] United Methodist missionaries overseas declined from 1,450 in 1968 to 824 in 1974; and the number of U.S. Catholic overseas missionaries dropped from 9,655 in 1969 to 7,649 in 1972.[5] A number of factors contributed to these declines—not least of which were political independence movements in Africa and other parts of the world.[6] According to one historian, with the onset of African independence in the mid-1900s, it became "transparently obvious that African autonomy in government must be paralleled in church affairs, and [therefore] church leadership roles were Africanized rapidly in the years that followed."[7] An early 1970s call by African leadership, including the All Africa Conference of Churches, to impose a temporary moratorium on missionaries made especially clear the intensity of the feelings about indigenizing African churches.[8]

Nevertheless, even as overseas mission involvements by American mainline denominations were tapering off, Africa mission involvements by American Charismatic and Pentecostal denominations were increasing.[9] Worldwide Pentecostal affiliation was placed in 1970 at more than 147,000,000 and in 1995, at more than 605,000,000.[10] That more than two-thirds of these Charismatic and Pentecostal Christians from the 1970 and 1995 totals were located in Africa[11] lends support to claims that Pentecostalism in Africa is one of the fastest growing religious movements in the world.[12]

That a great deal of this modern Pentecostalism traces its roots to late-nineteenth and early-twentieth century America also suggests a significant role for American Pentecostal and Charismatic missionaries in the growth of Pentecostalism in Africa.[13] While long-established U.S. Pentecostal groups such as the Assemblies of God and the predominantly black Pentecostal Assemblies of the World have both maintained significantly strong presences in Africa since the 1910s, a newer wave of American neo-Pentecostal and Charismatic churches began arriving in Africa in large numbers by the 1970s. This wave of neo-Pentecostal and Charismatic ministries, which have included groups such as Rhema Ministries, the Full Gospel Business Men's Fellowship, and many others, have gained tremendous followings and influence among the African masses and have also developed notable political and economic linkages from one African nation to another. The entrepreneurial aspects of many of these ministries are "essentially corporate transnational religious entities . . . that speedily ally with each other and a plethora of smaller independent churches on both practical business matters and matters of faith."[14]

Moreover, churches from the northern hemisphere—and especially U.S. Evangelical and Pentecostal churches—have effectively used print and electronic media sources as a means of extending their reach and influence within the developing world. Presently, close to 34,500 Christian periodicals, serials, magazines, journals, and newspapers globally circulate among approximately 50 million people; and approximately 4,000 Christian radio and television stations globally reach 510 million people per month with Christian programming.[15] Most of these media sources have emanated from the United States and Europe, with American television broadcast ministries such as the Trinity Broadcasting Network and the 700 Club having access to a particularly large number of African television markets and viewers. Although many Africans remain out of reach of these media relayed ministries, these ministries have penetrated some African contexts extensively.[16]

This changing of the guard is one of the central themes of this volume—appropriately so, given that it continues to outpace the limited amount of historical documentation and critical analysis it receives.[17] Chapters in this volume explore the increasing denominational, theological, and political diversity of U.S. church involvement in or with Africa, while providing important details about these contemporary involvements in countries such as Nigeria and South Africa and in other African contexts. Chapters also explore the sometimes culturally and politically insensitive (even neo-colonial) approaches of contemporary American Pentecostal and Evangelical missionaries toward Africa, comparing these approaches with similarly problematic approaches by mainline churches during the colonial era, and contrasting them with the more cautious and chastened approach to mainline denominational mission work in Africa from the mid-twentieth century to the present.

This volume drives home some of the hard lessons of missionary history that certain Evangelical and Pentecostal movements seem to be missing or ignoring in their contemporary involvements with Africa—lessons about appropriately accounting for the social positioning of *sending* churches, the social content of what is sent to Africa, and the social impact of American churches and their mission activities upon the African contexts to which they are sent. The colonial paradigm of foreign exploitation of Africa, then, serves as an implicit and sometimes explicit backdrop for evaluating the more recent U.S.-Africa interactions outlined in the various chapters. Conversely, *post-colonial* here alludes both to the volume's primary timeframe (1950s–present) and to an analytical standard for ecclesiastical and political relations between the United States and Africa—and that standard, as the authors employ here, most often takes the form of an emphasis on African democratic rights.

Historical Trajectories Within U.S.-Africa Relations

While this volume places churches at the center of analysis, this analysis does not approach churches in isolation from the broader range of social, cultural, and political forces that have influenced their attitudes, behaviors, and activities relative to Africa. Particularly, the U.S. government's approach to Africa—as it has variously conceived of and pursued American global interests—has significantly influenced the way that U.S. churches and the American public, broadly speaking, have been disposed toward Africa. Throughout the past century, U.S. churches have typically taken their cues from the U.S. government's behavior toward Africa—mirroring the government's vacillations between goodwill and self-interestedness, compassion and callousness.

Since the time that the United States outlawed its citizens from further purchasing or transporting slaves directly from Africa nearly two hundred years ago, the U.S. government has most often expressed inattention toward Africa (with certain notable exceptions).[18] This inattention to Africa has characterized the American public as well, with concern limited to more or less active cadres of African Americans (initially advocating "back-to-Africa" movements and then more general forms of cultural, political, and religious solidarity with Africa) and of internationally minded white Americans with entrepreneurial, humanitarian, or religious interests in Africa.

In particular, in the late eighteenth century white religious and civic leaders initiated the resettlement of freed blacks in Africa. Through the American Colonization Society, the organization founded to facilitate this activity, approximately twelve thousand African Americans left the United States for Africa during the first half of the nineteenth century to establish colonies along the west coast of Africa.[19] Some of the earliest involvement by U.S. corporations in Africa grew directly out of this episode.[20] During the latter half of the nineteenth century, however, black clergymen and lay leaders such as Alexander Crummell, Henry McNeil Turner, Martin Delaney, and William Blyden primarily propounded black emigrationism. Their efforts led to the exploration of a number of additional sites for black colonies, including the Niger Valley and non African locations such as Haiti and Canada. Land was actually purchased in Haiti and Canada toward this end and about 2,000 blacks were settled in each location.[21] In the early twentieth century, Marcus Garvey's United Negro Improvement Association, consisting of several million African Americans, envisioned returning to Africa to redeem the continent from colonialism.[22] Economic enterprises, including a factory and a steamship line of four ships, were planned to facilitate this endeavor, but neither the economic nor the political dreams of the movement ever fully materialized. Although each of these initiatives were of historical interest (then and now), only a small minority of Americans were concretely involved with Africa through these initiatives.

Africa commitments and involvements by the U.S. public and the U.S. government probably did not expand dramatically up through mid-1900s. However, by the late 1950s, interest in Africa did increase in conjunction with freedom movements in Africa and around the world that remained fairly dynamic—at least through the end of the Cold War and of apartheid in South Africa—and that along the way gained noticeably greater levels of institutionalization within both U.S. governmental and civil society sectors.

With respect to the changing U.S.-Africa climate beginning in the 1950s, the attention was partly constructive, partly less than constructive (to put it mildly)—and, in both instances, largely a response to the wave of decolonization sweeping across the African continent. With African independence from colonial rule, starting with Ghana's independence in 1957, Americans with pre-existing fealty toward Africa were energized, and new cadres of Africa supporters were mobilized toward positive engagement with Africa and African affairs. Beginning in the late 1950s, American students began pushing for a new relationship between the United States and the rest of the world—including Africa—and for fostering relationships based upon improved understanding of other cultures and more humane interactions with them.

Undoubtedly, the independence movement in Africa encouraged a different American approach to Africa, but so did the Civil Rights and Black Power movements in the United States; both forced a reconsideration of racial attitudes and practices. A theological outgrowth of these two movements was the Black Theology movement in the United States; which incorporated many of the black empowerment concerns voiced by the Civil Rights and Black Power movements. All three of these movements contributed to a growing solidarity between African Americans and continental Africans engaged in similar empowerment struggles—especially in southern Africa. Programmatically, the shifting racial equation coalescence on the African and North American continents produced Black Studies, Multicultural Studies, and Study Abroad programs on U.S. college campuses that allowed a significant number of students to connect with other cultures and contexts and to do so more on terms defined by those cultures and contexts. American students, and the broader public, became increasingly exposed to Africa through the writings of African novelists, historians, and social scientists; through relationships on campuses and in communities with an increasingly more visible African population residing within the United States; and through a growing number of opportunities for first hand travel in Africa, including the U.S. Peace Corps and organizations such as Operation Crossroads Africa (OCA). A chapter in this volume by Sandra J. Sarkela and Patrick Mazzeo examines the work of OCA and the Rev. James Robinson, who founded the organization in 1958 and was an early champion of African democratization and of U.S.-Africa partnerships.

A number of other U.S. nongovernmental organizations established from the 1950s through the 1970s focused on Africa, including the American Committee on Africa (1953), AFRICARE (1970), the Washington Office on Africa (1972), and TransAfrica (1977). These organizations, which have drawn on broad networks of support from within the business and civil society sectors (including churches), have monitored and lobbied the U.S. government on policies related to Africa, served as conduits of information and analysis to the American public, and mobilized resources toward African development concerns. A chapter in the volume by Lewis Baldwin details U.S. ecclesiastical and civic coalitions that formed in response to racial oppression and white minority rule in southern Africa (including activities centered in some of the above Africa advocacy organizations), and the impact of leading activists in the United States and South Africa, especially Martin Luther King Jr., on these coalitions.

As Africa emerged during the mid-1900s from the long season of oppression brought on by the nineteenth-century colonial scramble for Africa, it immediately became embroiled in another kind of scramble by northern hemisphere nations to determine the direction in which the continent would move. This time Africa was caught in a fierce *Cold War* competition between the United States and the Soviet Union to align nations with their respective ideological, geopolitical, and material interests. Cold War logic, wherein the U.S. objective was to prevent communist expansion, dominated the U.S. government's approach to Africa from at least the Kennedy Administration through the collapse of the Soviet Union in 1989. African independence, as well as U.S. anticommunist efforts in Cuba and Southeast Asia, picked up steam during Kennedy's presidency; both led Kennedy to take a closer look at developments in Africa than previous presidents had. The Johnson and Nixon administrations also approached Africa mostly out of a desire to prevent the spread of communist influence there. During this period the U.S. government began supporting African leaders who displayed an eagerness to oppose communist advancement within Africa, despite (and sometimes because of) their antidemocratic inclinations. This approach also comes through clearly during the Reagan administration's support of white minority rule in southern Africa. U.S. church relations with Africa did not escape the Cold War distortions of the 1950s through the 1980s. The chapters in this volume by Mark Hulsether and by Sarkela and Mazzeo discuss Cold War influences on mainline U.S. Protestant approaches to Africa during the 1950s and 1960s. My chapter on church-state relations examines the Cold War logic animating U.S. Evangelical and Pentecostal interactions with Africa during the 1980s.

Responding to communist expansion was not always the sole factor guiding U.S. government policy toward Africa during the Cold War years. Key segments of the foreign policy established during the Kennedy, Johnson, Ford, and Carter administrations, "believed in linking liberal policies at home with liberal policies abroad," which contributed to an anticolonial stance and promotion of foreign aid to developing nations on the part of these U.S. administrations as a "means of spreading the liberals' concepts of civil rights and of advancing the New Frontier to the most distant corners of the globe."[23] Nonetheless, the United States has responded to democratic rights and economic development in Africa rather sporadically—as demonstrated, for example, by the fact that the United States has been both a leading provider of the food assistance used to feed starving populations in Africa and a leading supplier of the weapons used to prop up nondemocratic governments and to feed the continent's frequent civil wars and domestic conflicts.

Once the Soviet Union was dissolved, bringing a sudden end to the Cold War, and once the last and most oppressive case of white minority rule gave way a few years later to majority rule in South Africa, U.S. government interest in Africa declined precipitously. Perhaps the retreat did not entirely resume pre-Cold War inattentiveness, but the U.S. government's unresponsiveness to major African crises during the 1990s is suggestive of the low priority placed on Africa in recent years. The 1994 genocide in Rwanda, in which one to two million Rwandans were killed while the United States and other western powers refused to intervene, particularly illustrates this recent egregious neglect. But so too was the U.S. government's failure to play a more active peacemaking role in the decade-long civil wars in Liberia and Sierra Leone during the 1990s, the civil conflict in the Democratic Republic of Congo during the early twenty-first century, and the extremely costly civil war that raged for decades in the Sudan. Two chapters in the volume look at efforts by U.S. churches to stand in the gap as peacemakers in situations of social conflict in Africa—Lutiniko Pedro's chapter on U.S. Mennonites in Angola and Stephen Angell's chapter on U.S. Quaker women in Kenya.

U.S.-Africa policy is central to the analysis of a number of chapters in the volume and, even where not explicitly referenced, forms the backdrop to the various discussions of church involvements in Africa. In either case, U.S. governmental relations with Africa is a central component of an interpretation of American ecclesiastical relations with Africa and of a hermeneutical reading of the chapters in this volume. Some of what should be asked, and is asked in one form or another by many of the volume's contributors, includes: (1) has church behavior toward Africa seemed to acknowledge the larger context of U.S. governmental relations with Africa and the potential or actual ecclesiastical alignments with U.S. governmental policy? and (2) whether acknowledging the governmental policy backdrop or not, in what ways have American church responses to Africa countered the shortcomings or complimented the strengths of U.S. governmental policy toward Africa?

While the case studies within the volume wrestle with some of the considerable social and political limitations of U.S. church involvement with Africa—limitations that are both intrinsic to church institutional life and a function of the constricting social policy and social structural contexts out of which they have operated—certain chapters within the volume consider ways U.S. churches have promoted or should promote ideals that attempt to transcend limitations within the church's social positioning. Dwight Hopkins' chapter focuses on the important social critique of racism and racial injustice that African-American theologians contributed to the U.S. and South African discourse on race. Similarly, Nico Koopman's chapter places U.S. and South African theologies in dialogue, exploring ways that theological frameworks within the two countries assist churches in breaking through the constrictions of the political, economic, and religious parochialism of their western contexts. Marsha Snulligan Haney's chapter underlines the importance of shared benefits and shared power as a post-colonial standard for missiological partnerships between U.S. and African churches. These themes of reciprocity, mutual respect, and commitment to a common good run throughout the volume and serve as important measurements for assessing and approaching social and ecclesiastical relations between the United States and Africa.

Part I

Churches and Democratic Rights in Africa

Chapter 1

Shifting Perspectives on Africa in Mainline Protestant Social Thought

The Case of the Christianity and Crisis *Magazine*

Mark Hulsether

"Among the many journals of opinion published in the United States is one of comparatively short years and small circulation, having a title that suggests a parochial concern relevant only to the very devout."[1] So began an article on the December 1, 1966 financial page of the *Rockland Record*, a newspaper serving a suburb of New York. Why should this newspaper care if, as its article discussed, the small Protestant journal *Christianity and Crisis* withdrew $25,000 from First National City Bank to protest its investments in South Africa?[2]

The *Record* provided clues. "With most periodicals the measure of influence is how many readers," it said. "With '*C&C*' as it is called in church circles, the measure of its readers is who they are." Quoting *Time* magazine, the *Record* judged that "[*C&C*'s] influence is well out of proportion to its size," with subscribers like former secretary of state John Foster Dulles, theologian Paul Tillich, liberal pundit Walter Lippmann, and civil rights leader Martin Luther King Jr.[3] *C&C* enjoyed the prestige of its founder Reinhold Niebuhr, one of the nation's most influential liberal intellectuals, and his longtime colleague and coeditor, John Coleman Bennett of Union Theological Seminary in New York. Its influence was strongest among liberal Protestant academics, clergy, and bureaucrats, including many leaders of mainline seminaries, religious social action agencies, and ecumenical organizations.[4]

C&C also gained attention from secular elites. Consider how it boosted the career of Ernest Lefever, who later helped to spearhead attacks on the programs of the World Council of Churches (WCC) in Africa and was nominated in 1981 to be Ronald Reagan's Assistant Secretary of State for Human Rights. According to Lefever, his big break came in 1954 when he wrote a *C&C* article pressing the WCC to be more realistic about communism. Supreme Court Justice Felix Frankfurter's notice of the article led Paul Nitze (the head of the State Department Policy Planning Staff) to arrange a grant for Lefever to work with him.[5] Although Lefever's career path is atypical for *C&C* because he was among the journal's most conservative writers, stories about *C&C*'s links to power are easy to multiply. Many prominent religious intellectuals, from Cornel West on the left to Michael Novak on the right, built their early reputations largely through writing in *C&C*. Senator Eugene McCarthy and Walter Lippmann helped with fund-raising. Nitze and famed anthropologist Margaret Mead served on its editorial board. Niebuhr served on George Kennan's Policy Planning Team at the State Department and was a key organizer of Americans for Democratic Action.

All this involvement meant that *C&C*'s trickle-down importance was considerable. In 1946 Niebuhr published an article in two versions, one for *C&C*'s seven thousand readers and one for *Life Magazine*'s four million.[6] *The New York Times* often reported on *C&C* editorials. Such evidence does not prove any direct correspondence between *C&C* and an average churchgoer's ideas, or even between *C&C* and the sermons of mainline ministers. It does suggest some broad correlation between trends inside *C&C* and among a wider mainline Protestant constituency.

The *Rockland Record*, thus, had some reason to care about *C&C*'s stance toward South African divestment. This concern in turn helps explain why the *Record* concluded with a warning shot across *C&C*'s bow. It used an argument that hit *C&C* where it hurt. *C&C* prided itself on religiously motivated actions for social justice that remained within the bounds of the pragmatically attainable; its watchword was responsible realism as opposed to idealistic utopianism. But the *Record* pointed out that the return on South African investments was 19 percent compared to an average of 11 percent elsewhere in the world. Therefore, the *Record* noted, *C&C*'s "impact on the realities of business with South Africa remains to be seen."[7]

Such skeptical comments were destined to increase. *C&C*'s protest against First National City Bank was only one blip amid *C&C*'s overall concerns in 1966, a year in which the journal threw itself into protesting the Vietnam War, struggled to come to terms with black power, and debated whether God was dead. Moreover, 1966 was only one moment in a five-decade process in which *C&C* played a key role: the transformation of liberal Protestant social thought in the postwar U.S., and especially the emergence of liberation theologies during the 1960s and 1970s. In this regard we might consider *C&C*'s divestment decision as the tip of an iceberg. As more and more of this iceberg came into view, the warning shots from *C&C*'s right became more insistent. *Newsweek* had praised Bennett's "astute commentary," but as *C&C* steered left the FBI placed his activities under surveillance.[8] *The New York Times* coverage began to drop off, and centrist commentators became less respectful. Meanwhile, attacking from the world of neoconservative foundations, Richard John Neuhaus called *C&C* the "little magazine that trashes the Reinhold Niebuhr legacy that it claims."[9] In 1993 *C&C* folded, mainly because of a general dwindling in resources at its two key institutional bases of support: Union Seminary and ecclesiastical bodies housed at the nearby Interchurch Center, including the WCC, the National Council of Churches, and several mainline denominations.

Despite *C&C*'s struggle to survive, its history was by no means a steady downhill slide after the 1960s. *C&C* remained one of the premier forums of Protestant debate on public issues, especially in the late 1970s (when its circulation peaked) and in the early 1980s. According to Gayraud Wilmore, during the 1960s and 1970s "it was difficult to find someone who was really making waves on the Christian social justice front who did not read *C&C*"; its "public was always small, but savvy . . . relatively free of the most doddering pieties and conservatism of the mainline, and yet influential enough to effect strategic changes in certain sectors."[10] After *C&C* folded, a struggle for ascendancy in mainline Christianity continued between neoconservatives and former *C&C* constituents who carried forward its legacy; although neoconservatives controlled a disproportionate share of financial resources, the sides were otherwise matched fairly evenly.

This article explores *C&C*'s writing on Africa, with special attention to the years leading up to its turn to liberation theologies. We will discuss both evolving coverage of African issues, and background presuppositions about theological ethics and U.S. global policies that informed this coverage. Within *C&C*'s discourse on world affairs, Africa was overshadowed by Europe in the 1940s, by both Asia and Europe in the 1950s, by Vietnam in the 1960s, and by Latin America in the 1970s and 1980s. Much of its writing on Africa, therefore, took place within wider treatments of relations between the U.S. government and/or the WCC on one side and the so-called third world on the other—a shorthand term we will use for former European colonies in Asia, Africa, and Latin America. In this context, *C&C* published a steady stream of commentary about Africa, culminating in the 1980s when South Africa was one of *C&C*'s top priorities.

C&C made striking changes within this stream of writing. Consider how its 1966 divestment decision fits within its long-term trajectory. Although *C&C* always criticized apartheid, thirteen years earlier one of its board members had written a glowing report on South African government plans for its bantustans, the notorious "homelands" imposed by the white minority government to keep the black majority divided, impoverished, and dependent. He saw a rosy future for bantustans through pro-Western economic development. Such paternalism and bullish hopes for African development survived into the 1960s; for example, a *C&C* writer could claim that "we have a clear obligation to take the Cold War to Africa" and that without the benefits of European colonization there would be widespread "cannibalism, slavery, and torture, all sanctioned by superstition."[11] At the same time, also leading up to *C&C*'s divestment decision, a growing stream of articles supported anticolonial movements—*C&C* writers backed South Africa's African National Congress (ANC) as early as 1952—and argued that capitalist development would reproduce paternalism and dependence. In later years, *C&C* valorized African liberation theologians like Desmond Tutu and defended the WCC's funding of armed revolutionaries in Southern Africa.

We cannot understand *C&C*'s positions on Africa apart from its overall transformation, which I have discussed in detail elsewhere.[12] Until the late 1960s, *C&C* was the voice of an editorial board of professors centered on Union Seminary; thereafter, an independent staff loosely related to Union ran the journal. *C&C* writers always worked within the tradition of theologically liberal and socially "prophetic" Protestantism; however, there was significant change in the perspectives from which they developed their arguments. *C&C* was founded with a paradigm that blended a stress on God's transcendent judgment on human pride, standoffishness toward Progressive optimism about social change (including the optimism of the left about revolution and of pacifists about peacemaking), and a commitment to liberal social action. Before the mid-1960s *C&C*'s specific applications of these themes moved in harmony with liberal U.S. elites. *C&C*'s personnel, perspective, and institutional matrix were almost entirely white male. Despite its rhetoric of critiquing pride and power, it was part of the social formation of Cold War liberalism; its top political concerns were anticommunism, New Deal type economic reform, and Western economic development. At one time or another *C&C* justified scenarios for nuclear war "in retaliation with all possible restraint," attacked the Kinsey Report for documenting "sexual perversions," worried that desegregating the army might be "going too far" strategically, and stated that "in the modern day domestic [as opposed to international] problems have been tolerably solved."[13]

Over time *C&C* listened to new voices and shifted toward standpoints that placed it in significantly greater tension with dominant social formations. We should not overstate the journal's early conservatism because some of the above examples are drawn from the more conservative side of its dialectical approach—an approach that its writers used to promote the boldest left-liberal activism that they perceived to be self-critical and constructive. More radical uses of this dialectic, nevertheless, came to the forefront. *C&C* became dissatisfied with the ways that its inherited positions assumed links to status quo power structures, and shifted toward liberation theologies that approached issues of social inequality from the standpoint of oppressed people and explored the possibilities of radical change. This shift polarized

C&C's constituents and led to different alliances. By the 1970s *C&C* advocated democratic socialism, feminism, and gay/lesbian rights; it could call the U.S. a parasite on the third world and support a demand for reparations from white churches to finance a revolutionary black power movement.[14] Whatever we say about continuity and change in *C&C*—and both are important—these are striking changes in the deployment of its moral reasoning and its place within structures of power. Let us explore how, within this framework, *C&C*'s stances toward Africa unfolded.

The "Classic" Vision of Cold War Liberalism in the Late 1940s and 1950s

C&C moved within the tradition of theologically liberal and socially "prophetic" Protestantism. During the early twentieth century, the formative years of *C&C*'s founders, this tradition took the form of the social gospel movement. Roughly speaking, the social gospel provided theological warrants and institutional support for liberal Progressivism.[15] Although it could express middle-class complacency and Anglo-American chauvinism, it could also take left-leaning activist forms. Niebuhr promoted the latter approach during the 1920s and 1930s. In his application, the prophetic books of the Bible were not otherworldly and apocalyptic; rather, Niebuhr stressed this-worldly exhortation and organizing for democratic socialism and against militarism. For most of his career he taught at Union Seminary and participated in various ecumenical groups, although he branched out from this base to a wide network of secular activism. His theology critiqued the shortcomings of the status quo in the name of God's will for social justice. Despite the social gospel's limitations, in the hands of Niebuhr and his allies during the interwar years its challenges to elite policies were not trivial.

Niebuhr's influence peaked in the 1940s—with *C&C* as a key forum he used to communicate with Protestant leaders—when he rearticulated the social gospel into what became known as "Christian realism." Now prophetic Christianity became less a protest against the sins of U.S. capitalism and militarism and more a "realistic" defense of U.S. nationalism against external enemies. At first Niebuhr mainly worried about Nazism. (*C&C*'s name reflects this; the original crisis that precipitated its founding in 1941 was the rise of Hitler.) Increasingly he focused on a crisis of communism; his prophetic attacks on totalitarianism targeted the sins of Stalin.

By the time Niebuhr founded *C&C*, he was calling on Christians to scale down their optimism about the prospects for peace and social justice—albeit without abandoning reform that was suitably "chastened"—and to pay more attention to the inevitable limits of human nature. At *C&C*'s birth, he used such arguments largely to attack social gospelers at *Christian Century* magazine who opposed U.S. participation in World War II. Their opposition was not based on any sympathy for Nazism or lack of concern for international issues; rather it reflected their judgment that the fundamental social conflict was internal to the U.S., between democratic socialists and anti-imperialists on one side versus a military-industrial complex supporting Henry Luce's vision of an "American Century" on the other.[16] In contrast to the *Christian Century*, Niebuhr reframed the central conflict as democracy and the U.S. military together versus external totalitarians on a global stage. He saw his opponents' advocacy of peaceful internationalism and anti-imperialism (a priority he had earlier shared) as highly inappropriate around 1940; he compared it to redesigning one's garden while a tornado threatened to destroy one's house. For Niebuhr, "the sin of imperialism . . . may well be a less dangerous form of selfishness than an irresponsible attitude toward the task of organizing the human community." All world powers (including the U.S.) needed to keep their pride in check—but fortunately the U.S. system had checks and balances that accomplished this goal better than most other countries. Moreover, "only those who have no sense of the profundities of history would deny that various nations and classes, various social groups and races, are at various times placed in such a position that a special measure of the divine mission in history falls upon them. In that sense God has chosen us in this fateful period."[17]

According to Niebuhr, responsible Christians understood the need to embrace lesser evils. In the 1940s this meant supporting the (less-than-pacifist) use of military force to uphold democracy and (less-than-egalitarian) global economic development against the greater evil of totalitarianism. If people who claimed Jesus as a role model felt uneasy about such compromises, they should review the teachings of St. Paul about the fallen human condition. They should trust in God to clean their dirty hands rather than try to save the world themselves. Critics called this position an apology for militarism and neocolonialism. Niebuhr himself called it "imperialistic realism," although he preferred "international responsibility."[18]

C&C's support for U.S. global policies in the late 1940s assumed the existence of a unified communist movement that threatened world conquest. Like many others in the U.S., *C&C* perceived communism as a threat to "democracy"—its shorthand term for a vision blending liberal political rights, freedom of religion, and a global free market system. Against this background, three themes provided the context for *C&C*'s writing on Africa: defense against communism, cautions about excessive reliance on military force, and the promotion of international economic development. Let us consider these in turn.

Since *C&C* had already argued that the "defensive" use of atomic bombs could be justified as a lesser evil, it easily endorsed other U.S. military projects that it perceived as defensive. Consider its stance toward the Truman Doctrine of 1947. This U.S. policy replaced Great Britain as the top colonial policeman in the Middle East, beginning with support for conservative Greek elites against a communist-led coalition and extending to a commitment to intervene anywhere in the world to assist "free peoples who are resisting subjugation by armed minorities or outside pressures." When Truman and his advisors prepared a speech to announce this policy, they scrapped their first draft, commenting that it "sound[ed] like an investment prospectus" when they needed to "scare the hell of out of the American people."[19] *C&C*'s editorial on the finished speech reflected similar priorities: it noted that U.S. interests in Middle Eastern oil could justify U.S. policy, but it stressed "a firm stand . . . [is] the most effective way to stop the expansionist drive of the Soviet Union."[20]

On issue after issue, *C&C*'s judgment on global issues flowed within the currents of liberal anticommunist opinion.[21] Economics and fear converged again in 1950 when the U.S. opted (in the NSC-68 document drafted by Nitze) for a military remobilization linked to escalating the Cold War. Throughout the late 1940s, U.S. leaders feared that reduced government spending might trigger another economic collapse like the Great Depression. They hoped to use Keynesian economic strategies to keep the economy humming, and their path of least resistance toward this end was to minimize state intervention that reduced corporate profits and to maximize opportunities for the U.S. to wield its economic power on a global "level playing field" of free trade. Military Keynesianism—concentrating government investment on a military buildup—seemed especially promising: it had revived the economy during World War II and it minimized corporate resistance to pro-labor dimensions of the New Deal. As 1950 approached, this path also appeared more politically viable in Congress than renewing the Marshall Plan (and related initiatives in Japan) to support the global economy. Dean Acheson recalled that "Korea came along and saved us"—that is, the Korean War eliminated the specter of Congress cutting funds for military Keynesianism.[22] Because the war began just as Mao triumphed in the Chinese revolution and the Soviet Union acquired atomic bombs, there was ample evidence for scaring the hell out of U.S. taxpayers. *C&C* speculated that "history may record that the Third World War began on June 25, 1950—if historians continue to inhabit the earth."[23] In light of this prediction, it is remarkable that *C&C* showed no doubt that U.S. policy in Korea was inevitable.

C&C's defense of U.S. military policy appeared within a matrix of writing focused more narrowly on theology.[24] Many of these articles reflected the involvement of *C&C* personnel in the ecumenical movement, especially around 1954 when the WCC met in Evanston, Illinois. *C&C* followed ecumenical news, and its articles were part of debates within the WCC.[25] How did theology relate to the Cold War? Niebuhr wrote of an "affinity at one point between democracy and Christianity: the toleration which democracy requires is difficult to maintain without Christian humility; and the challenges to pretensions of every kind which are furnished in the give and take of democratic life" provide "strong external supports for the Christian grace of humility."[26] According to other articles, "the perennial choice with which man is confronted—God or an idol—reduces itself, under contemporary conditions, to the stark alternative; *God or Stalin*." Communism had an "erroneous conception of human nature"—a "utopian illusion that the abolition of a social institution will redeem man of sin."[27] Secular leaders echoed these ideas. In 1948 Niebuhr appeared on the cover of the twenty-fifth anniversary issue of *Time*. *Time* and *Life Magazine* often featured him, as when *Time* reviewed his *Nature and Destiny of Man* under the title "Sin Rediscovered."[28]

C&C's first theme, military resistance to communism, was constantly shadowed by its second—cautions against overemphasizing military confrontation, whether as a result of a crusade mentality or unchristian pride and hatred. Sometimes its cautions did little more than exhort readers to support what U.S. government leaders had already decided, but to support it more reluctantly with a tragic sensibility. For example, let us reconsider *C&C*'s editorial on the Truman Doctrine. *C&C* would have preferred to see the U.S. intervene in Korea through the United Nations. When Truman spoke of "our date with destiny," *C&C* worried that this evoked Manifest Destiny. *C&C* also discussed evidence of Soviet weakness, thus qualifying U.S. claims about Soviet expansionism. It refused to endorse the war insofar as it was merely "for preservation of an economic system" and even compared U.S. allies in Greece to the notorious Spanish fascist Francisco Franco. *C&C* briefly acknowledged these issues, but overrode them with anticommunist arguments. It summed up its position with the idea that U.S. policy was tragic and must be undertaken self-critically.[29]

In the 1950s, *C&C*'s critiques of U.S. policy were sharpest (or least qualified) when discussing Asia. At times *C&C* merely sounded more critical without challenging any concrete policies because it stood with Democrats like Harry Truman against the Republican China Lobby; it stressed the bankruptcy of plans to roll back communism in Asia, and decried "hysterical journals" that hammered on the Democrats for their supposed "loss of China."[30] Its criticisms went further. *C&C* clearly regretted the legacy of imperialism and spoke forcefully against further military interventions. Bennett's 1950 article, "The Problem of Asiatic Communism," set forth reasoning used in many editorials about both Asia and Africa. Reflecting on a trip to Japan, Bennett identified the key problem of Asian societies as poverty and argued that "social revolution is overdue." For many Asians "Communism is the only movement that has a program that seems drastic enough to be relevant to the economic needs."[31] On Bennett's trip, listeners neither rallied to his rhetoric about freedom nor perceived a Soviet hand everywhere; they resisted Bennett's contention that communist ideas inevitably led to totalitarianism. Worst of all, said Bennett, Marxist propaganda had convinced them that Westerners were the real imperialists. In light of this situation, U.S. military pressure would make things worse. Asians needed programs modeled on the

New Deal and informed by Christian understandings of human nature. Only this approach could address core issues and stop the "threat of indirect aggression" through the spread of communist ideas.[32]

C&C's consensus on minimizing military strategies in the third world blended two lines of thought. One was Bennett's logic of relative trust and respect for revolutionary nationalists, linked to a critique of colonialism. In Africa the leading example was *C&C*'s attention to struggles in South Africa, where it was deeply disturbed by the rise of the National Party after 1948 and the theological defense of apartheid by the Dutch Reformed Church of South Africa. In 1952 *C&C* published a lengthy analysis by Z. K. Matthews championing the Defiance campaign of civil disobedience by the African National Congress.[33] Blended with this approach was a second line of thought: that military intervention was not a promising way to advance U.S. self-interest (whether or not this dovetailed with anticolonialism) in countries that lacked "viable" cultures for democracy. Although *C&C* would later use this second idea in sharp attacks on the arrogance of U.S. Vietnam policy, during the 1950s it was more like friendly advice to U.S. elites that they might not attain their goals by intervening in certain places—perhaps because local elites were corrupt, or too many people were leftists, or the economy was too far removed from industrial capitalism.

In all these arguments, *C&C*'s intentions were good; in general the journal is a fine example of an ideal that Melani McAlister calls "benevolent supremacy."[34] Nevertheless *C&C* often unpacked its idea of "unviable" civilizations with racist and/or paternalistic presuppositions. Writers judged that nations emerging from colonialism were like children and sprouting flowers not yet capable of democracy, that "millions of Africans are not yet ready for modern political leadership of any kind," and that Latin American Catholicism was "unable to develop that type of individual who is fitted for life in a democratic society." The problem in Latin America was that Protestant theology "creates responsible individuals who are the ideal citizens of a democracy, while the Catholic sacramental-sacerdotal system fails precisely at this point." Without help, the Latin American Catholic "will always continue to be a minor" who is "incapable of practicing liberty."[35] Statements like these were common well into the 1960s. According to Niebuhr, "democracy was not viable in unreconstructed feudal economies" like those in Latin America, where the leaders "obviously do not have the resources for correcting their own faults." In Africa, the West had been a "tutor in civilization to these primitive cultures" but they show a "fever of resentment." Speaking for *C&C*'s right wing, Lefever wrote that "in terms of health, economic well-being and respect for human rights . . . the net impact of European colonialism in every area has been good." Without it, "cruelty, cannibalism, slavery and torture, all sanctioned by superstition and abetted by self-serving witch doctors would be widespread."[36]

Although *C&C* never failed to note that sinful human nature gave all nations (including the U.S.) a tendency to abuse power, it normally assumed that imperialism was a European problem. Even so, according to Niebuhr, "Western imperialism was morally ambiguous rather than purely evil"; he found it "irrelevant" when Dutch Protestants repented after they "lost Indonesia" since the Dutch had "made solid contributions, advertently or inadvertently, to the budding Indonesian nation." He stated that communists should not describe the U.S. as imperialist, given that "we were never imperial in the classical sense of the word" and "the one portion of our 'empire,' namely the Philippines, was given its independence without a struggle." When twenty-nine nations formed the nonaligned movement at the Bandung Conference of 1955, Niebuhr conceded only one of their complaints: that the U.S. placed excessive stress on military solutions in its Asian policy, which "has given the colored part of the world this wrong picture of the realities."[37] Despite *C&C*'s many caveats about U.S. military policy and its desire to distance the United States from the taint of imperialism, *C&C*'s overall tension with U.S. policy on these fronts was consequently limited.

C&C's second geo-political theme—its qualified cautions about militarism and empire that we have been discussing—shaded into its third theme: full-fledged advocacy of nonmilitary forms of U.S. influence, which offered the hope of containing communism in a positive way. *C&C* enthusiastically supported economic development based on integration into the world capitalist market. This support does not mean that *C&C* favored the wide-open free market approach that Henry Luce championed in the Cold War era; and Milton Friedman propounded in later years. *C&C* saw such approaches fostering economic injustice and excessive individualism, whereas *C&C* favored government mechanisms, roughly modeled on the New Deal, for redistributing wealth within each country. Any proposal, however, that *C&C* judged incipiently communist was out of bounds, as were autarkic policies in Latin America and elsewhere.

In 1948 *C&C*'s board judged that the "present foreign policy . . . is essentially correct." The U.S. was like a doctor using the Marshall Plan to help heal an impoverished world; it should extend the Marshall Plan to Asia, carrying it out behind a shield of military containment from India to Japan. Failing this, *C&C* promoted a program called Point Four and a related WCC initiative. "If only the people of America could catch a vision of the enormous possibilities of this enterprise, and take fire!" preached one editorial, "so that again this country might be animated by a sense of mission . . . [and] a purpose broader and more constructive than that of the containment of Russian Communism by military might." By 1961 one article described Africa as a new front of the Cold War, where the U.S. might be "required to intervene" and where "our guiding principle must be to maintain access to all of Africa."[38] An article by a former member of Truman's Council of Economic

Advisors made it clear that this included economic access. After discussing "international economic integration," he concluded that the

> basic requirement is that each country be willing to give up possible gains in specific clashes of interest in order to reap for itself, and assume for others, the larger advantages of a peaceful, stable, prosperous, developing world. Responsibility in this as in other matters is correlative with strength. The lead must be taken by the powerful and prosperous.[39]

No doubt this advice was good in many contexts; however, *C&C* often used development as a panacea for problems that were more deeply rooted. For example, *C&C* repeatedly tried to imagine finessing the Israel-Palestine conflict through an economic development project modeled on the Tennessee Valley Authority, perhaps on the Jordan or Euphrates River. As a by-product of the imagined growth in prosperity, *C&C* hoped that Palestinians might be persuaded to give up their claims.[40] In general *C&C* touched lightly on the drawbacks of capitalist development for the people it disadvantaged. *C&C's* most flagrantly uncritical support for development appeared in a 1953 article on South Africa. Based on a short visit, Henry Pitney Van Dusen judged that the "wave of the future bears the cause not of Nationalism but of moderation." Speaking about the government technocrats who oversaw economic development in bantustans, he wrote, "I seldom have met a more competent or enlightened group of highly trained and informed social scientists." They had "detailed evidence of the well nigh limitless economic potential of the 'reserved areas.'" And they were committed to the "total advance of the population, not merely economic progress but economic, educational, social, cultural and spiritual factors in their organic unity."[41]

When reading *C&C's* calls for developmentalist solutions to third world conflicts, one is often unsure whether to interpret its arguments as prophetic critiques of the dangers and blindnesses of existing military policies or as something more like cheerleading for the American Century. In a sense it does not matter. In another sense, however, the point is crucial. *C&C's* rhetoric justifying U.S. economic expansion was very powerful because the rhetoric was most prone to self-deception and least vulnerable to critique when *C&C's* progressive vision of expansion through global capitalist development was implicit within overtly antiprogressive critiques designed to deflate alternative positions based on military force and/or socialist utopianism. *C&C* could easily second-guess U.S. elites when they launched military crusades because *C&C's* theology stressed how all regimes should keep their pride in check. When, however, the U.S. projected economic power and sought to create an ever-expanding market based on each group pursuing its self-interest—when it promoted a level playing field upon which the U.S. was the dominant force because its rivals had been largely leveled to rubble during World War II—*C&C* could present this view as an example of *criticizing* U.S. expansionism and imperial pretension. *C&C* managed to perceive the dominant strategies of global capitalism being undertaken with a defensive posture, in the name of a "humble acceptance of the fallen nature of humanity."[42]

Evolving Liberalism and Emerging Polarization, 1955 to 1965

After 1955 whenever a space for "responsible" cultural and political criticism opened in mainstream U.S. liberal opinion, *C&C* moved into it. Since the journal moved in harmony with the rise of Kennedy-style liberalism, we should not describe its overall stance as sharply critical of U.S. policy before the mid-1960s; nevertheless, its changes were not trivial. *C&C* withdrew its justifications for U.S. nuclear policy and identified deeply with the civil rights movement. It expanded its mental map of constituents, playing a key role in building alliances between elite Protestants and groups they had earlier excluded, notably liberal Catholics, black churches, and (after 1970) Christian feminists. Near the leading edge of this exploration—second only to civil rights and the Vietnam War in its impact—was *C&C*'s dialogue with Christians from Asia, Africa, and Latin America in the WCC.[43] Through this dialogue *C&C* increasingly focused on the gap between lived experience and the rhetoric of democratic responsibility in the former colonies.

None of these changes happened without resistance. Because *C&C* had always sought to be self-critical and to side with victims of oppression, it naturally considered the perspectives of blacks and third world colleagues as events forced these people into its field of vision. Because of *C&C*'s preference for peace, it naturally rethought the Cold War as 1950s anticommunism lost momentum. Whenever one *C&C* writer rethought an inherited position, however, another writer typically stepped forward in reaction, determined to pass on a Cold War vision intact.

In retrospect we know that these trends would ripen—that *C&C* would become frustrated with the status quo, advocate radical change, and identify with black militants and third world leaders who saw themselves separate from liberal elites and opposed to them. Already in 1966, one writer saw "no indication that anyone in political power really takes the gospel very seriously." He called churches to strengthen their alliance with oppressed people, even if this meant risking their "channel to the power structure of the nation through [their] influential members."[44] *C&C*, however, did not enjoy our advantages of hindsight between 1955 and 1965. Polarization remained in the future, and *C&C* saw itself as part of an ongoing New Deal coalition. Its goal was less to critique the limits of liberal policies than to overcome resistance to them. *C&C* sought a balance between its more liberal and more conservative writers, and most of its articles from its "far right" to "far left" endorsed policies of U.S. elites.[45]

During a debate about the Suez Crisis of 1956, *C&C*'s most forceful "pro-third world" writers supported (on the surface) nothing more radical than U.S. policy. This debate was nevertheless one of *C&C*'s first major controversies between writers who maintained a strong Cold War paradigm and those who began to focus on "North-South" issues.[46] During the crisis, Egyptian leader Gamal Abdel Nasser seized the Suez Canal in the name of pan-Arab nationalism. A British-French-Israeli military force then invaded Egypt to reclaim the canal. President Eisenhower and Secretary of State John Foster Dulles (a longtime *C&C* associate) were forced to choose between angering one ally or another, and they sided with Egypt. In this context *C&C*'s editors spoke about their "surprising disagreements."[47] Failing to reach consensus, they published a position paper by Kenneth Thompson with several critiques, igniting a long-running controversy.

For Thompson, the crisis represented a decline of NATO just when unity was desperately needed against the Soviets, who intervened in Hungary at the same time. He complained of a "legalistic-moralistic" approach in which "peace, anticolonialism, and the UN [were] invested with absolute ethical value." He saw this approach as a "substitute for discriminate moral and political judgments"; it formed "the new creed of a crusading, conservative...movement." While moralists talked abstractly about colonialism, European weakness "created a vacuum into which Soviet influence has flowed"—a result worse than colonialism. "Historians may record that with [the U.S. policy] we lost the 'Cold War' and paved the way to a third world war."[48] Niebuhr agreed, decrying "fatuous idealism" and stating that he normally opposed colonialism, but he could not do so when Egypt "develops imperialistic ambitions of its own, seeks to dominate the Islamic world and gets its hand on the life-line of European economy." UN condemnations of the European-Israeli intervention were irrelevant, Niebuhr judged, because "the UN without a strong Anglo-American core of power becomes a rudderless ship."[49]

At *C&C*'s anticolonialist pole, a reader from India attacked Thompson's "occidental centrism." Bennett charged that Thompson "sees the present crisis too exclusively in the context of the 'Cold War.'" Shrugging off the accusation of abstract moralism, Bennett proposed to talk about a specific "attack on Egyptians as a reversion to the worst kind of colonialism." He noted that Thompson refused to "see the problem even a little from the point of view of Egypt and the other Arab nations." Perhaps Thompson himself was the unrealistic theorist blinded by his presuppositions. Would United States support for Great Britain and France really advance United States interests? Would it not backfire as an anticommunist tactic by alienating most of the world's people? Could it really defend oil pipelines? Eisenhower and Dulles should be commended for respecting "the emerging Afro-Asian bloc which is, to be sure, dominated by undiscriminating anticolonial resentments but represents half of the world's people and has become a third force with which we and the Communists must reckon." Accused of ignoring a threat to U.S. vital interests, Bennett replied that if there were such interests, the United States could not defend them without Arab cooperation. Thompson revealed "the danger of thinking of Arabs as though they were like the American Indians and could be managed or pushed around by us."[50]

Such controversies were important for *C&C*'s transformation because they dramatized that not all conflicts translate well into Cold War morality plays. One of *C&C*'s best articles on the Middle East in the 1950s made a virtue of its inability to forge one single narrative; it presented the Middle East as a kaleidoscope of experience, which did not match Western assumptions.[51] Such testing of Cold War paradigms was not limited to the Middle East; on the contrary, it was generalized. For example, Herbert Butterfield called the United States and Great Britain to reorient their policies, since they had been "tripped into being on the wrong side of . . . the primary issue in international affairs" and had been "put in retreat by the problem of resentful people who are under some form of subjection." Defending the status quo was morally indefensible and had the practical effect of helping the Soviets. Butterfield denied that the Suez Crisis, the Algerian revolution, and other related conflicts should be compared to the Munich Crisis and the Cold War. Rather than "seek to hold the fort, to dam the flood," said Butterfield, the West should support alternatives to the neocolonial status quo that were equally committed to the material well-being of popular majorities as communism, but more committed to democratic freedom.[52]

Although tension was growing between Butterfield's vision and *C&C*'s classic paradigm, for the moment *C&C* channeled its hopes into support for Eisenhower's Mideast diplomacy, programs like Kennedy's Alliance for Progress, and various UN initiatives. In 1956 George Shepherd, a minister with experience in Uganda, endorsed the rising African voice in the UN and presented Father Trevor Huddleston's work in educating black South Africans as a model for Christian mission. He described the failure to defend Christian schools like Huddleston's against pressure from the apartheid government as a "sign of Western decadence, like our resignation to Mussolini's rape of Ethiopia." Shepherd condemned the Mau Mau rebellion in Kenya as "despicable terrorism," but presented the white reaction to it as equally bad; he encouraged churches to focus on underlying social justice issues rather than repression. According to Shepherd, the United States "is not economically tied into an empire" and has "historical sympathy with colonial peoples." As the Cold War cooled, the United States should collaborate with the UN to help colonialism evolve into "not simply a device of great evil but also a potential for great good as the means of transition from primitive societies into developed civilizations." According to Shepherd, the United States could act as "the mediating power of justice between the conflicting claims of the European colonial powers versus the ex-colonial and colonial peoples. In Christian terms this would be the introduction of the law of love in its transcendent respect for the dignity of each man, regardless of race, creed, or culture."[53]

In the early 1960s, most of *C&C*'s writing on economic development remained within the patterns we have already noted. It often remained paternalistic, as when Niebuhr bemoaned how the Congo crisis of the early 1960s was caused when "hapless Belgians set untutored tribesmen adrift before they could govern themselves." Often it extended familiar logic; for example, after the Cuban revolution, Thompson wrote that the United States had claimed a sphere of interest in the Americas because it "could not afford to allow imperialism in Latin America to go unanswered." Gunboat diplomacy had been morally ambiguous, but at least it "expressed the realities of the American position." Now, Cuba confronted the United States with a military threat if it allied with the Soviets and an economic threat if it successfully rebelled against "alleged American injustices." In the latter case "the symbolic effect elsewhere would be far-reaching and tragic." The best way forward was to increase economic development aid in Latin America.[54]

However, not all *C&C* analysis merely extended earlier trends during the decade after 1955. *C&C* theorized about development in more sophisticated ways, and variations emerged among the *kinds* of development it recommended. In an especially illuminating article, Elisha Greifer began with observing that radical ideas were gaining influence in many third world nations that faced intense poverty and injustice. He asked, "How, then, are we to think about the revolutionary temper which is so distasteful to our own?" Citing a book by Louis Hartz, Greifer argued that U.S. history had never provided conditions in which radicalism could become attractive since most U.S. citizens were liberal individualists.[55] Shifting gears from this view of distinctive U.S. identity to the vision of universal progress that often accompanied it, Greifer interpreted the "distasteful" revolutionaries using Walter Rostow's book, *The Stages of Economic Growth.* All nations modernized through stages similar to the rise of capitalism in Europe and the U.S.; however, unscrupulous radicals could exploit social turmoil and nostalgia at "danger points" during the transition from tradition to modernity. Greifer suggested that wise leaders should maintain stability by pursuing a responsible evolutionary road rather than overturning traditions too quickly. The issue was how to relate these insights to specific cases. For example, "should Castro be overthrown?"[56]

Armed with such theories, *C&C* had resources to support authoritarian allies of U.S. elites against revolutionaries in Africa and elsewhere, on the grounds that at least modernizing authoritarians, while not to be supported complacently, might be lesser evils and keep developing nations on track toward a democratic future. Reading such arguments, one might easily forget that they presupposed a universal "track" of development—in bad communist and good democratic variations—which every nation had to travel.

Greifer stated explicitly that "sooner or later all 'traditional' agrarian economies develop."[57] As they passed through Rostow's four stages—preconditions for take-off, take-off, drive to maturity, and high mass consumption—U.S. investment (both government aid and corporate speculation) might help jump-start their take-offs and speed their progress to maturity. Greifer's explicit statement of this theme, however, was somewhat atypical. Many *C&C* writers implicitly shared Griefer's faith in economic progress, while they explicitly offered a barrage of antiprogressive arguments stressing the limits of U.S. power to promote its ideals. Such arguments extended *C&C*'s earlier idea that since democracy was not "viable" in certain places, it was a utopian fantasy—at best sentimental and perhaps dangerous—to aspire for democracy everywhere. In this way *C&C* was able to understand its support for "modernizing" third world dictators as an alternative to liberal idealism, not as an example of such idealism.[58]

C&C's search for optimum techniques to manage a process of modernization could be—and at this time usually was—turned against revolutionaries such as Castro or Ghana's Kwame Nkrumah, either for moving too quickly or starting down the wrong (pro-communist) road to development. *C&C* could support the likes of Joseph Mobutu in Zaire, whose 1965 military coup it welcomed as the "statesmanlike act of a courageous man" whose "ambition is disciplined by an informed patriotism."[59] The logic of managing development, however, could also be turned around and deployed against U.S. policies, especially if one inquired about the practical limits of U.S. power. Even as Greifer aimed his intellectual guns at Cuba, he also asked whether—in the event that the U.S. overthrew Castro—a successor whom the U.S. picked would be more legitimate. If democracy was not viable in Cuba, perhaps Castro (not Batista) could be the preferred lesser evil. Even though Niebuhr stated that some third world dictators "may be bastards but are at least our bastards"—echoing Franklin Roosevelt's comment about the notorious Dominican strongman, Rafael Trujillo—*C&C* did not always agree with its government's application of this logic.[60] At some point "our bastards" could be seen not as realistically restraining others too impatient for change, but as themselves moving too slowly or ineptly. U.S. support for them could be criticized for its universalist pretensions, rather than lauded for restraining the universalist idealism of their left-wing adversaries.

Where did this crossover point fall? In the Dominican and Cuban cases *C&C* waffled, showing greater sympathy for the left than U.S. policymakers, but doing so more in the spirit of friendly advice than sharp dissent; for example, Bennett called Castro a "distasteful nuisance" but not an "intolerable danger."[61] In the case of Vietnam, *C&C* finished waffling by the mid-1960s; thereafter, an antigovernment application of this argument became its standard approach.

Prior to the 1960s, the WCC's ideas about what it called "areas of rapid social change" were similar to Griefer's on third world revolution. In 1955 the

WCC refocused its vision of "the responsible society"—its term for the same ideals of liberal democracy, anticommunism, and regulated capitalist development that *C&C* promoted—from Europe to the third world. It also shifted its postwar work with European refugees toward international development projects. The WCC exhorted first world Christians to appreciate "the economic implications of world community and the role of [Western] economic and technical aid." Addressing the third world, it sought "responsible emancipation" from tradition that successfully negotiated dangers much like Greifer's: a breakdown of rural life due to urbanization, the erosion of community morals, and the rise of communist movements.[62]

By the 1960s, many WCC leaders argued that such thinking, although sometimes helpful, could also be used to justify the repression of popular movements and to justify economic policies with mixed practical results for the majority of people. Ecumenical dialogue introduced *C&C* to perspectives unavailable in the mainstream U.S. press; it created cognitive dissonance when missionaries and trusted international colleagues began to "talk like communists." The following exchange illustrates dynamics that were played out in various ways.

A religion professor from Wake Forest University, McLeod Bryan, toured Africa. Upon his return, he wrote that Africa's "supreme test" was whether "African nationalism can keep open the frontiers that the outside forces of colonialism and Christianity cut through the jungle of closed, suspicious tribal communities." Could the "toddling democracies" of Africa achieve a nationalism that was "restrained and internally corrected by a transcendent Christian value system?" Or would radicals such as Nkrumah produce a "selfish black nationalism that destroys itself" in indiscriminate "anti-white hatred" and tribal warfare?[63]

Although Bryan saw independence and pan-African cooperation as generally positive, he was sorry to report that many Africans were guilty of "making of independence an absolute final good." Some Nigerians used Christian universalism to support pan-Africanism; thus, they replayed the errors of the social gospel, even to the extreme of using missionary hymns about "the golden age" [i.e. the millennium] as political campaign slogans. Luckily, some Africans understood that "realistic democracy can impose the necessary restraints" on one-party political systems. Bryan was pleased to report that in Nigeria he read "a line upon line, precept upon precept argument that some Nigerian had studied under Reinhold Niebuhr!" At least some Africans had learned that "absolute satisfaction of political ideals" and "absolute equality" were not practical possibilities.[64] In reply, an anonymous African wrote *C&C* to ask:

> Do Mr. Bryan and Niebuhr's students the world over really believe that one needs to be a Christian and opposed to the so-called Social Gospel in order to realize that . . . absolute satisfaction of political ideals is an

> impossibility? Since I do not know what he means by absolute equality I cannot say whether it is a practical possibility. . . . [However] any pagan with any amount of experience in interpersonal and inter-group living, let alone a politician, should be able to realize that life is a series of compromises.

This letter then inquired whether the Wake Forest faculty practiced what Bryan preached about racism. If so, they too

> would soon be labeled as followers of the Social Gospel school of theology, and thereby lose the respectability that comes with maintaining the sane and realistic balance between sanity and madness. African nationalists cannot afford to stand aside and make wise judgments on both sides of the struggle.[65]

At the emerging radical end of *C&C*'s political spectrum was the Nigerian lawyer Bola Ige, a leader of the Student Christian Federation and an important voice in the WCC. In 1961 Ige penned one of *C&C*'s more radical early statements on Africa, writing from a pan-African socialist stance and quoting liberally from Guinea's President Sekou Touré. Ige was acutely aware that not all African leaders were exemplary—indeed he complained that much of the "black bourgeoisie" was politically conservative and prone to "politico-economic harlotry." Nevertheless he was optimistic about the trends. He argued that anticolonial struggle should be "waged by us Africans alone" because Western entanglements reproduced paternalism and dependence.[66]

By the early 1960s, some of *C&C*'s core writers were considering this position. *C&C* produced a special issue on Africa in 1961, including not only Ige's article, but also an upbeat report on Julius Nyerere's government in Tanganyika, a book review about the Sharpeville Massacre in South Africa, and much reflection on how U.S. policy (both in the U.N. and on other fronts) could be less standoffish toward nationalist revolutionaries who were neutral, if not left-leaning, in the Cold War.[67] This shift was in the background when Bennett edited the preparatory documents for the WCC's Geneva Conference on Church and Society in 1966. Bennett wrote that the WCC's ideal of the responsible society needed revision: it reflected the needs of Western democracies but "does not fit the context . . . of nations which must first go through a period of revolution in which socially transforming justice has priority." He compared his second thoughts about this matter to his rethinking of social gospel pacifism during the 1930s. In both cases "the political choices may seem intolerable according to all the 'principles' learned in church in the past," but shifts were necessary in light of new situations.[68]

C&C's report on the Geneva Conference spoke of confrontations between third world delegates and North Americans. It noted that many U.S. delegates were offended by the conference's "resentment against the developed world's subtle but all-too-real economic imperialism." One delegate thought "Americans almost masochistic in responding to the criticism with silence."

Indian intellectual M. M. Thomas called attention to a third world colleague who perceived the silence as typical: "They think we're second-class citizens; they don't even reply to our criticisms."[69] This silence, however, was soon to change. *C&C* insider Paul Ramsey attacked the dominant position at Geneva in a book called *Who Speaks for the Churches?* He excoriated Protestant leaders for taking "prophetic" positions more radical than their rank-and-file constituents and insisted that they should keep silent unless they could speak from consensus. *C&C* debated Ramsey's arguments extensively—most often in the context of the Vietnam War and such issues as the arms race and sexual ethics that had already brought Ramsey's blood to the boiling point before his trip to Geneva.[70]

Although such sharp confrontations were increasingly common by the mid-1960s, Indian scholar Paul Devanandan's approach to developmentalism was more typical during the decade centered on 1960. He worried that accepting Western aid might undermine his nation's political independence, economic self-sufficiency, and cultural cohesion; nevertheless he argued that Western values could transform the caste system and Western aid could advance goals including national economic planning for socialism.[71] Around 1960 approaches like Devanandan's, written from third world standpoints and distinguishing between various uses of development aid, represented *C&C*'s most nuanced thinking about development. Such writing increasingly supplanted more paternalistic approaches that reflected U.S. government standpoints. Radicals who doubted whether there was a realistic pro-Western, social democratic "third force" in the former colonies remained a minority, but were gaining momentum.

The Turn to Liberation Theologies and Dependence Theory

In the late 1960s and 1970s, *C&C* continued to steer left, following a trajectory that roughly paralleled the civil rights and moderate antiwar movements. Its radicalization led to institutional crisis as *C&C*'s board fell apart in disputes pitting New Deal liberals (some of whom turned to neoconservatism) against student leftists and third world radicals. One editorial lamented that *C&C* had "relied on a tangible and active consensus" but "like our public discourse [this] has become fragmented."[72]

Since the late 1950s, the civil rights movement had been one of *C&C*'s highest priorities. It was fundamental in helping *C&C* rethink issues of race and adopt standpoints other than liberal, elite ones. Moreover, disagreements about black power were near the center of *C&C*'s breakdown of consensus. Although we cannot pursue these matters in detail, *C&C*'s coverage of domestic race issues intersected strongly with its analyses of Africa and other global issues. The Cold War spurred much of white liberals' initial interest in civil rights. As Mary Dudziak says,

> During the postwar years, other countries paid increasing attention to race discrimination in the United States. Voting rights abuses, lynching, school segregation, and antimiscegenation laws were discussed at length in newspapers around the world, and the international media continually questioned whether race discrimination made American democracy a hypocrisy.[73]

In this context, some *C&C* reports about civil rights seemed as equally worried about their impact on U.S. propaganda in Africa and Asia as about their consequences at home. *C&C* coverage shared the sentiment of a U.S. ambassador to India who stated that "I can think of no single thing that would be more helpful to us in Asia than the achievement of racial harmony in America."[74] Later, after *C&C* came to approach domestic racism less as a headache for U.S. diplomats and more from the standpoint of the civil rights movement, *C&C* insiders were closely associated with Martin Luther King Jr.'s work against the Vietnam War.[75]

C&C's other top priority, especially during the late 1960s, was Vietnam. Here again, we lack space to pursue the issue in detail; however, we should note that *C&C*'s rethinking of U.S. foreign policy, which we have explored in relation to issues like the Suez Crisis and the role of Niebuhrian theology in Nigeria, came to a head over Vietnam. *C&C* became a high-profile critic of U.S. policy. Many of its leaders were in the inner circle of the first major non-pacifist (or as they said, "responsible") religious peace organization—Clergy and Laity Concerned About Vietnam. As key *C&C* leaders questioned Cold War analyses of the war, conservative Niebuhrians at *C&C*'s hawkish pole were outraged. Meanwhile, heated debates unfolded between its antiwar activists who were liberal Niebuhrians and those who were more radical.[76]

As *C&C* flirted with radical analyses of the Vietnam War, its larger thinking about foreign relations moved in related directions. Increasingly, it embraced nationalist movements with anti-imperialist agendas in Latin America (especially Brazil and Central America), Asia (especially the Philippines), and Africa. It moved fastest where it had radical colleagues in missionary and ecumenical networks.[77] In the long run, the revolutionary nationalists who made the largest impact at *C&C* were Latin Americans. Their influence grew through a gradual process, beginning in the early 1960s and complete by the mid-1970s. Reports from Latin America helped spur *C&C*'s critique of the WCC's "responsible society," and by the 1970s *C&C* identified deeply with people such as El Salvador's Oscar Romero and Guatemala's Rigoberta Menchú. *C&C* promoted solidarity with the Latin American left and publicized human rights abuses ignored by the mainstream press. Some people in the magazine's circles took their solidarity so seriously that they volunteered as human shields against Central American armies and/or smuggled refugees from Central America into their communities, offering them sanctuary in their churches. In many places, because this movement served as the backbone of organizing against U.S. policy in Central America, Reagan ordered extensive illegal surveillance of churches.[78]

Southern Africa received considerable attention alongside Vietnam and Latin America. From the modest beginnings discussed above, *C&C* continued to support the campaign for South African divestment as the movement mushroomed during the 1970s and 1980s.[79] *C&C* championed the Christian Institute of Beyers Naudé and leaders such as Desmond Tutu, Allan Boesak, and Charles Villa-Vicencio. It devoted considerable attention to the *Kairos Document*, a manifesto of South African liberation theology.[80] *C&C* was largely supportive when the WCC's Program to Combat Racism (PCR), established in 1970, began to give financial support to revolutionary groups in Southern Africa—including the Patriotic Front in Zimbabwe, the Southwest African People's Organization in Namibia, and the ANC in South Africa. The PCR contributions were for humanitarian projects rather than buying arms; nevertheless they dramatized the WCC's intention to place itself unambiguously on the side of revolutionary change, as opposed to trying to stay neutral. Given *C&C*'s long tradition of counseling the tough-minded acceptance of tragic lesser evils and endorsing just wars against tyrannies that could not otherwise be dislodged, this step was not necessarily a difficult one to take. Neoconservatives such as Lefever (working from the Ethics and Public Policy Center at Georgetown University, a node in the network of neoconservative foundations and think tanks) nevertheless began to publicize the PCR's actions in an unflattering light. African issues became a key front in the battle between disaffected neoconservatives (who had left *C&C* by the mid-1970s) and the liberal-liberationist alliance that now controlled *C&C* and many mainline Protestant institutions. Ramsey's complaints about the Geneva Conference were recycled in this context—both his claim that the WCC did not speak for most Christians and that its Marxian social analyses were unpersuasive and dangerous.[81]

Insofar as it could, *C&C* focused on how elite policies affected specific Africans in concrete situations. For example, it discussed the repression of academic freedom and interracial education at the University College of Rhodesia in 1966, the Soweto uprising of 1976, the organization of South African's United Democratic Front (UDF) in 1984, and the politics of the global AIDS epidemic as it impacted Africa in the late 1980s.[82] In 1985 it invited readers to participate imaginatively in a funeral for slain UDF activists in Cradock, South Africa—which became an occasion for a sort of political rally and freedom march:

> As far as I could see in every direction people were standing, and they stood quietly for over four hours. I have never seen such discipline, such dignity, and such reverence among so many people. . . . Messages of support and solidarity came from all over the world. . . . Naudé leaned over to me and whispered, "You see, this is what the whites do

> not realize. They say the ANC has no support." . . . The pallbearers lifted the four coffins to their shoulders, and a procession of clergy led the way [to the cemetery]. On either side of the solemn procession, people stood eight and ten deep. Every one of them, every single person, had their fists raised. No one moved. The only sound in the crowd was the quiet singing of the black national anthem, '*Nkosi Sikelela iAfrika*' (God bless Africa).[83]

Although much of *C&C*'s writing on Africa after 1970 focused on the struggle against apartheid, it moved within a larger orbit of rethinking *C&C*'s developmentalism. In 1969 Paul Abrecht wrote as follows about Henry Luce's American Century:

> We can, looking backward, see that we shared much of [Luce's] optimism about the U.S. spreading her productive skill and culture over the world. We had great confidence in the ability of U.S. democracy to right wrong . . . [and] we believed that the U.S. as a world power could provide the answer to European colonialism. Today we are a little wiser.[84]

C&C increasingly abandoned the core premises of developmentalism: that Latin America, Asia, and Africa were following the same track to modernity as Europe and the U.S. and that by concentrating on their "comparative advantage"—that is, whatever the world market decreed that their capitalists could sell at the highest profit—they could "progress" faster down the universal path from underdevelopment to modernization. In the emerging paradigm of dependence theory, Northern industrial powers and their colonies had evolved together within the same world system. Northern wealth and Southern poverty both resulted largely from the exploitation of the South during this history. The South, thus, could not simply follow in the North's footsteps.[85]

C&C came to insist that it was ideological mystification to use the theory of supply and demand to posit equal relationships of international trade in which strategies of comparative advantage could be freely chosen in a free market. On the contrary, market choices in every nation were shaped by political policies such as tax incentives, labor laws, corporate welfare, and government investment in road building and arms production. International economics involved unequal relationships of dependence, in which stronger parties took advantage of weaker ones through means varying from pillage and slavery in the colonial era to neocolonial arrangements like the politics of international debt in the present.[86]

For example, the theory of comparative advantage in producing raw materials might consign a nation to sell cocoa on unpredictable terms to far larger industrial economies. Comparative advantage in the price of third world labor—that is, in human terms, starvation wages and appalling working conditions—was enabled by the repression of working-class movements by elites, often armed and funded by the North. Countries that tried to opt out of the world system, or to reform their economies in ways deemed too radical, were attacked as communist. Sometimes the combined power of Northern nations and their elite Southern allies destroyed such movements; sometimes they crippled them through embargoes, economic sabotage, and other means as lessons for people who might be tempted to try similar experiments.

Dependence analysis did not settle the question of how impoverished people who inherited this history could maximize their economic health. Should they try to withdraw from the global market or negotiate better terms within it?[87] In addition, dependence analysis could be misleading, insofar as it assumed that the lines between strong and weak parties were the same as national borders, as opposed to distinctions between international classes of elites and workers—so that, for example, Nigerian elites with children at Harvard could posture as oppressed while check-out clerks in U.S. supermarkets felt guilty as oppressors. Even so, the central realities of inequality and empire remained and were organized partly on national lines. Radical analyses informed by neo-Marxian theories overthrew the modernization paradigm in many parts of the third world, and *C&C* generally agreed.

We should not assume that all, or even most, of *C&C*'s writing after its radical turn was focused on politics and economics. Equally important was its transitional period when the theological paradigm inherited from the Niebuhrian model was transformed to liberation theologies. *C&C*'s theological transition during the 1950s and 1960s was far more complex than we can treat adequately here. Suffice it to say, the journal began to see its inherited theology as inadequate for addressing new challenges; it turned increasingly (despite objections from unreconstructed Niebuhrians) toward various forms of contextual ethics and secular theology. One voice in this conversation was the South African novelist Alan Paton. In 1960 Paton replied to critics who called him an extremist because he had decided "to choose justice and not injustice and not to seek some middle ground between them."

> The greatest danger to Christianity is [not communism but] pseudo-Christianity . . . [which] always prefers what it considers realism to love. . . . It says, 'you know, Paton, you are really talking a lot of bloody nonsense. . . . You don't understand human nature. You are trying to achieve the impossible.' . . . I think that ultimately if one wants to be a good man one must live by the law of love no matter what the cost of it may be.[88]

By the late 1960s, radical U.S. theologians such as Robert McAfee Brown, James Cone, and Rosemary Ruether joined with third world voices like Gustavo Gutierrez and Desmond Tutu to develop liberation theologies which correlated radical social activism with God's will and hegemonic policies with sin and oppression. When a neoconservative theologian objected to such politicization of theology and called on churches to stand aloof from all ideologies, Dorothee Soelle responded that neoconservatives would do better to ask why church people were turning toward radical positions. "Wouldn't it be thinkable that this has do with some major events in this century—say Auschwitz?" asked Soelle. "A spirituality that is stripped of human need, or any desire, becomes bloodless."[89] For Soelle, the practice of faith was a struggle against cynicism, exploitation, and the flattening of human relationships into commodities. Contrary to classic Marxian analyses, religion was not false consciousness. On the contrary, losing sight of utopian dimensions of religious meaning was exactly what capitalism wanted people to do. As Soelle confronted the many defeats of the left after the 1960s—which included not only large-scale political-economic changes but also the torture of one of her students in Argentina—her writings represented an effort to sustain hope, even in the seeming absence of objective foundations for it. This sustenance of hope was the heart of religion as she understood it.[90]

Conclusions

We have seen how *C&C* was founded to defend Western liberal freedoms—both democracy and a suitably regulated free market—against the threat of Nazism, and how it became a supporter of U.S. political economic goals during the Cold War era, including a stance of "benevolent supremacy" vis-à-vis the third world. By the 1970s, after the transformation we have traced, Dom Helder Camara, a Brazilian liberation theologian, penned a more typical *C&C* perspective on the U.S. global role. Invited to Harvard to receive an honorary doctorate of law, Camara asked "what kind of law?" He listed some possibilities and described how each was used against poor people. Then he turned to the four freedoms that the U.S. had proclaimed as the Western heritage to defend during World War II: freedom of speech and religion, freedom from want and fear. These "fundamental freedoms—portrayed so brilliantly on paper—soar like mockery, like jeers for the absolute majority of humanity," Camara said. For the sake of honesty, "Why not close . . . the schools of law and open schools of war?"[91]

By the 1970s, *C&C*'s spectrum of debate had been reconfigured. Until the journal folded in 1993, its new task was to pick up the pieces after the shattering of its earlier consensus and organize these pieces in new patterns—in relation both to longstanding concerns and to new ones including issues of gender and sexuality. Speaking about these developments in general terms is risky because they involved explorations in diverse directions rather than a search for any one unified vision. Analyzing specific positions of *C&C* in its later years necessitates proceeding concretely, case by case, grasping how any given case can be approached with diverse paradigms of analysis and priorities for action, which do not always move in harmony. Many of these explorations, nevertheless, were loosely linked through a shift toward approaching issues "from below"—from the perspective of people at the bottom of power hierarchies—and within specific local contexts and communities. The journal became a hub of communication among diverse people, often in tension but loosely linked, who were making related shifts. They ranged from moderately liberal to far left on the political spectrum.

For former readers of *C&C* who did not share the shifts in perspective that we have discussed, *C&C*'s emergent critiques called into question their inherited self-images as humane and practical realists. Whereas *C&C*'s earlier writing had encouraged them to identify with heroic leaders of U.S. government or business, its later writing made such identification difficult. If their standpoints did not shift along with *C&C*, changes in the journal could lead readers toward a sort of vacuum in which they complained about a lack of connection between *C&C*'s emergent writing and their lives—not only when *C&C* flirted with despair and/or romanticism about revolution (which sometimes did happen), but even when *C&C* advocated moderate and pragmatic tactics in support of nonelite agendas. Some people who began by perceiving this sort of vacuum moved on to nostalgia for a golden age of Niebuhrianism and laments about the loss of tough-minded realism in the world of liberal Protestant social thought.

In this context, let us return to the *Rockland Record*'s skeptical question about *C&C*'s $25,000 contribution to South African divestment. True enough, the realistic long-term impact of this action "remained to be seen," just as the *Record* stated; but it was often seen differently, depending on the standpoint and priorities of the seer. Granted, a rich U.S. banker and a militant Soweto student might look at the same facts and reach a similar conclusion—for example, that conditions in Soweto made efforts to overthrow apartheid inevitable. Despite this possibility, we should not underestimate the difference it makes—both for what one can see and what "realistic impacts" seem worth pursuing after seeing it—to look at the world from different standpoints.

C&C's shifts in political and theological standpoint were sufficiently profound that it is hard to judge even the most basic questions about the impact of *C&C*'s transformation. For example, to what degree should one interpret *C&C*'s early writing as savvy and commendable criticism of U.S. policies, as opposed to something more like uncritical baptism of them? Many liberationists after the 1960s charged that *C&C*'s earlier criticism had been overly cautious, if not fatally compromised, because of its style of weighing arguments in a "realistic" establishment voice. In contrast, classic Niebuhrians saw themselves lobbying policymakers in forceful terms, using a voice somewhat like a book reviewer who says "I like point A, and point B is solid, and I concur that point C is crucial, but let me say this about point D"—where the zinger about D calls everything else into question and would be considered the review's main point by readers who had ears to hear. Does a critic like Sharon Welch, who describes Niebuhrian theology as "an ideology of cultured despair," lack the ears to hear such zingers, so that she can only hear how *C&C* shared elite assumptions on points A, B, and C?[92] Or were *C&C*'s

early writings like reviews in which accepting points A, B, and C means supporting all the key issues, while the objection at point D merely corrects a spelling error? Did *C&C*'s critique have limited impact precisely when it was lauded as most influential, because the price of influence was agreement with elites on points A, B, and C?[93]

It is impossible to assess the zing in *C&C*'s zingers without thinking about its shifting constituencies. During the Cold War era, when *C&C* stood well to the right of writers such as W. E. B. DuBois who are valorized in liberationist genealogies, they were also trying to nudge policymakers in more liberal directions, and their ideas were significantly farther left than the Protestant laity to whom they hoped their views would trickle down.[94] *C&C* writers spoke to establishment insiders as insiders; often they explicitly adopted elite standpoints by using the word *we* interchangeably for the nation as a whole, government officials, the army, and themselves. As we have seen, insiders did listen; however, in time *C&C* moved toward a peasant's eye view of U.S. bomber planes and bottom-up perspectives on the struggle against South African apartheid. Adopting the standpoints of people further from centers of power—whether by publishing such people directly or imagining how they saw the world and trying to forge appropriate solidarities—*C&C* stressed the limitations of its former alliances and geared its message to a different set of readers.

If we approach the *Rockland Record*'s skeptical question about *C&C*'s impact from this direction, a different set of questions comes into view. When *C&C* lost the ear of elites, did its concrete impact become marginal? This assessment seems too harsh. *C&C* clearly contributed to social change through actions such as spearheading religious support for civil rights and anti-Vietnam War protest—even when this destroyed its alliance with the Johnson White House. In Africa it contributed by defending the PRC, strengthening ANC and UDF leaders, and promoting a divestiture campaign that had consequences far beyond *C&C*'s $25,000 contribution—even when such positions earned them contempt from neoconservatives.

Nevertheless, *C&C*'s concrete impact is hard to measure precisely. Studying *C&C* clearly helps as a rough barometer to understand background assumptions that have informed debates about Africa in liberal Protestant circles. To what extent did the journal's transformations represent a more sustained and helpful engagement with specific African issues? To what extent did they distract from other paths that might have had better results, either in Africa or in the U.S.? Is it appropriate for U.S. Christians to make alliances with certain African groups caught up in the conflicts of their continent, as opposed to other groups? There are no easy answers to such questions. We can only hope that after reviewing evolving ideas about Africa in this reasonably influential and representative journal, we are in a position to explore such questions in a more informed way, case by case.

Chapter 2

Rev. James H. Robinson and American Support for African Democracy and Nation-Building, 1950s–1970s

Sandra J. Sarkela and Patrick Mazzeo

A half century before the current American-led effort to promote democratization around the world, the words and deeds of Rev. Dr. James H. Robinson, Charismatic African-American Presbyterian minister and founder of Operation Crossroads Africa, captured the central components of today's ideological debates over democratization. The current language and vision of the U.S. State Department, especially the Bureau of Democracy, Human Rights, and Labor, was foreshadowed in many ways. Among these foreshadows was the prophetic, singular voice of this African-American visionary. Robinson represents one case study, outside the *Christianity and Crisis* circle, of a more limited, people-to-people, democracy-building approach that demanded the full participation of African Americans.[1] Drawing upon his religious values, his personal experiences confronting racism in the United States, the power of Communism as a competing ideology, and unrelenting hope for the future of Africa and all of the developing world, Robinson articulated a democratic project for Africa that was linked to the success of the democratic project for African Americans and for all disenfranchised peoples in the United States. This linkage is the central component of his vision for democracy and freedom in Africa.

James H. Robinson (1907–1972), the grandchild of slaves, had diverse commitments and involvements that included church ministry, social activism, racial/ethnic nationalism, universal humanism, and internationalism. Known as an outstanding orator and preacher, James Robinson voiced a message acknowledged by political, religious, and academic leaders from throughout the world, including Jawaharlal Nehru, John F. Kennedy, Jomo Kenyatta, Julius Nyerere, and countless others from the United States and Africa. With a passion drawn from trekking thousands of miles in the footprints of Africans, Robinson advocated his vision for a democratic African continent, with an optimism that was spurred on by faith, but with a cautiousness engendered by a realism about legacies of distortion within Africa's internal and external political relations. The breadth of issues and audiences Robinson addressed over thirty-five years are documented in a special collection at the Amistad Research Center at Tulane University. Drawing on documents from the Robinson Collection, this paper presents Robinson as one of the earliest U.S. advocates of democratization in Africa.

The paper begins with a brief overview of Robinson's leadership formation in historical context. We then present Robinson's perspectives about democracy in Africa as expressed particularly in speeches and sermons he delivered throughout the 1950s and 1960s. Four interlocking themes recur throughout his rhetoric. First, Robinson established a goal of democratic "freedom" as practiced in the West, for all nations, but especially for those emerging in Africa. Secondly, he argued for a democracy built upon strong Christian faith. Thirdly, he warned against Communist attacks on and corruptions of African freedom. Fourthly, he suggested a linkage between the African-American struggle for equality and justice in the United States and broader commitments to democratic expansion, the battle against Communism, and the development of strong Christian communities in Africa.

The essay concludes with thoughts about the significance of Robinson's discourse at the time and its place within current discussions of democratization, whether couched in terms of Samuel Huntington's "clash of civilizations" or of the neoconservative policy of promoting democracy through direct intervention. We note that while it may seem that Robinson's rhetoric reinforces certain aspects of the American policy climate of his time, he advocated tolerance of other cultures, warned that American-style democracy was not guaranteed to work well for others, and preached against hate and violence while supporting the value of Christian agape love as the ultimate foundation for conflict resolution.

Robinson's Cultural Influence and Cultural Influences on Robinson

Robinson's years as an influential voice in religious and political affairs began at least as early as 1938 when, as a newly ordained minister, he delivered the eulogy for the prominent African-American poet James Weldon Johnson. Other indications of Robinson's wide-ranging influence include his selection as the featured speaker for the prestigious Lyman Beecher Lecture series at Yale Divinity School in 1955; his testimony before the Committee on Foreign Relations in support of improved foreign aid in 1957; his address, "The Second Emancipation," delivered at Dartmouth College on the occasion of his honorary doctorate and published in *Vital Speeches*; and his keynote address at the American Negro Leadership Conference on Africa in 1967. These highlights pale, however, when compared to his untiring efforts between 1954 and 1972 to build relationships and understanding between North America and Africa. His involvements on behalf of his community, church, and the organization he founded, Operation Crossroads Africa, embodied his uncompromising solidarity with national and international struggles for self-determination and dignity. Despite his significant achievements and vision, Robinson's leadership contributions within the African and African-American freedom struggles remain under appreciated, if not largely overlooked.[2]

James Robinson was born in the "bottoms" of Knoxville, Tennessee. Robinson described the context of his upbringing this way: "Hemmed in by the muddy creek bank third, it was a world set apart and excluded."[3] The grandson of slaves and hard laboring parents, Robinson moved to Cleveland, Ohio, when his father joined the "great migration." Apparently, his Cleveland experience also left much to be desired:

> Except for paved streets over which I could romp freely, unsegregated schools, and a few personal friends of Italian and Polish parentage, the "Promised Land" failed to materialize. My disappointment was great. . . . In Cleveland, however, I only found toleration; I was accepted only at a distance. Worst of all I was ignored.[4]

Robinson joined the Presbyterian Church in 1931 and was given the opportunity to attend Lincoln University. An active and successful student leader, he brought his passion for both justice and faith to the many debates he engaged. Horace Mann Bond, President Honorarius of Lincoln University, described Lincoln during these years as a place of few diversions where "talk was a major sport."[5] It was an academic home to such seminal figures as Langston Hughes, Thurgood Marshall, John A. Davis, Kwame Nkrumah, and Benjamin Azikiwe. In the latter Robinson found inspiration:

> The issue took on new complications when Benjamin Azwkie (sic), an instructor, sought and failed to introduce a course in Negro History. Enlisting on Azwkie's side I became a speaker at protest meetings, spokesman before the faculty, and pamphleteer. Azwkie, the fiery and zealous son of an African chief, has tremendous personal appeal. Either loved or hated, he was the kind of fearless and uncompromising leader I could follow. It was a sad day for me when I learned that Azwkie would not be rehired at semester's end. I wanted to leave Lincoln but was too stubborn to quit. There were, after all, other important issues to face out and fight for. And one of the purposes of a man like Benjamin Azwkie was to inspire others to take up where he left off.[6]

After graduating as class valedictorian at Lincoln, Robinson attended Union Theological Seminary in New York City, graduating as President of his class in 1938. That same year he opened the Church of the Master and the Morningside Community Center. As an activist and young minister with an initial membership of less than fifty, he spoke out on behalf of his community's spiritual and material needs and saw the membership in his church grow significantly.

Not content to minister within the confines of his church and community center, Robinson helped establish the National Scholarship Service and Fund for Negro Students. He spearheaded the development of the Morningside Community Center, which provided broadly based community services, including community mental health services. In 1944 he was named chairperson of a campaign to expand Sydenham Hospital to Sydenham Interracial Hospital, offering patients access to African-American physicians and nurses. After receiving a gift of a parcel of land and an aging farmhouse in New Hampshire, he founded Rabbit Hollow, an interracial summer camp that relied on young volunteers for its day-to-day functioning. In 1948 he worked on Henry Wallace's Presidential campaign for the Progressive Party. Later in the 1950's Robinson ran for Manhattan borough president under the banner of the Liberal Party.

Robinson's reputation as an effective speaker and a motivator of young people continued to increase. It was in part the reason he was selected in 1951 for a 42,000-mile journey to Europe, the Middle East, and Asia. This first international foray under the auspices of the Presbyterian Board of Foreign Missions was planned to address students and youth leaders. Robinson wrote:

> In order to get some of what people were thinking, I tried to approach them with patience, humility, sincerity and understanding. During my journey I used 47 interpreters. I often slept with them on rice straw mats or on the floors of their mud walled, thatched roof houses. I ate with them on the farms, talked with them on the docks, went into churches and classrooms, spoke to them in foundries, met them in legislative halls, tarried at political rallies, talked for hours in decrepit eating places, joined them at water holes and mud ponds where they washed

> their clothes. My impressions were drawn from the endless conversations with thousands of individuals and hundreds of groups in discussion sessions which followed nearly all *the 500 speeches and sermons I gave* (italics added).[7]

Shortly after this first international excursion, an Indiana Parents Association accused Robinson of being a "communist sympathizer."[8] This accusation led the State Department to attempt to revoke his passport. Through the support of church allies, Robinson retained his passport in defiance of the State Department's initial demands. After a period of prolonged negotiations, Robinson resumed his travels in 1954.

On a national speaking tour in 1957, he challenged students at Occidental College to join him in working and learning in Africa. This year, of course, marks the independence of Ghana, the first country in sub-Saharan Africa to gain independence. That same year Robinson preached the Ghana Independence Sermon in the Washington Cathedral. In 1958 he founded Operation Crossroads Africa, a nongovernmental, nonprofit organization dedicated to building links between Africa and North America. That summer, groups of volunteers from the United States and Canada set out to work side by side with their African counterparts on small-scale community development projects. In commenting about Operation Crossroads Africa, Dr. Robinson said he believed that "the most important task in a shrinking world is the bringing of people into contact with peoples across all the old crumbling barriers of nation, culture, and race."[9]

For the next fourteen years, Robinson guided Operation Crossroads Africa and inspired thousands of volunteers on the mission he designed. The legacy of his vision resulted in the establishment of Canadian Crossroads International, a vibrant international, nonprofit organization that clearly traces its roots to the work of James Robinson.[10] In the United States, the organization survived a turbulent period between 1988 and 1995 and has expanded to include a specifically designated Diaspora program. With almost 10,000 former participants and projects in over thirty-five countries in Africa, the Caribbean, and now Brazil, James Robinson's dream has continued to bring people in contact across the barriers of nation, culture, and race.

Robinson's Thinking on Freedom and Democracy

Robinson's speeches and sermons throughout the 1950s and 1960s evidenced four interlocking themes: (1) democracy, nationalism, and self-determination; (2) democracy and institutionalized religion; (3) democracy and communism; and (4) democracy as a worldwide project requiring equal efforts in the United States and Africa. As early as 1953, after his first international speaking tour, he delivered a speech at Georgetown Presbyterian

Church in Washington, D.C. that contained these themes and outlined his commitment to the promotion of democracy throughout the world.

He opened with a statement consistent with the cold war rhetoric of the time. "There are two revolutions in the world. One is modern nationalism of Asia and Africa, and the other is imperialistic communism." He argued that America's free, democratic society inspired the new nationalism. In fighting the "pernicious force" of Communism, Robinson warned that the "means must never end in doing to ourselves and our institutions what communism seeks to do to us and others. Our means must be intelligent, creative and bold but always democratic." Those means, he suggested, should include the following eight points:

1. A commitment to "private agencies, foundation, individuals and groups" (rather than government agencies) as the primary means of bringing democracy to the world;
2. Immediate improvement in race relations in America, including taking advantage of "Negro leadership in the total struggle";
3. The creation of "labor centers for Asians and Africans" by American labor unions in order to close the door to Communist efforts in that area;
4. An emphasis on "personal witness" as the most effective tool for gaining commitment to a cause;
5. Respect for cultural differences;
6. Stronger U.S. alliances with its western allies in directing the "rising nationalism" toward the ends of freedom and democracy;
7. Supportiveness of countries such as India that have successfully transitioned from colonial rule to independent democracy, "even if they do not act and think precisely as we would like them to"; and
8. Establishment by the United States (given its global leadership status) of an international institution that trains people for international work and in language studies.[11]

Robinson's coalescing vision about America's strategic role in cultivating freedom and democracy abroad, and the success of his 1951 trip, resulted in a second overseas engagement in 1954 that focused on West Africa. As Robinson witnessed the changing future of Africa, the contours of his intellectual and programmatic focus became more apparent.

Through the lens of post-September 11 foreign policy shifts, with its growing emphasis on issues of security and the war on terrorism, Robinson's position may seem naïve and idealistic. As Mark Hulsether illustrates in chapter 1 of this volume, Robinson's views were within the range of contemporaneous progressive approaches to issues of development in general and in Africa specifically. Hulsether notes that the journal *Christianity and*

Crisis articulated three recurrent themes in discussions of Africa: the threat of communism, avoiding excessive military leverage, and economic development needs. These issues were framed theologically in the ongoing debate over the viability of the "social gospel" versus "Christian realism." As we document here, Robinson echoed the three themes in his speeches and writings; however, his emphasis on issues of development, equality, confronting racism, colonialism, and paternalism place him closer to the earlier social gospel perspective. He was immersed in the battle against racism, injustice, economic inequality, and political disenfranchisement and in the battle for human dignity during his entire life—as a student, in his early days in New York City, and as a champion for the democratic future of Africa.

Democracy and Nationalism

Robinson's trips abroad solidified his commitment to speaking out on behalf of struggling nations seeking self-determination and democracy. He linked nationalism and self-determination with democracy in two ways. First, he saw the rise of nationalism as the primary challenge to the maintenance of colonialism. The end of colonialism was a prerequisite for democracy. Secondly, his own experiences as an African American confronting the barriers of race, class, and ethnicity led him to see nationalism as an antidote to parochial ties that limited the possibility of democratic participation. What he did not see was that nationalism itself could take a decidedly antidemocratic turn. Furthermore, he believed:

> Nationalism, initiated by the Africans' contact with European colonials, fired by African students returning from foreign universities and by soldiers who fought in World War II, and encouraged by the rise and success of nationalism in Asia, is gripping the whole continent. . . . Africans are increasingly vocal in pleading their cause not only before the European governments but also at the United Nations. The cringing deference they formerly gave white men has turned to hostility, for they have learned that domination, poverty, hardship, servitude and discrimination need not be their lot forever.[12]

Recognizing the power of nationalism, he linked it to democratic participation and representation:

> The single most powerful force in Africa today is nationalism. And it is just beginning. More than all other forces combined, nationalism has awakened in the African a sense of pride and self-respect, a sense of destiny, and an *irrepressible desire to throe off the yokes of outside control* (italics added). In September 1954, in Enugu, Nigeria, I saw this self-respect written on the faces of hundreds of Africans, many of whom had walked twenty miles and more to see their new government ministers arrive at the parliament building when the Eastern Provinces Assembly opened.

> This was an occasion to remember, for it was the first time that all the ministers of the eastern Nigeria government were Africans and an African represented the British crown at the opening of the Assembly.[13]

For Robinson, "democracy" was both the formal process of participation that he found so inspiring in the previous example and a means to address the more far reaching and difficult challenges of social, economic, and religious life. Through democratic participation the just society was possible and social justice was achievable. As early as the late 1950s, before most countries achieved self-determination and statehood, he recognized the limitations and challenges to achieving stable, democratic, socially just societies. These obstacles to full political and social development included rural urban migration, overcrowding in cities that were not intended for such numbers with the concomitant social problems, wealth flowing out of the continent, foreign ownership of small businesses, failure to establish cooperatives that could compete with foreign owned small businesses, and failure to build strong democratic noncommunist labor unions. These issues were recurrent themes in Robinson's speeches and echoed his own life experience as an African American and as a social activist minister in Harlem. What he fought for in his Morningside Heights community was not dissimilar to what he advocated for in Africa—mainly, that the disenfranchised cannot solve their problems by themselves. Democracy was more than a ballot box; it required economic, political, and social empowerment.

Robinson's strategy for fueling democracy was personal witness. At the opening session of the orientation for OCA volunteers in 1960, he explained his vision of how these young people would help African nations develop and sustain viable democracies within their own historical and cultural norms:

> We know that nothing like nationalism can move from one continent to another without adjusting itself to the context of the area within which it finds life and vitality. We know also that there are improvements upon the democratic processes that Africans will make as they develop, expand and improve their institutions. What we hope to do is to share ideals and faith out of the context of our own situation in a way that will help foster self respect among Africans in their pursuit of their goals. When you get to Africa this summer, you will find in the structure of African tribal society many aspects of the democratic process which are as fine as any we have developed through all the years of our history in this country.[14]

The democracy he envisioned was one that grew out of existing traditions nurtured by the best that the West—and his model of Christianity—had to offer. The young volunteers of all religions, races, and ethnicities would model what it meant to build a nation in the interests of all. With a truly open, inclusive, and participatory process of decision-making, the old conflicts based on parochial divisions would no longer hold the future as hostage to the past. Unfortunately, what emerged was a failure of the nationalism/democracy linkage Robinson assumed. Many of the newly independent nations would use the rhetoric of nationalism to gain power and then fall back into the parochial, self-serving, ethnically bound politics of the part rather than the whole.

Democracy and Religion

For Robinson political democracy was integrally linked to the inclusive and egalitarian precepts he found within Christianity; therefore, for Robinson, promoting Christianity was a building block for democracy. For democracy to take root in Africa, Christianity had to be responsive to two religious urgencies. First, Robinson felt that western Christian churches needed to confront their paternalism and their racism. Second, countering the success of Islam required Christian churches that embraced racial justice and equality. In a speech expressing thanksgiving for Ghana's ascendance to independence, Robinson made explicit a somewhat chauvinistic understanding of the link between religion and freedom:

> The basic idea of a free society of free men is after all a moral idea. The individual and collective responsibility of a democratic society is grounded in a moral order which sustains the rights of men as children of God whom he loves as brothers. This is an order in which human personality is precious and every human being is sacred. Behind the advent of Ghana's freedom is the fundamental order of a universe grounded in the eternal purpose of Almighty God. No impersonal dialectic or contradictory notions can achieve good and just ends by using negative and despicable means. Ghana is the achievement of men of faith who believe in moral order, guided by a loving God to the end of a more equitable and secure society where "all men might have life and have it more abundantly. . . . Both we in the West and the people of Africa, despite all our failures and mistakes, owe more growth in social responsibility, political freedom and progress to religion than to any other single factor in our culture.[15]

Robinson appeared to believe that Christians were both obligated and well equipped to help build free and just societies around the world. He attempted to balance the collective and social responsibility of the brotherhood of believers with the individualistic ethos of American Protestantism. In this balancing act he saw the higher authority of his faith and its inseparability from the ideals of democracy, equality, self-determination, and justice.

Robinson viewed Islam as the great competitor to Christianity in Africa. He called Islam an "antagonist of great capacity" fighting for the same souls and bodies, but more so. He recognized that there were many factors in Islam's favor, which he articulated in a speech at Smith College in 1957 entitled "The Crescent, Sickle and Cross Over Africa":

> . . . the polygynous family system, nationalism and freedom which is a greater hunger than the hunger for food, the color of the Crescent's standard bearers which does not have the handicap of white western missionaries. . . . And of no less importance, Islam has achieved a brotherhood across race and color lines which Christianity has not effectively raised by the level of an idea and a hope. In fact, racism in Africa, as in so called Christian countries, is the Cross's greatest handicap in Africa.[16]

Robinson's analysis and interpretations of the future of Christianity and democracy in Africa were complicated. He believed that Islam's strengths were magnified by Christianity's failures. Particularly and most horribly for Robinson was the fact that American Protestant missionaries were almost exclusively white. Over and over again, Robinson voiced his frustration that racial segregation in the United States, whether *de jure* or *de facto*, seemed to have resulted in segregation in missionary work as well. He was acutely aware of the limited opportunities open to African Americans. Writing in *The Christian Century*, Robinson argued:

> The churches and missions have passed up a great reservoir of persons who could make a peculiarly effective witness in Africa—American Negroes. There are more Negroes of African origin in the United States than there are in all the rest of the world outside Africa. . . . But both our government and our churches have failed to make use of this potential to any extent. . . . Chester Bowles, formerly our ambassador to India, in an article he wrote after visiting Africa (Collier's magazine, June 10, 1955) strongly recommended that our government send Negro citizens there to represent it in various capacities. If this is a right move for the government, how much more so for the churches![17]

In 1962, foreshadowing the growth of the African Independent church movement, Robinson reminded the Presbyterian Church:

> With colonialism passing into oblivion, we can no longer justify missionary efforts that do not take African-Christians into full partnership in policy-making and administration. It is obligatory that we change as rapidly as possible from a missionary structure to a fraternal worker emphasis.[18]

Two challenges that Robinson often invoked, Islam and communism, tempered his hopes that Christianity and democracy would flourish in Africa. With a historic presence across the Sahel, Islam was well established in Africa before the large scale Christian missionary effort began. By the start of the twentieth century, the constituents of Islam were estimated to be over 30 percent of the continent's population in comparison to less than 10 percent Christian. Today, according to a variety of sources, Christianity has more adherents on the continent of Africa than Islam. Robinson's fear that Islam would succeed at the expense of Christianity proved wrong. Christianity found in Africa a fertile soil for both traditional denominations and the flourishing African Independent Churches.[19]

While he had profound respect for cultural traditions and differences, Robinson was committed to the belief that individual freedom, justice, and democracy were inherent in Christianity. From this perspective, then, Christian presence, witness, and vision were imperative for the survival and expansion of democracy in Africa. The first component of a Christian presence has succeeded and, according to Philip Jenkins (2003), will continue to do so; the second component, the expansion of true democratic forms, is still awaiting such success.

Democracy and Communism

If Islam was a worthy antagonist and competitor in Robinson's view, then Communism was not only a false prophet but a calculatingly deceptive one. Robinson's own experience with the progressive democratic left in New York City (the "Progressive Party" and the "Liberal Party") reinforced his ecclesiastical anticommunist impulse. Robinson commented about the Communist Party and movement that "Much of their work is secret and hidden as it is not their purpose to advertise their intentions, methods, and strategies."[20] His own positions reflected the dominant rhetoric of the time: Communism was an evil that promised many things but resulted in new forms of slavery and regimentation; it was a seductive ploy aimed at those who were disenfranchised at home and in Africa; the goals of the Communist movement were not self-determination and autonomy, but subjugation to an ideology. Stated in the best of cold war rhetoric and consistent with mainstream Protestant thought, Robinson asserted that Communism could be defined as "the fraudulent justification of the most heinous of means to achieve the most despicable of ends."[21] He believed Communism to have a powerful secular religious zeal. To promote a democratic/Christian tendency, the West needed a new counterforce. Surprisingly, his answer did not include more missionaries, but, rather, a cadre of social technicians "who will identify themselves with Africans in their reach for security, peace, equality, freedom and self-determination."[22]

Robinson did make clear, however, that the fight against Communism as an ideology should not be confused with a fight against a particular Communist person. In an argument he made in countless speeches and sermons, Robinson emphasized this distinction:

> While love must oppose and destroy whatever is against love such as prejudice, hate, indifference, injustice and Communism, it must not destroy those who have succumbed to these patterns of life. . . . Herein lies two important problems which trouble the soul of America, for we have allowed hatred of Communism to become hatred of Communists and hatred of things about people because of race, social condition,

> moral status or attitudes to become hatred of persons who are also dear and beloved to God.[23]

At the 1957 Baccalaureate Ceremony of Atlanta University, Morehouse College, and Spelman College, Robinson pitched his counter to the success of Communism. "(Y)ou cannot kill the ideas of communism with a gun. You'll have to outlive it, with a nobler idea in terms of people who are willing to count themselves as expendable to the way of their religion and their society."[24]

In that same year Robinson organized the first group of young North American volunteers who would work, live, and learn with African counterparts and in African communities. Operation Crossroads Africa began with deep roots in progressive Protestant social activism and gospel. In its early days many of the group leaders for this adventure in cross-cultural understanding were ministers, chaplains, teachers, and deacons. The goal of OCA was to give witness to the ideals that Robinson had long advanced. Robinson defined Operation Crossroads Africa as an organization that was neither black or white, Protestant or Jewish, liberal or conservative. It was about people to people witness in the name of the highest values of building community, exemplifying freedom and democracy, and reinforcing dignity. Though growing out of his ministry in the Presbyterian Church and mainline Protestant organizations, he also garnered early support from the National Conference on Christians and Jews. According to Ms. Laverne Brown, Rabbi Israel Moshowitz, a long time friend and coordinator of Robinson's first visit to the "Holy Land," served as Associate Director of OCA in it's first years.[25]

By the early 1960s James Robinson was already recognized as one of the most significant links with the newly emerging world of independent African nations and leaders. He was called upon to advise in the formation of the Peace Corps. In 1961 at a reception held for departing OCA volunteers on the lawn of the White House, President Kennedy acknowledged that James Robinson had created the "progenitor of the Peace Corps."

Democracy as a World System

Two events outside the vision of James Robinson have affected democracy as a world system. He was most concerned with linkages between African-American enfranchisement in the United States and democracy in Africa; however, the current global free market movement and the post-September 11 mark on the world, pose challenges unimagined in Robinson's time. Placing the rhetoric of James H. Robinson in the context of the early twenty-first century with an American agenda that openly and aggressive pursues "democratization," raises tensions between Islam and the West, and continues to struggle for democracy in Africa and equality in the United States, results in a vision of paradox and possibility. As with many others who dare to envision a future, Robinson was prophetic but miscalculated. He was right in placing Africa on the public agenda, pushing the religious establishment to incorporate "others" as equals, and in understanding the importance of volunteerism, self-help programs, technical assistance, and language training. He was premature in celebrating a democratic Africa, but not misplaced. Successful presidential transitions from Senegal to Tanzania and from South Africa to Ghana offer hopeful antidotes to events elsewhere on the continent. A deeper issue is the appropriating of democratization as a parliamentary movement rather than a social justice movement. Robinson's vision demanded both elements.

Rejecting the model of violent confrontation Robinson believed that democracy could take root in Africa as we adopted democratic possibilities and opportunities in the United States. Among the greatest assets of the States was the presence of the largest African derived population in the world. In 1964, for example, Robinson argued as the civil rights movement reached a climax in the United States:

> The present state of our racial affairs mutes our voice in world politics; it stymies our leadership of the forces of freedom; it embarrasses our friends and allies; it encourages our enemies; it confuses those who have not made up their minds as to which side of the ideological struggle they will join, and it drives some away from us in revulsion.[26]

He went on to chastise one politician in particular:

> One can only wish that Senator Fulbright could have been as creative in his dealings with our domestic race problems as with the myths of our foreign policy. In reply to questions about why he isn't as progressive and creative in race relations, Senator Fulbright fell prey to the greatest myth of all—that the problem of our domestic failure has no relation to our failures in foreign policies.[27]

In contrast to Fulbright, Robinson maintained that like Christianity and democracy, racial advances at home and abroad were inextricably linked. His Keynote Address to the second American Negro Leadership Conference on Africa, delivered on September 24, 1964, emphasized this linkage:

> Africa's rebirth and progress have had a powerful impact for good upon our own racial advance here in America. . . . It could not long maintain the paradox of spending billions for freedom abroad and doing nothing for the freedom of some of its citizens without the bounds of its own territory.[28]

The United States of the 1960s was vulnerable and forced to confront the hypocrisy of promoting democracy abroad while allowing it to wither at home. In the early stages of post-September 11 readjustments and the continued impoverishment of large segments of the African and African-American community, voices echo Robinson's earlier comments.

Robinson also did not anticipate the current internationalization of the free market paradigm whose staunchest defenders define the collective good as synonymous with what is good for the international financial and investment markets. He grounded his ideas about democracy in his real-life experience with the people who were to be empowered. This grounding was a tool for building self-respect, empowerment, and responsibility. It was a tool for building a just and hopeful life. His vision was not market-driven, though he advocated free markets; it was people-driven. James H. Robinson was articulating a vision of the place of democracy in Africa and, by extension, in the globe. He envisioned democratization based on the equality of peoples and nations. Democracy and freedom would ensure that all peoples in Africa and the United States would share a true brotherhood among God's children. That perspective was a world system view of democracy.

Conclusion

Located in a paradoxical space, Robinson's discourse foreshadows, on the one hand, elements of an ideology that could be identified with President George W. Bush, Samuel P. Huntington, or Richard John Neuhaus. On the other hand, Robinson can be easily linked with earlier social gospel traditions as well as contemporary antiglobalization, social justice rhetoric. The possibilities, hopes, and paradoxes are all present in Robinson's early, consistent, and unrelenting advocacy of Africa's place at the table of free nations and democratic people and of social justice at home.

Robinson's linkage of democracy and Christianity and his admonitions regarding Islam's power, growth, and implied democratic limitations preview positions now identified with neoconservative ideology. His clear refutation of the implied or actual use of force or violence, however, places him squarely in opposition to the "Christian realism" of the 1960s and to current practice of military-induced democratization. Additionally, his strong social justice message and support of nationalist agendas are linked today with international resistance to the neoliberal globalization manifesto.

His fears of Islam's growth in the face of Christianity's failing appear both tangible and muted—tangible in the ongoing tensions found in events across the continent from Sudan to Nigeria, and muted in the growth and vitality of Christianity across the continent. Linkages that Robinson assumed would lead to democratic florescence in Africa have not occurred. His conception of Christianity reinforced his vision of democracy. Robinson believed that democracy was rooted in the gospels. He preached that a true Christian faith began with the understanding that "Christ died to free us individually and collectively from the encumbrance of our sins. . . . The result of our Lord's sacrifice is to make us free in order that we might continue the interminable war against sin and evil."[29] This particular theology, for James Robinson, was readily adapted to the struggle against Communism and racism, agents and expressions of sin and evil. Conversely, this theology became an important building block of democracy, the system that sustained human freedom and justice. Theologically interesting, in practical terms the linkages between Christianity and democracy in Africa have not been fulfilled.

For Robinson, nationalism, the driving force in the founding of the United States, was an expression of the democratic impulse. It was a repudiation of outside control and exploitation. It allowed the peoples of a place to control the resources in their own interests. His concepts of democracy and nationalism were developed when the struggle against colonialism was at its height. Nationalism and self-determination were expressions of responsibility and by extension self-worth, dignity, and freedom. Robinson did not attend to nationalism's other face, authoritarianism and parochialism, in spite of its growing presence in the post-colonial period.

As with all individuals who attempt to effect change, what was as much wrong as right tempered the final verdict. This case study of the vision and advocacy of Rev. James H. Robinson becomes part of the "barometer" of understanding "background assumptions that have informed debates about Africa in liberal Protestant circles."[30] This introduction to the rhetoric, vision, determination, and accomplishments of one man, Dr. James H. Robinson, is testimony that personal witness was, and still remains, a path to freedom, justice, and equality in the name of democracy.

Chapter 3

Martin Luther King, Jr., a "Coalition of Conscience," and Freedom in South Africa

Lewis Baldwin

Martin Luther King Jr. often highlighted the need for "a real coalition of conscience"[1] in the crusade for equal rights and social justice. Here he had in mind the creation of "a grand alliance of labor, civil rights forces, and intellectual and religious leaders," a movement rooted in "spiritual and moral forces" and committed to the actualization of the highest humane, ethical ideal.[2] In King's estimation, this type of coalition reached its greatest maturity during the 1965 voting rights campaign in Selma, Alabama, when hundreds of blacks and whites, "nuns and priests, ministers and rabbis, labor organizers, lawyers, doctors, housemaids, and shopworkers" marched together, all "brimming with vitality and enjoying a rare comradeship." With the power and drama of the entire scene in perspective, King declared, "I knew I was seeing a microcosm of the mankind of the future in this moment of luminous and genuine brotherhood."[3]

This essay explores the joint efforts of Martin Luther King, Jr., George M. Houser, Donald Harrington, Charles Y. Trigg, Bishop James A. Pike, and numerous other American clergy to inspire national and international support, especially among religious leaders and institutions, for the anti-apartheid struggle in South Africa in the 1950s and 1960s. An examination of both primary and secondary sources indicates that these figures viewed

Jim Crow in the American South and apartheid in South Africa as manifestations of the same structure of evil and that the moral and theological challenge they put before the churches with respect to racial segregation extended beyond the United States to embrace the South African context. Some attention is also given to the ways in which King's legacy of struggle and ideas, especially his theological insights into the nature of social evil and his quest for community as the highest ethical ideal, continued to influence the attitudes and activities of clergy and churches toward South African apartheid in the decades after his death.[4]

King's Role within the Anti-Apartheid Coalition

King addressed the problems of the oppressed in South Africa from the time he assumed the pastorate of the Dexter Avenue Baptist Church in Montgomery, Alabama, in the mid-1950s. Standing in the tradition of his own father, the esteemed Baptist preacher and pastor Martin Luther King Sr., and of preacher-intellectuals like Benjamin E. Mays and Howard Thurman, King spoke of a close relationship between the African-American movement against Jim Crow and the black South African struggle against apartheid in his early speeches and sermons.[5] Interestingly enough, King equated both with "the struggle of Moses" and "his devoted followers as they sought to get out of Egypt." As he put it, "This is something of the story of every people struggling for freedom."[6]

While attending the independence celebrations in Ghana in 1957, King, in a conversation with the Anglican priest Michael Scott, who had worked with unwanted lepers in South Africa, put the relationship between the two struggles in more specific terms, comparing events in South Africa to those in Montgomery. He "expressed admiration for the bus boycott outside Johannesburg, with thousands of Africans actually walking ten to fifteen miles a day," and noted, in full agreement with Scott, that "Nonviolence in India and in Alabama 'did something to the oppressor', and so it will even in South Africa." The willingness to suffer without retaliation "will eventually make the oppressor ashamed of his method," King continued, "and the forces of both history and Providence are on the side of freedom." The content and moral tone of King's conversation with Scott resembled the ones he had with Bishop Ambrose Reeves of Johannesburg and Archbishop Trevor Huddleston of Tanganyika, and this conversation reinforced his conviction that clergymen had a unique leadership role to play not only in shaping world opinion regarding apartheid, but also in creating a climate for the triumph of justice and brotherhood.[7]

The beginning of the ANC's Defiance Campaign in South Africa in the early fifties provided much of the impetus for King to unite with other clergymen in supporting anti-apartheid activism inside and outside that country.

Walter Sisulu contacted King for support on behalf of the ANC because his respect for the civil rights leader was matched only by his admiration for the music and politics of Paul Robeson, the African-American artist and activist who supported the Defiance Campaign through his Council on African Affairs.[8] King responded favorably to Sisulu's request, but his involvement in anti-apartheid activities did not become considerable until a few years after the organization of Americans for South African Resistance (AFSAR) in 1951.

AFSAR was formed in New York by a group of clergymen and laymen, all of whom had either worked with or been influenced by A. J. Muste's Fellowship of Reconciliation (FOR), a Christian pacifist organization that began during World War I and taught that peace is not simply "an absence of war but a spirit of unity and harmony among peoples of all nationalities, races, and classes."[9] That group included liberal whites such as the Methodist minister George M. Houser of the Rocky Mountain Annual Conference; Donald Harrington, minister of the Community Church in New York; Charles Y. Trigg, pastor of the Salem Methodist Church in Harlem; Roger Baldwin, Director of the American Civil Liberties Union for several years; the Socialist leader Norman Thomas; and black activists A. Philip Randolph, Bayard Rustin, and Conrad Lynn. King's links with ministers and activists in the FOR meant that becoming involved with AFSAR was only natural for him, especially after it was reorganized and incorporated as the American Committee on Africa (ACOA) in May 1953.[10]

Recognizing bonds and obligations between African Americans and Africans, King had become a member of the ACOA by 1957. He was drawn to the ACOA for numerous reasons, aside from its advocacy of peaceful change and organized resistance against South African apartheid. First, was an interracial organization committed to the realization of the ethical ideal of the beloved community, which was, in King's thinking, the equivalent of the theological principle of the coming of the Kingdom of God on earth. Second, the ACOA was a national organization with international connections, committing its resources to a broader, deeper, and more positive relationship between the United States and all of Africa. Third, the ACOA did not isolate its moral concern for South Africa from the civil rights movement and anticolonial struggles throughout Africa. Finally, the organization comprised clergymen who shared King's belief in the morality and practicality of nonviolence as both a personal and social ethic—clergymen coming together with devoted laypersons to promote the gospel values of peace, justice, reconciliation, inclusiveness, and community as an avenue to a transformed world.[11]

One of King's first major initiatives in support of South African liberation occurred with his involvement with the worldwide "Declaration of Conscience," "a hard-hitting declaration" which asserted that "Freedom and human dignity are in grave jeopardy in the Union of South Africa today." Initiated under the auspices of the ACOA in 1957, this declaration brought together Eleanor Roosevelt, who served as the international chairman of the effort; Bishop James A. Pike, dean of the Episcopal Cathedral of St. John the Divine in New York, who was the U.S. chairman; and King, president of the Southern Christian Leadership Conference and pastor of Montgomery's Dexter Avenue Baptist Church, who was the U.S. vice chairman. The document urged churches, universities, trade unions, veteran groups, business and professional organizations, and, indeed, "all free associations" to make "December 10, 1957, Human Rights Day, a Day of Protest against the organized inhumanity of the South African government and its apartheid policies." It also challenged the white supremacist practices of "the Government of the Union of South Africa," insisting that it "honor its moral and legal obligations as a signatory to the United Nations Charter by honoring the Declaration of Human Rights."[12]

Due to its international appeal and the angry responses of representatives of the South African government, the "Declaration of Conscience" generated enormous publicity. It was signed by 123 world leaders, including religious leaders and theologians such as Albert Luthuli, the Methodist lay preacher, Zulu Chief, and ANC leader from South Africa; Bishop Ambrose Reeves; Rabbi Israel Goldstein; Erich Fromm; Michael Scott; Archbishop Trevor Huddleston; and Martin Buber and Reinhold Niebuhr, both of whom influenced King significantly at the levels of philosophy and methods.[13]

Much of the significance of the "Declaration of Conscience" lies in the fact that it united American and South African religious leaders in mind and spirit in a very special way. The Reverend Henry L. Bird, minister of St. Paul's Church in Bedford, Massachusetts, noted that "A Christian must speak out against such policies as those of the South African Government," and the Episcopal Bishop of West Virginia issued "a memorandum to all the clergy" in his diocese telling them to support the declaration "with a day of prayer." The Councils of Churches in Olympia, Washington, and Kansas City offered similar expressions of support. On the South African side, both Bishop Ambrose Reeves and Albert Luthuli lashed out at South African government officials who denounced the ACOA and the "Declaration of Conscience." In perhaps the most sweeping criticism, Luthuli attacked the apartheid government for branding King and the other sponsors of the declaration "as ultraliberalistic and smearing them as Communist," and he declared that such tactics "did not absolve South Africa from the charges made by leading individuals and statesmen throughout the world."[14] As American and South African religious leaders united their voices and various acts of protest against apartheid, King came to see just how powerful and effective a coalition of conscience could be when addressing global problems with both words and deeds.

After the "Declaration of Conscience" campaign, clergymen in the United States and abroad contacted King extensively about the best way to advance the anti-apartheid crusade to another level. Efforts in this regard were inspired largely by the stubbornness of the South African government, especially by its determination to convict and punish 156 anti-apartheid activists—whites, blacks, coloreds, and Indians—for what it considered acts of treason. In February, 1958, Bishop Ambrose Reeves, the chairman of the Treason Trials Defense Committee, wrote King, George Houser, and other ACOA members, urging them to continue their "efforts in the United States."[15] In a letter to King, Bishop James Pike, referring to Reeves's request, suggested "it seems especially appropriate that we should send to the religious press a letter signed by a number of concerned American churchmen." To encourage worldwide condemnation of the treason trials and to increase fund-raising efforts for political prisoners in South Africa, Pike, King, Houser, and other American clergymen drafted and signed "A Letter to the Religious Press." That letter read in part:

> As Christians and Americans we feel a grave responsibility to help meet the need in South Africa. The treason trials are a challenge to the people of goodwill around the world who realize that much is at stake. Not unmindful of our own failures in race relations in the United States, we nevertheless call for your support to help a people whose government sponsors a more rigid program of segregation.[16]

Many in the United States and abroad considered King unique among American clergy in that he symbolized, perhaps more than anyone else, the essential unity of the civil rights movement in America and the anti-apartheid struggle in South Africa. This regard was most certainly the case with Pike, Houser, and Donald Harrington, who often approached King about issues relative to both contexts. The same might be said of the Anglican priest Michael Scott, who consistently pushed King and other American clergy to take stronger stands against apartheid. In January, 1958, Scott praised King and the ACOA for launching the "Declaration of Conscience," but asserted that "We have felt for a long time that declarations of attitudes toward apartheid, while necessary, are insufficient to meet the serious challenge which it presents to the concept of civilization we in the West have sought to build and the United Nations was brought into existence to defend." Scott went on to recommend how the "Declaration of Conscience" could "be brought to bear in practical forms of action," noting how steps might be taken to exclude South Africa from the Olympic Games, to eliminate the restrictions imposed on non-European members of the nursing profession in South Africa, and to get rid of academic standards that prevent South African universities "from accepting non-European students."[17] While King took such recommendations to heart, he was hardly in a position to act on them in any serious ways. Even so, he commended Scott for keeping the South African problem before the world community. In an ACOA statement in 1959, King declared: "While Christianity has been timid in too much of

Africa, I am glad that Michael Scott—a clergyman—for more than a decade has represented the Herero people of South West Africa when South Africa refused to allow their representatives to appear before the UN."[18]

The black South African activist Albert J. Luthuli shared Scott's view of King and also the idea that American clergymen had critical roles to play in South Africa's movement toward freedom and multiracial democracy. When King's friend G. McLeod Bryan, a religious studies professor at North Carolina's Wake Forest College, visited Luthuli in South Africa in September 1959, the South African leader, under house arrest at the time, informed Bryan of his great respect and admiration for King. Bryan later wrote King, reporting that Luthuli

> told me that the greatest inspiration to him was your Stride Toward Freedom (that Bishop Reeves had put into his hands). Luthuli had been reading it in his cane fields the very day I visited him. He wished for copies to be put into the hands of his African National Congress. I told him I would put the request to you, believing that you would contribute this much and more to South African freedom. His eyes were the brightest when I referred to him as the "King" of South Africa. His odds are so much greater, but he is a profound Christian sharing your views.[19]

Bryan's report to King could not have been more significant, for both King and Luthuli embraced aspects of the philosophy of Mohandas K. Gandhi. Having a similar appreciation for Luthuli and his prophetic challenge to apartheid, and especially for the sit-ins and demonstrations he had led against segregation during the Defiance Campaign, King responded in December 1959:

> May I say that I too have admired you tremendously from a distance. I only regret that circumstances and spatial divisions have made it impossible for us to meet. But I admire your great witness and your dedication to the cause of freedom and human dignity. You have stood amid persecution, abuse, and oppression with a dignity and calmness of spirit seldom paralleled in human history. One day all of Africa will be proud of your achievement.[20]

The ACOA afforded an organizational framework through which King and Luthuli challenged the legitimacy of racial segregation. Both allowed their names to be used to promote the work of the ACOA, especially when appeals were being made for support from religious leaders and organizations. At the request of the ACOA, King became a sponsor of the new Africa Defense and Aid Fund in 1959. Aside from fund-raising activities to aid in the extensive legal costs and family hardships of South African political prisoners, he promoted special days of protest and conferences and workshops on apartheid; signed numerous letters, declarations, and appeals calling for freedom rallies and other acts of protest on behalf of oppressed South

Africans; and served as honorary chairman for some of the ACOA's Africa Freedom Day and Human Rights Day activities.[21] Undoubtedly, King's work with the ACOA, while secondary in importance to his other involvements, was an attractive feature for the growing number of socially prominent and politically minded American clergy who had become supporters of the organization's anti-apartheid activities by the end of the 1950s, among them Harry Emerson Fosdick, Robert McCracken, Reinhold Niebuhr, Adam Clayton Powell, Jr., and Howard Thurman.[22]

Most American clergy in the 1950s, however, remained essentially unfamiliar with the great depth and severity of the race problem in South Africa, knowing nothing of its relationship and similarities to that in the United States. The same applies in the case of King's efforts in the interest of South African freedom. Most white clergy lived comfortably with segregation in American institutions, even in their own churches, and were hardly prepared—spiritually, theologically, morally, or otherwise—to address in any serious way the problem as it existed abroad. Much of the same can be said of African-American clergymen, many of whom refused to actively support King and the civil rights cause in the U.S. Furthermore, since most of these preachers had not received formal training, they were ill-prepared to address world problems to any substantial degree in their sermons and activities.[23]

The 1960s brought new challenges for King and other American clergy who regarded the South African system as a barrier to world peace and community. In March 1960, the South African police shot down sixty-nine black peaceful protesters against Pass Laws at Sharpeville, a massacre that shook religious leaders and institutions throughout the world. King's name, along with that of George Houser, Donald Harrington, and other ACOA members, appeared on several letters highlighting and condemning this tremendous act of violent aggression. One letter signed by King called upon people of goodwill worldwide to "protest the cruel, inhuman massacre in Sharpeville" and to help "meet the needs of the families of those killed and wounded in South Africa."[24] On April 15, two weeks after the massacre, King, Niebuhr, Donald Harrington, and Rabbi Roland B. Gittelsohn of Boston united with some fifty politicians, lawyers, labor leaders, and intellectuals, under the auspices of Americans for Democratic Action (ADA), to urge the American government to take drastic action against the South African government:

> In view of the determination of the South African government to continue on its present appalling and disastrous course of action, we believe that further steps are urgently needed to impress upon it the deep concern with which the American people view its actions. We therefore urge that our ambassador be recalled to Washington for consultation on the situation and that, while these consultations are in progress, American purchases of gold from South Africa be suspended. As you know, these are measures long sanctified by diplomatic usage, and are a form of language among nations—strong language, but amply

> justified by the gravity of events. We are confident that the U.S. people will support you in these actions.[25]

King, Houser, and other clergy supporters of the ACOA took additional steps as they considered the tragedy at Sharpeville. Houser reported in 1961 that they had sent $19,050 "to South Africa in 1960 to support and sustain the families of the victims of the Sharpeville Massacre, to defend those arrested in the aftermath of the massacre, and to provide legal aid for those on trial, since 1956, for 'treason.'"[26] Aside from contributing financially, King gave the ACOA permission to use his name on all its printed material and responded favorably to the request that he "become a part of a national committee of 100 prominent citizens to push for a revised U.S. policy toward Southern Africa and Africa as a whole.'"[27] Perhaps more important for King, Houser, Harrington, and other ACOA affiliates, the naming of Albert Luthuli as the Nobel Peace Prize recipient in 1960 occurred only months after the shootings at Sharpeville, a gesture that reflected both the sentiments of the international community and Luthuli's own efforts to keep the anti-apartheid crusade in South Africa nonviolent despite the tragedy.[28]

Forbidden to travel and engage in political activity by the South African government, Luthuli was unable to personally accept the award until late 1961. In any case, this development helped set the context for Luthuli and King, who would himself receive the Nobel Peace Prize in 1964, to collaborate as cosponsors of "An Appeal for Action Against Apartheid," which was another call for an international protest against the racist regime of South Africa. Like the earlier "Declaration of Conscience," "An Appeal for Action Against Apartheid," drafted in 1962, was essentially an ACOA document. It defined apartheid as "the political, social, and economic domination of nearly 12 million nonwhites by 3 million whites" and recommended the following:

- Hold meetings and demonstrations on December 10, Human Rights Day.
- Urge your church, union lodge, or club to observe this day as one of protest.
- Urge your government to support economic sanctions.
- Write to your Mission to the United Nations urging adoption of a resolution calling for international isolation of South Africa.
- Don't buy South Africa's products.
- Don't trade or invest in South Africa.
- Translate public opinion into public action by explaining facts to all peoples, to groups to which you belong, and to countries of which you are citizens, until an effective international quarantine of apartheid is established.[29]

Religious leaders, politicians, social activists, educators, writers, journalists, labor leaders, and UN representatives were among the thousands who signed "An Appeal for Action Against Apartheid," a grand alliance that once again symbolized what King meant when he spoke in terms of a coalition of conscience. The names of Harrington, Fosdick, Niebuhr, and Pike, who had endorsed a "Declaration of Conscience" five years earlier, also appeared on the document along with those of Adam Clayton Powell, Jr., John A. Mackay, Rabbis Israel Goldstein and Abba Hillel Silver, and other American clergy.[30] Interestingly enough, these figures were united in spirit and purpose with Canon L. John Collins and Michael Scott of Great Britain, Bishop Trevor Huddleston of Tanganyika, Bishop Ambrose Reeves of Johannesburg, Martin Niemoller of the Evangelical Church in the Federal Republic of Germany, and numerous other clergy worldwide who also signed "An Appeal for Action Against Apartheid,"[31] with King and Luthuli best symbolizing the unity of the African-American and black South African struggles.

The effort to promote "An Appeal for Action Against Apartheid" occurred in conjunction with the rise of the American Negro Leadership Conference on Africa (ANLCA) in mid-June 1962. Organized by King, Roy Wilkins of the National Association for the Advancement of Colored People (NAACP), Whitney M. Young of the National Urban League, A. Philip Randolph of the Brotherhood of Sleeping Car Porters, James Farmer of the Congress of Racial Equality (CORE), and Dorothy Height of the National Council of Negro Women (NCNW), dubbed "the big six of the civil rights movement," the ANLCA was designed to give the African-American community a stronger voice in U.S. policy toward Africa. Backed from its origins by Houser, Harrington, and other liberal white ministers in the ACOA, it held several influential conferences in the 1960s, some of which targeted southern Jim Crow and South African apartheid. The ANLCA was sponsored by some twenty-eight organizations, but "it never lived up to its potential," mainly because "it was never able to establish an independent base in the black community," and especially in the black churches.[32] Strangely, most black and white American clergy remained virtually unfamiliar with the organization, despite King's references to what he termed "the American Negro's growing awareness of his world citizenship" and despite his often repeated claim that African Americans and South Africa's nonwhites shared "a common destiny"—"to live on in poverty and rejection or to walk proudly as free men in our own nations."[33]

King's disappointment with the failure of most American clergy to prophetically challenge racial discrimination had reached fever pitch by the early 1960s, as evidenced by his critique of the church and its leadership in his "Letter from the Birmingham City Jail" (1963). Aside from himself and leaders like Howard Thurman and Adam Clayton Powell, Jr., who had combined civil rights activism with a call for a boycott of South African goods, black preachers generally gave silent or noncommittal responses, approaches that King found inexcusable, especially since these figures, as he put it, are "freer, more independent, than any other person in the community."[34] White preachers presented an even greater problem for King, even as he considered the commitments of Houser, Harrington, Pike, and others to the elimination of white supremacy in both the United States and South Africa. Although Billy Graham, the great evangelist and dean of white preachers, spoke occasionally against Jim Crow and apartheid, he, like most Evangelical and fundamentalist leaders, was more concerned about maintaining his base of support, especially in the South, than in taking the type of radical steps needed to encourage genuine racial reconciliation and integration.[35]

On the whole, white churches continued to embrace what Bill J. Leonard calls "a theology for racism" in the sixties. Many preachers in the Southern Baptist Convention (SBC) turned to the Bible in defending racial segregation, a tendency that had disturbing implications for the struggles in America and South Africa. In a sermon entitled, "God the Original Segregator," Carey Daniel of Dallas, Texas, standing in the tradition of southern pro-slavery advocates in antebellum times, appealed to the myth of Ham in Genesis 10:32 to make his point. Southern Baptist preachers such as Wallie A. Criswell and Hugh Pyle commonly labeled the protest activities of King and other clergy *unbiblical*.[36] King dismissed such actions as "a glaring misrepresentation of what the scripture teaches"[37] and emphatically noted the blatant inconsistency between the SBC's support for apartheid and its declared mission to bring the whole world to Christ:

> You know the largest Protestant denomination in the South is the Southern Baptist Convention. And I happen to be a Baptist preacher. I pastor a big Baptist Church in Atlanta, Georgia. And do you know my church could never join the Southern Baptist Convention, because it's an all-white convention. Now it's denominational, and has a lot of money. . . . They send thousands and millions of dollars to Africa for the cause of missions. But do you know, an African student was studying at Mercer University in Georgia, and the First Baptist Church, white, of Macon, Georgia, where Mercer University is located, sponsored and gave him a scholarship to Mercer, and yet the young man, when he got here, decided he wanted to go to that church . . . and to sing in the choir. The pastor was for it, the assistant pastor, and the choir director, but do you know the members of that church refused to allow that young man to be a member while he was a student, refused to allow him to sing in the choir, and they voted the preacher, the assistant pastor, and the choir director out. . . . And if a Negro went to many of those churches today, they would be kicked out. . . .[38]

For King, the leadership of the SBC suffered from the same sickness as that of the Dutch Reformed Church (DRC) in South Africa, which formally endorsed apartheid. In both cases, he held, a deaf ear had always been turned to the oppressed and the victimized in society. Of the DRC, King lamented:

> Go to South Africa today. And there you will see some 14 million black men, women, boys and girls, segregated on 2 percent of their own land . . . having to use passes to walk the streets. Pretty soon you will discover that these vicious, inhuman apartheid practices are sanctioned, and to a large extent set up, by the Dutch Reformed Protestant Church. Over and over again, Chief Luthuli, that great black leading Christian, has knocked on the door of the church of South Africa . . . but always the response has been, "Get away from this door. We don't have time to bother with you. We're busy reciting our creedal system."[39]

King's affiliation with the ANLCA heightened the expectation that he would advance his activities on behalf of South African freedom to another level. Strangely enough, this involvement did not happen, even though George Houser, the Director of the ACOA, and other liberal white clergy in that organization often approached King with ideas about how he might become a more effective spokesman for oppressed South Africans. Although King's signature continued to appear on the ANLCA's and the ACOA's fundraising letters and petitions calling for U.S. government action against South Africa's white regime in the mid- and late 1960s, heavy involvements in civil rights campaigns in Birmingham, Washington, D. C., St. Augustine, Selma, Chicago, Memphis, and other cities, coupled with the decline in white liberal support for his SCLC and with his inability to gain entrance into South Africa, made it impossible for him to provide much beyond what might be regarded as symbolic support for the anti-apartheid cause.[40]

Even so, the demand for King to become a more powerful force in the crusade against South African racism was always there. Houser approached the civil rights leader in April 1963 as the Birmingham campaign was reaching a critical stage, suggesting that he appear before the UN General Assembly's committee on the apartheid policy of South Africa:

> I am reinforced in my opinion that it would have tremendous effect if you would be able to appear before the committee at a time agreeable to you and to their schedule. They are very enthusiastic about this, not only because of your position in this country, but also because you, along with Chief Luthuli, helped to initiate our *Appeal for Action Against Apartheid* around Human Rights Day last December 10th. Your appearance before the committee to make a brief statement would have great impact around the world and certainly in South Africa. It also would help bring this whole problem of the U.S. relationship to South Africa forcibly to the attention of officials in Washington. . . . Your participation in that struggle (in Birmingham) will make all the more effective what you can say about the struggle in Africa as well.[41]

Similar requests and challenges were put before King later. In June 1963, Enuga S. Reddy, the Indian activist and Gandhi admirer who served as

Principal Secretary of the UN Special Committee on the Policies of Apartheid of the Government of the Republic of South Africa, actually tried to arrange King's testimony at the U. N.; Collin Gonze, an ACOA staff person, prepared the rough draft of a statement for King to read on the occasion. Although King consented to testifying before the UN committee, a time agreeable for both parties was not found.[42] George Houser contacted King yet again in September 1963, a month after the celebrated "I Have a Dream" speech in Washington, D.C., urging him to make an appearance before the UN committee. "There was never a time more than the present when solidarity between African nationalist leaders and American civil rights leaders was more needed than at the present time," said Houser in a letter to King.[43] While other clergy in the ACOA agreed with Houser's challenge to King, growing commitments to the struggle in America made such an appearance impossible. Some actually felt that "perhaps Dr. King had been prevailed upon by the State Department not to speak before the UN committee," but this was apparently not the case.[44]

King's success in intersecting a core of dedicated black and liberal white clergymen in his civil rights campaigns in the 1960s was not duplicated in his efforts against South African apartheid. In the Albany Movement in 1962, numerous religious leaders protested with King and were arrested; much the same occurred in Birmingham in 1963 as Fred Shuttlesworth and other black preachers in the Alabama Christian Movement for Human Rights (ACHR) united with King and his SCLC in a series of street demonstrations.[45] This coalition of conscience comprised largely of clergymen became a more impressive force during the voting rights campaign in Selma in 1965 when some four hundred white priests, rabbis, and Protestant ministers participated. King called the Selma campaign "the warmest expression of religious unity of Catholic, Protestant, and Jew in the nation's history."[46] His general failure to organize American clergymen in a similar fashion to protest South Africa's racism is intriguing, especially in view of his conviction that the oppressed in America and South Africa were engaged in essentially the same struggle and also in his view of his frequent references to bonds and obligations between African Americans and peoples of color in South Africa. One can only conclude that the struggle in the United States consumed so much of the time, energy, and resources of the activist clergymen who were loyal to King that it was virtually impossible for most of them to constitute a formidable force in the crusade against South African apartheid.

Eugene Carson Blake, the Presbyterian clergyman and former president of the National Council of Churches (NCC), alluded to the painful silence of most American church leaders with respect to South Africa in a speech on "The Moral Responsibility of the Church in a Secular Society" in 1960. Delivering the Rauschenbusch Lecture at a convocation of the Colgate-Rochester Divinity School and the New York State Council of Churches, Blake observed that South Africa was "facing a political crisis so severe that even at our distance we can read about it almost everyday in our newspapers"; but he lamented that "a simple condemnation of the South African situation is hardly in order for an American churchman however much he agrees that the government policies of South Africa are leading that nation to a disaster both predictable and deserved." Convinced that "no responsible Christian Church in either" the United States or South Africa "finds Biblical grounds for racial prejudice," Blake attributed the silence of so many of his fellow clergymen to a range of factors, including fear, an excessively individualistic approach to the Christian faith, and the overriding sense that "our comfortable way of life may be upset, that our congregations will be divided if we apply the gospel to the social, economic, and political areas of life. . . ."[47] King had often raised these same concerns in his reflections on the moral responsibility of the church in relation to both Jim Crow and apartheid. Blake's own failure to become a strong, consistent, and uncompromising voice in the anti-apartheid crusade would heavily undermine the power of his words.

The Nobel Peace Prize led King to think more seriously about South Africa and other world problems that he, by his own admission, had not addressed to his satisfaction up to that point. Receiving the award in December 1964, King vowed to extend his work more and more beyond the boundaries of America.[48] Significantly, King "saw the award as an honour for the leaders of the struggle all over the world" and "mentioned especially Chief Albert Luthuli, a former Peace Prize winner, whose struggle . . . had been met with brutal oppression."[49] Clearly, King was thinking in terms of a global coalition of conscience, one geared toward the elimination of violence and oppression and the establishment of the beloved community. Unsurprisingly, he began to speak more forcefully and consistently on issues such as the Vietnam war, peace in the Middle East, and poverty in Asia, Africa, and other parts of the so-called third world, always challenging his fellow clergymen to do likewise.[50] Also, King delivered two extensive and thought-provoking speeches on South Africa—one immediately before and the other after he accepted the Nobel Peace Prize.

King gave the speech "Address on South African Independence" in London before a group of persons from America, India, Pakistan, the West Indies, South Africa, and other parts of Africa on December 7, 1964. In that address, he complained that Robert Sobukwe, Nelson Mandela, and "many hundreds" more were "wasting away in Robben Island Prison and scolded Great Britain and the United States for their economic support of South Africa. King also praised anti-apartheid activists in South Africa as one of the brightest hopes for avoiding "a race war," and he suggested that Great Britain and America should not "buy South African goods, not buy South African gold, " and "put an embargo on oil. . . ." In other words, throughout the fifties and early sixties, King spoke of the essential unity of the African-American and black South African struggles, also giving some attention to the dissimilarities between them:

> In our struggle for freedom and justice in the U. S., which has also been so long and arduous, we feel a powerful sense of identification with those in the far more deadly struggle for freedom in South Africa. We know how Africans there, and their friends of other races, strove for half a century to win their freedom by nonviolent methods; we have honored Chief Luthuli for his leadership, and we know how this nonviolence and restraint were only met by increasing violence from the State, increasing repression, culminating in the shootings at Sharpeville and all that has happened since. Clearly, there is much in Mississippi and Alabama to remind South Africans of their own country, yet even in Mississippi we can organize to register Negro voters, we can speak to the press, we can in short organize the people in nonviolent action. But in South Africa even the mildest form of nonviolent resistance meets with years of imprisonment. We can understand how in that situation people felt so desperate that they turned to other methods, such as sabotage.[51]

King knew that the lack of a natural rights tradition in South Africa, in contrast to its presence in the United States, made the anti-apartheid struggle unique, to say nothing of a range of other factors, such as tribalism, South Africa's racial composition, and "the means available to the oppressor" there. George Houser, Donald Harrington, and other clergy supporters of the ACOA and the ANLCA shared King's perspective on these matters; they applauded his "Address on South African Independence" as a major step in clarifying the relationship between the freedom movements in the United States and South Africa.[52]

King's longest speech on South Africa would be delivered on December 10, 1965, Human Rights Day, at Hunter College in New York, a few months after he had called for a Marshall Plan to benefit all African nations economically. Houser took the lead in planning the event, commenting in a letter to King:

> We feel that the American Committee on Africa should observe this day with a large meeting in New York, presenting speakers who will link the freedom struggle in our South with that in South Africa, where the fight is becoming so almost humanly impossible that they need every bit of hope and brotherly encouragement that we on the outside can possibly give them.... I know how very busy your own work keeps you. But I have noted your increasing concern for the deteriorating and humanly horrible situation in South Africa, and for this reason I feel sure that if it is in your power you will do this for us—not for ACOA—but for the millions of our co-workers who suffer in the land of apartheid.[53]

King's appearance at the Hunter College event attracted wide attention, and some 3,500 were present for what was called the civil rights leader's "South Africa Benefit Speech." Houser and other clergymen from both the ACOA and the ecclesiastical communities of New York also attended what up to that juncture was the largest event sponsored by the ACOA on behalf of a free South Africa.[54] In an atmosphere saturated with the spirit of freedom songs rendered by Miriam Makeba, the South African singing star, and Pete Seeger, the American folk and civil rights singer, King, who entitled his speech, "Let My People Go,"[55] in honor of Chief Luthuli, underscored America's failure to deal seriously and firmly with South Africa's apartheid regime and went on to remind nations everywhere of what he considered the only moral course toward a free, just, peaceful, racially integrated, and democratic South Africa:

> With respect to South Africa . . . our protest is so muted and peripheral it merely mildly disturbs the sensibilities of the segregationists, while our trade and investments substantially stimulate their economy to greater heights. We pat them on the wrist in permitting racially mixed receptions in our Embassy, and by exhibiting films depicting Negro artists. But we give them massive support through American investments in motor and rubber industries, by extending some forty million dollars in loans through our most distinguished banking and financial institutions, by purchasing gold and other minerals mined by black slave labor, by giving them a sugar quota, by maintaining three tracking stations there, and by providing them with the prestige of a nuclear reactor built with our technical cooperation and fueled with refined uranium supplied by us. . . . Have we the power to be more than peevish with South Africa, but yet refrain from acts of war? To list the extensive economic relations of the great powers with South Africa is to suggest a potent nonviolent path. The international potential of nonviolence has never been employed. Nonviolence has been practiced within the national borders of India, the U. S., and in regions of Africa with spectacular success. The time has come fully to utilize nonviolence through a massive international boycott which would involve the USSR, Great Britain, France, the U. S., Germany, and Japan. Millions of people can personally give expression to their abhorrence of the world's worst racism through such a far flung boycott. No nation professing a concern for man's dignity could avoid assuming its obligations if people of all states and races adopted a firm stand.[56]

The "South Africa Benefit Speech" highlighted the growing interracial character of the anti-apartheid crusade inside South Africa, a development King and other clergy in the ACOA considered immensely important. "Even more inspiring is the fact that in South Africa itself incredibly brave white people are risking their careers, their homes and their lives in the cause of human justice," King reported. Noting that "the powerful unity" of black and white South Africans alone "is stronger than the most potent and entrenched racism," King insisted, with intense feeling, "The time has come for an international alliance of peoples of all nations against racism." Obviously, King was pressing the need for a real global coalition of conscience, one that would work tirelessly toward a global beloved community, or a world in which humans attach great value to mutual acceptance, interpersonal and intergroup living, and shared power:

> The whole human race will benefit when it ends the abomination that has diminished the stature of man for too long. This is the task to which we are called by the suffering in South Africa, and our response should be swift and unstinting. Out of this struggle will come the glorious reality of the family of man.[57]

Interestingly enough, King never again participated in an event of this magnitude; nor did he give another speech on South Africa comparable to the one delivered at Hunter College. Responding to South African religious leaders, academics, and student organizations, from which he had long received invitations, King actually applied for a visa to visit South Africa in 1966, "to exchange cultural and human rights concerns," but representatives of the South African government denied him the privilege.[58] As he divided his time between activities in the South and a Chicago Freedom Movement in 1966 and between the planning of a Poor People's Campaign and active involvement in the antiwar movement and the Memphis sanitation strike in 1967–68, King found himself far too busy to exert a powerful and sustained influence on events in South Africa. When George Houser wrote him in January 1966 about participating in hearings on American policy toward South Africa before the Sub-Committee on Africa of the House Foreign Affairs Committee, King seemed interested but other commitments compelled him to decline the offer.[59] Liberal white and Jewish contributions to SCLC and King's campaigns began to drop sharply, making it difficult for him to pursue his own civil rights agenda in the United States, let alone the anti-apartheid activities of the ACOA and the ANLCA. The last couple of years or so of King's life, 1966–1968, consequently, were not particularly eventful in relation to the struggle in South Africa.

The serious challenge in those two years to King's belief in the potential for genuinely positive and lasting change in both South Africa and the United States led some of his critics to assume that he was not as hopeful or optimistic about the future of humankind. Indeed, this claim has some justification. A more militant phase and the call for black power, a trend that worried black and white clergy who embraced his cause, was eclipsing King's own nonviolent movement. King saw in both South Africa and the United States a growing, disturbing tendency among blacks and whites to justify racial separatism and to resort to violence as a means of settling racial conflict. King's hope for some type of permanent organization linking the concerns of African Americans and oppressed South Africans was essentially dashed as he witnessed the demise of the ANLCA. The death of Chief Luthuli, South Africa's prophet of peaceful change, in 1967, under strange and questionable circumstances, left him quite sad and bitter. This sense of reality, coupled with the insensitivity and unresponsiveness of the U.S. and South African governments, left King somewhat pessimistic about the possibility of the liberation of the oppressed in South Africa and the United States in the immediate future.[60]

Even so, King's challenge to American clergy and the churches around the apartheid issue never faded, especially since his greatest frustration was with the ways in which apartheid scarred and divided the body of Christ. In 1967, he referred to the Union of South Africa as "The classic example of organized and institutionalized racism" and reiterated the need for a worldwide coalition of conscience, led by religious leaders and institutions, to end racism in South Africa and throughout the globe.[61] King supported in principle the efforts of ACOA representatives to have South Africa barred from the 1968 Olympic Games in Mexico City and allowed his name to be used in connection with efforts to force the release of South African political prisoners and to raise funds for their families.[62] He also insisted that African Americans continue their leadership in bringing multiracial democracy to South Africa and cited the need for broader and more drastic forms of civil disobedience inside South Africa.[63] In early 1968, just prior to his assassination, King, surrounded by African-American clergy, actually evoked the memory of Albert Luthuli, comparing his nonviolent civil disobedience to that of Shadrach, Meshach, and Abednego in the Old Testament. Said he, "I'm convinced that if I had lived in South Africa I would have joined Chief Luthuli, the late Chief Luthuli, as he had his campaigns, openly to disobey those laws, and to refuse to comply with the pass system, where people had to have passes and all that stuff to walk the streets."[64]

King's death on April 4, 1968, meant that no other American clergyman of his stature remained to speak authoritatively to the South African situation. Black preachers such as Adam Clayton Powell Jr. and Jesse Jackson would become exceptions, and to a great extent Leon Sullivan would be. George Houser and other liberal white clergy associated with the ACOA would continue their anti-apartheid efforts, but nothing significant beyond the usual petition drives, appeals to the U.S. government, and fund-raising activity was achieved. Meeting in London with members of the International Defence and Aid Fund to discuss the South African problem within the context of global concerns on April 19–21, 1968, Houser and other ACOA representatives challenged religious leaders, social activists, and people of goodwill throughout the world to rededicate themselves to the crusade for South African freedom. They reminded all present that King's "constant struggle for racial justice and equality was a momentous influence not only in the United States, but also in Africa and throughout the world."[65]

Southern Africa Activism and the Coalition of Conscience after King's Death

King's powerful legacy of ideas and social activism was not lost on those American clergypersons who continued to protest against apartheid in the 1970s. Aside from supporting South African freedom fighters financially and morally, Houser and his fellow clergymen in the ACOA continued to promote King's image of the beloved community as the ideal for South Africa. They occasionally invited South Africans to meet with them and to update them on developments in their country. Of particular importance to them was South Africa's stubborn persistence in frustrating Namibia's quest for full independence. They supported the UN's 1976 *Resolution 385*, which condemned South Africa's "illegal occupation of Namibia, its growing military domination, and its oppressive rule," and which also called for "elections under UN supervision and control leading to independence."[66] The ACOA's positions on these matters were very much in line with views long held by King, who had consistently expressed an interest in the status of Southwest Africa.

African-American clergymen who had either worked closely with King or had been inspired by him sought to build on his efforts to bring the civil rights and anti-apartheid movements into full cooperation with each other. Ralph D. Abernathy, who succeeded King as president of the SCLC, and Jesse Jackson, who had headed the Operation Breadbasket arm of that organization under King, continued to advocate a nonviolent solution to the apartheid problem throughout the seventies. Along with Joseph Lowery, Walter Fauntroy, Bernard Lee, and other clergy who had assisted King in SCLC, they continued to echo King's call for the international community to reject military means while imposing diplomatic and economic sanctions against the South African government. In September 1976, Lee, the Executive Vice President of the SCLC, sent a strongly worded letter to the UN Secretary-General Kurt Waldheim, noting that the indiscriminate killing of South African blacks made it impossible for them "to continue the nonviolent tactics they learned from the late Dr. Martin Luther King Jr." Lee recommended that the UN dispatch a peacekeeping force to South Africa, a position that civil rights and anti-apartheid activists widely supported in the period following the Soweto uprising.[67] At times, King had advanced the idea of a larger UN role inside South Africa, especially as he considered the various ways in which world pressure could be brought to bear on the apartheid problem.

Despite the efforts of certain clergypersons in both the ACOA and the SCLC, the relationship between the civil rights and anti-apartheid struggles would never again be the same, and for obvious reasons. Both King and Luthuli, who had epitomized that relationship, had passed on, and the worldwide coalition of conscience they had sought to create in their assaults on apartheid, a coalition always somewhat fragile despite its effectiveness on some levels, gradually faded in the shadow of more militant forces. Moreover, there was a growing shift away from King's and Luthuli's conceptions of interracial community achieved through peaceful means, especially with the emergence of the Black Consciousness Movement (BCM) in South Africa under Stephen Biko and others, the rise of liberation theology there, the South African government's "violent repression of protests and the abundance of new martyrs," and the ANC's and Pan-African Congress's (PAC) increasing reliance on political activism and armed struggle. The PAC and black South African liberation theologians fully embraced the BCM's emphasis on black unity—even black separatism on some levels—and all of these groups, together with the ANC, sanctioned violent resistance in some cases.[68] Similar developments had occurred in the United States with Malcolm X and the rise of black power. In any case, these growing trends seemed to reflect what one newspaper columnist, referring to the 1970s, termed "King's fading legacy in South Africa."[69]

Some clergypersons in both the United States and South Africa continued to insist on the relevance of King's ideas and methods for the South African context; they sought, in their own unique ways, to advance that legacy in words and actions. American clergymen like Houser, Abernathy, Jackson, Fauntroy, Lowery, and Lee have already been mentioned in this regard. Also on the American side, Leon Sullivan—pastor of the Zion Baptist Church in Philadelphia, founder of the Opportunities Industrialization Centers of America (OIC) in 1964, and a member of the board of General Motors—figured prominently. In 1977, Sullivan introduced the "Sullivan Principles," a voluntary code of conduct for U.S. companies with affiliates in South Africa. This document advocated a policy of nondiscrimination in hiring practices, especially in quarters designed for eating and comfort, in work facilities, and in employment benefits. Imbued with the spirit of King and the civil rights movement, the "Sullivan Principles" were eventually adopted by churches, universities, and other institutions as a minimal standard of conduct for South Africa-related U.S. companies in which they owned stock. Indeed, the "Sullivan Principles," along with the founding of TransAfrica under Randall Robinson in 1977, symbolized the continuing unity of the civil rights and anti-apartheid movements in the post-King era. Both pushed for a more positive and aggressive U.S. policy toward South Africa, and some of the original sponsors of both had worked closely with King a decade earlier.[70]

On the South African side, clergymen like the Anglican Bishop Desmond Tutu and Allan Boesak of the Dutch Reformed Mission Church contributed significantly to keeping both King's and Luthuli's legacies alive inside South Africa. Tutu was quite conscious of King's importance when he explored the similarities between African and African-American liberation theologies in a 1975 essay; so was Boesak when he compared the ethics of King and Malcolm X in his doctoral dissertation at the Theological Academy of Kampen in the Netherlands in 1976.[71] Both men connected spiritually and intellectually with King, an ability not so readily evident among the more radical elements in the BCM, the PAC, the ANC, and the black theology movement. Tutu fully embraced King's view that racial separatism in all forms not only degrades human personality and denies the interrelatedness and interdependence of human beings, but also violates the parenthood of God and the essential oneness of God's creation. He frequently echoed King's belief that the love of God is inseparable from the love of neighbor; in many of his speeches and publications in the 1970s, he noted that "together we must learn to live as brothers or together we will be forced to perish as fools," a statement obviously taken from King.[72] This communitarian vision also registered in powerful ways with Boesak, who, like Tutu, found King's prophetic model of leadership useful for South Africans as they seriously entertained questions regarding the role of the minister and the church in an unjust and violent society.

In his *Farewell to Innocence: A Socio-Ethical Study on Black Theology and Black Power* (1977), Boesak, inspired largely by the African-American theologian and clergyman James H. Cone, contended that King helped create "a new consciousness" that "influenced black people in South Africa and all over the world." He also underscored the importance of King's reflections on "the relation between racism and capitalism" and noted that King urged the oppressed to develop "an unassailable and majestic sense of their own value," a "Black self-love," that could serve as "the creative precondition for a new black/white relationship." For Boesak, King's interpretation of black power as "a cry of disappointment," as "a psychological call to manhood," and as "a call to black people to amass their political and economic strength," was not an affirmation of racial separatism and violence, and in that sense had positive meaning and significance for African Americans and black South Africans alike. Interestingly enough, Boesak included King in a long history of African-American and black South African clergymen, comprised of Henry H. Garnet, Malcolm X, and Albert Luthuli, all of whom sought to transform their people's powerlessness into "creative and positive power."[73]

But Boseak and Tutu did not engage in an uncritical acceptance of King's ideas and methods when relating them to the South African context, a tendency not evident in Ralph Abernathy, Jesse Jackson, Bernard Lee, Walter Fauntroy, and other African-American clergy who had worked with King. While in general agreement with King's ideal of genuine human community achieved through nonviolent means, Boesak held that the South African situation was "such that political integration" or "black/white coalitions cannot be realistically discussed"; he reasoned that at times "retaliatory violence is necessary for the affirmation, the self-respect, the manhood of black people."[74] Tutu essentially agreed, suggesting that a violent response to oppression can sometimes be justified and unavoidable. After expressing his own preference for nonviolence at the South African Missiological Conference in 1977, Tutu explained why it was irrational for the world to expect oppressed South Africans to limit themselves to nonviolence as an absolute principle:

1. The Christian Church is not entirely pacifist;
2. Blacks are left wondering what practical alternatives are available, given the palpable failure of nonviolent forms of protest and opposition;

3. There is a hollow sound to white arguments for the way of nonviolence; given their at least tacit support for state and legal violence.[75]

Despite their questions about the applicability of certain aspects of King's methods to their own social, political, and cultural context, Tutu and Boesak were just as instrumental as Jackson, Lee, Fauntroy, and other African-American clergy when it came to making the King legacy a vital part of the debate over means and ends in the 1970s. Indeed, these men continued to symbolize that bridge between the struggles in America and South Africa. Andrew Young, the U.S. representative to the U.N., and also a clergyman who worked closely with King and the SCLC, captured the essence of that connection during an international tribute to King in Atlanta in 1979, insisting that the legacy of King could not be divorced from that of great nonviolent activists in South African history:

> Nonviolence came to us from Africa. It was Mahatma Gandhi who in his early protest used nonviolence against *apartheid*. It moved on to India. It was reborn again under the leadership of Chief Albert Luthuli. . . . We have seen it develop in such a way in the United States of America that is quite different from the experiences which occurred in other parts of the world. That is as it should be. But one of the things that concern me is that we in the United Nations and those of us who come out of this nonviolent tradition have always tended to think of nonviolence as it was last demonstrated in our own town. I would like to contend that what we see happening across the world today is very much influenced by a nonviolent understanding of how change can occur.[76]

Some black clergymen in America sought to work from a strong ecclesiastical base when addressing South African apartheid. In 1975 Bishop H. H. Brookins, who had previously been expelled from South Africa and Rhodesia because of his attacks on their racial practices, led the Bishop's Council of the African Methodist Episcopal Church (AME) in a call for black majority rule in both countries. In 1978 clergymen in the AME Church, the African Methodist Episcopal Zion Church (AMEZ), the National Baptist Convention of America, the National Baptist Convention, USA, and the Progressive National Convention united under the auspices of the National Council of Churches and asked major banks in the United States "to establish a policy that no new loans will be made nor existing loans renewed to the Pretoria, South Africa government."[77] These steps were aimed largely at forcing greater action against apartheid on the part of the NCC, an ecclesiastical body which, much like the larger World Council of Churches (WCC), had confined its activities mostly to the adoption of resolutions and petitions.[78] Fundamentalist and Evangelical clergymen in America were even less responsive to the cause; some, like Bob Jones and Jerry Falwell, supported racial segregation. Billy Graham, who had called King "an example of

Christian love" and who had predicted the demise of segregation in both the United States and South Africa in the 1960s, was a rare exception. Speaking to a racially mixed crowd of some 45,000 in Durban, South Africa in 1973, Graham warned that "If we don't become brothers, and become brothers fast, we will destroy ourselves in a worldwide racial conflagration." Graham went on to declare in a statement reminiscent of remarks that King had consistently made in the sixties that:

> This is not just a South African problem. This is a worldwide problem. America today has the finest civil rights laws the world has known, but the problem is deeper than the law. The problem is the human heart. We all need a new heart.[79]

King's philosophy and methods met perhaps their greatest test in South Africa in the 1980s. The obstacles to change in that country remained as formidable as ever. Polarization reached unprecedented levels along both racial and tribal boundaries as frightened and insecure whites moved increasingly to the right and as forces in the ANC and Inkatha clashed. Debates concerning violence and nonviolence occurred in the churches, the halls of academia, and the public square; a final, fatal confrontation between the races appeared more possible than at any time in the past. Frustrated with the lack of sufficient international pressure against South Africa, especially on the part of countries like the United States and Great Britain, even Allan Boesak, Desmond Tutu, and other proponents of nonviolence became less hopeful of a peaceful end to apartheid. In this "critical, quite traumatic period in the history of our land," as one black South African put it, the search for alternatives to a possible race war intensified, a search that involved not only a serious, critical study of classical Christian attitudes toward war and peace, but also a reexamination of Gandhian-Luthulian-Kingian principles.[80]

The continuing trend toward a more widespread, violent resistance to apartheid worried clergymen in the United States and South Africa, for it seemed so inevitable as black youth continued to seek military training in ANC guerrilla camps in Zambia and other countries, and as PAC guerrillas, who had spent years in bush camps in the Congo and China, persisted in their attempted incursions into South Africa. With this shifting moral and political climate in mind, Beyers Naude, the Dutch Reformed minister and the general secretary of the South African Council of Churches (SACC), raised an issue that weighed heavily on the thinking of American and South African clergy who had long refused to separate the civil rights movement from the anti-apartheid struggle. "Given the support of the major Western powers for apartheid, and the lacking unity of peace-loving forces," said Naude in 1986, "the crucial question" for South Africans "who admire Martin Luther King Jr." is "what relevance" his principles "have for their situation."[81] As had always been the case, there was no single, clearly stated answer to this question.

Walter Fauntroy and Andrew Young were among those clergy and former King aides who visited parts of southern Africa and discovered firsthand the difficulty of selling King's nonviolent methods in the eighties. In January 1987, they addressed a meeting of African political leaders in Gaborone, Botswana, where most appeared in no mood to talk about unconditional, unselfish love and the redemptive power of nonviolence. Fauntroy, also a congressman from Washington, D.C., briefly referred to King's birthday on that occasion, "but purposely avoided the mention of King's philosophy of nonviolent protest because he decided 'it is not relevant for the situation.'" Sensitive to the feelings of the black South Africans who were present, Fauntroy asserted "the violence of the South African government has suspended the moral obligation of pacifism." But when asked if King would agree with a violent response to apartheid at that particular point, Fauntroy emphatically responded, "He would not. He would have said that if the entire world turned violent, I would not."[82]

Andrew Young was much more aggressive in advocating King's approach at the Botswana meeting. He lectured African politicians and students on the peaceful elimination of American apartheid under King's leadership and advocated tolerance, patience, and quiet perseverance on the part of South African freedom fighters. "Chucks of skepticism from five hundred students greeted" Young's comments, and "one man on crutches hotly declared himself unlikely to believe a call for nonviolence from an American such as Young," who was accepted as a typical politician from the white West. "You are already violent, you have Star Wars, you have enough arms to do the job," cried the man. Young found himself grasping for words when the man alluded to the hypocrisy of an American government that encouraged pacifism among oppressed South Africans while supplying weapons to rebels in Angola. "The audience was suspicious of a theory apparently endorsing docility," reported the newspaper columnist Jim Galloway, "coming from a representative of a country they blamed almost entirely for South Africa's white regime." "The expression for patience is" far "too late," declared one politician in response to Young. The editor of a liberal South African journal fully agreed, insisting "King was okay for his time in his country, but the glamour and his time are gone."[83] After the meeting, Galloway concluded "in Gaborone, Botswana, twelve miles from the South African border, the Rev. Martin Luther King Jr. is a hard sell."[84]

Defending the power and relevance of King's legacy in the 1980s could not have been more difficult, especially since the South African government took numerous steps to destroy anti-apartheid activism in even its most peaceful and nonviolent forms. Control of black movements into towns was tightened, states of emergency were declared at times, new laws significantly expanded the South African armed forces, police arrests and detentions without charges rose, reports of torture and deaths continued unabatedly, and massacres occurred at Sebokeng, Crossroads, and Langa in 1984–1985.[85] Although black South African clergymen managed to lead peaceful marches and prayer vigils occasionally, Mokgethi Motlhabi, the director of the Equal Opportunities Council (EOC) in Johannesburg, pointed out that such activities seemed futile:

> King believed that unearned suffering is redemptive. In South Africa, though, self-suffering, rather than move the heart of the oppressor as both King and Gandhi thought was finally possible, seems to be an indication of weakness to him and thus something to be exploited to the full to drive home the point that it is a waste of time. . . . It seems . . . that people must first be exterminated before the oppressor's heart can be moved, if at all.[86]

In such a climate, even religious leaders came to terms with what appeared to be the inevitability of armed struggle and widespread bloodshed. "I know many peace-loving people who have been forced into violence," declared Motlalepula Chabaku, a black female minister in exile from South Africa. "They have suffered violence and in desperation they turn to counter-violence."[87] Any lingering questions about the vibrancy of King's legacy in this context were at least partially answered when the American religious thinker Walter Wink was told in the mid-eighties "the two dirtiest words in black South Africa today are 'nonviolence' and 'reconciliation.'"[88]

A few very vocal clergy continued to maintain that South Africa's brightest future hinged on the capacity to transcend racial divisions and a violent past. Desmond Tutu and Allan Boesak are cases in point. They continued to view King's nonviolent philosophy and beloved community vision, and his belief in the necessity for a coalition of conscience to address issues of racial injustice as the highest ethical ideals. Bishop Tutu, the 1984 Nobel Peace Prize recipient, unrelentingly called for nonviolent change in South Africa; yet he consistently insisted, "Should the West fail to impose economic sanctions" against South Africa's racist government, "it would, in my view, be justifiable for blacks to try to overthrow an unjust system violently." With Gandhi and King in mind, Tutu acknowledged, "There are some remarkable people who believe that no one is ever justified in using violence, even against the most horrendous evil." Referring to these as "absolute pacifists," Tutu noted that "I admire such persons deeply, but sadly I confess that I am made of less noble stuff." While describing himself as "a lover of peace," the Bishop expressed serious doubt that the type of nonviolent campaign advocated by Gandhi and King "would have saved the Jews from the Nazi holocaust," a point that had significant implications for South African liberation.[89]

Boesak was equally blunt in raising critical questions about the practicality of nonviolence in the South African context. While praising King and Albert Luthuli for their "theology of refusal," or for refusing to surrender to the violence of the status quo, Boesak contended in a 1984 publication that the incredible "hypocrisy of white Christians on the issue of violence" made it virtually impossible for oppressed South Africans to subscribe to nonviolence as an absolute principle. "You can hardly expect blacks to believe the gospel of nonviolence coming from those who, all through their history," argued Boesak, "have relied upon violence and military action to get what they wanted and to maintain unjust systems."[90] Such critical reflections did not amount to an outright rejection of King's approach and outlook. On April 3, 1988, the eve of the twentieth anniversary of the assassination of the civil rights leader, Boesak is said to have "preached to the memory of Martin Luther King, Jr.," an event that revealed the depth of his admiration and respect for King:

> He spoke passionately about what the martyred American prophet meant to him and South Africa. King is everywhere around Allan Boesak—his home and office are full of pictures, books, tapes, and momentos. Boesak is self-consciously a disciple of King, and makes regular reference to him and the freedom movement he led. Now more than ever, Allan Boesak and other South African church leaders are reflecting on King and the relevance of his radical nonviolence for the next phase of South Africa's history.[91]

King also remained important for South African clergymen Frank Chikane and Beyers Naude as they set the parameters of prophetic witness for South African Christians in the eighties. Chicane, General Secretary of the SACC, criticized the church in South Africa for not following King's example in putting the nonviolent method to the test.[92] Naude, Charles Villa-Vicencio, John W. deGruchy, and other church leaders and theologians agreed; they argued with increasingly loud voices that planned boycotts, strikes, acts of civil disobedience, international sanctions, and divestment were "the last nonviolent means left to break the evil of apartheid."[93] Such church leaders and theologians were responsible for keeping King's, Gandhi's, and Luthuli's ideas at the center of the debate over methods. Even the *Kairos Document*, developed by South African churches and religious thinkers in 1985 as a legitimate theological position on violence and nonviolence, reflected this continuing interest in ideas King, Gandhi, and Luthuli had advanced decades earlier.[94]

African-American clergypersons were among the strongest defenders of the King legacy and its significance for South Africa in the eighties. At a UN tribute to King in Atlanta in 1982, the Reverend Bernice King, his youngest daughter, mentioned that her father "was one of the very first American leaders to call for sanctions against apartheid"; she insisted that his "words and the challenge he laid before us are as relevant" for South Africa "today as they were in 1965."[95] Walter Fauntroy and William H. Gray, III, former King aides and part of a small group of clergy in the Congressional Black Caucus (CBC), used both their pulpits and the halls of Congress as forums for shaping public opinion in the United States around the apartheid problem, and their reaffirmation of King's call for international, nonviolent sanctions helped spark a congressional vote in favor of such measures in 1986.[96] Also, among hundreds of black ministers, Fauntroy, Gray, and Bernice King participated in protests at the South African embassy in Washington, D.C. in the 1980s and contributed to building the Free South Africa Movement that clearly reinforced the contributions of Randall Robinson and TransAfrica.[97]

The activities of Leon Sullivan, Joseph Lowery, and Jesse Jackson of People United to Save Humanity (PUSH) also deserve special attention. Inspired in some measure by King's vision for and activities on behalf of South African liberation, Sullivan called for a total withdrawal of U.S. businesses from South Africa in 1987, thus going far beyond what he had proposed a decade earlier. He "urged universities, pension funds, and labor unions to sell their estimated $80 billion in holdings in companies that continue their South African operations." In explaining this shift to a more radical posture, Sullivan remarked, "I'm taking a step beyond the 'Sullivan Principles' and attempting to use whatever abilities I have to bring every moral and economic and governmental force to bear for the cause of justice and freedom in the country."[98]

On December 10, 1983, "Human Rights Day," Joseph Lowery, who replaced Ralph Abernathy as president of the SCLC in 1977, handed out pamphlets containing King's and Chief Luthuli's 1962 appeal for world sanctions and also King's entire "South Africa Benefit Speech" at Hunter College on December 10, 1965. Lowery was fully conscious of King's and Luthuli's efforts to build a strong coalition of conscience around the apartheid issue:

> I am painfully aware of the failure of my own nation to act with courage and moral sensitivity in efforts to eliminate apartheid and express moral courage through sanctions and diplomatic means. It is indeed ironic, as it is sad, that a nation born out of the hunger for liberty and self-determination would defend or cooperate in any manner with such a tyrannical regime as the government of South Africa. We must urge the support and cooperation of the artists and athletes ban. Churches must refuse to do business with South Africa. And we must organize nationally to address the issue of doing business with corporations that do business with South Africa, individually as well as institutionally.[99]

In 1988, Lowery attacked conservative Republicans in the Reagan administration for ignoring the moral concerns and challenges emanating from apartheid. The SCLC leader joined an interdenominational group of clergypersons in urging President Ronald Reagan to "show the same concern for human rights in South Africa that he showed for human rights in the Soviet Union during the recent Moscow summit," asserting that "we don't want to see Mr. Reagan segregate his concern for human rights." For Lowery, such a challenge appeared all the more appropriate since Reagan had "assumed 'global leadership' in the fight for peace."[100]

Jesse Jackson echoed many of Lowery's and King's concerns as he took his prophetic witness against apartheid to various corners of the world. After a seventeen-day visit to southern Africa in late 1979, Jackson testified before the United States House of Representatives' Subcommittee on Africa, Committee on International Relations, expressing views that would become a vital part of his rhetoric as a presidential candidate in 1984 and 1988. "We have reached the countdown stage in the long struggle between the forces of freedom and institutionalized racism," Jackson noted. "It would be unwise, to say the least, for our country to be on the side of supporting moral bankruptcy and institutionalized racism." Jackson then repeated King's call for "world economic sanctions," declaring, "the human community cannot coexist with apartheid. It is a moral illegitimacy that we must fight."[101]

Early in 1985, Jackson toured parts of Europe and joined demonstrations against South African apartheid. In Bonn, West Germany, he locked arms with a hundred protesters representing the Christian Initiative to Free South Africa and Namibia Movement outside the South African embassy there. In words that recalled King's own analogy between the Jewish Holocaust and the slaughter of black South Africans over generations, Jackson reminded the protesters that apartheid was essentially a continuation of the Nazism that murdered six million Jews during World War II. "The same ethical grounds that were used for rejecting the Third Reich in Germany must be employed to stop the Fourth Reich in South Africa," he shouted.[102] Jackson continued to push this message in 1986 while visiting southern Africa's front-line states. In conversations with leaders from Angola, Botswana, Mozambique, Tanzania, Zambia, and Zimbabwe, he called for a kind of international coalition of conscience to press for the ending of South Africa's racist system and aggression against surrounding African states. Determined "to seize the moral offensive against apartheid" and to rebuild spiritual bridges between African Americans and black South Africans, he promised to urge the United States government to "impose tougher economic sanctions against South Africa" and to implement "a Marshall Plan" for the "respect, aid, trade, development, and defense of the southern region of Africa."[103]

The activities of clergymen like Jackson, Lowery, and Leon Sullivan were important enough, but there was no major, sustained effort to intersect large numbers of African-American pastors and their churches and denominations into the anti-apartheid crusade. Such a serious effort would have taken King's model of a coalition of conscience to yet another level. Certain major black church bodies made strong anti-apartheid statements, but mostly in the form of petitions and resolutions. Under the leadership of the Reverend Theodore Jemison, who had formerly advised King, the National Baptist Convention, USA, one of the largest black church organizations in America and in the world, pledged the resources of its seven million members for the support of black South Africans in 1985.[104] Four years later, "The Final Statement of the

Black Church Summit on South Africa" was issued, bringing together anti-apartheid sentiments held for more than a decade by the AME Church, the AME Zion Church, the Christian Methodist Episcopal Church (CME), the Church of God in Christ (COGIC), the National Baptist Convention of America, the National Baptist Convention, USA, and the Progressive National Baptist Convention. This statement expressed the churches' determination to "work for total, comprehensive new U. S. sanctions," to "keep the Southern Africa struggle before the U.S. public," "to "pray without ceasing for all the peoples of the region of South Africa," and to take other steps consistent with Christian values.[105]

Liberal white American clergy and their church bodies took similar positions. The United Methodist Church and the Presbyterian Church, USA, which had very vocal black minorities in their ranks, occasionally spoke to the immorality of apartheid while advocating interracial community as a more noble Christian ideal. In 1986, the National Council of Churches pushed for stronger economic sanctions against South Africa; still, most white clergy and churches either adopted a laissez-faire attitude and approach toward apartheid or embraced President Reagan's "Constructive Engagement" policy, which advised stronger economic links between the United States and South Africa. Strong action was rarely advised, let alone taken, by white pastors, despite the constant challenge that Leon Sullivan, Joseph Lowery, Jesse Jackson, and others put before the churches and synagogues of the United States. George Houser's relinquishment of the directorship of the ACOA in 1981 resulted in a gradual decline in liberal clergy influence on that organization's South Africa agenda. Generally speaking, the moral and spiritual laxity of the white ecclesiastical establishment in the face of apartheid practices, an issue King addressed probably more than any other clergyman up to his time, proved to be one of the great tragedies of the 1980s.[106]

The 1990s signaled a continuing decline in the activities of American clergy on behalf of South African freedom. African-American and liberal white clergypersons celebrated the release of Nelson Mandela in 1990, and sermons were preached that likened Mandela's emergence from Robben Island Prison to King's triumphs in the United States decades earlier. As the ANC moved from armed struggle to a more negotiating posture, and as South African clergypersons assumed the roles of "agents of reconciliation," calling for "peace talks" between the black South African community and President F. W. de Klerk's National Party, many American clergypersons concluded that apartheid was collapsing. De Klerk's lifting of the state of emergency and the decline of de jure apartheid in the early nineties reinforced this view, when even South Africa's Dutch Reformed Church abandoned its racist theology and policies. All too many clergypersons in the United States viewed the election of Nelson Mandela as South Africa's first black president in 1994 and the general establishment of multiracial democracy and black majority rule as the end of apartheid rule.[107] As Mandela himself pointed out at his inauguration, though, the greatest challenges stood ahead as South Africa sought to redefine itself over against a brutally oppressive and violent past.[108] Jesse Jackson, who led a U. S. delegation to South Africa for this historic event, strongly reiterated this point; his presence, along with Mandela's use of King's famous words in his inauguration address—"Free at last! Free at last!"—added to the powerful symbolism of the occasion.[109]

Mandela's decision to create a Government of National Unity (GNU) that included representatives from various racial and tribal backgrounds was the greatest tribute to King and the many clergypersons, in America and abroad, who had put their time and resources to the service of the anti-apartheid struggle. The GNU reflected King's model of the coalition of conscience and was amazingly consistent with his vision of the beloved community as the norm and goal of humanity. The Reverend Benjamin F. Chavis, the NAACP's executive director, widely praised Mandela's efforts to unite his country. Leon Sullivan, Jesse Jackson, Joseph Lowery, and William Gray were among those American clergymen who called for new business commitments to South Africa, noting especially the opportunities for black investment. Also, hundreds of American clergypersons visited South Africa throughout the late nineties, preaching the gospel and forging bonds of friendship and cooperation with their South African brothers and sisters.[110]

Although as an experiment the GNU had faltered by 1996, when the power of the ANC was consolidated and expanded, the effort to make South Africa a genuinely "rainbow nation" did not end. In fact, the effort continued as President Mandela joined Bishop Desmond Tutu and other South African clergymen in launching the Truth and Reconciliation Commission (TRC) in the mid and late 1990s, a development that stood as a powerful tribute to the legacy of King, Luthuli, and other anti-apartheid activists who had long advocated peaceful change, reconciliation, and interracial community for South Africa. Avoiding the extremes of Nuremberg-type trials and blanket amnesty or national amnesia with regard to those guilty of atrocities during the apartheid regime, the TRC chose to grant amnesty to such persons in exchange for a full disclosure of apartheid crimes. The TRC completed its work in 1998, a year before Mandela's presidency ended.[111] The task of compensating many of the victims of apartheid would be left to Mandela's successor, Thabo Mbeki, who was elected in 2000 and reelected in 2004.[112]

In the meantime, the transition toward multiracial democracy and the struggle for genuine reconciliation and community in South Africa are continuing. King's legacy of ideas and activism is still meaningful in that quest. King submitted that a multifaceted approach creates lasting human community in any society that seeks to overcome a history of bigotry and injustice. First, there is the need for religion, which, in its most authentic expression, transforms the heart and prepares one for an acceptance of the dignity and worth of every person, and for the essential oneness of humans as reflections of the divine image. Second, there is the necessity for education, which changes attitudes and internal feelings (i.e., prejudice, greed, hatred, etc.), and which, together with religion, breaks down the spiritual barriers to community. Third, legislation and court action are required as a means of regulating behavior and of breaking down the physical barriers to community. Finally, there is the necessity for the nonviolent resolution of conflict.[113] Over the last decade, South Africa, under its new system of government and with the assistance of its religious leaders and institutions, has sought to implement this fourfold approach on some levels. But the effort must move beyond expressions of goodwill, collective responsibility, and mutual acceptance to an emphasis on what King called "shared power." In other words, a serious encounter with the economic inequities and/or disparities must accompany the breakdown of social and political barriers. Only then can South African realize the fullness of community and peaceful coexistence.[114]

Chapter 4

A Transatlantic Comparison of a Black Theology of Liberation

Dwight N. Hopkins

Two of the most egregious social systems in the twentieth century have been racial segregation in the United States and apartheid in South Africa. This essay compares and contrasts the almost simultaneous rise of black theology of liberation on both sides of the Atlantic Ocean in their attempts to combat racism and apartheid. Since both segregation and apartheid were heavily undergirded by white Christian churches in the United States and South Africa, black Christians had to delve into their religious traditions in order to show that the norm of liberation was not alien to religiosity. Indeed, the common denominator for black theologians in the two countries meant that liberation lay at the heart of the message of Jesus Christ and that black power and the Christian religion were coterminous.

Black Theology in the U.S.

In the United States, the Black Power Movement, which grew out of the 1950s and 1960s Civil Rights Movement, resulted from several strands. First, despite the 1954 Supreme Court decision that separate was not equal and white liberals' hailing 1955 to 1965 as the decade of Negro progress, the masses of black people suffered. Between the successful 1955–1956 Montgomery bus boycott and the signing of the Voting Rights Act in 1965, the gap between black and white in every sphere in American society had widened. Despite the passage of the Civil Rights Acts of 1957, 1960 and 1964, and the Voting Rights Act of 1965, the myth of the decade of Negro progress applied only to a minute sector of the black community. In particular, the black middle class reaped whatever meager benefits resulted from the struggle for civil rights. The black poor, the overwhelming majority, languished in poverty and lack of significant societal gains.

Second, an increasing number of youth in the Civil Rights Movement voiced a growing disdain toward the hypocrisy of white liberalism. The Student Nonviolent Coordinating Committee (SNCC) mirrored this changing mood. In opposition to the local segregated Democratic Party, SNCC played a leading role in instituting the Mississippi Freedom Democratic Party (MFDP) as a representative of the state's loyal (black) majority for the presidential ticket of Lyndon Johnson. At the 1964 Democratic National Convention in Atlantic City, however, Lyndon Johnson, Hubert Humphrey, Walter Mondale and other white liberals on the convention's credentials committee, as well as black civil rights establishment leadership, supported the illegal, white, segregationist delegation from Mississippi.

The stage was set for Stokely Carmichael, newly elected chairman of SNCC. In June 1966, on the Meredith March Against Fear, Carmichael hurled the thunderbolt of Black Power from the backwoods of Greenwood, Mississippi. Carmichael received one graphic response to his declaration in October 1966. During that month a group of black, urban militants donned black outfits and patrolled the streets of Oakland, California, with carbines, rifles, and shotguns. The Black Panther Party for Self-Defense was born. In December 1966, Ron Karenga created the first Nguza Saba: The Seven Principles of Kwanzaa.

Further responses burned like prairie fire. Between 1965 and 1968 nearly three hundred urban rebellions exploded across America and thrust a new term into the national lexicon—the "long hot summer." The entire political and cultural scenery in black America underwent rapid alteration. The young, black revolutionary generation, whom Julius Lester knighted "the angry children of Malcolm X," had taken center stage.

Theological Themes

In the midst of Carmichael's Black Power cry, urban rebellions, and political, cultural trends in the black liberation movement, black theology burst forth. Black American pastors and laypersons found themselves caught with a theology suitable for the "We Shall Overcome" era of integrationism and liberalism, but apparently insufficient and irrelevant to the needs of the black community in the era of "I'm Black and I'm Proud!" In the hurricane eye of a black revolution, the ad hoc National Committee of Negro Churchmen (NCNC) coalesced. In the fall of 1968, Gayraud Wilmore, first chairman of the NCNC theological commission, described "the rising crescendo of voices from both the pulpit and pew demanding that black churchmen reexamine their beliefs; that unless they begin to speak and act relevantly in the present crisis they must prepare to die." The black revolution presented an ultimatum: unless black pastors "do their thing" in some kind of symbolic and actual disengagement from the "opprobrium of a white racist Christianity, they have no right to exist in the black community."[1]

The voices and protests of black people forced the issue of the role of Christianity in the black community. Thus black theology arose as an answer to the reality of black liberation moving against white racism. What did it mean to be black and Christian? Where was God and Jesus Christ in the urban rebellions? Was the black church simply serving an Uncle Tom, otherworldly role; or was it aiding in black control of the community and black people's destiny? Could blacks continue to uphold the theology of integrationism and liberalism—a theology where all power remained in the hands of white people? When stripped of its "whiteness," what did Christianity say to black Americans? Could black identity, culture, history, and language become authentic sources for the doing of theology? What did a blue-eyed, blond-haired, "hippie-looking" Jesus have to do with Black Power and black liberation?

Since contemporary black theology in the United States grew out of the National Committee of Negro Churchmen (NCNC), it is therefore important to explore NCNC's origin.[2] NCNC was comprised of black pastors and church executives, the majority in predominantly white denominations, who united to respond favorably to Black Power. The Reverend Leon W. Watts, one of the founders of NCNC, depicted the volatile environment at that time.

> In 1966 . . . everybody, including Martin Luther King, Jr.,, came out with a negative statement about Black Power. It was as if Stokely Carmichael had loosed some monster upon the country that was going to devour it, the way in which both black political leaders and the press came out in an almost unanimous voice opposing the concept of Black Power.[3]

When NCNC published its full-page Black Power apologia in the July 31, 1966, edition of *The New York Times*, the National Committee swam against the ecclesiological and societal tidal wave of anti-Black Power hysteria. In fact, the NCNC would not have formed were it not for the nationwide negative response to Black Power. As Leon Watts explains, "The National Committee of Negro Churchmen . . . had its beginnings in response to the way in which the press responded [rabidly] to Stokely Carmichaels' call for Black Power on the Meredith March." By focusing on black liberation over against integration, the Committee broke with King and the Civil Rights Movement.

The Reverend Dr. Calvin B. Marshall, another NCNC founder, states that black church people "found ourselves in a vacuum" and thus formed the Committee. The turbulence in the black community had caused black church people to choose between the "vacuum" of integrationism and the relevancy of black liberation. Marshall continues, "We had gotten to the point where we had to hear God speaking through what we [the black church and the black community] were going through." Where did the committee hear the Word of God? Previously the white church power structure had condoned only the formally educated and "reasonable" black church leaders such as Martin Luther King, Jr., No matter how many marches civil rights churches and organizations undertook against racism, the white church suspected that it shared the same theology with the black church. The white church could draw on a common theological framework and speak a common theological language.

In complete contradiction to this integrationist, theological contract, NCNC began to radically hear the Word of God elsewhere. Watts recounts how the Committee not only began to talk about what would be the response of the black church, to what Martin Luther King, Jr., was doing because many people were participating in the Civil Rights Movement as churches, but also began to take some account of Stokely Carmichael and the more militant groups such as the Black Muslims, Black Panthers, and Ron Karenga's group. The Committee had turned to the militant currents among the black poor to hear a "message from the Lord."

In 1967 in Dallas, Texas, NCNC held its first national convocation and formally established its theological commission. The Committee charged the commission to explore the uniqueness and profundity of the black religious experience in America. The commission had to articulate in clear theological terms the "differences and distinctions" between how black people and white people saw themselves as Christians. The black liberation movement required a theological response to the juxtaposition of "black" and "power." In short, the black churchmen turned to God to answer how black Christians could remain authentic witnesses of the gospel and not be either integrationists or segregationists.

In 1967 Dr. Nathan Wright, Jr., surfaced some major theological themes and began to address the theological roadblocks facing a nascent black theology:

> To the precise extent that Black Power affirms and extends God's truth and purposes, it is in that same degree possessed of a sacred and eternal nature. It is partially thus a sign of the presence of God's rule, which is what is meant by the term "the kingdom of God."[4]

Wright had pinpointed foundational, black theological issues—the positive relation of God to Black Power, the divine presence in Black Power, and Black Power as a revelation of God's rule. A year later, in 1968, at the second convocation of NCBC (*Negro* had been changed to *Black*) in St. Louis, the Committee had begun to use the phrase *black theology* to describe the encounter of God with the black experience. A *Time* magazine article reported on the gathering and described how "a number of speakers suggested that a major goal should be the creation of a fully developed black theology."[5]

Although the seeds of black theology in the United States sprouted with the formation of NCNC in 1966, not until the spring of 1969 would a little-known theologian bring those seeds to fruition. James H. Cone's *Black Theology and Black Power* appeared in March 1969. NCBC and the black church had finally received a scholarly work, which sharply presented the black religious experience, not merely as a challenge to the sociological practice of the white church, but as a devastating critique of the white *theology* dominant in white and black churches. Cone dropped a bombshell. Theologically, he argued that black power was the gospel of Jesus Christ![6]

The work of black theology in the United States also chastened racism in South Africa. "Back in the '60s," in the words of Rev. Watts, "the National Committee of Negro Churchmen was speaking out against apartheid. [The Committee] had written several documents" condemning white racism in South Africa. The statements of the NCBC and primarily the works of James Cone found a ready theological audience among blacks struggling to make sense out of God's relation to apartheid and the Black Consciousness Movement. In its own evolution, black theology in South Africa followed a course similar to the dynamics of black theology in the United States; thus, it is helpful to examine the historical backdrop and the political and cultural themes in South African society as preconditions to the theological themes in black theology in South Africa.

Black Theology in South Africa

Similar to the Civil Rights Movement's and Black Power Movement's relation to black theology in the United States, nonviolent Civil Disobedience protest and the Black Consciousness Movement (BCM) fostered the arrival of black theology in South Africa.

Civil Disobedience

At the beginning of the 1950s, the African National Congress (the primary voice of black resistance) included both an older, liberal tendency and a younger, more nationalist influence. The influx of younger leadership pushed the ANC from passive petitioning and court battles to civil disobedience. No longer would ANC rely primarily on elite black delegations' attempts to prick the white government's sense of justice. Tactics shifted from appeals to white supremacists to massive mobilization of boycotts, strikes, and marches in order to wrest away black rights from apartheid; yet, in the 1950s ANC still hoped to bring about black participation in the government nonviolently. The ANC wanted to have apartheid laws repealed and blacks granted the franchise; which, in the 1950s context, was a militant breaking of social laws. In fact, they believed a more militant approach would woo whites from apartheid policies. In other words, a shift to militant tactics remained within a liberal democratic strategy.

Underneath the social movement toward liberal democracy, a liberal Christian worldview existed. Many of the ANC leaders were trained in white missionary schools; many ANC rank and file were Christians. A missionary upbringing had taught older black activists of the 1950s that all protest movements were immoral and unethical unless whites and blacks worked together. In 1959 ANC's Africanist wing formally broke away and established the Pan-Africanist Congress (PAC). Like the ANC, PAC leadership and membership experienced Christian influences. At the founding PAC congress in 1959, a clergyman who headed the largest federation of African independent churches gave an address. Also, the PAC president, Robert Sobukwe, was a Methodist lay preacher. PAC attempted to build on the growing impatience and potential militancy of younger blacks and the African urban population.

Black Consciousness

Like the birth of Black Power, the Black Consciousness Movement initially rallied against the hypocrisy of white liberalism, primarily English speaking whites. By the mid-1960s the National Union of South African Students (NUSAS) played the leading role in white liberal defense of black rights. Due to the aftermath of the March 21, 1960, "Sharpeville Massacre," an immense political vacuum characterized the anti-apartheid scene of black South Africans. Fear gripped blacks to such a degree that the general population incorrectly believed political protest was illegal. NUSAS stepped in to fill this enormous void. Black students discovered that this liberal formation afforded one of the few remaining legal avenues for national dialogue among blacks; however, at a July 1967 NUSAS conference, black delegates were forced to live in appalling, segregated accommodations away from the conference site. This contradiction between liberal proclamation of multiracial equality, on the one hand, and NUSAS's persistent practical disregard for black student concerns, on the other, marked the beginning of the demise of a white-black, master-slave mentality in South Africa. A year later the South African Students Organization (SASO) formed; it held its inaugural conference in 1969.[7] Steve Bantu Biko, the father of Black Consciousness, chaired the youth organization. SASO's "Policy Manifesto" added weight to the deep pain inflicted on black students by the liberals. The Manifesto decried a scurrilous integration as a sham. "Integration does not mean an assimilation of Blacks into an already established set of norms drawn up and motivated by White society."[8]

In 1966 Biko attended Durban University and discovered an anomaly in black-white relations. He and his colleagues realized that "whites were in fact the main participants in [blacks'] oppression and at the same time the main participants in the opposition to that oppression." Biko referred to this situation as the "totality of white power." In particular, he pictured the white liberals as "playing their old game." They claimed a "monopoly on intelligence and moral judgment" and "set the pattern and pace" for black liberation. When the inevitable liberal backlash to black unity reared its ugly head, Biko retorted that white liberals "are the greatest racists for they refuse to credit us with any intelligence to know what we want."[9] In addition to white liberal hypocrisy, BCM attacked the overall apartheid system. Ownership of land ranked high among the grievances.

Finally, black South Africans absorbed lessons from American developments. In the United States, the 1955 to 1966 civil rights struggle and the 1966 Black Power Movement evidenced a political and cultural renaissance. Black South Africans diligently scoured the media for the latest news and shared works such as *The Autobiography of Malcolm X*, Stokely Carmichael's and Charles Hamilton's Black Power, Eldridge Cleaver's *Soul on Ice*, and James H. Cone's *Black Theology and Black Power*.

Theological Themes

The Black Consciousness Movement (BCM) sharply focused on a critical duplicity in faith faced by black South African Christians in general and black pastors in particular. On the one hand, they mouthed the Christianity learned from white European missionaries centuries past and the same religious doctrine that whites professed in contemporary South Africa. On the other hand, blacks muffled the burning beat of their own visceral faith encounter with Christ. Bonganjalo Goba, a participant in early black theology in South Africa, relates theology, black identity, and the black Christian dilemma:

> There was a feeling amongst those of us who were involved [in early black theology] that somehow we had experienced . . . a theological schizophrenia. We were split. . . . Part of our formation was terribly white, influenced by the western theology. . . . And there was another side to that in that we had our own [black] agenda which had never been addressed. So that the issue had to do with the identity crisis which we confronted.[10]

The BCM clashed head-on with black pastors' training and their avowed allegiance to an oppressive white theology and white Christianity. Like the political and cultural identity crises haunting BCM followers, the theological identity crisis gripped black church leaders. Goba comments further, "We were young pastors, most of us. The only academic theologian when black theology started was Dr. Manas Buthelezi . . . Most of us were simply pastors who were part of the Black Consciousness Movement."

In response to the racism of white Christianity, black theology in South Africa asserted its own theological agenda and incorporated the black reality of indigenous religious experience and struggle for liberation into the Christian hermeneutic. Manas Buthelezi, the father of contemporary black theology in South Africa, framed the essential ontological, existential, and theological query: If the gospel means anything, it must answer the "basic existential question 'Why did God create me black?'"[11] Around this basic issue, a constellation of other matters crystallized. Was Christianity ever meant for black people? How authentic was the church in catering to black needs? Did the white, apartheid designation "nonwhite" allow for the unity of blackness and Christianity? Did the Christian God support black acceptance of apartheid? What was God doing in a situation where blackness brought legal disenfranchisement and death in one's own land? What was God saying to black people who defined their life as appendages to white people? Why did blacks suffer because God had made them "nonwhites?" Did Jesus Christ belong to the Afrikaner and white, English speaking liberals; did blacks belong to the line of Ham? Did God reveal God's self in black people's political and cultural realities? Contrary to the white, passive Christ, blacks embraced Christ, the "fighting God" (in the words of Biko) who suffered with them under oppression and exemplified a vocation of struggle for freedom against spiritual and physical (systemic) wickedness. Because Jesus was poor, discriminated against, and exploited in his time, because blacks agonized in poverty, discrimination, and exploitation under apartheid, and because God incarnated in this particular oppressed Jesus, a meaningful contemporary symbol of God's presence in South Africa revealed a black Christ. God was a spirit of freedom and the black Christ was the liberator.[12]

In addition, black theology in South Africa struggled with eradicating the sacrilegious notion that black people survived through the grace of whites, not through the grace of God. The new interpretation had to force a break with the theological dependence on white authority. The authority question cut at the very substance of what it meant to be a Christian. How could black people claim faith in the lordship of Christ and the kingdom of God and, at the same time, desecrate their God-given humanity by kneeling before white apartheid? Biblically, the issue of authority and derivation of grace challenged black Christians to undertake a radical exegesis and rereading of Romans 13 and Revelations 13.

Finally, black theology in South Africa turned to its own indigenous cultures. In precolonial South Africa, African traditional religion exhibited a sophisticated understanding of the human person. There, Africans worshiped a good God, who bestowed goodness upon black people and, as a result, an inherent dignity in humanity. If stripped of this dignity, the African would sink to the level of beasts. Fortunately, African traditional religion coincided with Christianity's call for human liberation of oppressed humanity.

Though various Christian theological themes were debated wherever black people fathomed the relation of God and Christ to the black condition, the primary organizational vehicle for coordinating the discourse of black theology in South Africa was the Black Theology Project initiated by the University Christian Movement (UCM). By the end of 1969, black seminarians and pastors were discussing black theology, particularly as expressed in James H. Cone's *Black Theology and Black Power.* The project "came into being around 1970" and sponsored a series of meetings and seminars on black theology during 1970 and 1971.[13]

Similar Voices Across the Atlantic

To appreciate the historical dialogue, comparison, and contrasts between black theology of the United States and its South African counterpart, it is helpful to group representatives of both sides of the Atlantic into a paradigm I call the "political theologians" of black theology.

On the U.S. side, the political theologians give more weight to opposing racism in the white American political system, church, and theology. As a group they respond to Black Power's call for African Americans to fight the inhuman practices of white political power. They expose white people's use of religion and theology to justify the maintenance of white rule over black life. For them, black theology has to serve black people's daily struggle against the grip of a white power structure. They want to know how theology and the church aid in alleviating poor education, KKK terror, police brutality, insensitive and corrupt politicians, the hopeless job situation of black youth, rat infested ghettos, the lack of civil and human rights, and all situations in which whites control black humanity. To combat white supremacist power, the political theology group chooses theology as its area of resistance. The political theologians believe that fighting to alter the unjust and inhuman power relations in American society is a God-ordained gift for black people. They want to discover how black theology can be involved in that fight.

On the South African side, the political theological advocates maintain both a protest against black exclusion from participation with whites and a desire to work with whites toward the elimination of the latter's fracturing of human fellowship between the races. Like the Freedom Charter[14] and the African National Congress, the political trend defines the "will of the people" not simply by the black racial majority population, but by all who currently live in South Africa, black and white. All races are made in God's image; all, black and white together, have been granted equal calling to have dominion over God's grace of creation. The black political theological proponents share an extreme sensitivity to the bastardization of the gospel by the white apartheid government and its white church. They understand that an attack on the white power structure is both political and theological. It is political because the separation of the races undergirds the *raison d'etre* of apartheid, and theological because a heretical gospel confession and interpretation undergird white supremacy and the denial of racial fellowship. To disengage apartheid political policy, they must wage war on the theological justification. In brief, we discover a theology based on nonracialism (black and white together) versus a theology of apartheid.

Uniting with the *Kairos Document*,[15] the black political theologians would call the relations between the white Dutch Reformed Church and the apartheid government "state theology." State theology describes a situation in which both the oppressed and the oppressors pledge loyalty to the same church. For example, Christian policemen beat up and kill Christian children and torture Christian prisoners. State theology depicts the Afrikaner apartheid government as justifying the state's endemic violence, racism, and capitalism with Christian theology. Such a perverted theology supposedly gets its authority from scripture. It tells the oppressed in South Africa to obey the apartheid government automatically (Romans 13:1-7). It boasts biblical bases in Genesis 10 on human genealogy and in Genesis 11:1-9 on the tower of Babel. For the theology of apartheid, God condones violence against the poor and sanctions "separate development" of ethnic groups.

The black political theologians would also agree with the *Kairos Document*'s characterization of "church theology." This theology reflects the superficial, unproductive criticisms by the white, liberal English speaking churches. Church theology opts for "reconciliation" ("let's hear both sides of the story") without justice or confrontation with apartheid's evils. It makes appeals to the apartheid government but fails to focus on and support the people's struggles "below." Finally, it calls for nonviolence, thus equating the victims' practice of self-defense with the structural violence of apartheid.

Against state and church theologies, the black political theologians advocate "prophetic theology": a biblically based, action-oriented theology of oppressed people that fights external (white) and internal (black) oppressions and also uses social analysis of "the oppressor and the oppressed."

To compare both representatives of political theology, we begin with the U.S. side, that is, James H. Cone. For the South African perspective, we engage Allan A. Boesak.

James H. Cone

James H. Cone's black theology developed in response to the Civil Rights and Black Power movements of northern urban rebellions. He began his black theology by interpreting the black liberation movement through the systematic doctrines of "classical" theology. Cone's unique contribution emphasizes the liberation of the poor, especially the black poor, as the controlling norm of a political black theology.

In the early 1960s, throughout his graduate studies and earlier teaching career, Cone knew of the increased attacks on the black community. During 1967 while teaching at Adrian College in Adrian, Michigan, seventy miles from Detroit, that city's rebellion deeply affected him. He was, likewise, aware of other major urban rebellions and how of then-president Richard M. Nixon and F.B.I. director J. Edgar Hoover had planned the assassination of African-American human rights leaders. In this mix, the white academy toyed with esoteric issues like the Barth-Brunner debates and the "death of God" fad.

For Cone in 1968, therefore, the survival of his community and his own black identity were at stake. He had to write on black theology and black power. If Christianity had any meaning for powerless black America, Cone wrote, it placed black liberation of the poor at the core of the gospel. Thus he formulated his black theology in direct relation to the Black Power Movement and urban rebellions in the 1960s.[16] He perceived Black Power and black theology as colaborers in the field of black liberation: "Black Power and Black theology work on two separate but similar fronts. Both believe Blackness is the primary datum of human experience which must be reckoned with, for it is the reason for our oppression and the only tool for our liberation."[17]

Cone subscribed to a black theology that sought power for oppressed black people and a rearrangement of power to eliminate racist oppression and to enhance black freedom. Similar to Malcolm X's faith claim, Cone professed a religion whose primary theological cornerstone undergirded the political eradication of racial discrimination. Reviewing the birth of his black theology eighteen years later, he says, "I think when I first began [writing black theology], I saw the political as the most crucial. I still, in many ways, do." Wishing to "balance" the political, cultural dynamic "a lot more," now he more tightly interweaves his understanding of these two strands: "I see the political and the cultural now with the political really dependent upon the cultural. I don't see how you can sustain a political analysis and movement without cultural resources."[18]

Here too, one recognizes his penchant toward the black political trend. Though hindsight has informed his theological integration of the political with the cultural, Cone remains committed to a black theology that employs cultural resources for the political movement, the political liberation of black people.

I characterize the theological bent of Cone as a Black Christian Theology of Liberation. It is *black* because he equates the black experience with the primary datum of black theology. It is *Christian* because the foundation for his theology rests on inquiring, "What does the Christian gospel have to say to powerless black [people] whose existence is threatened daily by the insidious tentacles of white power?" It is *theology* because Cone reflects on the very presence of God "actively involved in the present-day affairs of [black people]." And it is about *liberation* because he surmises liberation as the "central idea for articulating the gospel of Jesus."[19] The Christian gospel of liberation and the liberation of the poor form the heart of Cone's systematic theology.

Liberation

What does the gospel of liberation mean in Cone's theological system? The target of liberation for him centers on the destruction of the structure of American white racism. This demonic system has crushed the African-American person to a nonperson. "The white structure of this American society," Cone elaborates, "personified in every racist must be at least part of what the New Testament meant by the demonic forces."[20] Though he later broadens the target to include women's oppression, capitalism, and imperialism, his entry point to the development of his black theology hinges on black people's struggles against racism.

For Cone, the human procession toward black liberation against this demonic structure originates in divine freedom. The freedom of God "is the source and content of human freedom." Grounded in divine freedom (meaning God's own free choice to create humans in freedom and to be with them in the realization of freedom and liberation in history), black liberation or black freedom denotes the divine will to execute human emancipation. The *imago dei* (God who is freedom in being, will, and function) mandates humanity's created state and *telos*. At the same time one cannot have divine freedom— and human freedom—without divine justice. Freedom or liberation accompanies justice. Divine justice makes black liberation more than a human effort and goal; it makes liberation a divine intent. God's righteousness changes God's freedom into a practical realization of human liberation in history.[21]

In addition to anchoring the concepts of divine freedom and divine justice/righteousness, liberation also links up with salvation and with "God's Kingdom" in Cone's theology. Salvation is no longer a supposedly inward calmness or elusive balm in the afterworld; thus it no longer creates opiates in support of racism. On the contrary, God, through Christ, saves humanity by entering the depths of oppression and liberating humanity from all human evils, including racism. Finally, Cone sounds a universal note of liberation in his theme of the kingdom. The kingdom stands for all the world's poor because they have nothing to expect from this world. Cemented in historical liberation, the kingdom embodies the poor's hope and empowers them toward organizing for practical liberation in history.[22]

Christology

God's liberation of black people through Christ's cross and resurrection marks the centrality of Cone's Christology. For Cone, the New Testament witness reveals Jesus' person as the Oppressed One. Because black people suffocate under extreme afflictions, the locus of Jesus' work is a black Christ identified with liberation from black suffering. The Bible tells the story of Jesus' oppression; the contemporary story tells of black people's oppression. In a word, the Oppressed One in black suffering expresses divine being and divine activity. Christ is black because of how Christ was revealed and because of where Christ seeks to be. Having intersected the liberation of the oppressed with the person and work of Christ and having situated that liberation in the black community, Cone boldly asserts in his first published book, "Christianity is not alien to Black Power; it is Black Power."[23]

Within the political theology trend, Cone dismisses J. Deotis Roberts's belief that blacks need a black Christ because of a psychocultural crisis.[24] Rather, Cone cites a distinction between the literal and symbolic nature of Christological blackness. In explaining the contrast, he offers a proviso for the possible interim nature of a black Christology. "I realize," he confesses, "that 'blackness' as a christological title may not be appropriate in the distant future or even in every human context in our present." For today the literalness of Christ's blackness arises from Christ's literally entering and converging with black oppression and black struggle. Cone continues to claim that Christ's symbolic status of blackness resides in Christ's "transcendent affirmation" that God has never left the universal oppressed alone.[25]

In order to fight white theology, Cone brings together both the Jesus of history with the Christ of faith to complement the liberation theme; we cannot have one without the other. Cone does argue that we know what and where Jesus is today based on what Jesus did while on earth. Cone, moreover, creates new political meaning in the crucifixion and resurrection around the thread of his liberation axis. Calvary and the empty tomb prove key in Cone's Christology. Jesus' "death and resurrection" reveal "that God is present in all dimensions of human liberation."[26]

Finally, Cone's black Christology privileges the poor. Christ died on the cross and rose from the dead in partiality to the liberation of the poor and the oppressed and in direct opposition to the satanic on earth. The being and work of Christ express the divine intent to liberate the oppressed. Christ rescues the downtrodden from the material bondage of "principalities and powers." In this liberation process the oppressors also realize their freedom because the object of their oppression—the now freed poor—no longer occupies an oppressed status.[27] The dialectical effect of Jesus Christ rendering deliverance for both the oppressed and the oppressor raises the question of the importance of reconciliation in Cone's black theology.

Reconciliation

Even though his first book expresses the thundering challenge of a manifesto against white people and their racism, Cone, however, never excludes the possibility of reconciliation. "I do not rule out the possibility of creative changes, even in the lives of oppressors. It is illegitimate to sit in judgment on another man," he argues, "deciding how he will or must respond. That is another form of oppression."[28]

The white oppressor might change and become reconciled with the black oppressed in the latter's liberation movement. Here too, within the black political theology trend, Cone differentiates his doctrine of reconciliation from Roberts'. The latter asserts a scriptural basis for reconciliation with white people as the essence of the Good News. In contrast, Cone develops his theme of reconciliation primarily and consistently with concern for the liberation of oppressed blacks. In order to yield meaningful and productive reconciliation, therefore, only the black community can set the conditions for reconciliation. On the other hand, the "white oppressor" suffers from an enslavement to racism and forfeits any capability to offer suitable reconciliation terms. Instead, the oppressed lay down "the rules of the game." The rule established by oppressed blacks aims at the heart of white racist power. In fact, Cone writes, "there will be no more talk about reconciliation until a redistribution of power has taken place. And until then, it would be advisable for whites to leave blacks alone."[29]

Cone describes two types of reconciliation—objective and subjective. Because Jesus Christ died on the cross and rose from the dead, the devil and satanic forces experienced defeat. The cross-resurrection triumph manifests the objective reconciliation. Now that God has objectively liberated the oppressed from the finality of demonic clutches such as white racism, oppressed humanity (African-American people) must assume its responsibility to subjectively fight with God in Christ against injustice. Divine victory of Calvary and the tomb objectively shattered the walls of hostility between white and black. Now the oppressed must act as if they are truly emancipated subjectively; that response means fighting with total effort against white racism and for freedom. This is subjective liberation. Cone, therefore, maintains the consistency of his liberation theme in both objective and subjective reconciliation.

He furthermore assigns the task of fighting white oppression as the example of what reconciliation implies for blacks. For whites reconciliation can only mean one thing—coming to God through black people.[30]

Allan A. Boesak

Word of God

Allan A. Boesak belonged to the Dutch Reformed Mission Church in South Africa, which the white Dutch Reformed Church (NGK) condescendingly considers a daughter church. He also has held the distinguished position of president of the World Alliance of Reformed Churches. In addition, he gave one of the major presentations at the founding of the United Democratic Front on South Africa (UDF) in 1983. The UDF falls within the political and theological lineage of the Freedom Charter movement. Boesak, therefore, was one of the premier theological spokespersons for the UDF-Freedom Charter political opposition.

Boesak concentrates on the evils of apartheid theology. The motivation for his theological project involved dethroning the theological support given by *his* Reformed tradition to the apartheid government. For instance, when the National Party came to power in 1948, the official white Dutch Reformed Church (NGK) newspaper *Die Kerkbode* stated, "As a church we have always worked purposefully for the separation of the races. In this regard apartheid can rightfully be called a church policy."[31]

Boesak was driven to undermine his church's theological backing for the apartheid state because the Afrikanner government was literally a collection of white racist politicians who were all NGK leaders. He felt called and challenged to confront his church for its continued justification of apartheid and of its initial suggestion to the government to establish apartheid in the 1940s.

The following existential and theological dilemma further influenced him: How can one be black and Reformed when the Reformed tradition sustained white supremacy of the (Reformed) apartheid government? Since Boesak chose to focus his theological energies on fundamentally changing the internal politics of the Dutch Reformed Church, he attempted to subvert the white NGK theology by rediscovering a radical wing in the Dutch Reformed tradition itself.

I picture Boesak's thought as a Black Theology of the Word of God. In my opinion he has expressed his Word of God perspective in diverse ways. In "Courage to Be Black" (*South African Outlook*, October 1975) and subsequent writings in the 1970s, he appeared to lean toward the Black Consciousness Movement and black theology. By 1987, apparently broadening his framework from "black" to "oppressed," he shifts toward a "theology of justice."

It is a question of shifting not from Black and Reformed to Black and Christian, but from Black and Reformed to oppressed and Christian because the oppression is suffered by Christians, and the oppression is sometimes perpetrated by Christians. Because Black and Reformed can no longer deal with what we have here today, we talk about Theology for Justice.[32] The manifestation of his theology may have shifted, but the supremacy of the Word of God—the norm regulating his God-talk—has remained constant throughout his theological career.

Boesak vehemently opposes apartheid because of its pseudo-gospel facade. Wrapped in the theological mantle of scripture, apartheid originated in the white NGK; the NGK leadership proposed apartheid to the government as a cultural way of life and political policy. Boesak insightfully describes this insidious apartheid-gospel connection: "Apartheid is more than an ideology, more than something that has been thought up to form the content of a particular political policy. Apartheid is also pseudo-gospel. It was born in the church. . . . The struggle against apartheid . . . is, therefore, more than merely a struggle against an evil ideology." The battlefront extends beyond the dethronement of a satanic political system. "It is," resumes Boesak, "more than a struggle for the liberation and wholeness of people, white as well as black, in South Africa. It is also finally a struggle for the integrity of the Gospel of Jesus Christ"—the Word of God.[33] In this way the white power structure (in this instance, the Afrikanner government) propped up separate development with the Bible.[34] The white "Christian" government and church indulge in idolatry by theologically justifying the deification of apartheid.

Boesak has dedicated his entire theology and ministry to the sovereignty of the Word of God. "The first thing I should mention, then," he confesses, "is the principle of the supremacy of the Word of God. In the Reformed tradition it is the Word of God that gives life to our words." The "Word of God" or "scripture," he continues, is the foundation of the Reformed church's life and witness in the world.[35] The Word of God or the Bible, however, does not kneel to uncritical accommodation to culture, neither to the apartheid pseudo-gospel nor even to the context that engenders black theology. The Word encounters and challenges black theology and the world. Out of that confrontation and under the supremacy of the Word, black theology becomes prophetic, critical, challenging, and transformational of all situations. Here Boesak wants to assert emphatically, in his view, the decisive role of the Word. In the final analysis, the liberation praxis of black theology submits not to the judgment of the situation of blackness, but to the liberating gospel of Jesus Christ. In the Reformed tradition, Boesak correctly claims, all of life falls under Jesus Christ's lordship. On this point he maintains consistency with his church tradition by accenting the supremacy of the Word; but he also breaks continuity by equating the Bible and Christ's lordship primarily with liberation. In fact, the content of the Word of God is the emancipation of all oppressed people; so, what God has done for Israel and revealed through the incarnation of Jesus Christ is, strictly speaking, liberation.[36]

Liberation

While not denying divine love, Boesak understands liberation of the *poor* as essential to the gospel proclamation. Neither a secondary aspect nor a tangential intersection with the gospel, liberation constitutes the substance and form of black theology's Word of God. "Black Theology is a theology of liberation," in Boesak's words. "By that we mean the following. Black Theology believes that liberation is not only 'part of' the gospel, or 'consistent with' the gospel; it is the content and framework of the gospel of Jesus Christ."[37]

Liberation ends alienation from God, neighbor, and oneself. It brings freedom from economic exploitation, dehumanization, and poverty. For Boesak, God liberates us to do God's will of justice. Liberation, then, frees one in human fulfillment for full service to God in order to emancipate the people of God; thus God's people, the church, proclaim a total liberation from all manifestations of sin and for a holistic humanity.

Describing prophetic proclamation, Boesak directly connects ultimate and penultimate liberation. The latter acts in anticipation of the former. In the prophetic task of freedom, he believes, the vision of the prophet in the fullness of the "Kingdom" (the Ultimate) is realized in the signs of the Kingdom—the cleansed lepers, the sight restored to the blind, and the justice rendered to the poor and downtrodden (the penultimate).[38] Today's partial freedom, then, mirrors apocalyptic signs of the kingdom coming.

Boesak's attention to the poor and the downtrodden also directs his aim of liberation against both the "external" and "internal" enemy. For instance, as God did with Israel of old, God demands justice from today's pharaoh, the external enemy (the white oppressor), as well as from the rich and powerful within contemporary Israel (black oppressors). As a result the truly free fight against any curtailment of freedom because God guarantees a thorough human liberation.

The Word of God, the Word of Liberation, consistently judges all human situations, regardless of color, with a singular divine yardstick. Accordingly, in Boesak's opinion, black emancipation should never duplicate white, bourgeois individualism. In one expression bourgeois individualism cloaks itself in individual selfishness at the expense of group well being. In another fashion it masquerades under the guise of an overly pious, otherworldly concern about heaven. In this last manner, it paralyzes and channels black people's effort into the escape mechanism of "heaven."

In a deeper sense, moreover, Boesak's consistent utilization of the liberating Word of God against all expressions of white and black oppression allows him to link racial discrimination with class exploitation. Posing the question "Is racism indeed the only issue?" in order to ferret out interconnecting examples of oppression against the poor, Boesak replies with this observation:

> It seems to us that there is a far deeper malady in the American and South African societies that manifests itself in the form of racism. . . . Even in South Africa there are signs that should circumstances but allow, some whites would be quite willing to replace the insecurity of institutional racism with the false security of the "black bourgeoisie." [Thus the issue is] the relation between racism and capitalism.[39]

The deeper malady in the form of racism, white over black, is the structural exploitation of classism, black over black. Boesak, then, desires a new South Africa, and by implication a new America, comprised of possibilities for true humanity. In the long term, God's purpose is for a black-white common world; hence, for an authentic liberation, blacks seek to share with whites dreams of a penultimate society of genuine humanness as a sign of the eschatological fullness of what it means to bear the *imago dei*, black and white. More specifically, Boesak depicts this image of liberation: "We are all committed to the struggle for a non-racist, open, democratic South Africa, a unitary state, one nation in which all citizens will have the rights accorded them by ordinance of almighty God."[40] In a word, commitment to nonracialism—liberation beyond racism and classism—affects the common ground for reconciliation.

Reconciliation

Boesak establishes several conditions for black-white reconciliation. First, reconciliation does not mean "feeling good"; it implies suffering and death. Christ had to die. Likewise, we too must prepare to sacrifice our lives for the sake of the other. "If white and black Christians fail to understand this," Boesak admonishes, "we will not be truly reconciled."[41] Second, in political terms reconciliation follows the attainment of righteousness and social justice. The South African system of privileges for the few must first give way to a democratic power sharing and an equal participation in rights and responsibilities for all.

Third, reconciliation exhibits the presence of both divine love and divine righteousness; but the love of God points to Yahweh's concretely taking the side of Yahweh's people against the oppressor pharaoh. Boesak places the role of God's love within the context of God's righteousness of liberation; divine love is God's open practice of doing justice. In reconciliation the Word of God activates liberation. God loves his people into freedom, and thus into reconciliation, through a love of justice. Justice is the condition for reconciliation.[42]

What does reconciliation signify for blacks and whites? For blacks, the "gateway" to true reconciliation, according to Boesak, opens when blacks say farewell to the white mentality. Blacks must affirm their blackness as part of the reconciliation process. They cannot reconcile with whites while hating their black selves and negating their "infinite worth before God." Black people have to grasp their *imago dei* as the constitution of their humanity.[43]

For whites, reconciliation entails their acceptance of black humanity. Even more, it summons whites to a commitment and faithfulness to the struggle of God's liberating Word of reconciling black-white relations through justice. In fact, Boesak recognizes whites who have already assumed the condition of blackness, that is, of already displaying commitment and faithfulness to the Word of God in the midst of oppression. At this point he makes the definition of "blackness" concrete in such a way that whites can enter blackness. "We must remember that in situations like ours blackness (the state of oppression) is not only a colour, it is a condition." He continues, therefore, to describe the role of whites:

> And it is within this perspective that the role of white Christians should be seen. . . . I speak of those white Christians who have understood their own white guilt in the oppression of black people as corporate responsibility, who have genuinely repented and have been genuinely converted.

These particular whites, in Boesak's assessment, have clearly committed themselves to the liberation struggle. They "have taken upon themselves the condition of blackness in South Africa" and are now part of the black church. They, therefore, have presumably met the conditions that lay the foundation for reconciliation.[44]

One has to emphasize that Boesak's reconciliation stands under the Word of God, a liberating Word. In reconciliation blacks and whites assume the condition of blackness based not on color but fundamentally on whoever witnesses to the Word in struggle. Neither blackness nor whiteness conditions the Word; "reconciliation and forgiveness find their meaning only when regarded against the background of God's liberating acts in Jesus Christ."[45]

Christology

In the previous section we saw how genuine theology, liberation, and reconciliation undergo the test of the Word of God in Boesak's approach to God-talk. In Christology, when he describes an emancipatory praxis under the Word of God, the liberating work and person of Jesus Christ pinpoint the substance of the Word. In the final analysis, the gospel of Jesus Christ judges all reflection and all action; the Word is the gospel.

Christ judges in the person of the Poor One and the Oppressed One. In Boesak's Christology Christ's birth in a barn and his parents' financial inability to bear him at an inn reveal him as the Son of the Poor. His lacking a place to "lay his head" (his homelessness) reveals a state of destitution. At the same time, Christ suffered oppression at the hands of the political state for preaching the

Word of God. He even bore unearned punishment from the wicked of his own people; yet, his person (divinity assuming Poverty and Oppression) lay the basis for his work on behalf of all poor and oppressed. He sounded good news for the marginalized, he sided with the dispossessed, effected liberation, and he fulfilled Yahweh's promise of deliverance for the captives.[46]

To the lordship of this Person and Work, Boesak pledges paramount allegiance. At all costs one clings to the confession of Christ as Lord. Consequently, the laws of the state and of self-preservation do not undermine the authority of Christ's Person and Work. Neither do the intimidating demands of a people, status quo, or ideology dictate to the followers of Christ. Here, drawing on progressive strands within his Reformed tradition, Boesak theologically justifies disobedience to apartheid and commitment to the Word in the liberation movement.

Divine lordship thrusts the faithful completely into the political arena. One has to trek the political path because even the "slightest fraction of life" falls under the lordship of Christ. Boesak employs a theological rationale for his claim of Christ's lordship. God created life and he is indivisible; hence, life is indivisible. Since the substance of the Word of God is the liberating lordship of Christ, Christ reigns over all life. Black and white are pulled into a loving family only with the oppressor's theology submitting to Christ's absolute lordship.

In this lordship Boesak also perceives faith and hope for the church. The certitude of Christ's past resurrection confirms his current reign. If Christ rose, he lives and rules over us today; therefore having risen from the dead, Christ guarantees us a future life in the eschaton. The ecclesia, then, witnesses as a church of the resurrection. The resurrected lordship cosmologically altered the balance of forces over sin's dominion, so the kingdom of sin likewise submits to the kingdom of Christ. This knowledge provides faith and hope for the church in the struggle between aggressive disloyalty to sin and unswerving allegiance to the kingdom.

In summary, Christ's lordship of liberation defeated the devil in political places. Christ rose from the clutches of evil persons and forever placed the faithful in God's kingdom of liberation.[47]

Transatlantic Dialogue

The comparison and contrasts between the two political theology representatives fall within a larger, historical transatlantic dialogue. It helps, then, to contextualize the history of the conversation about black theology between the United States and South Africa. Because black theology in South Africa sees itself as part of the overall theological developments in Africa and because U.S. black theology enters the transatlantic dialogue through contact with the generic African Theology, we begin with African Theology.

Black Theology Meets African Theology

The National Committee of Negro Churchmen (founded in 1966 and the first organization to develop black theology in the contemporary period) sent two observers to the 1969 Assembly of the All Africa Conference of Churches (AACC) in Abidjan, Ivory Coast.[48] At this meeting African-American delegates consciously began to link the movement for black power, the black church, and black theology in the United States with the developing liberation theology in Africa. As a result, the AACC decided to establish a "Round-Table Discussion on African Theology and Black Theology."

In 1971 Union Theological Seminary theologian James H. Cone and L. Maynard Catchings, chairperson of the Africa Commission of NCBC (the Committee had now changed its name from Negro to Black) and other black Americans met in Dar es Salaam, Tanzania with African theologians and church leadership.[49] The Christian Council of Tanzania and the NCBC Africa Commission cosponsored this event under the theme "Black Identity and Solidarity and the Role of the Church as a Medium for Social Change" with a focus on economic development, education, and theology.

This conference marked the first time in contemporary black church history that African Americans and Africans had talked face-to-face without a white missionary go-between. At this meeting, the clearest theological differences began to show. The twenty-eight black theologians accented strongly the political "liberation" of the black poor; and the sixteen African scholars and church leaders underscored the importance of "Africanization," especially taking into account the importance of translating Christianity from European culture into African culture.

In January 1972, under the theme "African Theology and Church Life," at an African consultation at the Makerere University (Kampala), black religion scholar George Thomas (then an Interdenominational Theological Center professor in Atlanta) delivered a major presentation on the relation between black theology and African religion.

In June 1973 at Union Theological Seminary (New York City), another consultation was held between six African and twelve black American delegates. John S. Mbiti headed the African group and C. Shelby Rooks (of the Society for the Study of Black Religion) led the black American contingent. As a result of this gathering, a larger meeting took place in December 1974 at the Ghana Institute for Management and Public Administration. On this occasion, the African delegates represented the theological commission of the AACC.[50] The theological debate between the political liberation of poor black Americans and the need to put the gospel message into African cultural forms (e.g., Africanization) continued.

The next meeting between African-American theologians and their African counterparts took place in Accra, Ghana (December 1977). James H. Cone and Gayraud S. Wilmore, along with a small group of black Americans, attended this consultation sponsored by the Ecumenical Association of Third World Theologians (EATWOT) in connection with the Pan-African Conference of Third World Theologians. The political, cultural and black theology-Africanization debates became even more focused; however, South African black theologians stood with the African-American emphasis on political liberation.[51]

The first direct discussions between black theologians in the United States and South African black theologians occurred at Union Theological Seminary (New York City) in December 1986. James Cone's presentation framed three of the major theological issues at the conference: gender, race and class social analysis, and the authority of scripture in the development of a black theology of liberation. Regarding social analysis, Cornel West's speech argued for the necessity of dissecting the many levels of power in all societies: exploitation, subjugation, domination, and repression.

South African theologians added their insight as well. Simon S. Maimela called for the use of Marxist analysis in the process of doing theology. Itumeleng Mosala questioned whether or not there are two Gods in the Bible: a liberating one and a reactionary one.

Roxanne Jordan (South Africa) and Kelly Brown (U.S.) raised concerns about the black female identity of God. They developed theologies from black women's unique experiences in their respective countries. Both Jordan and Brown showed how God and Christ revealed themselves in black women's political and cultural experiences. Together, they painted an integral womanist, black feminist theological process. Attacking the evils of gender, race, and class, black women across the Atlantic were creating a vibrant theology by combining political and cultural sources.[52]

In August 1993 the EATWOT sponsored a conference on the globalization of black theology. Held in South Africa, the conference's primary focus centered on the dialogue between black theology in the United States and South Africa. Issues of concern included culture, politics, women, the Bible and theology, theology and social analysis, and other topics. The agenda contained presentations from U.S. and South African theologians on the same topic as a way of organizing and enhancing dialogue of both black voices. This gathering showed several important theological developments.

First, it used a more comprehensive social analysis in black theology internationally because politics, economics, class, race, gender, sexual orientation, African indigenous religions, and African culture were all discussed and not pitted against each other. Second, black women from both sides of the Atlantic made their presence known by the presentations they gave, by the reoccurrence of (American) womanist and (South African black) feminist theological themes throughout the conference, and by the numbers of black women in both delegations.

Third, though the focus was on the United States and South Africa, black theologians throughout the world attended from Australia, Canada, the Caribbean, England, India, Latin America, the Netherlands, New Zealand, the Pacific Islands, other countries in Africa, and, of course, South Africa and the United States. In the theological history of American black theology's relation to the entire continent of Africa, it has been the close ties between South Africa and black Americans around the issues of political liberation and the beauty of God's gift of blackness which have encouraged a consistent and deep dialogue. This dialogue has helped to clarify the commonalities and differences between black theology of the United States and the rest of the African continent.[53]

The theological commonalities and differences between black theology in the United States and African theology vary.[54] First, both have much in their common ancestry. African Americans are not simply Americans, they are Americans with a difference. It is precisely this difference, this African difference, that continually reminds black people of their origin from their motherland which is Africa. It is conceivable, if it were possible, that many blacks in the United States could directly trace their family background to Africa, especially on the West Coast. In that sense, black Americans still have distant family and blood ties to the Continent.

In addition, black theology and African theology share a common history of struggle against white supremacy and its relation to the Christian gospel. Enslaved blacks in North America and Africans in their own homeland were introduced to the Bible by European missionaries. This history suggests a permanent negative commonality. Both sides of the Atlantic encountered the white supremacist attitudes and practices of whites from Europe and their descendants in North America. Whites and Europeans introduced the Bible to blacks and Africans only if they accepted a status of slavery, a subhuman position, or imitated white people.

Consequently, African Americans and Africans have from the very first day of contact with Europeans and whites experienced racial oppression and attitudes of arrogance. To become Christian, the test was to give up one's black and African identities along with one's natural resources. In return, the black person received white culture and fit into the white imperialist and slave economy as exploited workers. An African common wisdom saying states that when European Christian missionaries came to the Continent, they asked the Africans to pray. When all were through praying and opened up their eyes, white Christians had taken black people's land and natural resources in addition to opposing African indigenous culture. In return, Africans were left with the Bible and the clothing, culture, and capitalist individualistic lifestyles of Europe.

A similar process took place with enslaved African Americans. They received the Bible and white culture and were left without their full African culture. The introduction of Christianity meant white supremacy and arrogance and an attempt to take away wealth, resources, and black ways of being in the world. Both faced the question: Could one be black and Christian or could one be an African Christian? In other words, did they have to imitate Europeans and whites to become Christians?

Both black North American theology and African theology reject the oppressive interpretations of God from Europe and the United States, especially forms of liberal and conservative faith systems. Black theologians ask why and how is it possible for white Americans to do theology without taking seriously the history and ongoing reality of African-American suffering. African theologians reject oppressive theologies that tend to define African indigenous religions and cultures as subhuman, superstitious, or barbaric.

While victimized by a racist Christianity and theology, black and African theologies share in common their revolutionary reinterpretation of this distorted view of the gospel. They did not allow victimization to stop their God-given right to be their own pro-active agents and actors in this world. Through their own reinterpretations, enslaved African Americans created the foundation for a black theology of liberation in North America. They carried this idea out in the "Invisible Institution," the secret religious meetings of blacks during slavery. Africans took European and American missionary perspectives on the Bible and placed them within the context of African indigenous cultures, which existed prior to the arrival of European colonialism.

A final commonality is the rise of black and African women's voices onto the theological scene. In the United States, we find this reality in the development of womanist theology. On the Continent, this fact is shown in the election of the new president of EATWOT in December 1996 in the Philippines. For the first time in the history of EATWOT, a woman (Mercy Amba Oduyoye from Ghana) was chosen for the head office.

Commonalities have not blocked the surfacing of differences. The African-American experience is that of a minority population, stripped of its original land in Africa, removed from its African indigenous language, and forced to forget the memory of its ancestors in Africa. In contrast, the African experience is of a majority population whose memory of their ancestors remains in the grave sites and stories handed down to each generation through bloodlines and family storytellers. Africans are on the land which has been in their possession for centuries; therefore, they do not suffer from historical amnesia as much as black Americans. They can trace their ancestry back for centuries. In addition, they have a language completely different from Americans and Europeans, and perhaps most importantly have access to indigenous cultures and religions.

Theologically, black theology in the United States asks the question: what does God have to do with my blackness as a minority in a system of white supremacy? African theology poses the question: as a majority population with a vast indigenous culture, language and religion, how can I accept Christianity through my own indigenous culture?

The united front in African theology, however, is not as closed as we would think. Black theology in South Africa, like its counterpart in the United States, emphasizes political liberation and holds that the heart of the gospel message is liberation of the poor. Of all the countries on the Continent, South Africa was directly impacted by black theology from the United States (e.g., James H. Cone's book *Black Theology and Black Power*)[55] and was a source for the emergence of South African black theology. Because white supremacy was structurally part of the American power structure and because South African society was also built on institutionalized white skin privileges, black South Africans could accept American black theology more easily.

At the same time, the dominance of black theology should not obscure other expressions of theology in South Africa. For instance, scholars such as Gabriel M. Setiloane of Botswana and South Africa have led a strong Africanization or indigenization movement. Setiloane's *African Theology: An Introduction* puts him more in line with churches and theologians outside of South Africa who are less concerned with politics, economics, and class (e.g., key elements in black theology) and more concerned with language, ancestors, and indigenous rituals (e.g., key elements in African theology).[56]

Just as South African black scholars have different approaches to theology, so too does the rest of the Continent. In contrast to the general agreement among scholars who do African theology by following the Africanization process (e.g., the search to make the gospel relevant to African indigenous culture and religions), we find echoes of a stress on political liberation in certain French-speaking African countries above South Africa.[57]

In general terms, we can still say that, during the first period of contact, black theology in the United States emphasized the political dimensions of the gospel of Jesus Christ. This faith approach looked at systems of oppression and liberation around economic and political power. American black theologians saw blackness (e.g., the experiences of poor and working class black folk) as the main place where God revealed God's self to oppressed humanity; consequently, it was at the point of blackness where God was working to help in the liberation process. Black theologians, moreover, suspected that African theology's stress on culture meant that African scholars and church leaders were too conservative and probably supporters of capitalism. Still, it was the intricate thematic relation between U.S. and South African black theology that African Americans connected to their continent of origin.

Conclusion

What can black theology in the United States and South Africa say to each other? As we have discovered, both theologies share commonalities and dissimilarities. Both theologies arose in response to the racist and idolatrous claim of European and European American theologies. Such a claim unilaterally decreed itself as universal and normative; hence it ascribed blasphemy to the specificity and value of a black political and cultural theology. In contrast, black theologians insisted vehemently that genuine and authentic knowledge of God comes through revelations in Black Power and Black Consciousness. They believed God intentionally created them in God's own image. As God's children, their blackness bears beauty and acts as an essential datum for theological reflection. Moreover, Black Theology U.S. (BTUS) and Black Theology South Africa (BTSA) experienced God's presence as liberator in the black community's efforts toward liberation.

Because blacks suffer oppression and cry out for liberation and because Jesus Christ privileges the oppressed in the liberation struggle, Jesus Christ is black. For both theologies, Scripture also depicts a prototype liberation movement with the exodus as an emancipatory system *par excellence*; therefore, in the Bible and in blacks' lives, God sides with the poor. God calls the faithful, for example, the church, to fight alongside divinity in the movement to free the poor. Indeed, the poor are the subjects of their own history. Methodologically, this approach forces the theologian to start with a practical commitment to the poor and to listen attentively to their questions. Whether in the United States or South Africa, theorizing about God ensues as the second step. To exhibit a preference for the plight of the poor, black theological method admittedly and invariably solicits the aid of social analysis. In analyzing the black poor's particularity, black theology expresses solidarity with the liberation of the world's poor. In the liberation of the universal poor, the rich oppressor simultaneously attains liberation. Without black victims to oppress, the white "victimizer" would also enjoy the fruits of Jubilee.

But in the United States and South Africa, black womanist or black feminist theology has questioned the entire intercontinental dialogue. To speak honestly of God's presence among the poorest of the poor, black women submit, black male theology will have to reevaluate its own "liberation" presuppositions of black male theology. To successfully serve the black church and community, black theology also has to critically assess God's feminine attributes.

In addition to these similarities, BTUS and BTSA have different social contexts affecting the uniqueness of black theology in each country. In the United States blacks operate in a bourgeois democracy; South Africans did not have a constitution and the vote. In the United States a black minority status produces the omnipresent dilemma of potential genocide. On the other hand, the black majority reality posed the problem of what to do with a white minority elite in South Africa.

Further differences over land, culture, and foreparents' religion separate the black theological dialogue. Black Americans suffer from centuries of forced removal from their land and lack a precise lineage to their progenitors' culture. In contrast, black South Africans dwell close to their own land—the land of their ancestors, their cultural identity, and their African traditions. Black Americans have been stripped of a dominant consciousness of their ancestral religious mores. Relative to South Africans, they have successfully resolved their past indigenous African religions into their appropriation of Christianity. South African blacks' closeness to African traditional religions has caused more complications, though creative, in resolving indigenous religions with Christianity. For example, the question arises how to maintain the practical reverence for ancestors and simultaneously confess the decisive revelatory nature of Jesus Christ?

These disunities and unities between BTUS and BTSA fill in the outlines of our transatlantic investigation. Throughout, our single purpose has sought to answer one question: What is the common denominator between black theology in the United States and South African black theology? As a response, our study has verified that, in the main, the denominator common to the two theologies is a gospel of political and cultural liberation. Though black theologians are at variance regarding their shades of black theology, nevertheless, all would agree that the gospel of Jesus Christ has the potential to bring political and cultural freedom to the black poor.

Chapter 5

Quaker Women in Kenya and Human Rights Issues

Stephen W. Angell

Quakers traditionally have proclaimed a strong testimony of gender equality. From the time of their origins in seventeenth-century England, women of the Religious Society of Friends (also known as Quakers) have enjoyed full equality in ministry with Quaker men, something quite unusual three and a half centuries ago. More recently Quaker women in England and North America have been disproportionately active in the woman's suffrage and other women's rights movements. Quaker missionaries who came to Kenya emphasized this teaching. As Jeremiah Mogufu recalled, "In all matters, Friends taught equality. They were among the first to allow women in the pulpit because they believed that God speaks through everybody. Age, sex, or education has no distinction in their souls before God."[1] Elisha Wakube remarked, "The Kenyan Quakers have [a] testimon[y] which favour[s]. . . equality of all human beings," and in living up to this testimony, Kenyan Quakers have taken such stands as "promot[ing] girls' education [and] facilitat[ing] the participation of women in public life."[2] The purpose of this essay is to examine how this Quaker testimony of equality, which often has resulted in active advocacy of women's rights, has manifested itself in the quite different cultural context of twentieth- and twenty-first century Kenya.

The Quaker testimony of equality has deep and evolving roots, dating back to the period of Quaker origins in mid-seventeenth century England. "Christ has come to teach his people himself" through an inward light in each person, declared Quaker founder George Fox; this location of the divine inside every individual led early Quakers to what their contemporaries often regarded as dangerously radical stands toward a universalizing affirmation of humanity. For example, they insisted on addressing any person with "thee" or "thou," rather than the more polite "you"; and they refused to take off their hats in the presence of nobility. From their beginnings in the 1650s, women were regarded as having an equal right to preach the message of Christ, should they perceive Christ calling them to do so. Numerous tracts, most famously Margaret Fell's 1666 tract *Women's Speaking Justified, Proved and allowed by Scriptures, all such as speak by the Spirit and Power of the Lord Jesus*, presented the Quakers' case for gender equality in ministry. One notable fact about this tract is its authorship by a powerful widow, arguably the most influential woman in the Quaker movement, who three years later married Fox.[3] A ferocious revolt within the Quaker movement was touched off in the 1670s, in large part by Fox's and Fell's establishment of separate women's meetings for business. Their opponents were unhappy that these two influential leaders had sought fit to enhance women's powers by involving them in the denomination's decision-making processes, but Fox's and Fell's position in support of women's empowerment stood.[4]

In regard to differences of race and ethnicity, the Quaker testimony of equality was not initially as strong. In his visit to the West Indies and North America in the 1670s, Fox had been willing to countenance the slavery of Africans by Quaker owners, provided that the latter were diligent in providing religious instruction to the slaves in their households.[5] This position remained largely unchanged until the mid-eighteenth century, when a mild-mannered tailor and itinerant minister from New Jersey, John Woolman, gently but persistently persuaded the members of his own Philadelphia Yearly Meeting and of other Quaker bodies in North America to free their slaves. In 1758, for example, the Philadelphia Yearly Meeting reached a consensus that its members should no longer buy and sell slaves and that committees should circulate to the homes of Quaker slaveholders to urge them to free their slaves.[6] A more final step came one year after Woolman's death, in 1773, when the same Yearly Meeting decided that any member who still refused to emancipate their slaves should be removed from membership. Within a decade, every Quaker Yearly Meeting had followed Philadelphia's lead and the Quakers had become the first Christian denomination in North America to free itself of slavery.[7] Still, this step did not portend an absolute stance by Quakers on behalf of racial equality. By primarily informal means, African Americans were excluded from membership and segregated in attendance at many Quaker meetings in the late eighteenth and early nineteenth century.[8] While some Quakers played a notable role in antislavery movements and humanitarian work on behalf of African Americans, others stood aloof from such involvement. Some Quaker schools and institutions were not racially integrated until the mid-twentieth century, well after the start of the Friends' mission in Kenya.[9]

Seventeenth-century Quakers' advocacy for women had stopped short of any sustained argumentation on behalf of women's participation in politics; women's ministry indeed had been the main subject that they addressed. Their nineteenth-century descendants broadened the argument for women's equality in precisely this direction. Susan B. Anthony, who had a Quaker upbringing in New York, and Lucretia Mott were the two most notable Quakers to lend their efforts to the women's suffrage movement.[10] Even after American Quakers split into two contentious factions, the Hicksites and Orthodox, in 1827, both parties continued to deepen their advocacy for women's equality. By the late nineteenth century, Orthodox Quakers from the Midwest were the main supporters of Quaker missions. While not disavowing Victorian ideals about the sanctity of home and family, many Orthodox Quaker women were intimately involved in the Women's Christian Temperance Union, which took a firm stand on behalf of women's suffrage and many other social reforms. Emma Malone, along with her husband Walter, both Evangelical Quakers from Cleveland, Ohio, were the driving force in the establishment of the mission in Kenya in the opening years of the twentieth century. She enthusiastically embodied a "gender-inclusive credo" that regarded women "not as a special group, not even as equals, but simply as people."[11]

While the Quaker testimony of equality and human rights of women can be linked, it is important to note that they are not the same. Quakers understand the testimony of equality as a revelation, the result of a divine leading, perceived by each individual and the community through the workings of the "Inner Light" found within each person.[12] Quakers generally recognize the Christian Scriptures as another source of revelation. The human rights of women, as rooted in such documents as the United Nations' Universal Declaration of Human Rights, have more secular origins. Quakers have not always seen divine revelation and secular rationality to agree, although their doctrine of an Inner Light rooted in the human conscience often does provide a harmonizing mechanism.

As a result of the efforts of the Malones and others, the Friends Church in Kenya has been in existence since three American missionaries arrived in 1902, just slightly over a century ago. Membership statistics are not easy to come by, but according to the latest estimates of the thirteen Yearly Meetings of Quakers in Kenya, there are perhaps just under 150,000 Quakers in that East African country. When the roughly 25,000 Quakers in surrounding African countries (Rwanda, Burundi, Uganda, Tanzania, and Congo) are added in, roughly half of the current worldwide total of approximately 350,000 Quakers live in Africa.[13] When the rapid growth of African

Quakerism is added in, compared to the steady state or decline of many North American and British yearly meetings, it is obvious that African Quakers will become numerically predominant during the next century.

Of course, the significant cultural differences between Quakers in Kenya, a relatively poor nation, as compared to such wealthy nations as the United States, Great Britain, and Canada, where most of the world's other Quakers reside, do raise the question of how such Quaker traditions as a testimony of gender equality would translate into such a radically disparate context, if it would translate at all. An examination of the cultural transformations that would be necessary for Quaker understandings of gender equality to take root in Kenya is a significant task for this essay.

Willis Hotchkiss, Arthur Chilson, and Edgar Hole, the missionaries who set up the initial Friends Africa Industrial Mission in 1902, had been associated with the Friends Bible Institute in Cleveland, Ohio. Their Quaker faith had been heavily influenced by the Holiness Revivals that had swept through many Midwest Quaker meetings in the late nineteenth century, believing that before Christ's imminent return, it was essential to reach every man, woman, and child with the good news of Christ. They chose an uninhabited site at Kaimosi in western Kenya as the center of their mission and aimed to establish "a self-supporting, self-propagating native church." The Board of the Missions initially stipulated that no single men and women were to be sent to Kenya. Indeed, these three men were married; and after a few years of establishing the mission, Hole and Chilson brought their families to Kenya. (Hotchkiss eventually left to start another mission in Kenya, the African Inland Mission.)[14]

Most of the Luyia peoples among whom the three Quakers settled practiced a form of ancestor worship. Rituals to obtain the help of the spirits of the deceased, or at least to dissuade them from doing harm, were performed at family shrines. The spirits of the possessed might sometimes temporarily take over a living person, female or male; living persons susceptible to such possession might become known as prophets or diviners. In his *Sketches from the Dark Continent* (1901), Hotchkiss's judgment that African women were "the bulwarks of superstition" provided a faint hint of the leadership they often provided in their ancestral religions. He described a scene of "demon worship" where "forty or fifty women or girls . . . all . . . naked save for a strip of cloth about the loins" enter into a ritual dance. "No one utters a word, save now and then when one who has lost all semblance of reason, breaks forth with the most unearthly screams. She trembles from head to foot, and pays no attention to anything that goes about her. Yet they dare not stop: it would seem that their very lives depended upon their ability to keep going. They seem utterly at the mercy of some demoniacal power. And they tell me that this is indeed the case." Only the splash of cold water could dispel this spirit possession. "This is womanhood in Africa, womanhood without God! Oh God, what a pity! What a shame! Thou wouldst save, but there is no one to tell them!"[15] Women in Maragoli society (a subgroup of Luyia) were responsible for heavy tasks both in housework and in farming. Clifford Gilpin states that Maragoli men labored in the fields more than the men in most African societies, clearing away most of the brush and sharing in the work of cultivation and harvesting.[16]

The Friends Africa Industrial Mission, shortened in 1918 to "Friends Africa Mission" (FAM), was a multifaceted operation. Chilson and Hole were determined to harness the waterpower readily available at Kaimosi in order to grind corn and to saw logs, and this task they were eventually able to accomplish. Medical care was provided, as a young Quaker doctor, Elisha Blackburn, agreed to settle at Kaimosi. Levinus Painter characterized these advances, all realized by 1906, as "little short of amazing." The missionaries' most amazing accomplishment took longer: the establishment of a literary culture for the Maragoli (subgroup of Luyia) people with the transformation of their language, Luragoli, into written form by using the Latin alphabet, and then the translation of the Bible into Luragoli. The Gospel of Mark had been published in Luragoli by 1908; a collection of hymns, 1912; the New Testament, 1927; the entire Bible, with both testaments, 1951.[17] The existence of a fledgling literary culture would have been meaningless without literate natives to engage it, and so the establishment of schools became inevitable.

At first, the harvest of souls was slow. By 1913, eleven years after the mission's establishment, only 25 members had been received. In 1913, a new mission station was founded in Lugulu near the Uganda border among the Bukusu people; this station was successful and would eventually rival the original mission at Kaimosi, fifty miles to the South. By 1920, the mission had 331 members and 682 in training in five locations, for a total of 1,013 in some stage of affiliation; there were approximately 7,000 Quakers in Kenya by 1939, and 17,000 ten years after that.[18] The missionaries sought to encourage moral transformation among their converts. For example, they attempted to forbid polygamy, to prohibit female circumcision, and to do away with the bride price (the dowry that the family of a bridegroom would receive). While their earliest converts, mostly male, backed strongly the missionaries' efforts, in most of these areas, the resistance from their intended converts was quite stiff. Their campaign against female circumcision was perhaps the one that met the least initial resistance. Kenyan Quakers Peter Wanyama and Paul M'wbanga effectively disrupted some ceremonies of female circumcision. The Native Council of Kenya voted to abolish the practice in 1925; and, at least in some areas covered by the Friends Mission, the practice quickly disappeared among tribes, which admittedly had not often performed female circumcisions in the first place.[19] The issue reemerged, however, at a 1965 conference of Kenyan Quaker women, which resolved that the Christian Council of Kenya should study the ethical and health-related dimensions of female circumcision. This later interest arose from the fact that Quaker missions in Kenya had begun to receive converts in areas where female circumcision was more prevalent. "Since female circumcision is still practiced in the late 1990s, it attests to the complexities involved in overturning the practice including the status and standing of women in the communities that practiced it."[20]

The attempt to abolish the dowry (more properly known as a "bride price" or "bridewealth") was a very difficult campaign, despite the fact that the first Quaker convert in Kenya, Yohanna Amugune, offered to marry off his daughter without receipt of a bridewealth. None of his suspicious neighbors would take him up on such a surprising offer; and eventually Friends churches in Kenya made their peace with bridewealth in exchange for a role in negotiating it for each couple.[21] The church's involvement was initially intended to reduce the amount of the bride price. The same 1965 conference of Kenyan Quaker women recommended that the bridewealth be set at a level that would constitute "a token rather than a price," declining to recommend its complete abolition because, in Kenyan tradition, "it was the giving of bridewealth which made a marriage legal."[22] These kinds of moderating recommendations, however, have not been widely heeded. Jeremiah Mogufu writes, "Alas! This reduction has turned out to be too much addition."[23]

The struggle with polygamy of the Friends' mission has also been a multigenerational, drawn-out affair. Within the first decade, Quaker missionaries decided that no one employed by the mission could marry more than one wife and that anyone who already held such a position would forfeit it upon a second marriage.[24] This policy was later generalized to the position that no polygamist could become a member, although he might be welcome if he had married only twice and one of his wives had died. He could attend Friends' services, his wives and children would be welcome to join, but he himself would be forbidden to join.[25] While polygamists who were thus friendly to Friends would be respected and treated gently, this antipolygamy policy has still produced some backlash against Quakers, especially during the first half century of the mission's existence. In the 1940s, an anticolonial movement, Dini ya Masambwa ("Religion of an Ancestral Spirit"), was founded by a Bukusu man named Elijah Masinde, who told the foreigners to leave in order to permit his people to practice their original religion. As part of their revolt, they burned down the Friends' mission in Luguli. Masinde and several other leaders in the movement were former Quakers who had left the Friends' Church because of their opposition to the missionaries' prohibitions of polygamy.[26] While polygamy is a continuing part of the cultural fabric for Kenyan Quaker women and men, the complexities that this family system has caused has been often acknowledged.[27] A closely associated issue was levirate marriage, where, upon the decease of a married man, his wives would be wedded to a surviving brother. While this long-established custom had certain evident advantages in providing social security for vulnerable widows, Quaker missionaries opposed this practice for the equally obvious reason that it, too, encouraged polygamy.[28]

The earliest Kenyan converts, Amugune and Daudi Lung'aho, insisted on adding their own moral requirements to the moral teachings established by the American missionaries. For example, they noted that Maragoli women had observed a taboo against eating chickens or eggs. Some dread circumstance was said to follow from eating such foods: according to Amugune, it had been feared that the woman would be prevented from marrying; according to Lung'aho, it had been thought that she would be infertile, or possibly bear only deaf-mute children. In any case, they required, as a rite of passage, that any woman who wanted to belong to the Friends Church would have to summon up the courage to eat eggs and chicken, thus breaking a taboo.[29] In another telling of this tale, a speaker at a 1979 conference of Kenyan women Quakers spoke of "women in East Africa gain[ing] certain rights . . . [such as] eating the delicacies like eggs and chicken, which for a long time were denied to women and enjoyed exclusively by men."[30] Of course, this act may have seemed like both a fearful imposition and a regaining of rights, but Rasmussen seems correct to call it "a conscious expression on the part of both the women themselves and their husbands of their belief in the equality of men and women in the eyes of God."[31]

In a very male-dominated society such as the one Quaker missionaries encountered in Western Kenya, the mere introduction of ideas of gender equality often brought about changes in very basic mores. For example, men and women began to eat together at the same table, instead of men eating at the table and women and children on the floor. Edna Chilson noted that some Kenyan men had begun to consider whether they should walk with their wives instead of leaving them behind. "Being in America, you may not fully appreciate this move among these native Christians but it is a thing for which to praise God."[32]

Gender equality did not necessarily entail mixing with others of the opposite gender in public settings. For example, Kenyan Friends (like American Friends) initially required all men to sit on one side of the meetinghouse and all women to sit on the other side. This gender separation during worship has now formally been abolished, but Wakube states that it is still "not easy for people to mix" during worship time.[33]

Esther Mombo rightly concludes that such changes sought by Quaker missionaries in Luyia culture largely added up to an advocacy of "Victorian ideals of womanhood which stressed domesticity and female subordination." There was a basic asymmetry in what the American missionaries expected of women and men. Mombo writes, "while women were taught how to be Christian mothers, men were not taught how to be Christian men but they were given skills to help them live in a changing society." While women were taught to nurture the religious life within their own homes and among their neighbors, men were being groomed to be leaders.[34] Still, some aspects of the missionaries' program offered a fuller glimpse of women's equality, especially in their advocacy of education for both boys and girls.

The most important stance related to gender equality taken by the missionaries in the first three decades of the existence of the Friends' missions was to ensure that mission schools educated both girls and boys. They took this step against the opposition of the British colonial rulers and even more so of the Maragoli elders, both of whom would have liked for the Friends to have established classrooms for males only. Two wives of pioneer missionaries (Adelaide Hole and Deborah Rees) "did not wait for anyone's approval" in their work to educate girls and women.[35] While instruction in literacy at village schools began as early as 1903, a decisive step was the establishment of a girl's boarding school, roughly equivalent to an American junior high school, at Lirhanda in June 1921, with Adelaide and Edgar Hole and Roxie Reeves playing key roles in its founding. This girl's school had already been in existence eight months prior to the founding of an equivalent school for boys in Vihiga. The father of teenaged Rasoa Mutua,[36] one of the first students at the Girl's Boarding School, was staunchly opposed to her going to school; but Mutua enrolled anyway. When two African elders warned her father that it would cost him two cows to have her name removed from school rolls, he reluctantly permitted her to remain in school.[37]

Twelve years later, in 1933, it could still be said that "prejudice against education for girls was breaking down very slowly," although in the northern area served by Friends' missions, near Uganda, more girls were attending school than were boys as early as 1926.[38] By the 1940s, Kenyan opposition to education of girls was definitely waning. Dorothy Pitman, who arrived in 1944, wrote that, in her region of Kenya, "the parents accepted the need for girls to be educated and government officials were surprised to see so many girls in school where Quaker-trained teachers were employed and the Bible teaching of 'neither male nor female but all one in Christ' was put into practice by teachers and parents." By Pitman's era, Kenyan Quaker parents determined that an education might actually raise the bride price that could be expected when their daughter married; hence, the competition to fill the limited number of slots for girl's schooling had become quite keen.[39] The mere fact that the Girl's School was a boarding school was an important factor in freeing Kenyan Quaker girls to study. If girls enrolled in the school had stayed at home, household tasks would likely have taken up so much time that they would have little time left for study.[40]

The girl's lessons often focused on homemaking skills. Pitman noted that sewing was an especially "popular" subject.[41] Much of the justification advanced for educating girls had to do with their key roles in rearing children and domestic life. One proverb that contained this notion was the following: "Educate a girl and you educate a family; educate a boy and you educate an individual."[42] This emphasis on domestic roles for women is one reason that it is difficult to fit Kenyan Quaker missionaries from 1903 to 1950 into the modern feminist mold, as Samuel Thomas has observed.[43] But Quaker missionaries—especially the female ones—were also quite aware of the degree to which they were empowering Kenyan women, who would then be able to provide a broader transformative influence throughout the whole of Kenyan society. As early as 1932, Esther Ford, daughter of missionary Jefferson Ford, introduced a simple method of Bible study to Kenyan women at the village level. Although Esther stayed only a short time in Africa, her idea caught on among Kenyan women; when Kenyan women were able to hold their own conferences, they made certain that Bible study played a central role in them.[44] There would be much evidence to support Roxie Reeves' claim that "as [African women] become a bit more educated . . . [they] are bound to assert their rights to some extent."[45]

Reeves was certainly correct in intuiting that Kenyan Quaker women had broader aspirations than simply homemaking. Pitman reported in 1948, for example, that more Kenyan girls were "wanting to take teacher training."[46] Even those missionaries, like Pearl Spoon, who were more oriented toward directing women to domestic roles recognized the need for young Kenyan women "to do something constructive between the time they leave school and marriage." Consequently, she reported that, in addition to eight girls in teacher training, there were three training to be health workers and one going to high school.[47] Ruth Repogle observed that "African women are greatly concerned . . . to see that their daughters have greater opportunities upon reaching maturity than they themselves had."[48] One African Quaker, Priscilla Abwao, who eventually filled a number of high governmental positions during the period of transition to independence, completed the schooling available to her under Friends' auspices and "was obliged to go outside" the Friends' educational system to find the high school education that she needed to fulfill her career goals. Mildred White, writing in 1963, the year of Kenyan independence, found this limitation of the Friends' educational system to be "sobering to recall."[49]

In the area of theological training, however, Friends did provide further opportunities as early as the 1940s. In 1943, a veteran missionary, Jefferson Ford, opened the Friends Bible Institute in Lugulu. After four years of operation, the Institute had to close temporarily due to Ford's retirement, but it was reopened three years later in Kaimosi. In accordance with Friends' principles, the Institute was open to both male and female students from its inception. One of the three female students in the Institute's inaugural class was Rasoa Mutua. She had experienced a call to preach in 1921, while she was attending the Girl's Boarding School. Despite her marriage in 1923 and her bearing eight children, four of whom survived infancy, she did indeed minister to women throughout the district of Lugulu, often traveling with a baby. After her husband's death in 1940, she refused the offer of marriage from her brother-in-law as his third wife. Upon her refusal, he took her cow and chickens and set fire to her house. Still, she worked as a matron at the Girls' Boarding School, and the Christians in her village looked after her and provided her and her children with the necessities of life.[50] She attended the Institute for three years, graduating in 1946, and embarked on a much expanded ministerial career afterwards. She was particularly noted for her ministry in hospitals and prisons; she died in 1996 at the age of ninety-five.[51]

Mutua found support for leadership from strong women in her Bible reading. When "bringing the message" (a Quaker equivalent for "preaching") to an assembly of Tanzanian women in 1927, she chose as her topic Deborah, a female judge and military leader in ancient Israel (Judges 4). "I urged all of them to be like Deborah," she recalled.[52] While her worldview was much different after becoming Christian and Quaker, there was also some continuity with women's leadership in the ancestral religions. One similarity was her appeal to dreams and visions, a strong element of the inspiration of traditional African diviners, as well as many important figures in the Old and New Testaments. She recalled having been unconscious and "taken up as by an elevator to a very beautiful world. Once I was offered a banana but I would not take it. Had I eaten it, I would not have come back to this world. I stayed in the other world for two days. I was almost put out of the house as a corpse."[53] Other than stating that "we were saved by God," Mutua does not draw an explicit lesson from this vision; but in the context of her other autobiographical expressions, it bespeaks of a strong sense of mission or purpose—not only that she was saved by God, but that her life was preserved for a reason and that she and her listeners would best be advised to use their precious time to vigorously advance the cause of the Kingdom of God.

Mutua was a very significant minister in the development of the Friends' Church in Kenya, but she was only one among many. Wakube's 1990 work lists ninety-eight eminent female ministers among Kenyan Friends, fifty of whom were still living at the time of his writing and thirty of whom he adjudged as especially eminent.[54] The Friends Bible Institute (recently renamed the Friends Theological College) has enrolled female students since its inception, and it currently has about one third female students. In 2003, it enrolled a married woman, with the agreement of her husband and of her home congregation.[55] Some of the female graduates of the Friends Theological College are employed as pastors, but often as volunteers. Most of the paid pastoral positions go to male Quakers. A 1996 statement from the Sixth Friends World Committee for Consultation Mission and Service Conference held in Uganda includes the following pertinent comment: "We looked too at the questions of building trust between men and women, not hiding behind traditional roles which have little regard for the Quaker testimonies to equality and respect in each person. Yes, that means our partners too! The Clerk of the Section observed that no East African Yearly Meeting has ever had a woman as its presiding clerk or as a superintendent."[56] In other words, there does appear to be a rather definite "glass ceiling" among Kenyan

Friends when it comes to employment of women in ministerial vocations, despite the Quaker testimony of equality between the sexes.

Perhaps representative of female Kenyan pastors is Margaret Ngoya, daughter of Quaker parents and a mother of three prior to her conversion in 1973. She received a call to be trained in theology and afterwards, in 1982, became a volunteer pastor in the Nairobi Yearly Meeting, as no full-time jobs were available. For a while, she conducted seminars for youth and then was given a part-time pastoral position for a Friends meeting with more than 500 members. When she received a vision to build a new church, the women and young people in the church supported her endeavor; the men did not. Again, the testimony of equality did not seem to be much of a consideration when it came to paid employment for pastors. In 1990, she reflected that when male Quakers "saw that particular building going up they said to me they wanted a man. They looked for evil things about me. One of the committee members said, 'We want a man with a wife and children.' Praise God, I do not have a man but I do have Jesus. . . . I told them I came here to put up a church. Whether they employed me or not I must build that church." To handle all that her ministry required of her, she found that she needed to be "tough, courageous, loving, understanding, and kind."[57]

The two-decade period following the opening of the Friends Bible College saw the maturing of Kenyan Quakerism as a self-governing, indigenous church. The movement for *uhuru* (freedom, independence) with Kenyan Friends in relation to the overseas missionary boards and personnel proceeded fairly closely in parallel with the uhuru achieved by Kenya as a whole from Great Britain. East Africa Yearly Meeting (EAYM) was established in 1946. Since the Yearly Meeting is the basic Quaker structure for self-governance, with the founding of the Yearly Meeting, Kenyan Friends were authorized "to act as a corporate Christian body, to set up departments of religious work, to establish your own Christian ministry and to carry on evangelistic, educational and missionary service as a yearly meeting."[58] Eighteen years later, within months of the 1963 independence celebration for the nation of Kenya, all mission properties and funds held by the American missions within Kenya were turned over to EAYM in February 1964, after a careful transition process. Kenyan Friend Salome Nolega noted, "Only a blind person would say we were not mature enough to take over. So this was due and done at the right time."[59]

The independence process for Kenyan Friends did not empower men and women evenly. When the Yearly Meeting was formed in 1946, Kenyan men assumed all of the top administrative positions, as Kenyan women had feared would happen. Behind the scenes, women held some important positions. Rasoa Mutua and three other women were selected to serve on the board of the Yearly Meeting, and three other Kenyan Quaker women became members of the preacher's board. Women's concerns about their lack of voice were answered five years later, in 1951, by the establishment of a women's Yearly

Meeting. This new grouping, in fact, met for the first time in December 1952.[60] Two decades later, when responding to questions about women's issues during an American visit, Thomas Lung'aho, EAYM executive secretary, emphasized the existence of women's meetings at all levels, from the local to the national, as well as leadership positions assumed by some Quaker women in education and in government.[61]

This same time period saw several mass movements for self-rule by Kenyans, followed by Kenyan achievement of independence in 1963, an occasion in which Kenyan men and women were strongly united. The most famous of the uprisings against British rule was the Mau Mau rebellion of the 1950s, but there were several precursors of this. One such precursor was a female-led rebellion. In southern coastal Kenya (not an area where Quakers have a presence), the British attempt to eradicate native culture by destroying the *kaya*, sacred forest shrines, led Mekatilili Wa Menza to lead a rebellion against them in 1913. The British captured her and exiled her to Mumias for five years.[62] Mumias is only a few miles from such Kenyan Quaker centers as Kaimosi, so it is likely that Kenyan Friends would have learned of her during her exile.

In the 1940s, as mentioned above, a rebellion arose in the area of the Bukusu in the northern part of the area of western Kenya under Quaker influence. Led by Elijah Masinde, an ex-Quaker, this movement, Dini ya Masambwa, was dedicated to reviving traditional religious practices, recovering ancestral lands, and rejecting white supremacy in religion and politics. Quaker and Catholic churches were burned down and the agricultural department was also targeted by the rebels, as its land was ploughed up, its cattle set loose at night, and an agricultural officer's house was burnt down. Kenyan Quakers in good standing did not take part in this rebellion themselves; Elisha Wakube states that their testimony against secret societies prevented participation, and that they sought to follow Christ and Christ only.[63] At the same time, Kenyan Quakers did strenuously object to the repressive measures used in attempts to break up this movement and, moreover, appear to have had a patriotic pride about its confrontation with the colonial authorities, even if they did not agree with all of the methods used. Furthermore, they believed that American Friends missionaries (who, after all, were beneficiaries of an independence movement against the British some two centuries previously) should have been more understanding of the movement. Rose Adede (with others) wrote:

> The sad thing is that during the late 1940s literally hundreds of the Babukusu people were subjected to surveillance, interrogation, arrest, flogging, persecution, banishment, and in 1948 as many as eleven people were shot and killed by the colonial police at Malakisi—all this as a result of their participation in a mass movement whose twofold purposes were: a recovery of their ancestral lands and acquisition of free-

> dom of worshipping God anywhere at any time and in any way. Why was Friends Africa Mission not merciful to these people?[64]

The Mau Mau rebellion was considerably more tumultuous than Dini ya Masambwa. Unlike Dini ya Masambwa, it was not centered in western Kenya where Kenyan Quakerism was strongest, but rather in the area to the northeast of Nairobi. Kenyan Friends suffered as a result of the Mau Mau rebellion; for example, in January 1954, a Quaker leader was killed in the vicinity of Nairobi. Another Quaker pastor, whose congregation was at Nakuru, related being part of a group attacked by the Mau Mau, of whom only he escaped alive. Wilbur Beeson wrote, "Some of our own African Friends who lived in the danger area also have been persecuted and killed for their Christian faith."[65] For Kenyan Quakers, voicing support publicly for this movement at the time it occurred would have been impossible; however, in retrospect Kenyan Quakers have seen that the Mau Mau rebels raised compelling issues. Simeon Shitemi, for example, has described the Mau Mau movement as an understandable protest against the unjust appropriation of the best lands by the whites (both missionaries and others) for themselves.[66]

The parallels between the Mau Mau movement and the American Independence movement two centuries earlier are particularly close for Quakers in three ways: (1) for Quakers, both movements included a goal that they vigorously supported (freedom and independence) and that they experienced in conflict with a means that they could not support (using any means necessary to gain freedom); (2) in both cases, when Quakers attempted to witness to their own ideal of Christian nonviolence, they were exposed to "sufferings"; (3) in retrospect, both Kenyan and American Friends take patriotic pride in the freedom and independence achieved and do not dwell upon the violence that was used to achieve that desirable goal. In the case of the Mau Mau rebellion, Friends, both Kenyan and non-Kenyan, used nonviolent means whenever possible to alleviate the suffering of Kenyan Friends and to further the just goal of independence. For example, Friends went to the British authorities to witness for the character of those who had been imprisoned as Mau Mau supporters, and some of those for whom they testified were released.[67] Kenyan and English Friends joined in appeal for the release of Jomo Kenyatta, the man accused of heading the Mau Mau rebellion, who would later become president of Kenya. The government permitted these Friends to visit Kenyatta in 1961.[68] Priscilla Abwao, a Kenyan Friend who sat on the Legislative Council during the early 1960s while the plans for independence were proceeding, participated in the talks to write a constitution for her newly independent country at Lancaster House in London.[69]

The independence of Kenya and of Kenya Friends both were great and long-overdue accomplishments, events in which both Kenyan men and women could and did rejoice. These events also served understandably as a stimulus to a women's rights movement, for the same reasons that the American Independence movement eventually gave rise to a woman's suffrage movement. The same ideals of freedom and equality that underlay the independence of both Kenya and America would not be fully achieved until they would be fully reflected in the lives of both women and men in all independent countries. Maria Nzomo has written, for example, that Abwao's inclusion in the Kenyan delegation to draft the constitution "was an afterthought and [she] could hardly be expected to effectively represent women's gender concerns at that historical moment" and that when elections for the new Parliament took place, Abwao did not gain a seat.[70] The same incompleteness in inclusion of Kenyan women was evident in the workings of the East African Yearly Meeting of Friends. Men in the EAYM made all of the decisions and monopolized the paid positions; yet women provided most of the work on which Friends' Meetings in Kenya relied. "The Quaker tradition is kept by women," one of the leaders in Kenyan Quakerism has stated.[71]

As plans for full independence of the nation and the yearly meeting went forward, Kenyan women joined the United Society of Friends Women in 1962. Anne Webster observed, "This latter move caused the men to say that the women just want their own Yearly Meeting. The women partially accept this outlook, because they say the men do not really listen to them in the meetings in which they are in charge. It seems that the Christian and Quaker emphasis upon the equality of men and women before God is not being understood."[72] When, during the last quarter of the twentieth century, EAYM divided into a number of smaller yearly meetings (as of 2003, the number in Kenya is fourteen), most of the new yearly meetings set up their own chapters of the USFW.[73]

Since the height of the Kenyan independence movement occurred at about the same time as the climax of the American civil rights movement, perhaps it is not too surprising to find some echoes of the latter in the former. In the seventeen years of transition between the formation of the EAYM and its assumption of control over all Quaker property and funds in Kenya, the "integrationist" sympathies of the white Quaker missionaries was much in evidence. Racial integration was far less of a concern in a country with an overwhelming black majority than it was in a country where only a minority of persons was of African descent. In 1957, European Quakers and the EAYM cosponsored an international work camp, which undertook various construction projects for the Quaker hospital in Kaimosi, including the construction of a new ward for tuberculosis patients. One report on this work project stated that "The outward achievements of the camp, gratifying as they are, are not the most important. More important is the success of building human relationships and establishing the idea of voluntary international work camps for the promotion of peace in this country where the idea is so new. In Kenya, where racial segregation, if not an actual law, is still the practice in daily life, this camp with community living, housing, food and recreation is a shining novelty; no less the sight of young white men working hard along young Africans." Not everything was precisely equal, as European work campers stayed two years, whereas African work campers had only three-month terms despite their wish to stay longer. Indeed, this project in interracial cooperation seems to have been all male; there is no evidence of the inclusion of women.[74]

By 1961, there was an "integrated" and "thriving" Sunday School at the Friends Africa Mission in Kaimosi, with sixteen missionary children and 40 African children in attendance, according to the American Quaker journal, the *Friends Missionary Advocate*. Whites and Africans shared leadership, and classes were held in the schoolroom previously used for the missionaries' children. Noting that the class was bilingual, with songs and lessons in both English and Luragoli, the *Advocate* observed that "while the school achieves interracial unity, it provides that each child may hear the Bible lesson in a language that he can understand." An accompanying picture shows missionary children sitting together as a group toward the front of the classroom surrounded on the sides and in the back by their African classmates.[75] In any event, this concern with integration in Africa was a short-lived phenomenon in American Quaker journals. There is no mention of the topic following Kenyan independence in 1963.

The advent of Kenyan independence did not bring an end to human rights discourse in the conversations and interchange between Kenyan Quakers with their American and European Quaker counterparts. During the anti-apartheid struggle in South Africa, which reached its peak a decade or more after Kenyan independence, Kenyan Quakers were quite vocal in international gatherings in support of that struggle. It was of great assistance and comfort to all Quakers that there was a small (numbering in the hundreds), interracial group of Quakers in South Africa who were completely devoted to the antiapartheid movement. Rose Adede undoubtedly spoke for many Kenyans when, in a speech to the Friends World Committee on Consultation in 1987, she gently chided American Quakers for not doing more to achieve freedom for their South African brothers and sisters. "We do not even have to lift our eyes very high to see the suffering of Africans in South Africa." She praised the leadership that students in Quaker colleges had shown in their enthusiastic embrace of the South African divestment movement.[76]

Again, events have passed this particular issue by, with the 1994 South African elections ushering in an end to apartheid. In addressing American and European Quakers, Adede and others also have pointed to deeper economic injustices that have unfortunately proven far more durable. Describing the subsistence economy in which the vast majority of Kenyan women find themselves and the truly sacrificial level of giving required for poor persons to support the Kenyan Quaker churches, Adede appealed to the Quaker testimony of simplicity that cultivates a sensitivity "to what the luxuries cost the bodies of the poor and the hearts of the rich." Then she sought to prick the conscience of her listeners, asking how privileged American and European Quakers are living out that testimony of simplicity today.[77]

Along similar lines, Kenyan Quaker diplomat Simeon Shitemi decried the protective approach by privileged nations toward their own economies that then unjustly squeeze the economies of the poorer nations. In his view, Quakers in the more privileged nations have not been vigorous enough in their efforts to change this unjust situation. He asked, "What of the Society of Friends and the Church of Christ as a whole? While they compromise and rationalize, millions are starving and dying without food or shelter."[78] Adede has suggested that a more subtle form of racism is evident in such passivity in the face of economic injustice, arguing that the racism currently "found within the Quaker world . . . is insidious, cancerous, because it is forever protected by a veneer of self-righteousness and refusal to acknowledge that it exists!"[79] Lenah Mwenesi, longtime President of the United Society of Friends Women in the EAYM, cautioned Kenyan Quaker women not to become entirely preoccupied with their indignation against economic injustice: "Illiteracy, poverty, and inadequate health facilities have made leadership among our women in East Africa Yearly Meeting of Friends more difficult. However, some effort has been made to make some of our women realize that they are not the only needy ones in the world. For example, helping your neighbor extinguish the fire on her burning house does not require riches to do so."[80]

American Quakers, like other Americans, often have tended to undervalue economic rights that other peoples so desperately yearn for. John Woolman's life was one example of a countervailing trend among American Quakers, and there are others. For example, the *Friends Missionary Advocate* published an article on "Human Rights for Real" in 1968, to celebrate the twentieth anniversary of the adoption of the Universal Declaration of Human Rights. Dorothy Wesenbrink of the National Council of Churches wrote, "It seems as if Americans are all *for* human rights, and they tell themselves in their hearts and their neighbors over the fence, and thus being on the 'right' side of things, feel a pleasant glow of patriotic satisfaction. Part of the fatal charm of being *for* human rights has been that it is one of those causes which is so all-encompassing that it has seemed about impossible to do anything about it except reflect sentimentality upon its general goodness." She observed that part of human rights was economic: "Not only does everyone have the right to own property, but they also, according to the Declaration, should have the right to . . . work under favorable conditions, receiving (if a woman or a minority person) equal pay for equal work. The right to a just remuneration . . . and to a standard of living adequate for the health and well-being of each person and his family, are included."[81] On a worldwide basis, some American Quaker organizations actively address such issues: the American Friends Service Committee based in Philadelphia and the Right

Sharing of World Resources based in Richmond, Indiana, are two such examples. Still, American Quakers' quest to impart real meaning to these rights for citizens of poorer nations can get lost in the sentimental glow of which Wesenbrink has written.

Battles against racism and economic injustice have frequently united Kenyan Quaker women and men, but other human rights battles have raised more contention between the sexes. In December 1960, two leading Kenyan Quaker women, Lenah Mwenisi and Mellap Wakube, attended a United Nations Regional Women's Rights Seminar in Addis Ababa, Ethiopia. While the seminar was in progress, street fighting broke out in the city. For these Quaker women, it was a timely reminder of the need to work energetically for the interconnected aims of peace and human rights. Wakube wrote, "The rebels were starving. Bloodshed was everywhere. The best thing is for everyone to work for the promotion of peace and understanding throughout the world."[82] The conflict, however, did not cause them or other Kenyan women to lose sight of the cause for which they had come to Addis Ababa, to advance the rights of women. Indeed, Kenyan Quaker women, and other women in Kenya, have regularly looked to the advocacy of the United Nations on their behalf, in the way that their sisters in more advanced countries, and often with a more established set of precedents on women's rights issues, have not. For example, Maria Nzomo has written,

> Very little has been done to ensure that Kenya's domestic law conforms with international standards in respect to women's human rights. . . . Kenya should incorporate all the key international instruments concerning women's rights into our . . . law, including . . . the Beijing Declaration and Platform of Action of 1995.[83]

Joan Wena was a Kenyan Quaker who attended the Fourth UN Conference on Women in Beijing in September 1995. In her report on the conference, Wena mentioned that Kenyan men had been hostile to her participation in this conference. She sought to remind her male friends that "the woman is not fighting the man, because to her the man is not the enemy; in fact to her he is the best friend, the husband, the father of her children, the lifelong partner, the friend she loved enough to leave the security of her home for his." What women sought, Wena observed, was equal participation in family decision-making processes, equal regard for male and female children, and a relationship based on friendship and equality rather than domination and subservience. She found the Beijing experience to be an "exhilarating" and empowering one: "For me from the African front where Women are generally undervalued, it was heart warming to realize that this burden was not limited to African Woman but that it was a burden shared by women all over the world although the degree varied." While most Kenyan women "have no idea what their Human Rights are" and hence there must be "Mass Education to create awareness on gender equality," Wena stated that it was also necessary to have "a united front . . .

involving both men and women in struggling to improve the quality of human life."[84]

That (in Wena's words) *the degree* of undervaluing of women "varies" from place to place on our planet has been an observation made by many. Quaker women have sometimes commented on the severity of oppression of women that they have encountered in Kenya. At the Friends World Committee for Consultation in Kenya in 1991, Miriam Were and others lamented that "many African women die young of exhaustion from overwork" and then encouraged Kenyan "men to help their wives more."[85] Janet Minshall, a consultant to women's groups who visited Kenya twice during the 1980s, found that her work in Kenya funding small women's groups was made nearly impossible by the "extreme oppression of women" there. The immediate problem was that the women's husbands confiscated their profits instead of allowing them to be reinvested in the business, but as Minshall became more familiar with Kenyan culture, it appeared to her that gender oppression reached far deeper. "While it wasn't obvious at first, one soon came to notice that while all the women worked very hard in the fields, the men 'supervised' sitting under a tree, or visited with other men from nearby farms." In working with women's groups, she observed an absence of property or contractual rights for Kenyan women. There were other problems as well. Women "were cast off for younger wives with impunity and they and their children were then left without support. Women were legally blamed and exiled from their community if they were raped." In Minshall's view, Kenyan Quakers did recognize that such treatment of women was contrary to Quaker beliefs, including the testimony of equality. She sadly concluded, however, "many Friends did make an effort to break these traditional habits on the basis of their adopted Quaker faith, but the outside pressures to conform were enormous, and so they failed." Consequently, Minshall appears to have given up her work with Kenyan women's groups.[86]

Kenyan Quaker women might not challenge most or all of the features of the bleak picture painted by Minshall. They also have not been afforded the opportunity that she had as a Quaker from abroad to merely withdraw from the culture; thus, they have had to seek careful ways to safeguard their interests in a fashion that would build up cooperation and friendship across gender and ethnic lines. This recourse has certainly not been easy, but Kenyan Quaker women have been ingenious. Esther Mombo's work on Women's Meetings in the EAYM has provided much helpful detail on this aspect of the story. Similar to seventeenth-century Quakers, a key part of the story was the establishment of separate women's meetings at both local levels, beginning as early as the 1930s. They took place mostly during the middle of the week, on Thursday or Friday. They were of value as soon as World War II, when many Kenyan men were performing military service or were emigrant laborers, providing "a relief from the staleness of despondency which resulted from the increased hardships of war."[87] As mentioned above, the Women's Yearly Meeting was established in 1952. When problems arose about the lack of accountability of women's funds entrusted to the men's yearly meeting, the Women's Yearly Meeting opened its own bank account in 1961. The Women's Yearly Meeting has been indispensable in several very significant projects and ministries in Kenya. Rasoa Mutua and other women, for example, have largely carried out the Friends' prison ministry there. In addition, the fund-raising work of women enabled a meetinghouse to be constructed in the centrally located city of Kakamega. That meetinghouse officially opened in 1980. Mombo observes that "women developed skills of organization and leadership among themselves . . . is one of the successes of the Women's Yearly Meeting," but that the Yearly Meeting "never reached a point of being a voice of women in challenging the structures of the Meeting which sidelined them."[88] Recognizing the strength of women in this Yearly Meeting, the Right Sharing of World Resources, an organization of Quakers from around the world, have continued to support financially projects proposed by Kenyan Quaker women. They have done so after listening carefully to the women so that their procedures largely follow the protocols developed by Kenyan Quaker women themselves, including the opening of a bank account specific to each project.[89]

One article appearing in the journal of the United Society of Friends Women (the *Friends Missionary Advocate*) in 1969 advocated "planned parenthood [as] a basic human right." The author noted the tremendous demand, where readily available, for a range of contraceptive services and then asked, "Would you say that 'Every Child is a Wanted Child?' What does the population explosion of our world today say to you?"[90] While the author of this article, Thelma Hinshaw, was American, her perspective found some resonance among Kenyan Friends, among whom, even in monogamous households, there are often eight or more children.[91] Abigail Indire, a member of Nairobi Meeting, wrote in 1971, "Kenya has one of the highest population growth rates in the whole of Africa. Our meeting has realized the importance of educating people to space and limit their families in order to use the resources available at their disposal to uplift living standards among members of our society. It has heretofore resolved through our national conference that campaigns aimed at limiting and spacing of children so that people may live abundant lives should be encouraged wholeheartedly by members of our society. It has also been resolved that, if possible, the society should use the local women's meetings to teach people about family planning."[92] Some Friends meetings in Kenya have followed Indire's and Hinshaw's advice. Assemblies of Elgon Friends women in 1985 and 1986, for example, included discussion of family planning as one of a half-dozen major themes in their five-day gatherings.[93] Scholars have generally identified African feminism as "pro-natal."[94] That designation would certainly apply also to Kenyan Quaker women, but if these pro-family-planning statements are representative of Kenyan Friends, this would imply at least some measured limitation to pro-natalism in Quaker ranks.

This essay surely does not require an elaborate conclusion. Over the past century, views of women's rights and other human rights have continuously evolved and advanced among Kenyan and American Quakers, no less than among the other peoples of the world. I have attempted to forge a connection between two relatively radical concepts, the Quaker testimony of equality and the concept of human rights for women, and to record how these radical concepts have been lived out in a relatively recent, although also numerous, branch of the community that gave birth to the first of these concepts. Not all ideals are easily transferred across cultures. Still, it is clear that most putative human rights are strongly desired across all gender and cultural lines, including both economic ones such as adequate income to support one's family and political ones such as self-governance. It is surely not surprising that, when such high ideals have been set, they often find themselves in conflict with culture, both locally and worldwide; consequently, progress toward those ideals is sometimes slow and halting. It is also clear that struggles toward a fuller realization of human rights by Kenyan Quaker women, joined by Kenyan men and Quakers from abroad in many instances, have yielded significant fruit. There is clearly much more to do. Surely the high ideals exemplified on these pages should not be compromised, but Quakers and indeed all persons of good will should join together in a more concerted effort and with renewed dedication for a fuller realization of women's rights worldwide.

Chapter 6

Mennonites and Peace-Building in Angola

Lutiniko Landu Miguel Pedro

Introduction

Since the founding of the Anabaptist movement in Zurich in the sixteenth century, Anabaptists have been strongly associated with pacifism and peacemaking—including the Mennonite tradition, which will be the primary focus of this essay. Denny J. Weaver, for example, states that Anabaptists have placed a special emphasis on three things: "first, Jesus is the norm of truth. Second, the church that follows Jesus is a new social reality—a community. Third, peace, rejection of violence, and nonresistance are particular manifestations of following the example of Jesus."[1] John H. Redekop provides a longer, yet similar, list of basic Anabaptist characteristics, including the following: an emphasis on the New Testament and on the centrality of Jesus; the necessity of a "believers'" Church; the importance of discipleship; insistence on a church without social class differences; belief in the church as a covenant community; separation from the world; the church as a visible counterculture; and belief that the gospel includes a commitment to the way of peace modeled by the prince of peace.[2]

With these basic principles in mind, Hubert A. Henry and John H. Redekop recommend the following as a guiding precept for Anabaptist

Christians: "make every effort to obey the law; however, do not accept military service which involves training in how to kill fellow human beings who are also made in the image of God."[3] Today this position is considered somewhat extreme, and opinion about such issues among Mennonites and other Anabaptists is strongly divided. That among the members in my home Mennonite congregation—Igrjeja Evangelica dos Irmaos Menonitas em Angola (IEIMA), which is located in the Angolan province of Cunene—are a number of persons serving in the police force, which illustrates that while Mennonites throughout Africa share in common many of the characteristics outlined by Weaver and Redekop, including the emphasis on pacifism and peacemaking, these principles and priorities may not always be lived out, applied, or have precisely the same meaning or significance from context to context. This range in application is what I will show here in an examination of Mennonite peace-building and ministry in Angola.

The emphasis on peace-building is at the heart of the Mennonite tradition and derives from the concern Jesus showed for peace when stating to others: "Peace be with you" (John 20:21). The New Testament Greek uses the term *eirene*, which translates as simply "peace"; this verb comes from *eireneuo*, which means "live/be in peace." Peace, in this instance, alludes to the welfare of the whole human being and to a person being in harmony with his or her self and with others. Professor John S. Mbiti considers that harmony as the personal dimension of peace that comes out of a reconciled spirit and mind.[4] But there is also a social dimension to this peace, which David W. Schenk suggests has sometimes taken the form within Africa of people sharing food and other resources with each other as needed.[5]

This essay will specifically examine ways Mennonites have responded to the civil war context of Angola during the last quarter of the twentieth century. In a context where civil war produced extreme hardships and significant loss of life, Mennonites, including the Mennonite Brethren, the Evangelical Mennonites, and the Mennonite Community, acted sometimes on their own and sometimes in conjunction with fellow members of the Church Council in Angola (Conseilho das Igrejas Cristas em Angola "CICA") in peace-building activities within the context. Some of these activities included training workshops on peace-building and reconciliation, relief assistance to the dislocated civilians and demobilized fighters, and participation in various meetings intended to promote peace.

The chapter first explores Mennonite history in Africa, both in Angola and other parts of sub-Saharan Africa. Details of the civil conflict in Angola are then provided. The chapter then moves to a discussion of peace as an expression of deep desire among Angolans and as one of the fundamentals of Mennonite belief and truth. The chapter then looks at Mennonite peace-building activities and levels of responsiveness to urgent problems within Angola such as landmine removal, poverty, street children, disease, and neglect by other nations.[6]

History of Mennonite Involvement in Africa

Anabaptist presence in Africa resulted from the early twentieth century missionary activities of various American Mennonite churches (modalities) and teams of missionaries (sodalities). As E. M. Braekman notes, the Brethren expressed their interest in Africa, "first in partnership with the Baptists German Mission in Cameroon in 1895–1896, then in Congo with the Congo Inland Mission in 1912."[7]

A team of missionaries from North America established the Congo Inland Mission,[8] beginning their work in Bandundu and Kisai where they founded the Mennonite Community in Congo (Communauté Mennonite au Congo "CMCO"). In August 1962, tribal conflict between the Lulua and Luba people in Ndjoko Punda resulted in the birth of a new church called Evangelical Mennonite Community (Communauté Evangélique Mennonite "CEM"), with Reverend Matthew Kazadi as the leader of the sodality dissidents.[9] In 1920, Aaron Janzens began work on behalf of the Mennonite Brethren Mission, which became the Modality of Mennonite Brethren in Congo, known today as "Communauté des Eglises des Frères Mennonites au Congo" (CEFMC).[10] By the 1990s, a new wave of Mennonite evangelism produced many new Mennonite churches. The Mennonite churches in Congo eventually came together and reconciled in a sodality named Comite Nactional Inter-Mennonite (CONIM).

Mennonites first arrived in East Africa in 1934 when organizing a ministry in the Musoma district of northern Tanzania. These initial efforts were then extended into Kenya in 1965 and bore great fruit.[11] Mennonites gained official recognition from the Kenyan government in 1965 and immediately began church planting and relief work among socially marginalized populations, which they did in collaboration with the Mennonite Central Committee (MCC). In Ethiopia, the Eastern Mennonite Mission became active in social service provision beginning in 1945—operating a hospital and a school and engaging in other development work. The Mennonite church in Ethiopia was officially created in 1959. Local authorities observed the beneficial impact of MCC initiatives and provided authorization for further Mennonite church building in the country.[12] Mennonites have remained active in efforts to address the need for food, health, and peace within Ethiopia.[13] Mennonites have also been active in Somalia since 1953, when they planted a church there.

The primary areas of Mennonite activity in West Africa have included Ghana, Nigeria, and Burkina Faso. In Ghana, the first Mennonite church was founded in 1957 by a Ghanaian who was introduced to the Mennonite tradition in London. The founding of this congregation in Ghana was followed by a deployment of missionaries from the Mennonite Committee of Mission and Charity, which was an American organization parallel to the Mennonite Central Committee sent to Ghana to engage in evangelism and health care and social development initiatives.[14] In Nigeria, local independent churches in east Nigeria contacted Mennonites in Elkhart, Indiana, in 1958 to explore a partnership between Mennonites and these independent churches. In 1958, the first team of missionaries arrived in Nigeria and began work with about 3,000 Nigerians interested in becoming Mennonites. Many churches were planted, and Mennonite membership has continued to grow within the country.[15] Nigerian Mennonites have also engaged in peace-building activities through various workshops and training activities. In Burkina Faso, the MCC began its work there in the early 1970s. Through MCC contacts with Christian and Missionary Alliance congregations and missionaries, Mennonite missionaries were invited to plant churches in the southwestern part of the country. The first missionaries from Africa Inter-Mennonite Mission (AIMM) arrived in Burkina Faso during the later part of 1978.[16] Between 2001 and 2003, AIMM and Mennonite Brethren Mission and Services International (MBMSI) collaborated to plant churches in the capital city of Ouagadougo, and a missionary trained at the Centre Universitaire de Missiologie (CUM) in Congo was appointed to work as a missionary.[17] The Inter-African Mennonite Mission has provided peace-building workshops and training activities among Mennonites in Burkino Faso.

Brethren in Christ have established a significant presence in southern Africa as well, specifically in Zimbabwe, Zambia, Namibia, South Africa, Mozambique, and Angola. In Zimbabwe, the Brethren in Christ Church (BIC) began the work of church planting in Matopo in 1898. They experienced great success in Zimbabwe, especially with regard to their church planting initiatives. That both the largest Brethren in Christ congregation in the world and the Brethren in Christ congregation considered one of the fastest growing in the world are both located in Zimbabwe confirms this success. Several BIC missionaries crossed the Zambezi river into Zambia in 1906 and planted churches in two mission stations: Sikalongo (1924) and Nahumba/Choma (1954).[18] Urban church planting has been a high priority, resulting in more than 150 congregations, but leadership training has also been a central focus. The BIC began working in South Africa in 1988 in the Soshanguve township near Pretoria. Approximately ten BIC congregations are in South Africa, each promoting a "message of compassion, peace and reconciliation."[19] In Mozambique, the Evangelical Mennonites from Brazil began church planting in the 1990s and continue to operate in the province of Tete Center, primarily focusing their work on church planting and leadership training.[20]

Mennonites, including the MCC, are involved in medical work, agricultural development, publishing, and facilitation of leadership training through local educational institutions in Zimbabwe. In Namibia, the Mennonite Brethren from Angola initiated work there in 1998. Additional missionaries were sent in 2000 and planted a Brethren Church. Brethren churches in

Namibia responded to needs such as leadership training, material assistance, and evangelism.

Angola has three Mennonite communities: Igreja Comunidade Menonitas em Angola or ICMA, (which is the Mennonite Community of Churches in Angola); Igreja Evangélica Menonita em Angola or IEMA, (which is the Mennonite Evangelical Church in Angola); and Igreja Evangélica dos Irmãos Menonitas em Angola or IEIMA (which is the Evangelical Church of Mennonite Brethren in Angola). All of these churches resulted from the involvement of Angolan refugees in Congo with Mennonite ministries in that country. The IEIMA is the first of these three Mennonite groups to be established in Angola, founded as it was in 1982. In 1986, a conflict within the Mennonite Brethren group (IEIMA) over sharing power and the lack of opportunities for leadership training led to a division with some of the community remaining with the Mennonite Brethren and others splitting off to form the Mennonite Evangelical Church in Angola (IEMA).[21] In 1991, the Evangelical Mennonites (IEMA) established a fraternal relationship with the Evangelical Church of Congo (CEM).[22] The ICMA began its work in 1990, starting with church planting in Luanda. This Church has its roots in Methodism in Angola and in Congo—where they joined the Mennonites of Communaute Mennonite au Congo (CMCO).[23] Despite the separate tracks of Mennonite activity historically in Angola, the three Mennonite groups willingly united in a new structure named Conferencia Inter-Menonita em Angola (Inter-Mennonite Conference in Angola) that was created in collaboration with MCC in 2003. Some of the social ministries of Angolan Mennonites will be discussed in the following section.

Civil Conflict in Angola

Brendan Salisbury refers to Angola as a "forgotten country."[24] In certain ways that description is accurate—at least as it relates to receiving aid from the advanced industrialized nations. However, Angola is widely known for its civil conflict, which dates back to the year of Angolan independence in 1975. A country of about six million at the time, Angola was one of a handful of Portugese colonies in Africa, including Mozambique, Cape Verde, and Guinea Biseau. In response to Portugese colonial presence in Angola, three primary liberation groups emerged: the Frente de Libertacao de Angola (FNLA), the Movimento Popular de Libertacao de Angola (MPLA), and Uniao Nacional de Independencia Total de Angola (UNITA). Tensions between the three groups arose over ideology and power, and in the months preceding Angola's independence from Portugal (July 1975), open hostilities broke out between FNLA and MPLA. The tensions and hostilities between the groups increased in the months leading up to the

November 1975 elections which would determine the post-independence government that would be the successor to Portugese colonial rule. The MPLA won the election, but not without enormous bloodshed leading up to the elections. Full-scale civil war broke out in Angola just after the 1975 election. Abebe Zegeye describes aspects of the fighting:

> Intense fighting between FNLA and MPLA forces continued throughout August, as did MPLA attacks on UNITA positions along the Southern coast. By late August, however, a peace had fallen over both battlefields. This had less to do with reconciliation than preparation for final confrontation that all sides predicted was coming. In fact, both the FNLA and the MPLA had drawn the same conclusion: whichever group occupied Luanda on 11 November was likely to become the international recognized government of Africa's newest nation.[25]

By the end of 1975, 60,000 to 70,000 Africans had been killed in the battle to control the capital city Luanda.

The MPLA gained support from the Soviet Union and Cuba, due largely to the declared socialist intentions of the MPLA. The FNLA had significant support from Zaire, while the UNITA had strong backing from the South African government and eventually from the United States. The election of the MPLA, therefore, took on major geopolitical implications, coming as it did at the height of Cold War tensions between the United States and the Soviet Union. As a consequence, the MPLA electoral victory was not welcomed by the United States or South Africa; nor was it welcomed or accepted by the FNLA or UNITA.

After the proclamation of independence on November 11, 1975, the FNLA's forces abandoned fighting and many of them joined the armed forces of Angola (Forças Armadas Angolanas). The FNLA's leader, Holden Roberto, was said to have refused to engage in further fighting over power despite pressures from some combatants to hold onto the northern portion of the country that was under FNLA control. According to Father Simon, "Roberto had a vision in which God told him 'why would you want to destroy the town and my people over a selfish desire for power?' When he got up he ordered his troops not to attack Luanda."[26] Most of the people in the northern part of the country fled to the Republic of Congo as refugees both before and after Angola's independence.

With Roberto no longer contending for power, UNITA, headed by Jonas Savimbi, remained as the chief opposition to the MPLA—and the fighting became centered in the southern part of Angola, the section controlled by Savimbi and UNTA. The fighting between UNITA and the MPLA in the southern part of the country had a devastating impact on that region and on the country as a whole. During the period of civil conflict, many people suffered starvation due to the fact that famine was structured as means of slaughtering people. One source commented on Savimbi's role in this tactic:

"According to human rights groups, Savimbi used the famine to his strategic and political ends by using food as either reward or punishment. . . . (and was) singled out for hampering UN efforts to open corridors for food convoys."[27] Many persons from southern Angola fled to Zambia as refugees. As stated in one report: "By March 1976, some 50,000 Angolans, mostly Ovimbundu, had fled to Zambia"[28] As late as 2003, Angolan refugees were still present in Zambia in large numbers, including in a refugee camp in Maheba (which I visited) where many Angolans were still longing to return home. After many attempts at peace, the most binding of these attempts occurred when both sides signed a memorandum of peace between the MPLA government and UNITA (called the Leuna Memorandum) on April 4, 2002. Still, only Savimbi's death during a battle in 2002 assured the end of conflict between UNITA and the government. Angolans are happy for the peace we now have after almost thirty years of civil conflict.

Mennonite Peace-Building During and After the Civil Conflict

Now we have entered into a very challenging period of recovery. In the words of President Jose Eduardo dos Santos: "O futuro comeca agora" (Let the future begin now)."[29] But where do we begin reconstruction of the country? The economy, the educational sector, the health sector all need repair. There are urgent needs to provide for demobilized troops, displaced people, and families who have experienced human and material loss. There is significant damage to the land after decades of war, including scores of landmines scattered about the countryside that unsuspecting civilians continue to detonate. The future of Angola hangs between danger and opportunity—and this challenge has been bequeathed to Angola's leaders from every sector, including the religious sector. Mennonites have contributed significantly to this process.

During and after the time of civil conflict in Angola, each of the three strands of Mennonites within Angola (the IEIMA, the IEMA, and the ICMA) pursued peace and engaged in relief and development initiatives. In the months preceding and following the Luena Memorandum, the influx of displaced persons into Luanda and other cities controlled by the government resulted in large numbers of families living without access to food, clean water, and proper sanitation within these urban contexts. Mennonite churches, alongside other church groups, helped displaced persons resettle in rural areas once the areas were declared safe and helped them search for their lost family members. The church council in Angola, Conselho das Igrejas Cristas em Angola (CICA), primarily facilitated these initiatives, which were effective in mobilizing many different churches in the effort to assist the displaced.

Member churches of CICA (including the Mennonite churches) were involved in worship services and marches focusing on peace that were organized by CICA and the Inter-Ecclesial Committee for Peace in Angola, or "Comite Inter-Eclesial Pela Paz em Angola (COIEPA). COIEPA brought together a number of ecclesiastical bodies that were not necessarily involved in CICA, including an alliance of Evangelical churches called Allianca dos Evangelicos em Angola (AEA) and a Catholic organization called Conselho Episcopal Angola e Sao Tome Principe (CEAST). The peace gatherings organized by CICA and COIEPA have included the annual freedom day celebrations held at the national stadium and attended by various national leaders.

Under their own auspices, Mennonites also organized numerous conferences and seminars that focused on peace. In 1992, after national elections in Angola that were riddled with violence, IEIMA held a seminar in one of its congregations in which a visiting Brethren missionary from Congo shared his eyewitness account of violence in the UNITA-controlled areas of Uige and Malange, including massacres of their residents and the destruction of churches. Mennonite churches were among the churches destroyed in Malange, Mennonite pastors barely escaped arrest, and many Mennonite members fled to Congo.

In 1998 Mennonites organized another seminar focusing on peace-building and held it at the Centro de Formacao e Cultura de Angola (CEFOCA). The seminar, featuring a number of speakers with expertise in conflict resolution, was attended by almost one hundred participants who received certificates naming them as peace advisors. The seminar focused on how to live in peace with one's neighbor during civil conflict. That the MCC provided materials on peace-building for the seminar demonstrates once again the close collaboration between Mennonites in the United States and in Angola. Mennonites sponsored additional peace conferences, including one sponsored in 2000 by the IEIMA's Instituto Biblico e de Missiologia em Angola and attended by persons from many denominations, and one held in 2001 at the Centre Kimbanguist in Luanda, which is a large African Independent Church originating in Zaire.

The partnerships that Angolan Mennonites have enjoyed with Mennonites from around the world have certainly contributed to Mennonite peace-building initiatives within Angola. North American Mennonites, operating through the MCC, assisted Angolan Mennonite churches and the CICA through food and financial aid contributions and frequent visits to Angola. With respect to food contributions, MCC shipped containers of food on several occasions during the early 2000s that the CICA and Mennonite churches distributed to needy persons throughout Luanda. The MCC's Global Family Project helped facilitate school construction projects where many Angolan children have received educational opportunities they otherwise might not have had. Education is obviously critical to Angola's reconstruction and to its future. MCC also played an important role in providing formal and informal training opportunities within Angola on matters related to leadership development and peace-building. The Mennonite Brethren Mission and Service International (MBMSI), located in the United States and Canada, assisted the IEIMA in responding to Angolan refugees forced to flee from Malange and Uige to Congo. Through these partnerships with Mennonites in the United States, Angolan Mennonites have been encouraged in their commitments and strengthened in their capacities for peace-building and development work within Angola.

Conclusion

Angolans are grateful for the peace that has come to our country. Still, many challenges lie ahead that must be addressed to ensure a lasting peace in Angola. Mennonites are united behind a program of peace-building, both within our new Mennonite structure (the Conferencia Inter-Menonita em Angola) and in collaboration with other denominations through CICA. Together we are committed to trying to resolve some of the social and spiritual challenges our people are facing. We have committed ourselves to programs related to social integration, evangelism and mission, community development, and education. Perhaps, our greatest emphasis should be on education.

Emerging from such a protracted civil war, people are struggling not only with the physical reconstruction of the country but also with the spiritual and emotional reconstruction of the people. Education is key to both of these objectives. Daniel Ntoni Nzinga, the leader of COIEPA, captured this dual challenge by referring to a "landmine mentality" operating among the Angolan people. By this he meant not only that our land has been mined but our mentality has also been mined.[30] For example, we have people who have been trained over the course of a thirty-year civil war to kill their neighbor. Now that these fighters have been demobilized, they are without jobs, but the only way they know to survive is by violating other people through theft or other means. Education is a means for reorienting our people who are suffering from mental or psychological distortions created by years of civil conflict. Our secular and theological schools should focus, therefore, not only on skill development but also on creating a culture of peace and social responsibility.

Since the health of Angolans is also key to a lasting peace in Angola, we must be attentive to primary care needs of Angolans. Churches through the CICA have responded to families who have lost loved ones to civil violence and also to AIDS and Ebola. We must also engage in more preventive health care and preventive education. For these reasons our educational programs should shift toward preparing future leaders to be responsive to all sectors of life and to a broad range of human needs. Our churches should seek a greater voice in national discussions of economic, political, and social life.

Theologians and church leaders must join in with jurists, educators, physicians, professors, and others in deciding these issues that are so crucial to our national reconstruction. Finally, we acknowledge once again the role played by our international partners who did not abandon us and who shared with us their presence, skills, and resources. Partnerships such as these will be just as essential to our reconstruction as they were to our survival during the civil conflict.

Today Angola is at a point "where danger and opportunity meet, where the future is in the balance and where events can go either way," to borrow a phrase from theologian David Bosch.[31] We stand between danger and opportunity, and if we do not take the right steps today, the future may turn out badly. We must be guided by a commitment to peace—even that peace that is not from this world.[32]

Part II

Revivalistic Churches, Ecclesiastical Expansion, and Ethical Challenges

Chapter 7

American Evangelists and Church-State Dilemmas in Multiple African Contexts

R. Drew Smith

In 1985 Rev. Jerry Falwell, founder of the "Moral Majority," visited South Africa, where he met with South African President P. W. Botha and other government officials and pro-government community leaders. Although his visit occurred at a time when anti-apartheid activism was at its height and reports of terror and injustices against black South Africans were provided daily, Falwell assessed that racial progress was being made in South Africa and apartheid was "gradually being put off the scene" by the South African government. He also condemned the imposition of sanctions on South Africa as a means of bringing about change in the country (although this strategy was widely supported within the United States and South Africa at the time). Instead, Falwell announced his intention to invest in South African gold krugerrands and in companies doing business in South Africa, and pledged a million dollar campaign by the Moral Majority to encourage other Americans to do likewise. In addition to his failure to meet with South African anti-apartheid leaders during his visit, Falwell characterized Desmond Tutu as a "phony," stating in a news conference after his visit that Tutu was "no more a spokesman for the black majority than I am." Although Falwell later apologized for calling Tutu a phony, his antipathy for South African anti-apartheid activists was extended in subsequent months to

Nelson Mandela, whom he dismissed as a communist and a terrorist requiring careful watching. Falwell also urged a boycott of the HBO cable station for airing a dramatized biography of Mandela's life.[1]

Support for the white minority government in South Africa during the late 1980s also came from fellow American televangelist Pat Robertson. Robertson, founder of the Christian Broadcasting Network, devoted significant network airtime to interviews with white South Africans and pro-government black South Africans, as well as to "pleas for viewers to pray for stability" in South Africa. Robertson also dispatched Ben Kinchlow to South Africa (the black cohost of the "700 Club") to conduct an interview with South Africa's foreign minister that focused on the negative consequences of imposing sanctions on South Africa.

A few years later, with apartheid having given way to majority rule in South Africa, Robertson moved on to other controversial Africa involvements. The Zairian President Mobutu Sese Seko, when faced with opposition in 1992 from pro-democracy activists and armed rebel groups, turned his soldiers loose on thousands of persons participating in a peaceful, pro-democracy rally. Estimates were that Mobutu's soldiers shot and killed up to 250 protestors. Three weeks later, Robertson made an appearance on Zairian national television, where he hailed Mobutu as a "fine Christian and a democrat." Robertson maintained his support of Mobutu through 1995, lobbying the Clinton administration and Congress to reverse Mobutu's U.S. travel ban while arguing that Mobutu had reformed his ways. Unknown to many people at the time was Robertson's engagement in diamond-mining operations in Zaire for a number of years as part of a mining and timber contract with Mobutu. By 1995, the operation was declared a failure and Robertson pulled out.[2]

Not long after Robertson's retreat from Zaire, he transferred his mining and timber operations to war-torn Liberia, entering into a business and political alliance with Liberia's warlord-turned-President, Charles Taylor. Robertson signed a mining agreement with Taylor in 1999 that granted mining concessions to Robertson's mining company and a 10 percent equity interest in the company to the Liberian government. Robertson also began making public defenses of Taylor, whose troops or armed proxies were believed responsible for hundreds of thousands of deaths in Liberia and in neighboring countries: "This man Taylor is not the monster everybody makes him out to be," Robertson stated.[3] He also defended Taylor on religious grounds, proclaiming that Taylor "definitely has Christian sentiments" and arguing that the U.S. sanctions against Liberia and withholding of military support for Taylor's government "were undermining a Christian, Baptist president to bring in Muslim rebels to take over the country."[4] A number of Robertson's Evangelical colleagues in the United States publicly distanced themselves from Robertson's support of Taylor. One Southern Baptist leader remarked: "I would say that Pat Robertson is way out on his own, in a leaking life raft, on this one."[5]

It is unclear, however, that contemporary alliances between American evangelists and problematic political regimes in Africa are unique to Pat Robertson (or to Jerry Falwell). In fact, what will be shown here is that Robertson's and Falwell's involvements with Africa are simply a more politically and ecclesiastically troubling variant of what has been a large, and seemingly increasing, pattern of opportunistic outreach by American evangelists to top governmental leadership in Africa. When these Africa-related outreaches by theologically conservative American Protestants are placed alongside their equally close interactions over the past few decades with political officials within the United States, what becomes evident is a growing receptivity among this sector of Christians to close collaborations with government in general.

There has been important scholarly attention paid to this apparent shift in the conservative Protestant understanding and configuration of church-state relations within the United States—specifically as a feature of 1970s and 1980s activism among white Evangelicals and of African-American church-based activism during and after the Civil Rights Movement.[6] While church-state relations are an important dimension of the present analysis, so too are state-to-state relations—which, in this case, mean U.S. governmental relations with African states.

Falwell's and Robertson's public support of the South African government during the 1980s took place within a context where South Africa's President Botha was one of many anticommunist proxies of the U.S. government during intense global competition between western-bloc and communist-bloc nations. Subsequently, Robertson's collaborations with Mobutu and Taylor (which he defended by extolling the Christian virtues of the two presidents) and similar alliances between American evangelists and African governments during the late 1990s and early 2000s took place while the "Islamic threat" was crystallizing as the guiding ideological principal of post-Cold War U.S. foreign policy. This 1990s emphasis upon Islam as a global security concern within U.S. foreign policy snowballed with the spread of indigenous Islamic fundamentalism in Nigeria and Sudan and with the transplanting of Middle Eastern Islamic insurgents into African countries, as evidenced in the1998 U.S. Embassy bombings in Kenya and Tanzania, allegedly carried out by Al Qaeda operatives. Clearly, then, in both the Cold War and post-Cold War contexts of U.S.-Africa relations, the United States has given priority to its own global security and strategic positioning over Africa's social progress or development during these periods.

Peter Schraeder has aptly characterized this history of U.S. foreign relations with Africa as "Africa as a solution for non-African problems."[7] While Schraeder is referring mainly to the proxy status of Africa within U.S. global security strategies, I also find Schraeder's characterization useful as a description of how certain American Protestant leaders have pursued Africa involvements toward what are ultimately American, rather than African, ecclesiastical and social ends. In providing certain American evangelists with convenient opportunities for bolstering their ministries, public profiles, financial situations, or social objectives within the United States, Africa has functioned as mere backdrop to an otherwise American story line—in much the same way as it did for Johnny Weismueller in Tarzan or Humphrey Bogart in The African Queen.

Governmental relations, then—both church-to-government and government-to-government—provide a theoretical lens through which to analyze Africa involvements of contemporary American evangelists. Specifically, I am here interested in how the ideological framing of U.S. foreign policy and a growing emphasis by theologically conservative Protestants on temporal influence served as sources of legitimation for alliances between a cadre of high-profile American evangelists and problematic regimes in Africa.

American Missions and U.S.-Africa Policy: A Problematic Symbiosis

Two waves of missionary ferment have impacted Africa. European mission churches largely dominated an initial period of missionary ferment lasting into the mid-1900s. U.S.-based churches were an important factor in some African countries as well, with both theologically liberal and conservative churches venturing forth to Africa from the United States during this period. Liberia and South Africa received some of the earliest attention from U.S. churches, with a few other countries in South-Central Africa (such as Zaire and Zambia) and in West Africa (such as Nigeria and Ghana) also serving as early recipients of these churches.

African-American Baptist and Methodist groups were among the very first U.S. churches to establish a mission presence in Africa. One of the first and largest of these initiatives was certainly Liberia, established as a haven for freed American slaves. Approximately 12,000 freed slaves traveled to Liberia between 1820 and 1861 when the U.S. Civil War disrupted emigration. This episode in American colonization was sponsored largely by an American church-based group appropriately called the American Colonization Society—with active support from the U.S. government. The majority of American slaves that repatriated to Liberia were Baptists and Methodists, possessing a strong commitment to converting the native populations within the territory. Much of this early mission outreach to the native populations in Liberia was linked with the American Colonization Society.

In addition, other American church groups began sending missionaries to Liberia in the 1800s (not as repatriates but as representatives of their home church groups in the United States). American Presbyterians established a presence in 1833; the Protestant Episcopal Church arrived in 1836; the Southern Baptist Convention came during the mid-1800s, left in 1875, then returned in 1960; American Lutherans arrived in 1860; an African-American church group, the African Methodist Episcopal Church (AME), sent missionaries to Liberia in 1873, followed closely behind by a closely related denomination, the African Methodist Episcopal Zion Church (AMEZ), who sent missionaries to Liberia in 1876. By 1897, two African-American Baptist groups were operating in Liberia, the National Baptist Convention, USA and the Lott Carey Baptist Foreign Mission, which had ties to more than one group of African-American Baptists. In 1919 an African-American Pentecostal group, the Pentecostal Assemblies of the World, began operations in Liberia. Much later, in 1960, the Southern Baptist Convention sent missionaries to Liberia (although they were present in other places within Africa earlier, including Nigeria, where they sent missionaries prior to World War I).

The AME church was also among the first U.S. churches to establish a presence in South Africa (arriving in 1892). They were also present in neighboring countries at about the same time, including Northern Rhodesia (Zambia), where they arrived at the beginning of the twentieth century. The National Baptist Convention, USA and the AMEZ church also began operating in South Africa during the 1900s. A predominantly white Pentecostal group, the Assemblies of God, arrived in South Africa in 1917. U.S. churches active in Zaire included the American Baptists the northern, antislavery wing of U.S. Baptists, who arrived in Zaire in the 1870s; the Southern Presbyterians, the formerly pro-slavery wing of U.S. Presbyterians, who arrived in 1891; the Disciples of Christ, who arrived in 1897; the Assemblies of God, who arrived in 1918; and the AME church, which arrived in 1957.[8]

It is also interesting to note that Zaire, Liberia, and South Africa (and later, Nigeria, Angola, and Sudan), were countries where American business activity was entrenched, with strong political support from the U.S. government. In Zaire, these activities were initiated as early as the 1880s, when the U.S. became the first country to establish formal political ties with Belgium's King Leopold's private annexation of the land that would come to be called Zaire. This political recognition was followed closely behind by the establishment of a number of U.S. corporations in Leopold's territory, including companies involved in the extraction of the territory's abundant natural resources (including copper and oil) and companies involved in manufacturing industries and trade. A vigorous opponent of economic exploitation in Zaire during the late-1800s and early 1900s was the American Baptist Church, who was able to press through certain reforms. Later on, neither American Baptists nor other U.S. mission churches featured prominently in political resistance to colonial rule in Zaire—they focused their attention, primarily and with great success, on educational activities.

By the 1970s American corporations displayed an even larger presence in Zaire, as they were integrally involved in the construction of a dam on the Zaire river, the development of the longest direct current electric line in the world at that time, road construction, offshore oil rigs, and a General Motors plant.[9] Zaire had also by this time become a bulwark in the United States' anticommunism strategies in Africa, with President Mobutu working closely with the CIA and the U.S. State Department in efforts to fend off communist influence within South-Central and Southern Africa. The Mobutu era, then, very much built upon the foundations established by Belgium's Leopold, with Mobutu treating Zaire like his own private colony and cash cow. The result of many years of this pattern was that Mobutu became one of the wealthiest men in the world while the Zairian people were among the poorest and most politically beleaguered in the world.

Robertson's business and political alliances with Mobutu in the 1980s were, therefore, built on well-established precedent; so too were Robertson's alliances with Charles Taylor in Liberia. Throughout Liberia's history, repatriated American slaves and their descendents (who came to be referred to as Americo-Liberians) influenced Liberia's social and political affairs in ways disproportionate to their small numbers. From the outset, this was an exercise in American domination of native populations, down to the naming of the country and its capital city, Monrovia, which was named after U.S. President James Monroe. At least seven major battles occurred between the colonists and native populations between 1822 and 1843, with the U.S. Navy often called upon to intervene on behalf of the colonists.[10] In the early 1900s, there were also charges, confirmed by the U.S. State Department and the League of Nations, that Americo-Liberian government officials were trafficking locally in slaves.

In 1926, an American corporation, Firestone, was granted a lease of a million acres of land by the Liberian government and established the largest rubber plantation in the world at that time. Between 1926 and 1977, Firestone's profit margin was estimated at approximately $415 million dollars, with 25 percent of that going to the Liberian government and 75 percent transferred into Firestone's coffers in the United States. Another American corporation operating in Liberia, the National Iron Ore Company, shipped approximately $300 million worth of iron ore out of Liberia between 1962 and 1973. As Paul Gifford notes, these companies provided enormous benefits to the Liberian officials, whom the companies bought off, but they proved exploitative of the people both through the favorable allotments of the country's natural resources they received and (at least with Firestone) through labor practices that were just short of indentured servitude.[11]

Just as the repatriated Christian slaves and initial American church groups during the 1800s were aligned with forces of political domination, the legacies of these transplanted Protestants and of newer ecclesiastical arrivals into the 1900s were much the same. Gifford concludes that Christian churches in

Liberia were "structures of dominance" and a "pillar on which the whole oppressive structure was built."[12] He also argues, interestingly enough, that church complicity with political and economic oppression in Liberia was partly a function of financial pressures and obligations on the part of these church groups and the need to preserve their political and funding networks within the United States and Liberia.[13] Robertson's involvement with Taylor was very much in keeping with these kinds of calculations.

One American church group with a role somewhat distinctive from many other American church groups—at least in southern Africa—was the AME church. Founded in Philadelphia in 1787 by black Americans protesting segregation within Methodism in the United States, AMEs, committed in a fairly systematic and outspoken ways to Black Nationalist ideas, first established mission churches in South Africa in 1892.[14] White settler and colonial governments of southern Africa viewed the AME missionaries with great suspicion because as a black-run institution, they undermined white control. For example, when the AME Bishop Henry McNeil Turner traveled to South Africa in the 1890s, he reportedly "alarmed" white South Africans by his condemnations of "white imperial oppression" and his promotion of "Africa for the Africans" and "African separate development."[15] The colonial administration in Northern Rhodesia (Zambia) also banned the AME church for a period of time shortly after their arrival in that country in the early 1900s.[16] Churches such as the AMEs, therefore, proved important because of their ability to function as political organizations that provided contexts for advancing the hopes of African independence, which stirred in the hearts of many Africans who were suffering under colonial rule. In fact, African-American missionaries in general, though their numbers were relatively small in Africa compared to white American missionaries, were the most likely of these missionaries (except as outlined in the Liberian case) to be sympathetic to African social grievances and hopes of empowerment and to be greeted with suspicion and hostility by white colonial authorities.[17]

The onset of African decolonization during the late 1950s brought with it a new set of calculations with respect to both governmental and ecclesiastical relations between the United States and Africa. With respect to governmental relations, U.S. foreign policy swerved between two concerns. First, with independence sweeping across the continent, the United States had sympathies at points with African nation-building and social development. Duignan and Gann point out, however, that "Anticolonialism came to be interpreted as a policy that was moral in itself, as a device for expanding American trade, and as a means for strengthening the American position where the newly independent states were endowed with a voting strength in the United Nations. . . ." Anticolonialism, moreover, was seen as a "weapon in the cold war," which came to be a dominant consideration for every Presidential administration from Kennedy through Reagan (with the possible exception of the Carter administration).[18] Although the United States did not participate in the "scramble for Africa" that led to the carving up and colonization of Africa by European nations, they were very much at the center of the new "scramble for Africa" embodied in the Cold War competition between western and communist bloc nations over influence within Africa.

During the 1950s through the 1970s, U.S. churches involved in African affairs (whether based in the U.S. or in Africa) were most vocally and visibly aligned with nation-building and social development priorities within Africa. Whether through the various denominational mission boards located in the United States or their mission initiatives within African nations, most U.S. churches concerned themselves mainly with contributing to such things as the educational and health care infrastructure of African nations and to consolidating their ecclesiastical presence in their African mission sites by solidifying their support among the African populations they served and among the newly independent African governments.

Adrian Hastings comments on the role many mission churches played in rural and remote areas as bridges between rural populations and the central governments of these African countries. During the colonial period, these ecclesiastical bridges between African governments and African population groups often undergirded colonial arrangements in ways that would lead the African populace to resent some churches. In cases where churches were viewed as especially supportive of colonial interests, these churches sometimes faced retribution after decolonization and independent rule had been achieved—as was the case with some Catholic churches in Zaire.[19] Hastings notes, however, that in most cases, newly independent African governments were happy to draw upon the institutional strengths of mission churches as resources in the nation-building process and that the churches, for the most part, "were only too glad to be allowed to bless and participate in it all—even to bow and scrape on occasion."[20]

Cold War approaches to Africa would nevertheless gain quite an ecclesiastical boost with the emergence in the late 1970s of the so-called Religious Right—(referring to a politicized wing of theologically conservative churches that had historically remained aloof from politics). Jerry Falwell and Pat Robertson were leading figures within the development of this movement. As one American religion scholar observes, by 1983, Falwell "emerged as the most outspoken defender of President Reagan's arms policy and critic of the nuclear freeze and other disarmament proposals that might leave the United States in a position of inferiority vis-à-vis the Soviet Union."[21] Falwell's anticommunist activism with respect to the African context mostly singled out the South African situation. As Falwell sided with the apartheid government in South Africa, he defended his position by way of various anticommunist assessments. Falwell warned, for example, that South Africans need "our coercive and patient encouragement to clean up their act while at the same time not passing them over to the Soviets,"[22] and sounded alarm about "a red river of communism" threatening to engulf South Africa.[23]

The emergence of the Religious Right in political affairs coincided to some extent with a second period of African mission ferment which, as Paul Gifford points out, drew heavily on U.S.-based Evangelical, Charismatic, and Pentecostal churches, especially from the 1970s forward.[24] David Barrett and his coauthors have placed worldwide Pentecostal affiliation in 1970 at more than 147,000,000, and in 1995 at more than 605,000,000.[25] More than two-thirds of these Charismatic and Pentecostal Christians from the 1970 and 1995 totals were located in Africa.[26] Patrick Johnstone estimates that between 1960 and 2000, Evangelicals tripled from roughly 5 to 15 percent of Africa's population and that Pentecostals increased from about one to about 6 percent.[27] Another indicator of the vitality of this wave of Evangelical and Pentecostal ferment in Africa, and of American church contributions to this wave, comes from an inventory of U.S.-based ministries operating in one specific country—Zambia. Approximately half of the U.S. denominations there have arrived since 1960, and most of these denominations could be classified as Evangelical, Charismatic, or Pentecostal. Of the forty or so U.S. parachurch organizations ministering in Zambia, almost all have arrived since the mid-1960s, and all but one or two could be classified as Evangelical, Charismatic, or Pentecostal.[28] It is important to note, however, that as theologically conservative American church groups were arriving in large numbers, theologically liberal American churches were significantly downsizing their mission operations in Africa (and around the world) and working mainly through local ministry partners in African contexts. This shift, in certain respects, cleared the way for this new wave of theologically conservative mission groups.

Robertson's forays into Southern Africa and West Africa took place within this context, but in his case and in the cases of a number of other American evangelists, their Evangelical work within Africa clearly took political sides in quite politically conflicted contexts. For example, Robertson's 700 Club began broadcasting in Zaire in the 1990s with Robertson certainly benefiting from his access to millions of Zairians. As William Reno points out, this television access by Robertson (and by fellow U.S. televangelist Jimmy Swaggert) also resulted from Mobutu's desire to counter the influence within Zaire of Catholic Archbishop Monsengwo, who was an ardent opponent of Mobutu. Apparently, Mobutu got what he hoped for out of the deal, with Robertson prone to publicly celebrating Mobutu's Christian inclinations and Swaggert fervently preaching a gospel that deemphasized social conditions—thereby offering an alternative to the theological view of the Catholic Archbishop, in which Zairian social suffering was more central.[29] Despite the religious buttressing he received from these U.S. based ministries, Mobutu's reign did not last out the 1990s.

In Liberia, large-scale spiritual revival initiatives accompanied Robertson's financial dealings with Taylor. In both the business and revival activities, Robertson worked closely with a fellow American evangelist, Bishop John

Gimenez of the Rock Church in Virginia Beach, who served as Robertson's point man in Liberia. Gimenez, who owns a radio station in Liberia and has invested in a Rock Church school and hospital there, assisted Robertson in successfully organizing a three-day crusade called "Liberia for Jesus." Taylor (who donated $100,000 to the initiative) and 75,000 Liberians attended the crusade that was held at the main stadium in Monrovia. Taylor heaped public praise on Gimenez and Robertson for their leadership and, while speaking at the crusade itself, proclaimed Jesus to be the President of Liberia. He then laid prostrate on the stage and urged that others should also prostrate themselves before God. A Rock Church representative was quoted after the crusade as saying: "I have never seen a president giving his country to the Lord this way, prostrating in submission among a huge crowd like this one. He is a mighty man of God."[30] A spokesperson for Robertson also remarked during a Christian Broadcasting Network show that Taylor stands "as a symbol of the nation's corporate surrender to the sovereignty of Jesus."[31] By 2003, Taylor, faced with an armed insurrection in Liberia against his leadership, resigned and moved to Nigeria. Now, a UN-backed tribunal in Sierra Leone has convened to hear testimony about Taylor's war crimes against the people and the nation of Sierra Leone. Apparently, with Taylor's demise, Robertson may be eyeing another African leader behind whom to throw his support. A statement posted on the Christian Broadcasting Network website celebrates the President of Benin, Matthew Kerekou, commending him for being a born-again Christian, a convert from Marxism to Jesus, and a "hope for all of Africa." The statement also makes clear that Christian Broadcasting Network has operated in Benin since 1997 and that representatives of the television network frequently enjoy private audiences with President Kerekou in his Presidential Office.[32]

American Evangelicals were also highly enthusiastic during the 1990s and into the early 2000s about Zambia's president, Frederick Chiluba, largely due to his official designation of Zambia as a Christian nation. It was not unusual for Chiluba to grant private audiences to visiting American evangelists. Richard Roberts, President of Oral Roberts University, was hosted by Chiluba while conducting evangelistic crusades in the country, and evangelist Ernest Angley from Ohio conducted lengthy television interviews with Chiluba. Although Chiluba was also popular among Zambians (at least during his first term in office), Zambians opposed his attempt to amend the constitution to allow for a third term in office; they were already concerned about Chiluba's leadership due to worsening economic conditions and charges of political corruption. Chiluba solicited support from American televangelist Benny Hinn—with whom Chiluba had shared a stage at a massive 1995 Christian crusade in Zambia—citing "great forces of opposition against his bid." Hinn contacted Paul Crouch, the founder of the Trinity Broadcasting Network, which broadcasts through a local affiliate in Zambia, so that appeals for prayer on Chiluba's behalf were made over the television airwaves.[33] In the end, Chiluba was unsuccessful in holding onto power and was later brought up on charges of financial malfeasance during the course of his presidency.[34]

Then there is the very public support that a number of high profile African-American clergymen gave to General Sani Abacha's regime during the mid-1990s. Nigerians and the international community widely opposed Abacha's Presidency for its corruption and brutality; yet Henry Lyons, who headed the largest African-American Baptist Convention, and Maurice Dawkins, a black Baptist minister who ran for the U.S. Senate, received hundreds of thousands of dollars from the Abacha regime to press American government officials to soften their opposition to Abacha.[35] Lyons also attempted to broker oil deals with the Nigerian government, but the negotiations were never concluded—primarily because Lyons was arrested and imprisoned in the United States in 1997 for fraudulent financial dealings. Things also went decidedly bad for Abacha, who died suddenly in the late 1990s. The democratically elected and more highly regarded successor to Abacha, General Olesegun Obasanjo, was awarded an honorary doctorate degree by Oral Roberts University (ORU), most likely since ORU was attempting to establish a presence in Nigeria among what is considered one of the most rapidly expanding Evangelical and Pentecostal populations in the world. Obasanjo, who professes to be a born-again Christian, routinely grants audiences to American evangelists visiting in Nigeria.[36]

Conclusion

As troubling and problematic as the high profile Africa involvements of Robertson, Falwell, and other American evangelists have been, they have in almost every instance been consistent with, or at least patterned after, the approach of the U.S. government to the African nations in question. Robertson's involvements with Mobutu and Taylor caused a stir within the U.S. State Department at the time,[37] but it was not because Robertson's actions violated State Department sensibilities or patterns of involvement relative to Zaire and Liberia. In fact, the U.S. government helped establish and was principle backer of Mobutu's self-serving reign and, with respect to Taylor, worked to gain acceptance from the Liberian people and from neighboring countries for Taylor's rule.[38] Robertson encountered criticism, therefore, not because his actions diverged dramatically from precedents established by the U.S. government, but because he did not follow the U.S. government's lead when they chose to withdraw support from Mobutu or when they pretended to have nothing to do with Taylor's rule. It could also be argued that Robertson's support of Taylor and Mobutu was very much in line with the emerging emphasis during the 1990s on supporting regimes that could serve as counterweights to Islamic militancy. With respect to

Robertson's and Falwell's earlier support of the Botha regime, their positioning on this issue was hand and glove with Reagan administration policy.

Generally speaking, U.S. mission involvements in Africa—particularly as part of the post-1970s wave of missionary arrivals—have been far better, seemingly, at serving American governmental and ecclesiastical interests than at serving African interests. The ideological alignments by churches with U.S. foreign policy (both during the colonial era and in more recent decades where conservative mission groups have been dominant) have been sometimes explicit, sometimes implicit; but, in either case, the underlying concern of U.S. missionary activity in Africa has been, too often, with its own ecclesiastical aggrandizement. Certainly, there have been numerous exceptions to this, but not nearly enough (the exceptions represented primarily by postcolonial liberal mission groups, despite their scaled-down presence). Throughout, the U.S. government has pretty much had its way—but that is not unusual. African presidents, as discussed here, gained valuable religious endorsement for presidencies badly in need of moral buttress—although for these particular presidents, it did little to transform their political images or fortunes. The clear casualties in all this, it seems safe to say, have been American ecclesiastical integrity and African people's hopes for social progress and progressive allies. Hopefully, after nearly two hundred years of getting this relationship mostly wrong, U.S. churches will do better in the twenty-first century in developing relations with Africa centered on integrity and commitments to African social progress.

Chapter 8

American Pentecostalism and the Growth of Pentecostal-Charismatic Movements in Nigeria

Matthews A. Ojo

Introduction

In a leading article on the new phase of African Christianity, Paul Gifford has argued that the doctrinal emphasis on prosperity within the emerging Pentecostal and Charismatic movements in Africa derived its doctrinal and ideological roots from the North American Pentecostal churches and organizations.[1] Elsewhere, Gifford further strengthened his argument about strong ideological, financial, and organizational links between African Pentecostal movements and their U.S. counterparts.[2] Other scholars similarly affirmed, though with little evidence, the American impact on African Pentecostalism.[3]

Among historical links used to justify this conclusion is that of an early holiness-Pentecostal minister in Illinois, John Alexander Dowie of the Christian Catholic Apostolic Church in Zion, who has sometimes been noted for influencing the formation of Pentecostalism in South Africa. Allan Anderson, however, states that "after about 1910 . . . North American Pentecostalism had no further direct influence on the progress of Pentecostalism in South Africa."[4] In addition, Ogbu Kalu argues that Nigerian Pentecostalism "is not an offshoot of Azusa Street revival . . . or an extension of American electronic church or a creation of televangelists. It has a certain uniqueness which could best be understood from its fit in African primal worldview. . . . Its problems and idioms are sourced from the interior of African spirituality."[5] This assertion supports what I have argued elsewhere, mainly that the interconnections between American Pentecostalism and Nigerian Pentecostalism do not necessarily result in what could be considered as an ideological or a doctrinal imposition within the Nigerian context, given that Christianity as a world religion shares certain features in common across cultures and boundaries.[6] In the contemporary global world, these increased interconnections between religious groups may be self-initiated, direct contacts between religious groups or may be facilitated vicariously through the media. Global Pentecostalism thus falls into the realm of what Karla Poewe has described as a form of global culture.[7]

America-centric scholars have sometimes adopted a Western anthropological approach that suggests external influences account for the vibrancy of contemporary Pentecostals in Africa. In this way they imply that influence merely flows one way—from the United States to Africa—while ruling out other possible directionalities. It is important, therefore, to move from a superficial analysis of African Pentecostalism as a derivative of American capitalist and corporate culture and examine, instead, the internal dynamics of the African Pentecostal movements. There is a need, then, to critically examine the roots of Pentecostal revival in many African countries, especially since the 1970s, before generalizing about the influence of American Pentecostalism on other Pentecostal movements in the world.

This essay outlines interconnections between American Pentecostalism and the growing Pentecostal and Charismatic movements in Nigeria from a historical perspective. Such a historical analysis provides evidence of the nature of the changing relationship between American Christianity and various forms of Christian expressions in Africa. It is argued here that dynamic local religious and social environments have enabled the Nigerian movements to look to more than one source for appropriating elements that have proved helpful to them in their spirituality. Although American Pentecostalism has been a source of inspiration, creativity, and entrepreneurship for Nigerian churches, American Pentecostalism has had little political impact within Nigeria because Nigerian Pentecostals have not seen it as an ideological matrix but mainly as a religious matrix—a source of confirmation of certain passages and prophecies in the Bible. Although Nigerian Pentecostalism has had its peculiar indigenous origin, in the course of its growth it has benefited from Pentecostal movements in other countries. Pentecostalism in South Korea provided Nigerians in the early 1980s with the concept and practice of house churches and mega churches, and Great Britain provided examples of a healthy blending of Pentecostalism with the mainline Protestant churches.

The Beginnings of Pentecostalism in Nigeria

Christian mission agencies, mainly from Europe, were responsible for the planting of Christianity in Nigeria in the 1840s. Although some missionaries of the Church of Scotland Mission came from the West Indies, these men and women had little contact with American Christianity and, hence, did not convey any uniquely American features in their mission work. Nineteenth- and early twentieth-century Baptist work, nevertheless, was overwhelming an American initiative inaugurated by the Foreign Mission Board (now the International Missions Board) of the Southern Baptist Convention. Most of the Baptist missionaries were Americans and made a noticeable impact in two areas. First, they introduced a democratic and congregational model of church government in contrast to the episcopal polity of the churches brought from Europe. Secondly, the Baptists in Nigeria and in the United States promoted separation of church and state, although this idea had little impact in colonial Nigeria where British colonial administration legislated on all spheres of national life. Even during the independence era, political leaders have made no concrete attempt to promote the separation of church and state. Although the 1999 Nigerian constitution in Section 10 affirmed a "no state religion" clause, in practice various regional and state governments have clearly supported religious establishments and functionaries in many ways. Another American church, the Seventh Day Adventist, which began mission work in Nigeria in 1914, did not have much impact because of its slow growth and little membership.

Various scholars have confirmed that Pentecostalism in Nigeria had an indigenous origin, taking its root from two revivalist movements.[8] Garrick Sokari Braide, a local Anglican evangelist in the southeastern riverine areas of the Niger Native Pastorate (an administration framework that the Church Missionary Society created to foster indigenous leadership), stimulated a revival in the first and second decades of the twentieth century in the Anglican churches in that area. Its emphasis on healing, prophecy, Christian purity, and the leading of the Holy Spirit sustained a religious movement that the colonial administration and the Anglican church opposed and persecuted. After Braide's death in 1916, the followers established the Christ Army Church to carry on the activities of the movement, although it lacked the vigor with which it had begun early in the decade.[9]

In Ijebu Ode, about 90 kilometers from Lagos, Sophia Odulami, who in 1918 claimed that God had procured healing through the use of water for the rampaging influenza epidemic at that time, founded a group called the Diamond Society. This group was the first in southwestern Nigeria that laid claim to such Pentecostal practices as healing, prophecy, vigorous prayers, dreams, and visions. In 1920 the Diamond Society corresponded with the

Faith Tabernacle Congregation in Philadelphia, Pennsylvania (a holiness-Pentecostal church with emphasis on moral purity and the rejection of any human medication to treat illnesses). The members of Diamond Society, having satisfied themselves that the doctrines of the Faith Tabernacle Congregation were biblical and similar to what they had earlier believed, affiliated with that church in 1923. From then on, the church's official magazine, *Sword of the Spirit*, along with other church literature, was circulated in southwestern Nigeria.[10] After the group was expelled from the Anglican Church due to the refusal of its members to baptize their infants, it adopted Faith Tabernacle as its new name.

This affiliation was the first institutional relationship between any Pentecostal group in Nigeria and a counterpart in the United States. The Nigerian group severed the relationship in 1926 when they were dismayed by an adultery case involving the pastor of the American church. The initiation of the Nigerian church in severing the relationship serves as an important indicator of this congregation's independence and its unwillingness to accept things American without a good cause. Thereafter, in the late 1920s, another short-lived affiliation was established with a Pentecostal group, Truth and Life Gospel Mission, which was based in Canada. Other than the benefits of Pentecostal literature sent from North America, the Nigerian Faith Tabernacle maintained its doctrinal and organizational independence.

When the Faith Tabernacle affiliated in 1930 with The Apostolic Church headquartered in Bradford, England, its previous American affiliation ceased altogether. In September 1931, The Apostolic Church sent missionaries to Nigeria who subsequently ordained Nigerians as pastors and evangelists, thereby creating an institutional framework for a trans-national religious network in the country. This initiative had a far-reaching impact on Pentecostalism in the country throughout the 1940s and beyond. Significantly, the coming of the Apostolic Church produced the popular acceptance of baptism of the Holy Spirit and various manifestations of the Holy Spirit—both of which are major doctrinal emphases within global Pentecostalism. T. N. Turnbull, a historian of the British Apostolic Church, confirmed the indigenous growth of Pentecostalism in Nigeria when he wrote:

> The extensive Missionary work we have in Nigeria is because of Revivals in which the work was born, nursed and fed into vigorous growth. The Revival did not begin with the advent of The Apostolic Church missionaries, but the Holy Spirit had already commenced His work in some parts of the country a few years before, through the instrumentality of others. . . .When our Missionaries arrived they found many Churches already opened. This movement's previous teaching had been of a strong fundamental character, and they were outstanding Evangelically, believing in Divine Healing.[11]

In 1939 another American Pentecostal church, the Assemblies of God, responded to an invitation made by the Church of Jesus Christ, a group of Nigerian Pentecostals seeking legitimacy under the hostile colonial environment. By the 1950s, the extensive evangelistic activities of this church among the Igbos of Eastern Nigeria produced numerous churches in the country led by indigenous leaders and by a few American missionaries. In the 1940s, the Foursquare Gospel Church and the Apostolic Faith Mission, two classical American Pentecostal churches, established branches in South Western Nigeria before spreading to other parts of the country in the 1950s and 1960s.

In the mid-1960s, the pattern of American connection with Nigerian Pentecostalism changed. It moved from the existing pattern of denominationally based missionary endeavors to the activities of independent freelance Pentecostal evangelists and churches. It is necessary to explore the background of this new expression of Pentecostalism in Nigeria through the activities of an important freelance evangelist, S. G. Elton. Elton, who came to Nigeria in February 1937 as one of the missionaries of the Apostolic Church in Nigeria, had by the early 1940s become the missionary overseer of the church in western Nigeria. In 1953, Elton invited Rev. Thomas and Evelyn Wyatt of the Latter Rain Revival movement of Los Angeles to conduct healing and evangelistic campaigns in South Western Nigeria. From this bold endeavor, which was displeasing to the Apostolic Church in England, resulted Elton's resignation as a missionary of that church when he did not accept his recall to England. Thereafter he became an itinerant and independent Pentecostal evangelist. By the late 1960s, he had established contacts with a number of American Pentecostal organizations and acted as their representative in Nigeria. Consequently, Pastor Elton used literature to propagate Pentecostal doctrines from a neutral ground. Elton's influence as a Pentecostal evangelist was considerable, especially in the literate communities of the universities where he had frequent invitations. Indeed, he became a link between the old classical Pentecostalism and the new Charismatic Renewal of the 1970s.

On the platform of cooperation that Elton established, T. L. Osborn, a prominent American Pentecostal televangelist, first visited Nigeria in the mid-1960s. After Osborn's visit, Pentecostal literature, including tracts, magazines, and books, flooded the country. Those coming from Osborn were quite noticeable and freely distributed. In the early 1970s, many more American Pentecostal evangelists came into the country, bringing literature and, in some instances, conducting seminars or evangelistic campaigns. A few, such as T. L. Osborn, Oral Roberts, and Gordon and Freda Lindsay, financed and supported indigenous initiatives in the area of church planting.

During this same period, some American Pentecostal evangelists sponsored regular broadcasts of their evangelistic programs on Nigeria's radio stations. Although not all of these efforts were coordinated centrally, their cumulative impact was great. First, the converts from these Pentecostal activities were organized into independent congregations, thus extending and strengthening the growth of religious independence in the country. Secondly, the financial and organizational support from the United States promoted a rapid growth of Pentecostalism in the country and also produced a corps of pioneering independent leaders. Soon afterwards, taking cues from the American model, some indigenous Pentecostal evangelists began producing and distributing free literature and supporting other local evangelistic efforts. Among these early leaders were Pa O. Martins of the Free Gospel Mission in Lagos, Benson Idahosa of the Church of God Mission in Benin City, Stephen Okafor of the Hour of Freedom Evangelistic Association in Onitsha, and Joshua Durojaiye of the Calvary Apostolic Church in Ibadan. By the late 1970s, a high degree of independence within Pentecostalism had ensued.

The mid-1970s witnessed the greatest influx of American Pentecostal literature into the country. Among these were the booklets and tracts of T. L. Osborn, Oral Roberts, Kenneth Hagin, Gordon Lindsay, and Morris Cerullo—all of whom were prominent American televangelists. Some visited Nigeria and conducted crusades while others sent their tracts and booklets freely into the country. For example, in 1973, Reggy Thomas of the Revival Fires, along with T. L. Osborn, conducted crusades at Ibadan, while Brother Argemiro of the Free Gospel Mission conducted a crusade in Lagos. The year ended with the Morris Cerullo crusades, held in Ibadan in mid-December.[12] Early in 1974, T. L. Osborn organized a workshop on evangelism in Benin City. During this workshop, vehicles, tape recorders and generators to be used in mass evangelism were distributed. This evangelistic program had a major impact on the campuses, as some students abandoned their studies to become full time evangelists.[13]

Pastor J. O. Durojaiye, a leader of one of the indigenous Pentecostal churches in Ibadan and host to one of the American evangelists, summarized the events thus:

> 1973 was a year of so many revivals and crusades in Nigeria all because the Holy Spirit had come to stay. . . . Christianity is now gaining ground in Nigeria like the forest fire. Here and there bells ring, and today we have several thousands of servants of God in Nigeria deceminating (sic) the gospel of Jesus Christ round the world. . . . Finally, the Holy Spirit in Nigeria took the control of all. Over the radio He went and broadcast daily through His servants about the power that is in the blood of Jesus Christ. From the Baptist Witness to the Billy Graham broadcast and to several other Christian broadcasts, the Holy Spirit has always been in the studio to travel by its natural route—Air—to the homes through the radio set.[14]

Prior to the 1970s, Pentecostal doctrines were largely confined to the classical Pentecostal churches and within a few independent Pentecostal organizations, thus limiting their influence to a small circle. The major influx of Pentecostal evangelists, radio broadcasts, and literature that strongly promoted the rapid spread of Pentecostalism in the country came in the early 1970s. The large constituency of young people who were mobile aided the growth of Pentecostalism across social and cultural boundaries. More importantly, since these Pentecostal activities were promoted on the periphery of the existing mainline Protestant and Pentecostal churches, they greatly facilitated religious entrepreneurship and independence in the Nigerian context. Consequently, before then no social and religious change had been achieved on such a massive scale among both the elite class and the grassroots. Eventually, these Pentecostal activities would stimulate new forms of Pentecostal spirituality in the country and open avenues for further affiliation and interrelationship with American Pentecostalism.

American Pentecostalism and the Charismatic Revival of the 1970s

A major Pentecostal revival broke out among youths in the early 1970s, particularly among matriculants and graduates of Nigeria's tertiary institutions of learning. The revival, which had its origins among members of the Christian Union, an Evangelical group at the University of Ibadan, centered on the baptism of the Holy Spirit and speaking in tongues. Although this revival began as an indigenous initiative, by 1972 American Pentecostal literature had penetrated the Christian circles and eventually altered the nature and progress of the revival. By the mid-1970s the revival had spread to the point of becoming the basis of a broad, influential Charismatic movement within Nigerian Christianity.

As in earlier cases, Pentecostal literature from the United States paved the way for American insertion into this revival. Nigerian leaders quite likely received inspiration of various kinds from this literature. For example, leaders of World Action Team for Christ (WATC), a group that evolved from the revival in the University of Ibadan, received along with other American literature a periodical called the *Miracle Word*, which was the official magazine of Franklin Hall Ministry, a Pentecostal denomination headquartered in Phoenix, Arizona. These leaders were fascinated with the testimonies of miraculous healings and divine protection that the magazine featured regularly.[15] The evangelistic activities of WATC lent prominence to Franklin Hall's teachings, thereby contributing to his popularity in certain Charismatic quarters in Nigeria between 1973 and 1976. In fact, Franklin Hall became the focus of American Pentecostalism in the mid-1970s because he had the most sustained ministry among college students. Later in 1975, Hall himself came to Nigeria to give credence to his teachings.

Hall had been a leading figure in the Latter Rain Revival movement within the United States from the late 1940s. His teachings could be condensed into the following three elements. Firstly, Hall taught that repentance from sins and the acceptance of Christ as one's Saviour, (what he termed "heart-felt" salvation as commonly preached by many preachers), touches only the soul. A full salvation, which he called "body-felt salvation," must affect the body as well.[16] Therefore, those who have body-felt salvation will never be sick, get tired, die, or even have body odors.[17] Since body-felt salvation protects one from diseases, it follows that immediately upon obtaining body-felt salvation, one receives "Holy Ghost Clothing of Fire," which gives an everlasting protection.[18]

Secondly, Hall emphasized fasting and prayer. He taught that before fasting, natural and carnal things occupy one's mind, but with fasting one gradually eliminates the food, sex, and greed appetites.[19] Hall added that when one fasts, the energy that should have been used for food digestion now turns into a bonfire, which consumes all the waste in the body and gives protection over diseases.[20] Thirdly, he taught that Christians could keep their eyes open when praying so that they could see God's glory.

Although Franklin Hall Ministry was influential within Nigeria, the aspects of the Christian life stressed by WATC were often different from those emphasized by Franklin Hall Ministry. While Hall focused his teachings on healing and divine protection, WATC was preoccupied with evangelism—using the Pentecostal experience as a basis for that evangelism. This difference clearly indicates that Nigerians did not accept everything that emanated from American Pentecostal literature or ministries.

Other evangelists who held extreme views and who circulated their tracts and pamphlets within the "Charismatic Renewal" in Nigeria were William Branham and Neil Frisby, two American Pentecostal prophet-healers. Branham, who died in December 1965, ignited the American Pentecostal healing revival, which began about 1947 and spread throughout the 1950s and 1960s. Branham condemned denominations as pagan organizations and urged rebaptized Christians to come out of the organized systems of the churches. In addition, Branham accepted the "Jesus Only" doctrine and refuted the Trinitarian doctrine by insisting on baptism "in the name of Jesus only."[21] Likewise, Neil Frisby claimed that he was the end-time prophet with the end-time message. According to him, God gave Noah the end-time message for his age; and likewise God had also called him to declare the end-time message to this age. He added that a time would come when the various world governments would confiscate all Bibles, and true Christians would be left with the scrolls containing Frisby's end-time messages.[22] The introduction of the doctrines and literature of certain of these American evangelists, particularly Franklin Hall, caused division within the existing Evangelical groups on the campuses and the emerging Charismatic movements because some of these teachings were considered either extremist or heretical. In response, some Nigerian Evangelical Christians published tracts to refute the teachings of some of these American evangelists.

In the continuous growth of the Charismatic Renewal, some profound changes also took place. The church planting activities of Rev. S. G. Elton spread the Pentecostal faith in the country and thus aided the rapid routinization of the revival into a new denomination within the country. Among the early Nigerian leaders, Benson Idahosa was greatly influenced by Elton and benefited greatly from American support. In the early part of his ministry, he promoted his American benefactors, but later became a leader of African Pentecostalism on his own.

Benson Idahosa, who died on March 12, 1998, had founded a small independent prayer group in 1969, which was later named the Church of God Mission.[23] Thereafter, Elton facilitated linkage with American Pentecostal evangelists a contact with Gordon and Freda Lindsay, founders of Christ for the Nations in Dallas, Texas. He enabled Idahosa to attend a Bible College in the United States in 1971. Upon Idahosa's return in 1972, he took up the practice of church planting and within a short time had planted satellite churches around Benin City.[24]

The church-planting concept launched Idahosa into the limelight as an energetic itinerant Pentecostal minister in the country. Soon he became a favourite preacher within many Pentecostal circles. Besides, he was the first African evangelist to promote the "gospel of prosperity," "productive faith," and miracles. By the late 1980s, these new doctrinal emphases had spread widely through Idahosa's weekly television broadcasts and his numerous evangelistic activities. So successful was Idahosa that in 1981, he was consecrated the Archbishop of the Church of God Mission International.[25] He thus became the first Archbishop within African Pentecostalism.

More important for the growth of Pentecostalism in Nigeria and West Africa were the various trans-national religious networks that were facilitated through the educational and ministerial opportunities provided by Idahosa. Through these activities, he had a more lasting impact on the African religious scene, particularly on the Charismatic movements in Ghana in the 1980s. Scholarships provided by Idahosa enabled some Ghanaians to come to Nigeria for training in his Bible College throughout the 1980s and early 1990s. The nine-month Bible and theological training brought together Africans from many nations, with Ghanaian forming the largest number.[26]

Indeed, Idahosa's scholarship strategy became an effective means of sustaining substantial religious and social transformation in Africa. It exported the Nigerian Pentecostal model and concepts across West Africa as most of Idahosa's disciples returned to their countries with strong Pentecostal convictions. Among these trained in Idahosa's school was Duncan Williams, who established the Christian Action Faith Ministries International (CAFM) as Ghana's first Charismatic church in 1979. Besides, the Associate Bishop of the CAFM, Bishop James Saah, was for more than a decade the editor of the

Redemption Faith Magazine while in Nigeria. There is also Bishop Charles Agyem-Asare who trained in Nigeria in 1986 and later established the World Miracle Bible Church as one of the largest Charismatic churches in Ghana.[27] Likewise, Pastor Suleiman Umar returned to Niamey, Niger Republic after his training under Idahosa and established *Eglise Vie Abondante* in 1990 as the first independent Charismatic church in the country.[28] Idahosa's style of bold preaching and his ethic of hard work were reflected in many of his disciples. Indeed, Idahosa instilled the idea of religious entrepreneurship in those he trained, and this influence helped bring independence to Pentecostal Christianity in several West African countries. Decades later, many of Idahosa's disciples became pioneers in their countries.

Another American Pentecostal organization that has had some impact on Nigerian Pentecostalism since the mid-1980s is the Full Gospel Business Men's Fellowship International (FGBMFI). It was established in the United States in the early 1950s by Demos Shakarian and his wife, both Armenian Christians, whose grandparents immigrated to California in the nineteenth century. With the growth of Charismatic Renewal in the United States in the 1960s, FGBMFI also gained popularity as an interdenominational Pentecostal organization patronized primarily by upper and middle-class white Americans. First introduced to Port Harcourt, Nigeria in 1983, it made little impact until 1984 and 1985, when branches were established in Ibadan and Lagos.[29] It then witnessed tremendous growth, and branches were established in many towns. By the early 1990s, membership in the FGBMFI had become a social index of success among middle-class Nigerians—lecturers, managers, professionals, and so on. Its monthly breakfast or lunch meetings held in hotels attracted large number of nominal Christians who normally would have had nothing to do with Charismatic organizations.

By the mid-1990s, other Nigerians had facilitated the spread of Pentecostalism into other African countries and had created networking with a number of the Pentecostal organizations in the West African region. Furthermore, a burgeoning trade produced exchanges of Pentecostal products such as recorded audiocassettes and videocassettes, home video films on religious themes, and devotional literature (mostly produced in Nigeria and distributed widely in the West African sub-region). These products provided a continuous flow of Nigerian Pentecostal culture into other West African countries; hence, they have become tangible resources for strengthening the networks initiated by Nigeria.

Pentecostalism's rapid expansion and the networking created have been remarkable because they have stimulated other social changes in the West African sub-region. They have encouraged cultural interchanges, provided theological and ideological support for doctrinal emphases and practices, promoted trade, and created a power base for Nigerian churches. These networks also provided theological and ideological support for Pentecostal and

Charismatic movements as they tried to bring the concepts of evil and spiritual warfare onto the agenda of social and political discourses, thereby facilitating new forms of religious expression and political understanding.

By the mid-1990s, Nigerian Pentecostalism had supplanted American Pentecostalism in the West African region. First, it has promoted religious entrepreneurship on a larger scale than has ever been known. Secondly, it has created large networks reliant upon Nigeria rather than upon the United States. Thirdly, it has set the pace for the production and consumption of religious products marketed through media: audiocassettes, videocassettes, CDs, and so forth. The negotiation between the local and the foreign, which in the 1970s and 1980s was between the American Pentecostal brand and the Nigerian one, by the late 1990s had become a contest between the Nigerian and other African brands.

Social Implications for Nigeria

Nigerian Pentecostalism has its roots in a marginalized Christian community of revivalists from the second decade of the twentieth century. It expanded in the 1970s among the mobile, young, educated elite who, though small in number, had an immeasurable influence in the Nigerian society. The involvement of this class of people changed certain features of the movement, removing it from its restricted space and making it a popular religion—partly as a result of access to the media. By the 1980s, the Pentecostal and Charismatic movements had become a major force in Nigerian Christianity.

The social dimension of Pentecostalism in Nigeria—judging by the wide range of activities in which they are involved, such as healing services, anointing and breakthrough services, evangelistic campaigns, drama ministries, empowerment services, and others—tends to depict a very vibrant religious movement that is responding to the felt needs of millions of Nigerians within a contemporary dislocated society. Indeed, Nigerian Pentecostals and Charismatics are pragmatic in their approach to personal and social issues. Although their marketing techniques and the appropriation of media technologies may reflect the influence of western capitalism and American Pentecostalism, their obsession with power and its manifestation in every sphere of personal life reflects a deep-rooted connection to a traditional African worldview. In fact, the Nigerian religious and social environment has never departed from its overtly religious worldview. The specific religious phenomenon of Pentecostalism in Nigeria, though deriving some inspiration from foreign models including American Pentecostalism, is still clearly indigenous.

Nigeria during the 1970s certainly provided fertile ground for American Pentecostalism as religious actors established linkages in the two countries.

Initially, the quest for a global outlook, modernization, and trappings of success led Nigerian Pentecostalism to establish relationships with American Pentecostal organizations. These linkages granted access to the global world of Pentecostalism, provided moral and financial support to the burgeoning Pentecostal movements in Nigeria, facilitated organizational stability, inspired them to greater heights as new opportunities were opened, and produced a personality-cult leadership style as the Nigerians emulated American televangelists. Eventually, the American faith preachers and their literature fueled Nigeria's revival during the 1970s, as these literatures offered quasi-theological training when access to Bible colleges and seminaries were unavailable to Nigerian Pentecostals. The open air and large evangelistic meetings of T. L. Osborn, Oral Roberts, Morris Cerullo, and others in the 1960s and 1970s set a standard for many Nigerian Pentecostals and helped to create the megachurch phenomenon in Nigeria. For their part, American televangelists found justification for their social and mission-related activities, thereby guaranteeing continuous support from their home partners and "faith supporters." The Americans also obtained a sense of fulfilment as they tried to export the American brand of faith gospel and prosperity gospel to the impoverished African continent, and also sought to influence U.S. foreign policy in support of Christian rights in certain African countries.

American Pentecostalism has had a limited, but distinct political impact within the Nigerian context. Specifically, the trans-national religious influence of global Pentecostalism has contributed to the evolution of civil society and to a moral community able to exert certain pressures on the political spheres. First, the doctrinal emphases on the new birth emphasized personal morality in ways that strongly challenged the endemic corruption and ineptness of governance in the country. The doctrinal emphases in these instances indirectly were antiestablishment and challenged the status quo; hence, their political implication could not be ignored. Pentecostal teachings about personal empowerment through the Holy Spirit, moreover, sustained a certain degree of self-reliance, and created alternative centers of power for solving human needs—against the background of failure of the centralized state. Consequently, Pentecostalism with diverse impetus from home and abroad and with its appeal to the grassroots conflicted with the orientation towards centralization under many African regimes—both civilian and military. Certainly, in these ways, Pentecostalism within Nigeria has had a politically empowering effect, with American Pentecostalism contributing to this process.

Secondly, from the late 1970s, Nigerian Charismatics used prophecies to stir Christians toward socio-political actions, drawing from a theology that affirmed that matters occurring in the spiritual realm have implications for the socio-economic and political developments of any nation. Politically, in many instances this theology constructed alternative forms of citizenship for believers within a moral sphere where forces of good always triumph over satanic agents that caused socioeconomic and political crises. These Charismatics subsequently developed religious and political influence extending beyond Nigeria to include other African nations. Evangelism supplied the locomotion for this belief, and evangelistic thrusts into other African nations projected Nigeria's image as the "big brother" of Africa. By the 1990s, Pentecostalism extended Nigeria's religious influence across Africa.

Thirdly, Nigerian Pentecostalism received moral support indirectly from the Christian right in the United States in its struggle against Islam. At the root of the Pentecostal struggle with evil forces is its competition with Islam over public space. During the late 1980s and early 1990s, Pentecostal discourse included an overt demonization of Islamic groups. Moreover, the introduction of Sharia in certain Northern states from 1999 made Christians aware of the possibility of "an Islamization agenda" and caused further deterioration in Christian-Muslim relations. As Christian-Muslim relations deteriorated following the religious and political crises, Pentecostals increasingly depicted Islam as an enemy or in satanic metaphors. Pentecostals often used expressions such as "the religion of the bondwoman," "the religion of force and violence," "the slaves," and "the spirit of anti-Christ" in referring to Islam. Pentecostal spiritual warfare fought not only against demons—real and imagined—but equally against sectarian religion and Islam. The covert and overt actions of some state-level governments and the federal government in preference for Islam did not help matters. Overall, Pentecostal attitudes toward Islam have been negative and aggressive.

Fourthly, association of political actors with Pentecostal churches has tended to confer a degree of legitimacy on their political actions. While most prominent politicians come from the mainline Protestant churches, they nevertheless openly court Pentecostals because these politicians believe that they can politically use the preponderant influence of the pastor to mobilize large congregations. Pentecostal churches have also sought to increase their own social relevance by giving religious support to political actors.

Overall, the interconnections with American Pentecostalism have enabled the Nigerian Pentecostal organizations to develop sophisticated entrepreneurial strategies, to venture into the world of modern media technologies, to develop elaborate networking within and outside Africa, and to appropriate American faith theologies in support of a broader attitude of religious triumphalism. Many Nigerian Pentecostal pastors, moreover, have adopted the model of celebrity Christianity (something taken from American Pentecostalism), but that model is sustained by a patriarchal African culture of hero worship and limited accountability. The overemphasis on money and material prosperity, as some commentators suggest, is part of the American induced spirituality of the 1980s. In sum, inspiration and support for the evolution and expansion of Nigerian Pentecostal movements are the major contributions of American Pentecostalism on the Nigerian religious scene.

Chapter 9

U.S. Evangelicals, Racial Politics, and Social Transition in Contemporary South Africa

R. Drew Smith

Evangelical Christians from the United States have strongly influenced South African ecclesiastical and social affairs for over a hundred years. Pentecostal missionaries from the United States arrived in South Africa in the first few years of the twentieth century, and many more would follow in the period between then and the first few years of the twenty-first century. Some of these missionaries would play a central role in the founding of ministries that would evolve into institutions of great numerical, cultural, and social significance within South Africa. Even where U.S. Evangelicals were not involved at the founding stages of South African ministries, collaborations and partnerships between U.S. Evangelicals and preestablished South African ministries also occurred with some frequency and in ways that impacted the ecclesiastical and social framework within South Africa. Race, and more specifically racial conflict, has been at the center of South African life during much of the U.S. Evangelicals' involvement in the country. This essay examines U.S. Evangelical responses to this central feature of South African social life, from the early twentieth century through the contemporary post-apartheid context.

The term "Evangelicals" is used here to include Baptists, Pentecostals, Seventh Day Adventists, Charismatic Christians, and other nondenominational churches and parachurch ministries that emphasize a personal confession of faith in Christ and (with respect to Pentecostal and Charismatic Christians) a "baptism by the Holy Spirit" as evidenced by "speaking in tongues" or spiritual gifts such as prophesying or supernatural healing powers. This grouping of churches constitutes a substantial percentage of South African Christians. By one estimate, approximately 40 percent of the forty-five million people who live in South Africa are said to be Pentecostal or Charismatic Christians.[1] Another measure of the size of the Evangelical population in South Africa are the self-reported figures of the recently formed Evangelical Alliance of South Africa, which brought together twenty different Evangelical groups into a structure that would permit collaborative approaches to some aspects of their ministry and witness. According to descriptive information disseminated on the group, it represents over twenty million Evangelical Christians within South Africa. The present essay focuses mainly on the attitudes and actions of the some of the oldest Evangelical groups within South Africa, groups in which whites have historically exercised control over the ecclesiastical structures and affairs of what have been racially segmented denominations. These groups include the Apostolic Faith Mission, the Full Gospel Church of God, the Assemblies of God, the Seventh Day Adventists, and the Baptists—who all maintained separate white and nonwhite sections of their respective denominations for most of the last century.

This study examines the development of racial segregation within these denominations, including the steps toward desegregation and racial reconciliation in each instance. Reconciliation is analyzed here not only as a function of structural unification of these denominational groups, but also of the level of acknowledgement of past wrongs, and the degree of instrumental change and redress that is pursued, within both ecclesiastical structures and culture, and by way of support for social policies aimed at redressing inequalities and imbalances at the societal level. The essay argues that Evangelicals drugged their feet in reforming their ecclesiastical structures and have shown even less enthusiasm for supporting social policies that concretely address the racial inequalities that continue to permeate South African society. Testimony from South Africa's Truth and Reconciliation Commission and media accounts are the main sources from which the essay draws.

Racially Segregated Churches and Apartheid Politics

In South Africa, the Dutch Reformed church, the Apostolic Faith Mission, the Assemblies of God, the Full Gospel Church of God, the Lutheran church, and the Seventh Day Adventist church have been separated into racial subsections, for the most part, since these groups were established in South Africa—some as early as the 1700s and 1800s. Baptists were also racially segregated, though in a slightly less formalized way. In these instances, blacks, whites, and coloreds formed their own independent communions, becoming concentrated within these separate and (from a resource and social authority standpoint) unequal ecclesiastical bodies beginning in the opening decades of the twentieth century. In the cases of Evangelical churches such as the Apostolic Faith Mission, the Assemblies of God, the Full Gospel Church of God, the Seventh Day Adventists, and the Baptists, U.S. missionaries and U.S. ecclesiastical sponsorships and partnerships were central to the development and sometimes the origins of these church ministries within South Africa.

Racial politicization and polarization within the churches of South Africa proceeded practically unabated until the dawning of the twentieth-century ecumenical movement. The move of churches away from their problematic racial alignments, beginning in the 1950s (and in these instances only some of the mainline, English speaking churches such as the Methodist and Congregational churches were doing so), often grew out of black activism within the larger civil society. The emergence of black empowerment organizations, such as the African National Congress (ANC) in South Africa in 1912, inspired some of the terms of the ecclesiastical and civic discussion. Also, progressive forces in South Africa were mobilizing against apartheid under the banner of the Defiance Campaign. Organized by the ANC in 1952, this coordinated protest mobilized tens of thousands of black freedom fighters, gaining fairly minimal support among the white church community. As Charles Villa-Vicencio points out, despite the existence of a few white clergy allies of the campaign, white churches largely rejected the campaign, branding it as "excessive and responsible for unnecessary suffering."[2]

From the early years of apartheid until its demise in the early 1990s, the white English-speaking churches in South Africa limited their resistance activities mainly to declarations and consultations, including the Freedom Charter, issued in the 1950s as a broad manifesto of "nonracialism," and the Cottesloe Statement. Issued in response to the 1960 Sharpeville massacre, the Cottesloe Statement advanced a number of important declarations about race in South Africa, including that apartheid in general and policies such as the prohibition on mixed marriages were irreconcilable with Scripture, that political rights for coloreds should be pursued, and that persons should not be barred from church membership based on race or color.[3] These and other initiatives emanating from English-speaking churches from the 1940s through the 1960s served as the beginning steps of a South African "confessional movement" that gained greater formalization through Bishop Manus Buthelezi's successful efforts to have the South African racial crisis declared a *status confessionis* by the Lutheran World Federation in 1977, and through Dr. Allan Boesak's analogous success with the World Alliance of Reformed Churches in 1982.

While not all anti-apartheid discourse within English-speaking churches translated into concrete ecclesiastical reforms during the apartheid era, some initiatives do stand out in this regard. For example, English-speaking churches offered up sufficient resistance to the Native Laws Bill of 1957 (which contained a "church clause" that made it "virtually impossible for black people to worship in churches located in white areas") so that it was slightly modified. The Methodist church in particular had already formally announced that it would not comply with the bill and that racial unity would stand as official policy within the Methodist church.[4] In 1967, the London Missionary Society, the Bantu Congregational Board, and the Congregational Union of South Africa took a more significant step toward ecclesiastical reconciliation. The churches agreed to unite as the United Congregational Church of Southern Africa (UCCSA) and immediately invited the Anglicans, Presbyterians, and Methodists to join the union. The South African Association of the Disciples of Christ would later join the UCCSA in 1972.[5] Both the Congregational churches and the Disciples of Christ churches were churches with U.S. parent bodies.

Within South Africa, the Dutch Reformed, Seventh Day Adventist, Lutheran, Baptist, Pentecostal, and Charismatic churches remained largely segregated along race lines throughout most of the twentieth century. The Dutch Reformed churches made some efforts during the 1950s to face up to racial divisions, including five conferences on race convened by the Federal Missionary Council of the Dutch Reformed Churches between 1950 and 1953. Dutch Reformed churches also participated in the Cottesloe conference of 1960, endorsing many of its racial reforms, but eventually recanting and resigning its World Council of Churches membership after South Africa's Prime Minister, Hendrick Verwoerd, roundly condemned the conference. The first significant movement by the white Dutch Reformed Church toward racial reconciliation did not take place until after the NGK (the Dutch Reformed Church) was suspended from the World Alliance of Reformed Churches in 1982 for its racial policies. In 1990 the NGK and the colored NGS agreed to unite and form the United Reform Church (the VGK)—though choosing not to unite at the time with the black NG churches. Although the VGK adopted a statement at the time that declared apartheid to be a sin, the VGK's failure to really confront the racial issue, given its exclusion of black churches, apparently led to an alternative alliance in 1994 between black and colored churches, which took on the name of the Uniting Reformed Church of Southern Africa.

Also in 1990, a church conference held in the South African town of Rustenburg spawned significant new breakthroughs on racial reconciliation among the Dutch Reformed churches and other racially divided churches. Rustenburg, which was hailed as a "conference of confessions," reportedly brought together "approximately 230 church leaders from more than 80 denominations and parachurch organizations," representing "more than 90% of Christians in South Africa."[6] The first morning, a confession of the NGK's "guilt of negligence" relative to apartheid established the tone of the event.

Although many warmly received the confession, the black and colored Dutch Reformed churches approached it with skepticism, sensing that the confession, "like others they had heard before, was too general and all-inclusive." Apparently, neither the South African Council of Churches (SACC) nor the World Alliance of Reformed Churches (WARC) was totally persuaded by the confession. At the SACC's annual conference a few months after Rustenburg, the SACC turned down a request by the NGK for observer status pending further progress by the DRC in concretely opposing apartheid and desegregating its churches.[7] The WARC refused as late as 1997 to readmit the NGK until it condemned apartheid "in its fundamental nature"—something the Rustenburg apology was not believed to have done.[8] Not until October 1998 had the NGK resolved that "apartheid [w]as wrong and sinful, not simply in its effects and operations, but in its fundamental nature." Even here, however, the NGK maintained its resistance to the idea of uniting with its black "daughter" churches.[9]

The NGK was not the only church in South Africa that continued to drag its feet on racial reform through the 1990s. Efforts to unite black and white Lutheran churches during the 1970s failed due to resistance by whites, eventually resulting in further ossification of racial divisions as the four independent black synods abandoned hopes of racial reconciliation and organized apart from white Lutherans into the Evangelical Lutheran Church of South Africa.[10] White South African Lutherans also became increasingly out of step with their larger Lutheran communion, the Lutheran World Federation (LWF). At its 1977 assembly in Dar es Salaam, the LWF delegates accepted a confessional statement that called on their churches in southern Africa to demonstrate their Christian unity by unequivocally rejecting apartheid. The failure by white churches to do so led delegates at the 1984 LWF assembly to pronounce white Lutheran churches in southern Africa officially withdrawn from LWF membership, given their unwillingness to unify Lutheran churches in South Africa and Namibia.[11]

Racial segregation was a fact of life within such mainline churches as the Dutch Reformed churches and the Lutheran churches, and it was also a formal characteristic of Pentecostal and other Evangelical churches, including the Full Gospel Church of God, the Assemblies of God, the Seventh Day Adventists, and the Baptists. With respect to the Pentecostals, some have argued, in fact, that there is a strong connection between white Pentecostalism in the United States and both the early twentieth-century expansion of the Pentecostal movement in South Africa and the public policy codification of racial segregation within South African society, which occurred at about the same time. Religion scholar Nico Horn, citing published interviews of American Pentecostal evangelist John Lake (who arrived in South Africa in 1908), notes that Lake, in private conversations with Prime Minister Louis Botha and in a public speech before the South African Parliament, outlined a segregationist "native policy" that provided theoretical foundations for segregationist laws implemented by the Union of South Africa in the early 1900s.[12] Horn argues, moreover, that the widespread paternalism in South Africa by white Pentecostals toward blacks, and the racial demarcations of Pentecostal church ministries and structures, beginning with the segregation of white baptisms from black baptisms within the Apostolic Faith Mission church in 1908, helped position Pentecostal churches and the broader society for the more rigid racial segregation of South African society that resulted from the 1948 establishment of apartheid.[13]

The Apostolic Faith Mission, the Full Gospel Church of God, and the Assemblies of God are among the oldest Pentecostal groups in South Africa. All three are connected to missionaries connected with the U.S. Pentecostal movement that emerged in the last decade of the nineteenth century and the first decade of the twentieth century. Lake is credited with mission work in South Africa that resulted in the founding of the Apostolic Faith Mission in 1910. The Full Gospel Church of God in South Africa specifically traces its history back to the missionary efforts of a Pentecostal missionary, George Bowie, deployed to South Africa in 1909 by the Bethal Pentecostal Assembly of Newark, New Jersey. His ministry led to the founding in 1910 of the Pentecostal Mission in South Africa, which later became the Full Gospel Church of God. Its U.S. ties were further strengthened in 1951 when it amalgamated with the Church of God, Cleveland, Tennessee. The Assemblies of God in South Africa grew out of the missionary work of an American couple who arrived in South Africa in 1908, Henry and Anna Turney; the work of a Canadian couple who arrived in South Africa the same year, Charles and Emma Chawner; and an English missionary named Hannah James. The Turneys and Hannah James ministered together in Pretoria where they founded South Africa's first Pentecostal church. When the Assemblies of God denomination was founded in the United States in 1914, James and the Turneys sought affiliation with the new denomination and were granted missionary status of the denomination in 1917. Henry Turney then registered the Assemblies of God through the Department of the Interior in Pretoria as a denomination officially operating in South Africa.[14] In 1925, the Assemblies of God in South Africa became the South African District of the Assemblies of God in America, but in 1932 reverted to a less formal relationship with the U.S. Assemblies of God in order to more easily work with partner churches from Canada and elsewhere.[15]

Each of these South African Pentecostal denominations was racially segregated virtually from the outset. The Apostolic Faith Mission was organized as a largely white denomination, while black Pentecostals influenced by Lake developed what became the Zion Christian Church (now one of the largest churches in South Africa). As early as 1925, and continuing throughout much of the twentieth century, the Full Gospel Church of God was divided along racial lines into white, colored, Indian, and black sections, with the overall administrative structure of the denomination dominated by whites.[16]

Although black congregations within the denomination exerted pressure to eradicate formal racial divisions within the denomination, these pressures were largely resisted within the denomination's white-dominated leadership structures. A 1990 date was eventually set for uniting the church but was delayed indefinitely by whites who resisted taking such actions. In response to this resistance, most black churches, colored churches, and Indian churches, along with a few white churches, formed a separate body in 1990 called the United Assemblies Association of the Full Gospel Church while most of the white churches along with a small number of black churches formed the Irene Association.[17]

The Assemblies of God differed from other Pentecostal groups in South Africa in both the intent and the extent of racial segregation within their churches. Initially, ministry by Assembly of God missionaries and ministers in South Africa was entirely among the black population. Some work began among the colored population as early as 1921 and then expanded significantly in subsequent decades. Work among whites began in 1935 and among Indian communities a short while later. Apparently, the denomination made no ideological decision to divide its ministries along racial lines; nevertheless, in practice Assemblies of God churches were divided into "sections" that were usually racially distinct. It is noteworthy, however, that the Executive Council of the denomination, the chief governing board of the denomination at the national level, was always fully integrated. Because the Executive Council operated largely on the basis of proportional representation of the various sections of the national church, blacks outnumbered every other racial group on the Executive Council by a large margin, given that the Assemblies of God membership within South Africa was predominantly black. Peter Watt summarizes the situation as follows:

> The multiracial nature of the Assemblies of God did not arise from a white church inviting blacks into its membership. Uncharacteristically for South Africa, the Assemblies of God was a black church that invited whites into its membership. . . . That such a thing could happen in South Africa as early as 1937 is remarkable.[18]

Significantly, a number of U.S.-related Evangelical churches and parachurch ministries, many of which arrived or were organized in South Africa during the 1970s and 1980s, also operated on a largely nonsegregated basis within their ministries. Included were groups such as Rhema ministries, Youth for Christ, Youth With a Mission, Navigators, Campus Crusade for Christ, Vineyard Ministries, and Full Gospel Businessmen's Fellowship International. Nevertheless, with respect to racial policies at the broader societal level, these newer Evangelical ministries and older ones such as the Assemblies of God were characterized by an overall acquiescence to the racially oppressive status quo—despite whatever racial integration may have existed within their church ministry structures and practices.

Baptists first arrived in South Africa from England and Germany in the early 1800s and established a congregation as early as 1819. Baptists organized into an association in 1877 called the Baptist Union, which whites controlled, but which included congregations from other racial communities. Nearly a century after white Baptists from England and Germany first arrived in South Africa, black Baptist missionaries from the United States came to South Africa in 1899 as representatives of an African-American mission organization called the Lott Carey Convention that ministers formerly affiliated with the National Baptist Convention formed in 1897—the largest African-American Christian body in the United States. The Lott Carey Convention ministered and engaged in mission work among black South Africans, working independently of the Baptist Union for about fifteen years. But a 1915 South Africa law that prohibited further immigration into South Africa of "colored people," including missionaries, led to a request by the Lott Carey Convention for formal cooperation with the Baptist Union of South Africa. In fact, the South African government refused to recognize "Native" Baptist churches unless they "were commissioned by the South African Baptist Union."[19] This arrangement did not last long, given that the black Baptist congregations within the Baptist Union withdrew in 1927 and started their own association called the Bantu Baptist Association (and changed their name in 1965 to the Baptist Convention of South Africa). In 1966, the Baptist Convention of South Africa rejoined the Baptist Union as one of five segregated racial-ethnic divisions within the Baptist Union's structure—the five being white, black, colored, Indian, and Afrikaans. Again, Black Baptist congregations objected to the nature and terms of their relationship with the largely white-controlled structure of the Baptist Union, and many of the black congregations collectively withdrew from the Baptist Union in 1987 in order to operate as an independent black Baptist Convention.[20] While the Baptist Convention distanced itself from the Baptist Union, it maintained a close relationship with the African-American based Lott Carey Convention, with the Carey Convention contributing hundreds of thousands of dollars of support to the South Africa Baptist Convention. The South Africa Baptist Convention has also been in active partnership with the foreign mission board of the American Baptist Churches, headquartered in Valley Forge, Pennsylvania.

Racial segregation within Evangelical denominations was only one aspect of the concession these churches made to the racially oppressive social system within South Africa. These churches were also implicitly and explicitly supportive of the South African government despite, and sometimes because of, its promotion of "separate development" for the country's various racial groups (i.e., apartheid). Looking retrospectively at the 1987 withdrawal of black congregations from the Baptist Union, Pastor Terry Rae, General Secretary of the Baptist Union during the 1990s, suggested that it was understandable given that "the Baptist Union's white leadership had not worked through the issues of being the 'favoured' culture in an Apartheid South Africa," nor had they shown sufficient sensitivity to how apartheid impacted black communities.[21] Pastor Gerald Honey, former Moderator of the predominantly white section of the Full Gospel Church was a bit more direct in recalling the political positioning of white Full Gospel churches during apartheid. He stated: "We did not confront the practices of the State. We worked within the rules of the government of the day and submitted to the powers that be."[22]

Pastor Honey's phrase "working within the rule of the government" alludes to the range of ways people accepted the segregationist status quo and embraced norms and practices inherent to the apartheid system as part of daily life. At some levels this acceptance may have had a kind of routine, unexamined quality for many white Christians, but for many others it also operated at a level of significant intentionality and purposefulness. Such participation could take the form of policy activism, as Nico Horn points out in reference to a conservative Pentecostal/Charismatic fellowship known as Christian Action for South Africa (CASA). As late as 1989 CASA, "encouraged the government to maintain the ban on the African National Congress and the Pan African Congress, to retain Mr. Nelson Mandela until he had renounced violence, and to keep the death penalty intact."[23] Similarly, Pastor Colin Lavoy, a national leader within the Assemblies of God in South Africa, recalled that Evangelical leaders "frequently participated in government commissions," including "the John Vorster Commission that led to the closing of the Christian Institute and the banning of Doctor Beyers Naude." He also noted that Evangelical leaders often "traveled around the world" countering the anti-apartheid positions of the South African Council of Churches, while "claiming to speak for 11 million Evangelical Pentecostal Christians."[24]

Churches were also active participants in the internal security functions of the apartheid state. Often cited is the example of the Apostolic Faith Mission deacon who engaged in the torturing of Apostolic Faith Mission pastor and well-known anti-apartheid activist Frank Chikane, who, after torturing Chikane, left to attend Sunday morning worship service. Pastor Moss Ntlha, General Secretary of the Evangelical Alliance of South Africa, outlines another way, admittedly a more subtle one, that Evangelical churches actively participated in state internal security operations. He refers to efforts, particularly during the 1980s, when the South African government "aggressively . . . recruit[ed] a number of Evangelical groupings to become a part of its counter-revolutionary strategy." As illustration of the point, he cites government initiatives during this period in which thousands of black township youth were sent to all-expenses-paid youth camps where white Evangelists were deployed "to proclaim the Gospel to these young people as a way . . . of neutralizing them from their political commitments."[25]

One church leader, Ray McCauley, President of the International Federation of Christian Churches and Pastor of Rhema Ministries in South Africa, accounted for the role of Evangelical churches during apartheid:

> It's sad to admit that we often hid behind our so-called spirituality and ignored the stark reality of the dark events of the apartheid age. . . . Paralyzed by false respect for government authority, most of your White Charismatic and Pentecostal church followers were simply spectators to the horrible acts of abuse to humanity in this country. When we should have been comforting and praying for those in desperate need, we sometimes joined the cheering crowds and urged on the gladiators who in this modern day was a ruthless security force machine that crushed any foe that dared to shout freedom. . . . We must confess that many of us allowed ourselves to be swayed and manipulated by a government propaganda machine that tried to portray freedom fighters as the enemies of the church and of Christianity in particular.[26]

In the aftermath of apartheid, a number of church leaders have admitted that their churches have actively collaborated with apartheid; these leaders have attempted to rationalize their actions, as McCauley does to some extent, by arguing either that people on both sides were guilty of atrocities or that, in any event, powerful forces within the apartheid state or media manipulated white churches. One of the more telling examples of this response is the following statement by the President of the Apostolic Faith Mission, Pastor Isak Burger:

> . . . the State being the major employer during the apartheid years, many of our members worked for it. Whichever way we may look at it, we helped to keep the system going and thereby prolonged the hurt of apartheid. In the more gruesome arena people were slain and injured on both sides of the line . . . There came days when people on all sides became severely frustrated and vented their anger unilaterally. There were traitors on all sides, some did it for money—life was hard, at times hunger pains and cold put out minds the virtues of morality and ethics. Others did it because they thought they were doing the nation and God a service, fighting what they had been indoctrinated to believe was ungodly. . . . But one needs to look at the days we were living in, be it far from me to push blame recklessly onto another establishment. The fact is that the ordinary man in the street was dependent on the media for information. The State machinery controlled the print and the electronic media by way of legislation or direct holding, as was the case of the SABC. . . . Whites were steadily being indoctrinated through liberal doses of contorted and distorted information, while people of colour were increasingly being incensed. Should we not have been more critical of what we were told, should we not have challenged and resisted more? The questions are many and the answer to all of them is: "Yes, we all failed terribly." However, the fact is that by the time most of us were born, the National Party already was in power. I was born and reared in an environment in which one did not challenge— I'm stating this as a fact, I'm not using it in mitigation.[27]

In the years leading up to and just after the 1994 elections, Dirkie Smit comments on a tendency on the part of white Christians to place the blame for apartheid on someone other than themselves:

> People everywhere wish to excuse themselves for what happened in the past. We begin to talk everywhere about "their" guilt; children, the younger generation, begin to feel this way about their parents, and are already innocent in their own eyes; whites from other language groups begin to feel this way about Afrikaners; ordinary Afrikaners begin to feel this way about the earlier politicians (adopting the attitude that "we did not know, we were not there, we were always against it," (as if the politicians elected themselves); the politicians may begin to feel this way about members of the security forces (as if the latter devised the system themselves and committed their deeds out of sheer evil). The chain of denial of guilt and accusations of others is potentially endless and—as we have learned from other countries—potentially devastating in the long run.[28]

Nonetheless, the late 1980s and early 1990s did represent a period of progress on race issues among some Evangelical churches. First of all, a progressive Pentecostal group calling itself Relevant Pentecostal Witness was organized in May of 1989, immediately countering CASA's pro-apartheid policies by calling for the government to "lift the ban on political parties, to release Nelson Mandela and to repeal the death penalty." Also, many regarded the broad involvement by Pentecostal and Charismatic churches in the Rustenburg Conference as an important step forward. As important as these kinds of declarations may have been, the political gradualism among Evangelical churches was evidenced in the fact that when apartheid officially came to an end with the 1994 election of Nelson Mandela as President of South Africa, the Apostolic Faith Mission, the Full Gospel Church, the Baptists, the Seventh Day Adventists, and (in their own way) the Assemblies of God were still structurally divided into racially segregated sections within their respective church bodies.

Desegregation and Evangelical Social Policy in the Post-Apartheid Context

The release of Nelson Mandela from prison in 1990 and the 1994 elections that brought him and the African National Congress (ANC) to power certainly signaled momentous changes within South Africa, but they were also portents of enormous changes still to come under the leadership of the ANC government. The ANC came into office with a commitment to moving South Africa toward significantly greater racial inclusivity and equality in as short a time as possible. Pursuant to that goal, the ANC government began implementing formal policies and encouraging social practices that would facilitate racial inclusiveness and fairness within every social and institutional sector within South Africa. Two of the primary policy approaches to this were Affirmative Action and Black Economic Empowerment. Through affirmative action, black professionals were rapidly integrated into the leadership structures of governmental, educational, civic, cultural, and business institutions from which they had been largely excluded in previous years. Perhaps even more significant was the integration of the student populations of South Africa's primary, secondary, and tertiary institutions. Schools with long and rich histories that were once almost exclusively white have been transformed, virtually overnight, into institutions that more accurately reflect the diversity of the country. The ANC's Black Economic Empowerment initiative has served as a strategy for increasing black business and financial shareholding by encouraging the white-dominated business and financial sector to include blacks as partners and investors. While voluntary, businesses that do not have black partners and investors are largely ineligible to compete for government contracts that are often an indispensable source of revenue for South African businesses; consequently, many businesses have brought in black partners and investors, with these businesses competing successfully for an estimated 150 billion rand worth of business with the South African government between 1994 and 2005.[29]

With the ANC government charting a course intended to bring about racial transformation within South African institutions, and with many of the mainline Protestant churches such as the Anglicans, Congregationalists, Presbyterians, and Lutherans operating within nonsegregated church structures and expressing support for the ANC's racial inclusivity policies, the racially segregated Evangelical churches were clearly out of step with the times. Not only had their ecclesiastical structures remained largely unchanged, but they had also taken few steps, if any, to come to terms with their political alignments within South Africa's past or within the new political circumstances emerging around them. Feeling the need to act, Evangelical churches finally decided to tackle, at the very least, the issue of their problematic ecclesiastical structures.

In a nationally televised Easter service in 1996, the Apostolic Faith Mission became, in the words of Pastor Burger who heads the denomination, "the first church denomination to unify since the advent of (South African) democracy."[30] The onstage embrace between Burger and Frank Chikane symbolized an end to almost ninety years of racial segregation within the denomination—which included refusing to recognize legally the membership of blacks who belonged to the denomination until a 1991 revision of the denomination's constitution made allowances for this recognition.[31] In 1996 the Seventh Day Adventists (SDA) also formalized steps toward unifying their racially segregated structures. Although the Cape (or colored) conference of the SDA had petitioned without success for the merger of the separate white, colored, and African conferences at each of the annual conferences since 1970, only in 1994 did SDA churches move toward establishing a merger committee. Over the next two years, their racially distinct conferences merged, with the exception of the Cape where white members in the Cape voted the merger down. Those resisting the merger argued that it had to do with finances and not race given that virtually all the churches in the Cape conference had some colored or African members already.[32]

In 1997 Full Gospel Church of God officially desegregated. Following a series of dialogues between the leadership of the predominantly white branch and the branch containing most of the black, colored, and Indian members of the denomination, a public ceremony was held to confirm and celebrate an agreement between the two sides to unite fully and formally. During the ceremony both men commented upon the historical divisions within the church. Pastor Honey, the leader of the Irene Assemblies (the predominantly white section of the church) said: "We ask God to forgive us for allowing our vision and focus to be clouded and so compromised." He went on to say: "We the Irene Assemblies of the Full Gospel Church of God, pledge our allegiance to the one Full Gospel Church of God of Southern Africa and commit ourselves anew to work together in a diversified unity. We bow in deep repentant humility before an Almighty God and request forgiveness of all those who have been pained and still suffer consequences of the past injustices in our land." Pastor Naidoo, the leader of the United Assemblies Association (the section to which most people of color belonged) responded: "The evil in the earth-bound system of apartheid was that it put vast numbers of us across the colour line at a disadvantage through no fault of our own, but due to a circumstance of birth." Both men embraced before what was reported to have been a quite contrite and emotionally overwhelmed audience filled with members from both branches of the church.[33] Another quite interesting dimension of the Full Gospel Church's unification is that a U.S. denomination, the Church of God, Cleveland, Tennessee, apparently played a significant role in encouraging the two sides of the Full Gospel Church to unite.[34]

The Baptist Union and the Baptist Convention began talks about uniting the two groups in 1991 and continued these discussions until reaching an impasse in 1996. The Baptist Convention actually withdrew from these discussions, referring to them as "an exercise in futility," given "the intransigent and contradictory actions of the (Baptist Union) that negate the spirit of reconciliation." With dialogue broken down between the two groups, missionaries connected with the Southern Baptist Convention in the United States engaged in efforts in 1996 to bring the two sides back into dialogue, which resulted in a renewed commitment by the two groups to continue to work toward reconciliation. In 1997 and 1998 the Southern Baptist Convention and the American Baptist Churches sponsored a series of conferences designed to facilitate dialogue between the Baptist Union and Baptist Convention. Over the next few years, the Baptist Union and Baptist

Convention continued to dialogue, including a large gathering of leaders and parishioners from both sides in 1998 in which there was an outpouring of contrition, confession, and forgiveness. In 1999, three other groups of South African Baptists (the Baptist Association of South Africa, the Baptist Mission of South Africa, and the Afrikaanse Baptiste Kerk) asked to join these efforts to bring about unification of Baptists in South Africa. In 2001, all five Baptist groups united into a single, unified structure known as the South African Baptist Alliance.[35]

Also noteworthy here is the role played by church groups within the United States in facilitating some of these reconciliation efforts. The Southern Baptist Convention and the American Baptist Churches sponsored two important dialogues in South Africa among South African Baptists that proved to be important steps toward unification among South African Baptists.[36] Also, as mentioned above, the Church of God–Cleveland, Tennessee helped facilitate dialogue that led to the unification of the Full Gospel Church of God.[37] Despite these examples of engagement by U.S. Evangelicals on race matters, Horn nevertheless argues that the lack of pressure from the world community of Pentecostals on South African Pentecostals during apartheid needs to be contrasted with the pressure that the global community of Reformed churches placed on the Dutch Reformed Church, that virtually every other global church placed on its counterpart within South Africa, and that the global political, business, sports, and entertainment placed on their respective counterparts within South Africa.[38]

Certainly, structural unification of these various Evangelical denominations was slow in coming,[39] given that it took these denominations an additional two to seven years beyond the official 1994 dissolution of the apartheid system to desegregate their church structures. These structural unifications and the confessional processes that occurred as part of these denominational reformations were nevertheless significant and instructive with respect to the possibilities for negotiating conflict. The same could be said about church participation in the Truth and Reconciliation Commission (TRC) process. The TRC was built into the constitutional framework of the new South Africa as a means of helping South Africans account for the atrocities of the apartheid era, but through a controlled process that provided amnesty (in some cases) to persons testifying before the Commission in return for disclosure of their human rights crimes and violations. It was hoped that this process would maximize disclosure, which, given the extent of the atrocities connected with the apartheid system and the limits on the new government's capacity (and desire) to conduct an investigative process, was more likely to happen voluntarily. It was also hoped that the TRC process would help the country, in some respect, to heal and move on. Over the course of almost six years (ending in 2001), approximately 27,000 persons presented testimony as part of the TRC hearings. Roughly 7,000 perpetrators applied for amnesty, with approximately 850 receiving it. Testimony was received at the TRC from a limited number of church groups, but Evangelical groups testifying included the Apostolic Faith Mission, the Evangelical Alliance of South Africa, Rhema Ministries, and the Baptist Union and Baptist Convention.

Many of the Evangelical churches, including the Pentecostal and Charismatic churches, seemed to have settled on approaches for dealing with race in the post-apartheid era that promote what Anthony Balcomb refers to as "alternative community," which emphasizes "reconciliation, self-determination, and the inability of politics to provide meaningful solutions."[40] This kind of community draws partly on deeply rooted Evangelical understandings of the church as *ekklesia* (meaning a "called out assembly"), which exists as separate from, and sometimes over-and-against, secular society. As an *ekklesia,* the church distinguishes itself from secular society in its methods and, often, its goals; pursuant to this self-understanding, churches function within this tradition as alternative communities (drawing on Balcomb's language) that are internally directed, internally resourced, and internally regulated.

Historically, Evangelical distancing from secular approaches and resources has resulted sometimes in a sectarian aloofness, an institutional marginality, or both. In the last two decades, however, Evangelicals (both Pentecostal and non-Pentecostal) have embraced methods and styles that in earlier years would likely have been considered too "worldly" (including worship styles heavily influenced by popular music and artistic expression; extensive use of modern media and communications technologies; and even a greater concern with social issues). In addition, and perhaps as a result of these new methods and styles, Evangelicals have enjoyed a massive influx of members and resources (both in South Africa and elsewhere in the world). A doctrinal emphasis on self-determination, along with the incorporation of new methods, members, and material resources, has fueled an expansion of denominational infrastructure, parachurch ministries, and congregational-level ministries among Evangelicals. With respect to congregational expansion, many of the congregations emerging as part of a recent wave of large-membership congregations known as "megachurches" (typically meaning congregations with 3,000 or more persons in attendance from Sunday to Sunday) are within the Evangelical family of churches.

In South Africa, for example, Rhema Ministries, founded in 1979 by Pastor Ray McCauley and a handful of members, has a current membership estimated as high as 35,000 people, a full time staff of 750 people, a multimillion dollar church campus in suburban Johannesburg, a hospital, a men's shelter, a women's shelter, four orphanages, a home for street children, and a large ministry to impoverished drug and alcohol abusers.[41] The racially diverse membership is predominantly black and largely middle class, although McCauley is a white South African who worked as a bouncer in South Africa prior to attending Bible College in Tulsa, Oklahoma. Rhema's sizeable membership and institutional resources have gained it significant ecclesiastical influence, but its social involvements and demographic profile also serve as something of a model for other Evangelical churches within South Africa who are pursuing ways to be socially relevant, but within an Evangelical doctrinal framework.

For Rhema and Evangelical churches on similar trajectories, the pursuit of racially integrated ministries and of social service responses to poverty is viewed as socially and theologically appropriate correctives to past racial imbalances. Integration of the ecclesiastical structures and worship life advances these churches beyond previous segregation, while social service responses to poverty serve as concrete demonstration of church concern with apartheid's legacy of social inequality—and, in both instances, churches reposition socially while avoiding (at least for now) a commitment to some of the larger (and, perhaps in their view) more contentious structural transformational goals of the ANC government. While this political response is not entirely symbolic, it certainly has significant limitations.

Part of the appeal of this approach for Evangelicals, and part of the problem with it politically speaking, is that the social realm requiring concern and obligation in this instance does not extend much beyond the relatively narrow and essentially *private* denominational or congregational grouping in question. In its desegregated form, the denomination or congregation possesses a racially enlarged sense of *groupness*; in its provision of services to the poor, it broadens its class base as poor people are welcomed as clients and sometimes as members. In spite of such enlargement and broadening, the *social constituency* and *collective good* embraced in these instances has been defined in theological and institutional ways that fall far short of a broadly construed South African public or public agenda.

McCauley's ministry may be a little harder to classify in this way than other large, white-led Evangelical ministries such as Hatfield Christian Church, Elim Full Gospel Church of God, or Cornerstone Assemblies of God church, (all three located in Pretoria), and many other ministries just like them across South Africa, which go little beyond integrating their congregations and providing charity to the poor as ways of responding to South Africa's historic racial imbalances. McCauley is somewhat different since he has, on occasion, made strong public statements in support of "restorative justice" and was one of only a handful of Evangelical pastors who appeared before the TRC (even if his testimony intentionally stressed the culpability of people on all sides of the social conflict). In fact, during his testimony before the TRC he made what could be considered an especially strong statement about restorative justice:

> Restitution or reparation has to happen. There is hardly a White person in South Africa who did not benefit in some way—no matter how small, from apartheid. We benefited in the field of education, business, sports, arts and in everyday life by having better bus services, train services—

> and I'm the first to admit today, that I got benefits from the apartheid system. Maybe I didn't get it deliberately to mistreat or deprive others but Black people certainly never enjoyed the rights and privileges that I did when I was at school and when I was a young man. So we have to face the challenge of restitution head-on. The issue of land acquisition is key to giving people a sense of dignity and belonging, and my sincere prayer is, that those church organizations that hold unused property will generously show the hand of true Christian charity—this could be—in some areas, a wonderful example of restitution.[42]

McCauley and Rhema Ministries are also active members of the Evangelical Alliance of South Africa (TEASA), which is headed by one of the most politically outspoken Evangelical pastors in South Africa, Moss Ntlha. Pastor Ntlha not only made some of the most detailed and revealing statements in his testimony to the TRC about the complicity of Evangelicals with the apartheid regime, but he has continued to be outspoken on the need for an effective public policy responsive to the problem of poverty within South Africa. He stated: "Reconciliation is not cheap grace, but is attended by a willingness to suffer in solidarity with victims." Ntlha went on to say that the "burden for the nation's reconciliation project was inordinately carried by the poor and most vulnerable victims of apartheid" and that there was a need for reconciliation not only between the races but between economic classes.[43]

It is important to note, however, that mainline churches have made much stronger statements on restorative justice and have followed up with actions designed to achieve their stated objectives. For example, the Southern African Catholic Bishops Conference made the following statement in response to the final report issued by the TRC:

> The report has been the focus of many deeply emotional challenges that have tested the resolve of our society to come to terms with its past. However, the delivery of the report to the President today marks the beginning of the equally important challenge of ensuring reparation for the communities and individuals who suffered severe damage as a result of apartheid abuses. Since the delivery of the first TRC report, the question of reparations has remained unresolved. Our society will be reconciled to the extent that the perpetrators and beneficiaries of apartheid crimes open their hearts to ensuring that apartheid's social and economic imbalances are overcome through reparations programmes for the reconstruction and development of poor communities. While significant progress has been made in regard to the provision of housing and education, more effective programmes must be implemented for job creation, land reform, and the treatment of people with HIV and AIDS. When that happens, then the work of Truth and Reconciliation will be complete. . . . While the government must play a strong role in guaranteeing reparations in the spirit of the TRC, this is not the responsibility of the government alone. Private companies, banks, and individuals who made huge profits under apartheid must also be held accountable for reparations, both within South Africa and internationally.[44]

The South African Council of Churches (SACC), comprised primarily of mainline churches and a few Evangelical groups (including the Apostolic Faith Mission and the International Federation of Christian Churches, an Evangelical consortium headed by Ray McCauley), has also been a leading voice on restorative justice issues. SACC issued a statement calling on "all institutions that benefited from apartheid to make reparations and (calling) on churches, in particular, to lead by example (e.g., by establishing a bursary fund for the children of victims of apartheid, by returning land to its original owners, etc.)."[45] Although these statements are important, churches are unlikely to voluntarily relinquish land in the interest of justice, despite prodding by groups such as the SACC and Rhema. According to a study of the land redistribution issue:

> The churches themselves generally consider their ownership of land to be legitimate as they hold title deeds. Some consider that the churches obtained ownership of the land through the unjust dispossession of black communities; others argue that some churches gave sanctuary to communities threatened by state policy; and yet others consider churches to have been "neutral"—observing the destruction of communities without doing anything about it. It is estimated that churches own more than seven percent of land in South Africa, but to date most churches have not made available a reliable inventory of their land.[46]

Consequently, some church groups have gone beyond statements and taken further steps to attempt to insure restorative justice. The SACC was one of the few church groups to support class action suits filed in U.S. courts in 2002 by South African groups seeking reparations from U.S. and European corporations who benefited from apartheid. Archbishop (ret.) Desmond Tutu has also been a leading champion of this cause. Commenting on the strategic value of the court cases as a means of seeking justice for South Africans, Tutu remarked: "I do not see why victims of the apartheid regime should not take the chance to get substantial reparations payments, seeing that the victims of Nazi Germany did that very successfully. The apartheid system was nearly as odious as the Third Reich."[47] Even when South African President, Thabo Mbeki, and former President, Nelson Mandela, came out forcefully against the suits, the SACC, and even more so Archbishop Tutu, continued to support the suits. In a statement Tutu issued to the presiding judge hearing a motion by the South African government to dismiss the suits, Tutu opposed any action to dismiss the suits and countered arguments that the South African government and others put forward, including the argument that the suits would "deter future foreign investment in South Africa." The South African government criticized Tutu for his position, but one of the organizations sponsoring the suit praised him as a "leader of the people" who has "stood side by side with the poor and the oppressed of (South Africa)."[48] Evangelical churches apparently chose to steer clear of this issue entirely, despite its importance as a means of operationalizing the matter of restorative justice.

Where Evangelical churches have been vocal on public policy issues in the post-apartheid context (apart from the support for restorative justice by McCauley and Ntlha), the concern has been limited to opposing constitutional support for abortion and gay rights. Anthony Balcomb remarks: ". . . many of the Evangelicals who were at best apolitical and at worst upholders of the status quo in the old regime have now become vociferous opponents of the liberalization of society, especially in the areas of abortion and gay rights."[49] This involvement was part of what Allan Anderson refers to as a larger "paradigm shift" by Pentecostals, beginning with the election of the ANC government in 1994: "Those conservative Whites who had seen the old order as a 'good force' now saw the ANC government as an 'evil' force . . ."[50] In mid-1995, for example, a coalition of fundamentalist church groups came together and formed a group called "The Christian Voice," whose first order of business was organizing a march on Parliament to protest, among other things, "the exclusion of the words 'Almighty God' from the Constitution."[51] Conservative Protestants met a year later at a conference on "Christianity and Democracy" at Potchefstroom for the primary purpose, according to some observers, of persuading Christians to "get involved in politics to struggle against the new Constitution in order to defend their 'Christian principles.'"[52] A conference attendee from one of the more liberal denominations in South Africa summed up the spirit of the conference (and, perhaps of this entire conservative strategy) this way:

> It was almost impossible to place any debate in the context of social and economic justice. The conference was dominated by a fundamentalistic interpretation of life and faith (in which) there was no place for the prophetic tradition of liberation theology.[53]

The conservative Christian attack on ANC secularism has also been used as a means of directly opposing specific legislation aimed at black empowerment. The "Promotion of Equality and Prevention of Unfair Discrimination Bill" was singled out by some within conservative Protestant camps as an example of the South African "Constitution and laws . . . placing themselves above God's laws." One of the concerns voiced in this instance was that the legislation could require Christians to employ persons "living in sin"—an argument that appears particularly specious as a basis for opposing a bill designed to prevent wide-scale discrimination against blacks, coloreds, and Asians in the workplace.[54] Policy correctives to long-term discrimination against blacks, therefore, are opposed by many of the same white Protestants whose ecclesiastical confessions were intended to admit to the historical severity of racism. The failure of most of the politically conservative denominations in South Africa to connect sentiments of reconciliation with actions that address fundamental antagonisms between blacks and whites has been among the foremost hindrances to reconciliation efforts and to the redemption of the social image of Evangelicalism within South Africa.

Conclusion

Significant changes have occurred within South African society over the last fifteen years, and while important reforms have taken place within Evangelical churches and ministries, these reforms have hardly been at a scale or a pace consistent with the transformations occurring at the broader societal level. Structural unifications and formal apologies were imperative steps to take, but more is possible—and needed—both ecclesiastically and socially. Building community at ecclesiastical and social levels does not occur simply because previously institutionalized barriers are removed. Community building is difficult to achieve when benefits are not mutually shared and burdens are not mutually borne across the communities in question—and in a context such as South Africa, where benefits and burdens have been distributed so inequitably and where those inequities have been embedded within the social and ecclesiastical structures of the country, apologies and steps toward integration need to be accompanied by social action that deals concretely with entrenched inequalities.

It would appear that whatever momentum South African Evangelicals may have had in this direction during the 1990s has slowed. Moss Ntlha assesses the current situation this way:

> Not much has been done by Evangelicals beyond confession. After the TRC a lot of events were held where Evangelicals could restate their confessions, but that was about it. In terms of the economic issue, apartheid still continues. We have found that we have not really done anything to move beyond economic divisions. There has been a lack of rigorous projects.[55]

The report issued by the TRC on the role of faith communities reaches a similar conclusion about the current trajectory of many of these groups, including Evangelical churches, and then leaves off with a challenge:

> . . . sadly, it must be observed that faith communities seem to (be) claiming that "now that society has changed" they can go on building-up their own institutions. (One of the reasons) for having faith communities as part of the TRC process, therefore, is to remind them that . . . they have a moral obligation to be involved in the transformation of a society they so profoundly affected.[56]

The willingness of South African Evangelicals to rise to this challenge remains to be seen.

Part III

Considering the Future: American and African Perspectives

Chapter 10

The Changing Nature of Christianity and the Challenge of U.S.-Africa Mission Partnerships

Marsha Snulligan Haney

Introduction

The growth in mission, postmodernity, ethnic, and postcolonial studies within academia, as well as numerous ecclesiastical dialogues and exchanges related to contemporary existential and mission praxis, afford opportunities for churches in Africa and the United States to articulate the need for more mutually satisfying relations on every level of involvement: denominational connections, ecumenical movements, and religious studies activities sponsored by universities and by mission organizations and agencies. In this essay a vast array of themes, debates, and illustrations are referenced to represent the diversity of denominational and ecumenical partnerships that serve as evidence of the challenges facing Africa and U.S. churches in mission. Included are the following: the All Africa Council of Churches, Seventh Assembly in Addis Ababa, Ethiopia (1977); the Africa and U.S. Christian contingency that sponsored and supported the meeting of the Parliament of World Religions, Cape Town, South Africa (1999); the final report on the Dialogue Between the African Independent or Instituted Churches and the World Alliance of Reformed Churches (2003); the approach of the AME Church (U.S.) toward key leadership issues facing the AME Church in Africa

(2004); the meeting of the World Alliance of Reformed Churches, Accra, Ghana (2004); and, the provocative keynote address of African leaders to the U.S. Committee of World Council of Churches (Atlanta, October 2004).

The relationship that has existed between African and U.S. churches has been dynamic, though one not always appreciated from one generation to another of ecclesiastical or public sector leaders. Because of the western mindset and tendency to sharply separate secular and religious life, the dynamic character of global mission relations has often been illusive, particularly the political implications of religious partnerships. With the phenomenal late twentieth- and early twenty-first-century growth of Christianity in Africa, Asia, and Latin America, U.S. churches—sometimes freely, sometimes grudgingly—have found themselves redefining, reevaluating, reassessing, and restructuring their relationship to churches, beliefs and traditions within these contexts, including, and perhaps especially, in African contexts.

Christian unity between African and U.S. churches—in the midst of evolving sensibilities and sensitivities globally about acceptable and unacceptable ways to approach issues of culture, ethnicity, gender, economics, linguistics, and sociological and political dynamics; and against the backdrop of varying mission histories—remains illusive, not in theory, but in practice.[1] Without a doubt, African and U.S. church relations stand at a critical historical juncture. As it has been observed:

> Africa clearly has a distinctive and growing place in Christian history, yet many parts of the African Christian story are too little known, not least within Africa itself. Furthermore, in Western Christian consciousness, the continent continues to be regarded as a forbidding and dangerous mass, known chiefly for its capacity to generate the stuff of which newspaper profits are assured: rampant corruption, political dysfunction, recurring family and genocidal civil wars. A parallel and more significant reality, which features a richly diverse and thriving range of Christian congregations whose churches serve as centers of human normalcy, integrity, and hope, escapes notice.[2]

Just as the churches clearly need to assume the posture of mutual respect and partnership, the question must be raised as to whether the U.S. church is capable of responding to this challenge. As the late missiologist David Bosch has mused, "Is it not because it [Western Christianity] has not looked at these and related issues from a missiological viewpoint that the Western church still is . . . a nineteenth-century middle-class church struggling to come to terms with the twentieth century on the eve of the twenty-first?"[3] The twentieth-century belief that Protestant missions was an integral part of the cultural expansion of Euro-American peoples continues to have a negative impact on both U.S. and African churches, even to the point that "empire" and "empire religion" have become newly designated terms used to describe how some African and other global churches perceive and experience U.S. Protestant churches in mission partnership.

As attention turns to the matter of the need for mutual respect and equality in global mission relationships, the inextricability of missiological belief and practice is emphasized in the following discussion, with the first emphasis on mission as history. Second, because practices convey and embody belief (orthodoxy) and because Christians perform their faith (orthopraxy) consciously and unconsciously, attention is given to mission personnel (missionaries and mission advocates) and their role and impact as conveyers of the Christian message. The third section, which focuses on mission as contextualized theology, stresses the need to reaffirm the truth that Christian mission does not originate with humans, but with God and God's deepest desire that humans may flourish in all of life, not merely exist or survive. Because of the need to enable the church in Africa as well as the church in the United States to respond faithfully to the changing climate of global mission engagement, in the final section ten themes are presented as key indicators of missional challenges. While emphasizing the African realities, the challenges clearly articulate the need for U.S. churches to learn how to assume a listening posture that will lead toward a renewed commitment to genuine mission partnership, based on a vision of true mutual respect and appreciation. Represented is a missiological perspective that refuses to engage in mission attitudes, beliefs, and behaviors and/or practices that emerge from any other center than that which is embodied in the missional theme, "that all may have life" (John 10).[4]

Mission as History

While the language of missiology may be new and the implications newly considered in light of the growing literature of mission, post-colonial, and ethnic studies, it is, and always has been, incumbent upon every faith community in every generation to engage in mission. The concept of missio Dei is an attempt to usher forth a new type of missiology (or study of Christian mission) whereby mission is primarily viewed not as an activity of the church, but rather as an attribute and activity of God.[5] Given the variations of encounters within the historical African and U.S. Christian mission interchange (which involved not only key leaders but also key corresponding factors such as biblical hermeneutics, theological perspectives, organizational structures, political perspectives, and cultural understandings), both churches have discovered that identifying a common missional frame of reference for developing solutions for the present and future is not an easy task. It is one that requires the churches in Africa and the United States to interact with integrity, honesty, and courage with one another and with a willingness to move beyond traditional interpretations and analyses of one another in order to address critical issues and concerns with the urgency they deserve.

Although the Nubian, Coptic, Ethiopian, and Orthodox churches existed and engaged in Christian missions in Africa 1600 years before the Roman Catholic and Protestant (western) churches invaded and engaged in evangelism and church planting on the continent, the latter engaged in a form of mission practice and missiological theorizing shaped by a Eurocentric worldview that forever changed the perception of life as universal. As it has been noted,

> the Enlightenment period profoundly influenced mission thinking and practice, "the more so since the entire modern missionary enterprise is, to a very real extent, a child of the Enlightenment. It was, after all, the new expansionist worldview which pushed Europe's horizons beyond ...and paved the way for a worldwide Christian missionary outreach. ...I have shown that the very term used for this ecclesiastical and cultural expansion, namely "mission," was conceived as a concomitant of Western imperial outreach.[6]

During the early stages of modern mission history, three primary factors are identified as crucial to this era of foreign (global) mission. First is the notion of the *sending churches*. The churches of France, Great Britain, Portugal and the Netherlands often represented the state authorities. By the year 1817, however, American churches had joined the missionary enterprise to such a great extent that it has been noted, "the missionary cause had become the great passion of the American churches and . . . foreign missions had become the new orthodoxy."[7]

Secondly, there is the notion of the *frontier*. In this instance, Africa in the nineteenth century was viewed as a geographical area and social context to be conquered, and in need of the salvation that only the West could provide. The idea of "Manifest Destiny" is illustrative of how, in the western missionary enterprise, theological and ideological underpinnings worked together to represent Africa as the "dark continent"—that unknown frontier which was to be civilized and changed. Concerning mission and Manifest Destiny, the following observation is instructive:

> . . . at one point or another in recent history, virtually every white nation regarded itself as being chosen for a particular destiny and as having a unique charisma: the Germans, the French, the Russians, the British, the Americans, the Afrikaners, the Dutch. It was only to be expected that the nationalistic spirit, in due time, be absorbed into missionary ideology, and Christians of a specific nation would develop the conviction that they had an exceptional role to play in the advancement of the kingdom of God through the missionary enterprise.[8]

Thirdly, there is the concept of the *mission field*. Blinded quite often by their own ethnocentrism, yet fueled by their commitment to Christ, the missionaries (European and North American) often created mission fields that functioned as centers of money, power, influence, and cultural forms often structured on social and economic systems similar to those back home. For better or worse, Africans living in closest proximity to the mission station were impacted greatest by the presence of the missionaries, the perceptions of the missionaries, and the mission station.[9]

Not until the early twentieth century did this form of mission thinking and practice (i.e., missiology) slowly give way to another form. The second form was marked by the development of the *indigenous church*. A survey of the development of the earliest recorded mission policy statements in several countries (e.g., Ghana, Sudan, and South Africa) show that this action usually began with the ordination of the national (then translated "native") pastor. The national pastor, usually trained and educated at the mission station and in the manner and doctrine of the sending church, often served as an apprentice to the missionary. The missionary from the United States, regardless of denominational or mission society affiliation, remained the dominant figure. The sending Protestant church structures and relationships were of such a nature that the younger, indigenous churches that were birthed were heavily dependent upon the mission churches. The dependence included not just finances, but also ecclesiastical structures, theological constructs, and liturgical categorizations.

A third type of missiology became evident during the mid-twentieth century. The 1950s and 1960s saw a period of political and social struggle throughout various African countries that coincided in many ways with the struggle for civil rights in segregated America. In this era of foreign missions, the three features previously mentioned were still evident—the sending of American Protestant churches, the designation of Africa as the mission field, and the development of indigenous churches—but now the creation of the *National Church* has replaced the indigenous ordained pastor model. The church planted by U.S. churches eventually began to take the form of the national church as a result of much internal and external struggle. It began to claim its God-given sense of self and purpose, and the concepts of self-propagating, self-determination, and self-governing were embraced as paramount—self-theologizing as a mission mandate would not be recognized until later. Actions, such as the call by the Presbyterian Church of East Africa in the 1970s for a moratorium in U.S.–Africa missions, exemplify this mindset.[10] While missionaries and mission advocates began to advocate for contextualization, Protestant missionaries began to engage in a process referred to as indigenization; the Roman Catholics espoused a similar process called enculturation. Both processes of contextualizing the faith led to the encompassing of self-theologizing, a critical aspect of global Christian missions often lacking in earlier missiological thinking. While some churches planted by American Protestant denominations began to voice their resentment of their dependence upon foreign church leadership and resources, others eagerly sought it.

Over the next few decades, the church in Africa, in an effort to become more authentic to the African culture and worldview, began to engage in more critical self-reflection in light of its own reading of the Word of God. Consequently, it began to develop a more culturally appropriate base from within its own African context. The use of vernacular languages in Christian missions, the use of culturally appropriate models and methods of education, attention to familial structures and patterns of life, and attention the character of the churches and ministries began to reflect more appreciation for the African way of life.

At this juncture, noting the dichotomy between the mission and the church is important. The mission existed as a separate entity or organization working to support and extend the national church, but with its own organization. Institutions such as schools, hospitals, and clinics are, for the most part, still related to the mission concept. This continued relation is due primarily to the fact that the required degree of financial support and technical assistance that the church depends on to maintain the mission is beyond the capacity of the national church. Hindsight indicates that the ecclesiastical dependence that exists between the African churches and American Protestant churches is a mirror image of the relationship that existed between the African economy and the World Bank. In the earlier versions of this model of mission, the sending church, no longer related directly to the national church in Africa, but related through the body of missionaries on the African "mission field." As a consequence, issues of trust and integrity become keen.

During the last quarter of the twentieth century, transnational church relations, undergoing yet another transition, continued to demonstrate differing models of overseas mission support, including (1) denominations in Africa relating directly to denominations in the United States and (2) African denominations relating to specific mission agencies or organizations in the United States (such as Lott Carey and Carver Foreign Missions). A relatively new phenomenon has also emerged—that of U.S. congregations (especially mega churches) bypassing denominational systems and providing support directly to specific African congregations and/or mission projects of their own selection and choice.

This brief and simplified overview of mission-as-mission history demonstrates the obvious need for a new mission model. One need is to acknowledge that the church, the national church, must be the base from which mission takes place in every context, in that it is best suited to provide the space to address current tensions and conflicts. The primary responsibility for mission (whether emphasizing a social concern with meeting human needs, or evangelism and church planting), lies with the church in each land; that the American Protestant church and the Africa church are not ends in themselves is important to remember.[11] A new understanding of Christian missions, holistically concerned about all of life, will, therefore, direct its attention outward, away from the church, and toward a world in need of hope, healing, and health.

The bases for mission in the contemporary African context must now be viewed as a partnership between U.S. and African churches within a broader, truly global context, and no longer as one church against another. The frontier is the invisible line that separates church from the world, faith from non-faith, love from hate, peace from hostility, justice from injustice. The frontier is no longer viewed simply in geographic terms, but also in terms of spaces where there is need and neglect, where marginalized persons seek not only to survive, but to flourish.[12] The world is viewed as the object of mission, and the church on every inhabited continent is viewed as the primary agent of Christian mission. The field of mission service is wherever there is a call to bear witness to the love, grace, and power of God. The missionary vocation is that of being sent by the church to the frontier of faith. Both the African church and the American church participate in the sending, commissioning, and supporting of mission. The manifold implications of the need for a new paradigm of mission based on mutuality in mission may be summarized as follows:

1. The priority of mission (*missio Dei*) over against relationships with the West;
2. The call to Christian missions is a call to participate creatively in the transnational nature of the church, whether locally, nationally, or globally;
3. Mission models cannot be transported from one culture to another, but must develop from within each culture and be confirmed by the Spirit of God;
4. Churches must recognize that they engage in genuine mission only when their activities transform persons and systems according to the image and plan of God as revealed in Christ;
5. Each church in a mission partnership needs to have opportunities to initiate new programs, seek new partners, and respond to new opportunities;
6. Mission resources (both funds and personnel) must be freed up and mobilized for new outreach and for cutting edge mission projects;
7. Systems of justice must replace systems of global white supremacy;[13]
8. A perspective of mutuality in mission emphasizes the need for sending and receiving in the world, including the world that exist within the United States;[14]
9. An understanding of the terrain of mission needs to include the entire world, not simply one geographical area; and
10. Mission, spirituality, and development must be perceived as interrelated if they are to bring people holistic solutions based upon a holistic understanding of the gospel.[15]

Mission as Missionaries and Mission Advocates

An essential aspect of missiology that has been the target of much discussion among mission consultations held since the 1960s, particularly related to Africa, has been the role of the missionary. Within the last quarter century, persons willing to cross geographical, social, cultural, and linguistic boundaries have often been caught in the middle of tensions over what it means for churches, U.S. and African, to become "giving" and "receiving" churches in mission. While researchers have contributed to an understanding of the lives and varying motivations of key historical figures involved in African missions, they cannot deny the central role that missionaries (as men, women, and families who live, work, and serve intimately in cross-cultural contexts) have played in the development of new patterns of mission partnerships.

While U.S. academia tends overwhelmingly toward an uncritical, negative depiction of the role and impact of missionaries in relation to Africa, African scholars and churches have offered a more balanced perspective. Consider this observation from African missiologist Jehu Hanicles:

> It is no secret that the often hegemonic nature of the Western missionary enterprise meant that it almost everywhere provoked powerful resistance within non-European societies. This was certainly the case in the African experience . . . but it is a matter of record that his [missionary Henry Venn's] ideas exerted a profound influence on the development of African Christianity and also contributed to the growth of African nationalism, political consciousness, and nation building. The point made here is that while the relative handful of African Christian leaders who initiated protest movements and championed radical (sometimes grandiose) visions of African Christianity are important components in the story, they invariably drew upon intellectual currents that were the product of multiple contributions and the wider religious environment. Equally important, their efforts were shaped by the decisions and contributions of ordinary women and women whose actions provided vital links in the chain of events. Without this common element there would be no revolutions to write about.[16]

His observation significantly points to the dialogical nature of intercultural intellectuality and of the communications process in general, and to the universality and holistic nature of the Christian faith in particular. Moreover, African scholars Lamin Sanneh[17] and J. N. K. Mugambi[18] provide alternative assessments of the cumulative value of the presence of U.S. missionaries, especially as their presence relates to preserving indigenous languages and education and to enabling Africans to participate actively in transnational projects. Only within recent years, however, has research and scholarship emerged that provides fresh insights into the lives of significant U.S. missionaries such as Edward Wilmot Blyden, Henry McNeil Turner, Maria Fearing, and the William Shepherd family.[19] For example, *William Shepherd: Congo's African American Livingstone* by William E. Phipps brings to the forefront the biography of a late nineteenth-, early twentieth-century missionary whose emphasis on religion, human rights, and education helps mitigate Belgian oppressions of the Congolese people—thereby making him one of the first international human rights advocates.

In terms of missionary practice, by the 1970s the majority of the Reformed churches within the United States no longer initiated the "sending" of missionaries; instead, U.S. missionaries were "sent" only for a specified period of time and only when they were "requested" or "invited" by the partners or connectional churches in Africa in order to meet a particular need for expertise. On both continents consciousness and intentionality about the meaning of mission partnerships developed more deeply than ever before.

This development also reflected the growing autonomy and self-reliance of the African church. Defining the terms and parameters of missionary operations or activities was now viewed as the prerogative of the African church. Church to church relations began to replace the older form of mission organization outreach most evident in the preceding types of missiology. These relations were possible because the missionary force was integrated into the structure of the national church.[20] More and more, the direction of missions became understood as "a two way street." Every church, regardless of its geographical location, was increasingly understood to have a mandate under the gospel to "send" and "receive," to listen and to learn, to witness and to teach. In one sense, the concept of mutuality in mission is but a natural consequence of growth and maturity related to living as religious bodies interconnected by a common faith identity. It also speaks to the historical development of the transnational nature of the church, and the need for persons willing to welcome the challenge of serving as a living symbol of the unity of the Christian faith beyond familiar contexts. To suggest that these emerging concepts impacted the lives of missionaries without struggle, however, gives an incomplete picture.

The U.S. missionary living in Africa faced a new question: To whom was he or she now accountable? Was it the church in Africa or the church in the United States? Letters, conversations, and journals of U.S. missionaries recorded during the mid-1960s, when transitional forces were the greatest, often reveal an uncertain sense of church loyalty and personal identity. Given current twenty-first century contexts of violence, terrorism, and war and the contemporary reactions to the "global empire" of the United States, those persons and families who do accept the challenge to serve the church overseas do so with a keener sense of awareness about the complexities of the world. Necessary skills for cross-cultural missionary workers today include not only a concern with the spiritual needs of others, but also an understanding of the impact of globalization on local communities, a concern for changing church-state relations, a concern for promoting sustainable economic development, and the ability to closely examine the role of reconciliation in a variety of contexts. Persons engaging in Christian missions in Africa in the midst of tremendous challenges to the physical and spiritual well being of contemporary Africans must do so as persons who are informed, caring, and knowledgeable of lessons learned from a history of racism, colonialization, impoverishment, and imperialism that has impacted U.S. church relationships with Africa. Another essential role U.S. missionaries and mission advocates must take seriously is educating U.S. Christians about how others live out their faith—sometimes in conditions of extreme suffering and persecution—while also suggesting ways U.S. Christians, broadly construed, might show solidarity with Africans in these circumstances. This activity could take many of its cues from ways African Christians both respond to situations of great need and pay tribute to the faith, dignity, and courage demonstrated by the church-at-large in Africa.[21]

What about missionaries *from* Africa? African missionaries and church leaders, both those who reside in the United States and those within Africa who view the "Great Commission" as mission mandatory for all Christians, are challenged by what it means to be a missionary 'to' and "within" the U.S. context. African Christian scholars, students, and church leaders serving congregations in the United States and developing ministries to respond to African refugees and immigrant populations within the United States are challenged by the need to help U.S. churches to define the concept of mutual partnership in this reversed scenario. For example, how is mutuality in missions achieved when lines of accountability related to African missionaries in the United States are unclear and/or when Africans in the United States are left out of the church decision-making process?

While the desire for true and genuine mission partnership and the discourse related to mission partnerships is in transition, what is revealed is the lack of a clearly articulated theology and mission praxis related to the two-directional nature of missions. This ambiguity has partly contributed to a decline in missionary personnel and financial support. During the last few decades, this decline, in turn, has led Protestant American churches to pursue a strong affirmation of the *African-church-for-Africa* approach to mission. This goal has been supported in various forms by a variety of mission advocacy groups such as the Religious Action Network (Washington, D.C.); the American Committee on Africa (New York); the Africa Desk of the Presbyterian Church U.S. (Washington, D.C.); the Maria Fearing Partnership Fund, Inc (Atlanta); and Religious Heritage of the African World, (Interdenominational Theological Center).[22] Through such partnerships African leaders, missionaries, and advocates find common ground in their commitment to a better future for Africa.

For African church leaders who have lived in the United States and are impacted by its decisions, the vagueness inherent in the "partners in mission" concept continues to beg clarification. A recent illustration of this ambiguity is seen in the actions that the Episcopal Church in the United States took in 2004 to affirm the ordination of homosexual persons to

Christian ministry. Although African church leaders understood somewhat that U.S. churches were attempting to take seriously their theological role within the social diversity of twenty-first-century U.S. society, they do not interpret Scripture and the role of the church in the same manner as their U.S. counterparts in this instance. Consequently, African church leaders find themselves in conflict with U.S. churches, and new issues have arisen over matters of ecclesiastical authority and identity—particularly within the worldwide Anglican communion.

The church of Africa, in fact, is no longer viewing itself merely as a recipient—either of resources, ideas, or culture—but as a base of operations from which a new thrust in mission is to take place. As the AACC stated, "While there are poor people in Africa, Africa is not poor." Difficult days remain ahead. From the standpoint of the African national churches, they are dissatisfied that the churches in the United States and Europe, in spite of the rhetoric of partnership, are making more and more critical decisions that impact ecclesiastical and social affairs in Africa. From the perspective of the European and U.S. mission boards and denominational agencies, African churches seem slow to respond and are preoccupied with their own survival and well being. Only through a commitment to a dialogical process among transnational churches (U.S. and African), however, can the concept of mutuality in mission enable a partnership capable of engaging in just and right relations.

Mission Praxis and the Changing Nature of Global Christianity

By framing the discourse on missiology as a reflection on the Christian transformation of the person and of the community, we are better able to embrace and appreciate the religious and theological insights provided by contemporary African theologians and missiologists such as Mercy Oduyoye, Lamin Sannah, and Jean-Marc Ela.[23] Based on an understanding of missiology as authentic, faithful, and holistic response to *missio Dei*, the two primary disciplines undergirding this perspective are theology and anthropology: theology because we begin with an understanding of God and his purpose for humanity (expressed in the concept *missio Dei*, "the mission of God"), and cultural anthropology because God's intent and purpose must be communicated to humans in communities shaped by culture (*imago Dei*, humans as created in "the image of God"). Common to both concepts are the beliefs that human identity, including ethnic identity, is a gift from God (divine origins) and that what we do with it (human response) is our gift to God. Both the spiritual mission of the church and the mission of social transformation are, therefore, decisive.

The changing nature of Christianity worldwide is making this contemporary reality a challenge for the U.S. church. More and more global missiologists are acknowledging what has been observed for some time now—"the coming of the Third Church." The "First Church" refers to the church that existed during the first thousand years of Christian history, dominated by the Eastern Church in the Eastern part of the Roman Empire, including the North African, Nubian, Egyptian and Ethiopian Churches. The second millennium saw the rise of the European and Western Church, located in the Western part of what used to be the Christian empire, including the North Atlantic churches. Current philosophical, religious, theological, and educational constructs pertaining to the meaning of "church" and "humanity" continue to make use of theological themes, language, and categories reflective of an historical situation dominated by Europe and North America.

This phase in mission history, however, is rapidly giving way to a new era. In the third millennium, the Christian church is experiencing the growing strength and influence of the Third Church (churches existing in the southern half of the global hemisphere, sometimes referred to as the Southern Church). From a global perspective, missiologists are convinced that the most important church developments in the future will come from the Southern Church, which includes the Church in Africa.[24] If in the new world arena churches strive for a theologically and ethically centered sense of Christian missions, then theologians, scholars, and advocates for an African-centered missiology have an enormous responsibility to learn and convey what Africa has to teach the rest of the church. How do we build on insights gained from those who have gone before us, those who have contemplated similar mission issues in their day, those who were committed to a just and righteous understanding of mission and witness in the various contexts in which we live, and work, and worship? What do we need to know? What new ways of thinking are required?

This points to an essential character of the praxis of Christian mission in general, and that is that Christian mission must demonstrate and communicate a concern for the progression of the whole person—the spiritual, the social, the intellectual, and the emotional. Clearly, given the postmodern world in which we live, we are called to reenvision what it means to be part of a larger, complex religious world, and to understand our primary leadership task is to proclaim (in word, deed, and lifestyle) the Christian gospel in such a way that enables persons to engage in critical self-examination that will lead to a more faithful response to God's mission, or the *missio Dei*. Christian scholarship, pastoral care, and reflective action must address, in a way that values persons as individuals and as committed participants in community and relationships, the spiritual hunger that so many people express and that is intensified by violence and fear in our societies.

Only as scholars, theological educators, and ministerial leaders grow in this understanding and knowledge are they able to appreciate African-centered Christianity as offering a corrective to the current persisting theological hegemony. By moving the question of what it means to be African and Christian from the margins of theological inquiry to the center and by presenting Christian missiology as an authentic pathway toward human transformation, ten missiological themes are emphasized and presented for further consideration.

First, attention to the *Church as a reflection of African experience* (socio-political-religious) recognizes the importance of an African-centered biblical hermeneutics, and of the significance of God as revealed through an African-centered biblical hermeneutics but also recognizes that, for Africans, God's revelation is known not only through Scripture, but also through the human efforts that put into practice God's love as revealed in Christ. According to worldview theory, the church aims to help persons catch the vision and experience the transforming power of God, the call to Christian discipleship, and the call to Christian ministry as theologically related to the whole of human life. The insights of African Christianity, whether western transplanted or indigenous, demonstrate a deep awareness that in a rapidly changing world, African spirituality and theology has to express itself in everyday living if it is to be truly authentic. It must bear fruit on many fronts: in worship, liturgy and preaching, as well as in the market place and every aspect of public life.

Second, there is recognition that the encounter between *gospel and culture* is at its core a lively and dynamic interaction of values, ethics, traditions, morality, and discernment. How faith and socio-political-religious practices come together in the life of an African faith community often determines which theological source (experience, scripture, tradition, or culture) will serve as the point of departure for authentic Christian reflection. The ongoing cultural interface between tradition, social change, and the spirit and the message of the gospel will help determine which models of contextual theology emerge as African Christians and their invited guests (i.e., missionaries) seek to engage in theological reflection, advocacy, and action that are both explicit and meaningful.

Third, doing theology from a missiological perspective requires an *interdisciplinary approach* that will help church leaders and their faith communities recognize how their lives relate to a wide variety of challenges and opportunities in the secular world. An interdisciplinary approach not only promotes a multidimensional gospel for multidimensional human needs, it also communicates a holistic concern for persons: relationships that must be restored, bodies that are in need of healing, minds that must be taught, spirits that must be encouraged, and personalities that must be transformed. Missiology views an interdisciplinary approach as the only way to address holistically and authentically the complex challenges facing African Christian women, men, and children in the twenty-first century. The dialectical relationship between theology and other disciplines is particularly important today because of the complexity of critical issues now confronting persons, families, communities, societies, and nations.

Fourth, further *interreligious dialogue* between Christians and non-Christian believers is becoming crucial for both African Christians and

Christians in the United States.[25] What can the U.S. church learn from countries in Africa, such as The Gambia and the Republic of Cameroon, where Muslims and Christians have long histories of harmonious relations and are appreciate the gifts of each others' heritages? If peaceful coexistence within a religiously plural situation is to be achieved, respect and appreciation for interfaith and interreligious dialogue is mandatory. Practitioners of traditional African religious beliefs, Muslims, Fulani Jews, Bah'ais, Christians, and other faith communities seek to bear witness "unapologetically" to the essential elements of their faith through sacred rituals, rites, writings, worship, and other activities. They also are concerned with presenting their beliefs as capable of offering something valuable to our collective humanity.

The tragedy of September 11, 2001, has beneficially produced a heightened emphasis on various types of interfaith dialogue. As individual faith communities communicate effectively about salvation and human liberation, truth and justice, and reconciliation and peace, they must do so in neighborhoods, communities, and social contexts where people of various faiths encounter one another in shared space—including the workplace, the market place, schools, and entertainment and leisure venues.

Fifth, it is hoped that attention to *African centered worldviews and theories* within U.S. models of learning will reaffirm social and religious commitments to enter into partnership with the reconstruction and development of Africa on various levels. African-centered thinking and practice (especially in urban and metropolitan centers where large numbers of Africans reside) have contributed greatly to a social discourse as Africans have communicated their point of view through cultural arts and aesthetics, educational programs and curricula, entrepreneurial activities, holistic health initiatives, and community development enterprises. This contribution is occurring at a time in history when U.S. society is grappling with the question, "Can there be a public theology in the twenty-first century in view of ethnic, religious, class, economic, and philosophical differences?" African and U.S. churches have the opportunity to respond in the affirmative. As mutual partners, an empowering missiology has the responsibility to expose and critique the presuppositions of colonialist, imperialist, and the other worldviews and interactions that persist in disregarding, distorting, and undermining a missiological concern for the personhood and humanity of all individuals.

Sixth, in the *emerging global context*, where contextual theologies become more pronounced, influential, and interactive, possibilities increase that Western and non-Western Christian traditions and northern and southern hemisphere churches may interact to enrich one another. It is hoped that important meetings of various church bodies within Africa may present new lenses for reading world realities at both local and global levels. Given the burgeoning access to Christianity in Africa, Asia, and Central and Latin America at the dawning of the twenty-first century, more and more African scholars, missiologists, and other leaders are demonstrating an ability and willingness to engage in an understanding of local mission and ministry realities that reflect an understanding of global connections and interactions. Examples would include the present African leaders heading up the United Nations, the World Alliance of Reformed Churches, the Lutheran World Federation, and the World Council of Churches.[26]

Understandably, the church in the United States is having problems grappling with the new reality of the growing non-Western church and the implications of this reality for the future of Christianity. It has been reported that in response to the "browning of Christianity" (as described in *The Next Christendom: The Coming of Global Christianity*), one prominent church leader asked, "What can we do to stop it?" Yet, for those who remain fixed and, therefore, marginalized within the former historical mission paradigms, these new developments on the horizon offer much excitement and hope.

Seventh, the *cultural integrity of Christian partnerships* has received a growing emphasis. The fact that some historical paradigms of Christian partnership are not meeting the felt needs of a growing number of Africans is being articulated more today than in the past. For instance, whereas in the past Christian contributions of educational materials were accepted without question, today there is an increased desire for African-centered Christian educational curricula. It is now acknowledged that African children and youth are not receiving from classical models premised on western theological conceptions of divinity, beauty, power, and individualism an adequate view of themselves as having been created in the image of God. African-centered philosophy, which is centered on persons at all stages of the life cycle, prepares and sustains young people to live creatively with faith, courage, and confidence in a violent capitalistic and often dehumanizing world, a world consumed by superficiality and concerned only with the obvious and the shallow, where quick fixes abound. Important progress in developing African-centered curricula has been made, but much more needs to be done.[27]

Eighth, African Christian theology and Christian education must be done from the *perspective of the people* (that is, the laity and not simply from the perspective of clergy and scholars). Traditional wisdom contained in certain proverbs and adages emphasizes the importance of people as diverse and necessary—for example, "I am because we are." This perspective underlies what it means to be human. It also points to the need for a mission-conscious church to cultivate its Christian identity through an emphasis on the communal nature of being—linking the past, present, and future. In such congregations, denominations, and seminaries, African-centered theological insights and religious education models instruct people on the need to trust in the presence of God's spirit in their midst and in the manifestation of God's will and purpose within the faith community. The outcomes are twofold: the Christian message will be more culturally accessible for groups of people within each context, but also contextual models of theology allow people (women, men, and youth) to utilize cultural elements consistent with the gospel. As a result, the self-perception and self-worth of a people are elevated.

Ninth, the *reign of God*, said to be the central theme in both the Hebrew Scriptures and in Jesus' life and message, is also penultimate in an African-centered Christian theology. The experience of those who gathered in Accra at the 2004 World Alliance of Reformed Churches meeting confirms this penultimate position. A renewed sense of Christian identity based on the reign of God provides a powerful spiritual and missional motivator. It stands as a corrective to the modern missionary movement described as primarily linked to a traditionalist, colonialist, and imperialistic interpretation of the Christian mission as one of "being sent." Instead, Christian mission and witness when informed by an African Christian spirituality stresses that the goal is "to be human as we go about daily living." The proclamation of this message in word, deed, and lifestyle already is a missiological phenomenon, but requires more research. The power of God to form, shape, and empower Christian ministry is being illustrated in a variety of contexts, even in the midst of seemingly hopeless situations. The reign of God issues forth an invitation to discern God among the human brokenness around us; it empowers women, men, youth, and children to choose daily to participate in those things that produce life for all.

Finally, the tenth theme related to the intersection of missiology and our concern for Africa is the foundational relationship between *spirituality and mission strategy*. Christians throughout the world urgently need to question how Christian spirituality can become a more tangible and available resource in helping people tackle massive social changes that have transformed modern life while leaving persons spiritually hungry and searching. Missiology, from an African-centered perspective, suggests that spirituality has no validity if it does not lead to social action that vividly demonstrates the difference that faith in Jesus Christ makes. The interconnectedness of spirituality and social responsibility, as we live and move in the tension of God's grace in the here and now, requires that our lives reflect, in contextually and theologically appropriate ways, a sense of human responsibility and accountability to both God and our fellow human beings. This challenge faces transnational church partnerships—how to enable personal and communal spirituality to inform and transform social, political, and religious realities in the world in which we are called to live, move, and have our being. Both spirituality and social responsibility are necessary and inextricably linked within an authentic biblical understanding of lived experience.

Conclusion

Missiology, in focusing attention on *missio Dei*, acknowledges that, in fact, all theology is contextual and that Christian theology is the product of a specific group of people in a particular time, place, and space who are seeking to respond faithfully to the God revealed in Jesus Christ. The foregoing missiological themes summarize the learning possibilities for U.S. churches as they reflect on the need for healthy relationships that support and nurture transnational partnerships based on mutuality in Christian mission. Churches of the United States and Africa must be willing and able to engage in critical mission praxis as the conduit for understanding the power of God at work reforming and transforming personal, cultural, and societal attitudes, behaviors and systems by utilizing the theological resources we should already possess through our Christian baptism and confirmation. Again, because practices convey and embody belief and because we perform our faith in word, deed, and lifestyle, even when we are unaware of it, we must be reminded that God is the originator of mission. *Missio Dei* results from God's initiative, having been rooted in God's purposes to restore, to heal, and to give life. Ours is the challenge of a renewed commitment to genuine mission partnership, both with God and one another, grounded in mission praxis that is rooted in the One that came "that all may have life" (John 10).[28]

Chapter 11

Contemporary Public Theology in the United States and South Africa

A Dialogue

Nico Koopman

The famous South African journalist Allister Sparks argues that the dawning of democracy and freedom within South Africa has contributed to improved living conditions among South Africans. He describes the achievements of the young democracy as follows:

> We have entrenched a new democratic Constitution . . . and bedded it down through four national, provincial and local elections which have been manifestly peaceful and fair. We have a Constitutional Court presided over by world-class jurists to interpret and defend it, and we have established a number of other institutions to give effect to the Constitution. . . . We have scrapped all the old race laws, guaranteed freedom of speech and the press, abolished the death penalty, legalized abortion on demand, protected the rights of gay people, and advanced women in many spheres of life. We have brought clean water to more than 9 million people who did not have it before, electricity to more than 2 million, and telephones . . . to 1.5 million. We have integrated, at least nominally, more than 30,000 public schools that used to be racially segregated, as well as all the country's universities and other institutions of higher learning, raised the literacy rate of 15-to-24-year-olds to 95%, and brought free health care to millions of children. . . . We have resuscitated an economy that was on its deathbed . . . generally winning universal praise for establishing a sound macroeconomic

> base from which hopefully to build future prosperity. It is indeed another country.[1]

Yet, in a clear and courageous way, the renowned South African economist Sampie Terreblanche portrays the work unfinished in South Africa with regard to social and economic justice. Terreblanche refers to the 2000 report of South African Statistics, which states that in 1996 at least 41 percent of all households were living in poverty, i.e., were living with an income between 601 and 1000 rand. He also refers to statistics that paint an even gloomier picture, including 1995 figures showing that 65 percent of black people between the ages of sixteen and twenty-four were unemployed.[2] In 1999, 4.2 million blacks remained out of work, with working-age blacks under age twenty-nine accounting for almost half that number.[3]

The dawning of South African democracy has certainly brought with it many new considerations for churches with respect to their role within South African public life. The challenge is no longer to break down apartheid, but to participate in the building of a new society, including responding to a wide range of social development needs. This unfinished business within South Africa's contemporary social development closely parallels unfinished business within U.S. society. Cornel West speaks to this business: "Twenty-one percent of all children live in poverty; 52 percent of young brown brothers and sisters live in poverty; and 51 percent of black children live in utter poverty in the richest nation in the history of the world." He also cites James Cone's estimate that 1 percent of the U.S. population owns 30 percent of the wealth while 80 percent of their fellow citizens wrestle with long-term tendencies of wage stagnation since 1973.[4] With the United States and South African contexts presenting their respective churches with similarly daunting challenges, to what extent are churches within the two contexts speaking the same language as they attempt to respond to these challenges?

In the years of the struggle against apartheid, the theological scene in South Africa was influenced by theological approaches such as political theology, liberation theology, black theology, feminist theology (or womanist theology as this approach is labeled amongst blacks in Africa), forms of African theology, and political theology. With race now receding somewhat as one of the central points of conflict within South Africa (and the United States) and with class disparities becoming more severe within both contexts, this essay strives to describe the relationship between public theological discourse in the U.S. and public theology in the New South Africa, and the relevance of either of these discourses, especially to the South African context.

The emphasis of Black theologians like James Cone and Cornel West on the priority of the poor and marginalized in theological discourse is investigated. Moreover, the plea of West for the involvement of theology in thorough technical economic discussions in its attempt to serve the need of the poor is explored. The contributions of U.S. theologians like James Gustafson and David Tracy on the direct involvement of theology in the modern-postmodern pluralistic public sphere is also investigated. Lastly, by appealing to the work of Stanley Hauerwas, the challenge to actualize the potential of inner-church practices for public life is investigated. An attempt is made to identify the influence of these different approaches to public theological discourse on the public theology discussion in the South African context.

What is Public Theology?

The definition of public theology varies within the growing literature on the subject. In tracing its genealogy, U.S. theologian Max Stackhouse states that theologians like Ernst Troeltsch, Abraham Kuyper, Walter Rauschenbusch, Reinhold Niebuhr, Paul Tillich, Martin Luther King, James Luther Adams, and Paul Ramsey contributed to the contemporary development of public theology, although they did not use the concept public theology. According to Stackhouse, the North American theologian Martin Marty used this concept for the first time in 1974 in an article titled "Reinhold Niebuhr: Public Theology and the American Experience."[5]

At a descriptive level, U.S. theologian Linell Cady understands the task of public theology, firstly, to "sustain, interpret, critique, and reform a particular religious worldview and its concomitant way of life" and, secondly, to "contribute to the upbuilding and the critical transformation of our public life."[6] U.S. theologian Robert Benne offers the distinction that public theology "refers to the engagement of a living religious tradition with its public environment—the economic, political and cultural spheres of our common life."[7] The South African theologian John de Gruchy describes public theology similarly, but cautions against the idea of a universal public theology—preferring to speak in terms of shared commonalities in approach and substance by theologians seeking to engage the public realm within particular localities.[8]

These definitions of public theology fall within two schools of thought: the Chicago school and the Yale school. The Chicago school, with David Tracy as its most eminent representative, recognizes the fact that the fragmentation of rationality within particular contexts inhibits the possibility of acquiring universal consensus on public issues in a pluralistic context. This school, however, reckons that it is important to explain, justify, and defend theological claims in a "public" way and to seek at least a degree of consensus and universality. In this way public theology reaches its aim of addressing issues that affect society as a whole and of dealing with these issues in a way accessible to everyone in the public sphere. The Yale school, with representatives like George Lindbeck, Hans Frei, Paul Homer, Ronald Thieman, and Stanley Hauerwas, views the task of theology not as making faith claims rationally accessible in the public sphere or seeking public consensus.

Rather, theology should simply describe the way in which Christian truth claims function within a particular faith community. According to the South African theologian Ernst Conradie, public theology needs the approaches of both the so-called Chicago and Yale schools of theology.[9]

These various theological schools and approaches coming out of the United States have influenced South African theologians at many points, but in what ways has the U.S. influence contributed to an effective public witness by South African theologians and churches? The following section explores implications of these U.S. schools of thought for public theology within South Africa as it has gained expression in numerous ways within South African society.

Multiple Faces of Public Theology Within South Africa

David Tracy has received much attention in South Africa for his distinction of three publics (i.e., reference groups or social locations) that are engaged in theology: the church, the academy, and the broader society.[10] Tracy thinks that all theology is, in some meaningful sense, church theology, i.e., ecclesial theology. Theology develops from within the church as both a pneumatological and sociological body. When he refers to the church as one of the publics of theology, he has this sociological nature of the church especially in mind.[11]

Theology and the Broader Society

In examining the broader society as one of theology's "publics," South African theologian Dirkie Smit identifies four spheres in a modern democratic society with which churches and theology engage. The political sphere of the public focuses on themes such as the relationship between theology and the state, government, political power, and the control and regulating of public life. The economic sphere focuses on themes such as the relationship between theology and the so-called autonomous market-economy, globalization, ecology, science, and technology. Civil society focuses on themes such as the relationship between theology and the institutions, organizations, associations, and movements of civil society which, independent of the state and economy, strive to enhance the quality of life, satisfy human needs, foster the interests of the populace, change the nature of society, and build the common good. Schools, legal bodies, cultural associations, sports clubs, and neighborhood structures are all institutions of civil society—as are churches (sociologically speaking). A fourth sphere, public opinion, focuses on themes relating to the relationship between theology and the pluralistic public discourse on matters such as the nature of society, common foundational values for society, common challenges, and common priorities for society.[12]

The dialogue and engagement of theology with these spheres take place in four ways according to North American theologian James Gustafson.[13] The first typology among his four varieties of *moral discourse* is *prophetic discourse*, which takes the form of indictment at times and a more utopian form at other times. Indictment points to the roots of moral or social problems. Utopian discourse evokes a hopeful vision. It proclaims an ideal state of affairs in the future and motivates people towards its realization. Within *narrative discourse*, the second of these typologies, stories and parables are told of significant events and of moral heroes in the community and tradition. These stories sustain common memory in a community and shape the consciences, moral identities, and characters of members of the community. More than a rigorous casuistic argument, stories provide illumination and help in the process of moral decision-making. A third typology, *ethical or technical discourse*, uses philosophical and rigorous modes of moral argumentation. Logic, precision in use of concepts like justice and rights, and the identification of the rational grounds of autonomous ethics (which might be backed by Christian convictions possibly shared by nonbelievers), are typical features of this discourse. Lastly, *policy discourse* deals with questions such as what is desirable within the constraints of what is possible, what power do we have to effect change, what the time frames are for the achievement of ends, and whether we have all the necessary information and knowledge. Policy discourse entails that we have to distinguish between matters of ethical principle and the inferences we draw for policy. We can be more certain about the first than the second. In the dialogue and engagement of theology with the various spheres of society on issues like social and economic justice, attention is to be given to all these discourses. The vision of an alternative society that energizes and opens innovative possibilities should be spelled out. Clear critique where injustices exist should be voiced. The grass roots stories of poverty and suffering are to be heard, as well as stories of achievements and successes. The technical discourse is of immense importance because it suggests that it is not enough to spell out broad principles and visions of justice. The hard work of critical, scientific, interdisciplinary, and intersectoral analysis and deliberation, even if it leads to only preliminary solutions, is of crucial importance. Engagement with these various discourses paves the way for appropriate interventions in the policymaking processes on different levels of governance and authority within the various spheres of society.[14]

In engaging these spheres theology must resist the temptation to relegate itself to a prophetic discourse of critique and indictment. In the same vein responsible theology does not merely spell out the vision of a good society. The road of partnership that institutions like the South African Council of Churches currently opt for is perhaps the most fruitful path to follow. In this cooperation theology must not be coopted by the agenda of the state. A guiding principle for this cooperation is to continually ask what the impact of dialogue, cooperation, compromises, and policies are on poor and vulnerable people. A cherished notion in Christian theology about which Liberation Theology reminded us during the 1960s to 1980s is the conviction that God is especially the God of the poor, the destitute, and the wronged. The acid test for our social and economic discourses, policies, and priorities is the question of how they impact on the most vulnerable in society.[15]

While the approaches of the so-called Chicago and Yale schools are very helpful for the public theology discourse in South Africa, the question remains as to whether these theologies adequately address the plight of the poor, the wronged, and the marginalized. In this regard the lessons that we had learned from black theology in the United States and in South Africa, as well as from Liberation Theology in Latin America, remain of crucial importance.

Reminders from black theologians such as James Cone and Cornel West should be heeded strongly in order to prevent us from making compromises at the expense of the most vulnerable. This compromising is a big danger among South African churches who have opted to cooperate with government and other agents of society in the hopes of building a more humane society. South Africans, in the context of their young democracy, can learn from black theologians in the United States who operate within a more established democracy. A number of African-American theologians think that despite the existence of a mature democracy, the nineteenth century abolition of slavery, and the successes of the mid-twentieth century civil rights movement, many people in the United States still suffer, not only under racism, but also under poverty.

In 1999 James Cone wrote an essay entitled "Looking Back, Going Forward" in a book of critical essays celebrating the thirtieth birthday of his famous book *Black Theology*. In this essay Cone pleads that theologians not lose sight of the prophetic dimension of theology, which easily happens amongst black theologians as they seek acceptance from the white establishment. Cone makes his case in passionate language:

> The anger I felt while writing Black Theology and Black Power was fueled by the assassination of Martin Luther King Jr. Thirty years later as I prepared the Aims of Religion address on the anniversary date of King's death, I am still just as angry, because America, when viewed from the perspective of the black poor, is no closer to King's dream of a just society than when he was killed. While the black middle class has made considerable economic progress, the underclass, despite America's robust economy, is worse off in 1998 than in 1968. While the statistics are well known, they still fail to shock or outrage most Americans. One-third of young black males are involved in the criminal justice system. One-half of black babies are born in poverty, and their life expectancy in the urban ghetto is lower than that of Bangladesh.[16]

In South Africa's young democracy, where we have achieved political liberation but not economic liberation, the picture that Cone sketches looks familiar. His appeal for critical prophetic speaking in order to address poverty and economic injustice deserves our serious attention.

Jon Sobrino adds a further dimension to this concern about the danger of social irrelevance within theology, and even within Liberation Theologies:

> Poverty is increasing in the third world, the gap between the rich and the poor countries is widening, there are wars—more than a hundred since the last world war and all of them in the 'Third World.' Cultures are being lost through the imposition of foreign commercial cultures. . . . Oppression is not a fashion. The cries of the oppressed keep rising to heaven . . . more and more loudly. God goes on hearing these cries, condemning oppression and strengthening liberation. . . . What I ask myself is what a theology is going to do if it ignores this fundamental fact of God's creation as it is. How can a theology call itself 'Christian' if it bypasses the crucifixion of whole people and their need for resurrection, even though its books have been talking about crucifixion and resurrection for twenty centuries? Therefore if those doing liberation theology are not doing it well, let others do it and do it better, but someone must keep on doing it.[17]

As Cone and Sobrino make clear, any theology that claims to be faithful to the Christian gospel will have to pay adequate attention to this agenda. Within South Africa this agenda has not been dealt with sufficiently.

Cornel West lends support to this deficiency, but also asks that theologians familiarize themselves more with technical modes of engaging public life, especially economic life. In his famous book *Prophesy Deliverance! An Afro-American Revolutionary Christianity*, West illustrates that prophetic speaking cannot be done adequately without thorough technical analysis. He is partly suggesting here that it is infinitely more difficult to engage in discussions about what society should look like ideally than it is to criticize, oppose and negate current social arrangements. Says West:

> Black theologians all agree that black liberation has something to do with ameliorating the socioeconomic conditions of black people. But it is not clear what this amelioration amounts to. There is little discussion in their writings about what the liberating society will be like. The notion and the process of liberation are often mentioned, but, surprisingly, one is hard put to find a sketch of what liberation would actually mean in the everyday lives of black people, what power they would possess, and what resources they would have access to. To address the issue of poverty and of economic injustice prophetically, we need to develop a thorough understanding of the internal dynamics of the society from which people must be liberated. Without this clear-cut social theory about what is, it is difficult to say anything significant about what can be. The possibility of liberation is found only within the depths of the

> actuality of oppression. Without an adequate social theory, this possibility is precluded.

In pointing out the lack of an adequate social theory within black theological approaches, West spells out the questions that such a social theory should be addressing:

> An undisputable claim of black theology is America's unfair treatment of black people. What is less apparent is the way in which black theologians understand the internal dynamics of liberal capitalist America, how it functions, why it operates the way it does, who possess substantive power, and where it is headed. As noted earlier, black theologians do not utilize a social theory that relates the oppression of black people to the overall makeup of America's system of production, foreign policy, political arrangement, and cultural practices.[18]

West does not suggest that black theologians do not engage in technical discourse; rather, he thinks that they do so insufficiently. They analyze racial injustices without engaging in analyses of the national and international economies and of culture and power relations in these spheres. As South African theologians, we can intensely identify with West's proposals. During the years of struggle, we were quite clear on the evils that we oppose—racism, classism, sexism, economic injustice, the gap between rich and poor. In a new complex context of democratization, modernization, globalization, and postmodernism, we need this analysis for the sake of faithful living today.

Theology and the Academic Public

Tracy describes the academy as that public or social location of theology where critical scientific dialogue takes place with other academic disciplines. In its engagement with the academy, theology is challenged to provide arguments that all reasonable people from diverse religious and secular traditions can recognize as reasonable. In this discourse, appeals are made to universal faculties such as experience, intelligence, and rationality. Claims are stated with appropriate warrants, backings, and rebuttal procedures. He also pleads that although theologians confess allegiance to a specific religious tradition or to a praxis movement bearing religious significance, they abstract themselves from these faith commitments for the sake of critical analysis of religious and theological claims by outsiders and by those who belong to the tradition.[19] Many theologians of course, would oppose Tracy on this point. They would specifically argue that abstracting and distancing oneself from one's faith commitments is not a prerequisite for critical and honest introspection into the cognitive claims of faith traditions. Such withdrawal, premised on the idea of being scientifically honest, is actually viewed as dishonesty.

In the encounter with the academic public, theology makes the choice for scientific reflection, for making faith convictions as far as possible rationally accessible to all reasonable people, and for constructing arguments that pass the test of coherency, consistency and logical reasoning. Theology, however, does not have to distance itself from its faith commitments, but takes care that such commitments do not exclude scientific scrutiny. The age-old Christian notion of *fides quaerens intellectum* (faith seeking understanding) that Anselm of Canterbury framed in the eleventh and twelfth centuries needs fresh application in this dialogue of theology with the academic public.[20]

The U.S. theologian Stanley Hauerwas explores the tensions between faith and reason and between theology and broader social discourses in ways that are both intriguing and relevant with respect to the contemporary South African context. In various publications over more than three decades, Hauerwas has reminded us about central notions in Christian theology like character and virtue, narrative, community, identity, and teleology.[21] Hauerwas's famous one-liner perhaps best describes his views on the public role of the church: "As such the church does not have a social ethic; the church is a social ethic."[22] For him the task of the church is to be clear about its identity and faith convictions and to live in this world faithful to that identity:

> I am in fact challenging the very idea that Christian social ethics is primarily an attempt to make the world more peaceable or just. Put starkly, the first social ethical task of the church is to be the church—the servant community. Such a claim may well sound self-serving until we remember that what makes the church the church is its faithful manifestation of the peaceable kingdom in the world.[23]

Hauerwas's strong plea for a revaluation of the identity of the church has caused much misunderstanding amongst many of his readers. Many have accused him of sectarianism.[24] Hauerwas's approach, however, gains important support from scholars such as British theologian Nigel Biggar. In an article on the public relevance of Hauerwas's theology, Biggar argues that Hauerwas's emphasis on the identity and *telos* of the church not be understood as an attempt to withdraw from society.[25] Rather, says Biggar, Hauerwas accentuates the identity of the church so that the church can fulfill its public role more faithfully. To fulfill its role faithfully, the church should rethink what it means to be the church. It should rediscover its particular vocation. The church embarks on this task "not because it has ceased to care about the wider world, but precisely because it cares to discharge its own peculiar and vital service to it properly."[26] Through this emphasis, Biggar reckons, Hauerwas succeeds not only in confirming the church's identity, but also paving the way for the church to say something unique, unfamiliar, and original to society. Hauerwas's emphasis on the church's identity, then, is not for the sake of the church exclusively, but for the sake of the world. Only where the church discovers its true identity can it offer something peculiar and vital to the world.

South Africa's *liberation struggle* churches and *status quo* churches would do well to heed Hauerwas's emphasis on the *why* and *how* of church engagement. South African churches should involve themselves in society not simply to place themselves in the service of democracy and nation building, but to be faithful to the triune God. Formerly struggling churches so dearly want the new government, which consists mainly of former comrades in the struggle, to be successful. This desire leads easily to the trap of *Constantinianism*, by which is meant positioning churches in such a way toward government that they become coopted by the agenda of the government. Simultaneously, former status quo churches within South Africa may become copted out of their desire to show support of the new political and economic system for the sake of repenting for their involvement in apartheid, and for the sake of regaining credibility amongst fellow South Africans. Hauerwas's reminder about our unique motivation and contribution in the light of our identity as the church serves as an important guideline for how South African churches and theologians attempt to rationalize their faith.

Theology and the Churches

For various reasons churches have the potential for making a significant contribution to addressing the challenges in society, e.g., to the realizing of social and economic rights, but primarily because of the high percentage of people belonging to religions in South African society. The dawning of modernization in neither its institutionalized forms of a democratic state, a market-driven economy, an advanced civil society, and a sophisticated public media, nor in its *Zeitgeist* of individualism and rationalism has led to an overwhelming secularization of South African society. On the contrary, recent statistics indicate that more than ninety percent of South Africans belong to some form of religion. The percentage of religious practitioners specifically identifying themselves as Christians, currently estimated at about 80 percent of South Africans, has continued to increase in the last few years.[27]

Dirkie Smit suggests that churches operate institutionally out of various modes in interfacing with society, including worship related activities, local congregational activities and practices, denominations, and ecumenical bodies. Smit identifies two other modes related to the church more as an organism than as an institution, namely, individual Christians in their normal daily roles in family, work, neighborhood, etc., and individual Christians in their involvements with voluntary organizations.[28] How these modes could potentially translate into social impact is as follows: *worship services* have the potential to transform people into people committed to justice and the social and economic transformation of society; various *practices of congregations* (both related to spiritual formation and social services) may enhance the realization of a society of humaneness; *denominations and ecumenical bodies* may engage in a range of programmatic activities intended to show solidarity with the marginalized and the wronged; and *individual Christians in their normal daily roles and in voluntary organizations* may bring into these two contexts spiritual resources derived from their institutional church involvements that move these contexts in truly progressive directions.

We can return to Hauerwas's analysis once again to reinforce these points about the inherent public nature of normal church practices. To demonstrate the public nature of Hauerwas's approach it is important to cite some examples in his work where he demonstrates how practices that are essential elements of church identity impact on public life.[29] Hauerwas contends that when Christians "pray, baptize, eat meals, rejoice at the birth of a child, grieve at illness and death, re-roof church buildings, and so on," they strengthen the engagement of the church with society through such visible acts.[30] Elsewhere, Hauerwas and William Willimon add to this list of visible Christian acts, noting the strong public impact Christians have when they "are faithful to their promises, love their enemies, tell the truth, honor the poor, suffer for righteousness, and thereby testify to the amazing community-creating power of God."[31]

The sacraments of *baptism* and the *eucharist* also have public theological significance. According to Hauerwas, these sacraments are essential to Christian self-understanding and practice. They are not only motives or causes for our social work, they are our effective social work. In them we see most clearly the marks of God's kingdom in the world.[32] He cites an example of a congregation whose practice of the eucharist incorporated meal-sharing with impoverished residents of their neighborhood. In this instance, the eucharist enlarged the congregation's self-understanding to include a public dimension and served as a visible witness to the society. Says Hauerwas, the congregation perceived "that we were not simply another social agency that does a little good, but a people called out to witness to God's presence in the world. That presence which comes in the meal we share sustained that church's ability to be present in that neighborhood as a symbol that all was not lost."[33]

Hauerwas also writes about the public significance of *prayer*: "(P)rayer is the way we let God loose in the world. Prayer, therefore, though a common activity, is a dangerous one, for God's presence is not easily controlled. God is a wild presence calling us to ways of life we had not imagined possible."[34] In a debate about prayers in public schools he emphasizes the public nature of prayer explicitly: "For if Christians reclaim prayer as an end in itself rather than a way to confirm the 'Christian nature' of our society, we will perform our most important civic responsibility. As Origen argued, what more important public service can we render than to pray that the emperor recognizes his or her status as a creature of God? Such a prayer is no less significant in a society that believes 'the people' have in fact become the emperor."[35]

The practice of *preaching* also has public significance. It forms Christians into a people of witness. Preaching that challenge people with the story of Jesus and his kingdom helps them to hear and see in new ways. The preaching of the church shows hospitality to strangers by inviting them to share the story of Jesus. In this act of hospitality and in this engagement with strangers, we learn more fully to hear the story of God. "Without the constant challenge of the stranger—who often, interestingly enough, is but one side of ourselves—we are tempted to lose the power of Jesus' story because we have so conventionalized it."[36]

Hauerwas even indicates that the way Christians approach issues of *sexuality* impacts on public life. Christians bring children into the world because they believe, despite evidence to the contrary, that God has not abandoned this world. As such, children are a sign of our hope for the world. Marriage and family are central institutions that affirm that God is bringing his kingdom into this world through the providential ordering of history. The faithfulness and commitment to exclusive relations implied in marriage witnesses to God's pledge to his people, Israel and the church, that through his exclusive commitment, all people will be brought into God's kingdom.[37] Sexual behaviour, according to Hauerwas, is not private, but public. What we do with our bodies impacts the body of Christ, of which we are part through baptism, as well as society. With Willimon he states "God desires us and enlists our aid in reclaiming a lost creation. Salvation of the world turns on our obedience, on how we have sex and handle property and watch our words." Hauerwas and Willimon articulate the involvement of God in all spheres of life in a striking way: "Any God who won't tell you what to do with your pots and pans and genitals isn't worth worshipping."[38]

During the struggle against apartheid, so-called struggle churches held this understanding of the public nature of normal church practices. This was reflected in the various worship services held in local congregations. The national and provincial councils of churches and the management bodies of denominations provided liturgies for special services. Hymns, catechesis, pastoral care, theological education, and many other ecclesiastical practices acknowledged an inherent public nature and mandate. Days of prayer were regularly held for public causes, e.g., for the liberation of jailed political leaders such as Nelson Mandela, for exiled leaders such as Oliver Tambo, and for the unbanning of liberation movements such as the African National Congress. In 1986 South African churches even prayed for the fall of the apartheid regime.[39]

Attention to Hauerwas's approach might help South African churches in our young democracy to revalue this inherent public nature of normal church practices. Maybe this realization will pave the way for a restoration of a lively and constructive participation of churches in South African society.

His work, however, has important limitations. Hauerwas does not sufficiently offer constructive suggestions on how the public role of churches should be fulfilled when dialogue and cooperation with other religious and nonreligious traditions are required. Churches certainly bring a unique contribution to the public arena, but churches also need assistance with developing appropriate ways to communicate their message in a pluralistic society. Failure to develop these ways lends strength to criticisms of Christian sectarianism leveled at the kind of approach outlined here. U.S. theologian Lewis Mudge, for example, while appreciative of Hauerwas's approach, argues that civil coexistence by Christians with other religious traditions without substantive engagement between these various religious traditions may contribute to a cultural Christianization and churchification of the world—given Christian dominance in the western world and given Hauerwas's and other Christians' resistance to ideas of religious relativism.[40]

Hauerwas does not deal explicitly with the questions about the direct public involvement of churches. His agenda focuses predominantly on highlighting the identity and calling of the church and the consequent vital, unique and indispensable contribution that Christians are to make in society. In that endeavor, at least, he seems to be successful.

Conclusion

South African theologians realize that we live in a globalized world. We are very much aware of the higher levels of interconnectedness and interdependence of nations, and we, in fact, cherish this development. For us, it is an expression of greater ecumenicity, greater interaction, and greater fellowship among the inhabitants of the one great household of God on earth.

As people doing theology in the context of a very young democracy, we are open to learning from the experiences of our brothers and sisters who strive for faithfulness to God in the context of more established democracies. In our quest to discern the significance of faith in the triune God for public life, we have learned certain important lessons from our engagement and dialogue with theologians in the United States.

This engagement confirms our assumption that the faithfulness of any public theology is measured in terms of its attention to the agenda of the poor, the marginalized, and the destitute. Especially U.S. black theologians confirm this truth and even suggest creative ways of serving this truth in the context of the dominance of the global market economy. This emphasis is also the guiding principle for three other premises within public theological discourse—namely, engagement with questions posed by a modern/postmodern, pluralistic public sphere; the challenge of actualizing the potential that church practices hold for public life; and the need to prioritize the plight of the poor and suffering in society.

The fact that this article mainly focused on the contribution of U.S. scholars might create the impression that there is no reciprocity and mutuality in our engagement with each other. This is, however, not the case. U.S. theologians seriously attended to and learned from the theological discourses in South Africa during our struggle against apartheid. They also have strived to learn from the theological engagement during our transition to democracy, especially theology's role in the work of the Truth and Reconciliation Commission established in the mid-1990s to investigate the political crimes during apartheid and to foster reconciliation and reparation. We hope that our brothers and sisters in the United States might be enriched also by our future quests to strengthen democracy, to wipe out poverty, to overcome diseases like HIV/AIDS and tuberculosis, to enhance peace and reconciliation, and to address moral degeneration. We trust that this engagement with each other not only facilitates reciprocal learning, but also paves the way for existential participation in our respective contexts.

Conclusion

R. Drew Smith

The volume speaks to important cultural, ideological, organizational, and historical dimensions of contemporary U.S. Protestant involvements with Africa. What serves as a common subtext from chapter to chapter is the degree of emphasis American Protestants placed on social policy in their engagement with African affairs and contexts—with social policy understood both in terms of U.S. and local African policy frameworks. Although chapter contributors varied (as did the Protestant actors detailed in the chapters), in the extent to which they explicitly considered social policy, the American Protestants described in the volume generally approached complexities related to the broader political and social policy contexts of their Africa involvements in one of four ways.

First, some American Protestants acted out of presumed political neutrality. The idea that Christian institutions and individuals are able to operate within an historical context while they remain innocent of its politics has endured throughout much of Christian history. This idea also has dominated contemporary American Evangelicalism and Pentecostalism and their involvement in Africa. One example covered within the volume was the aloofness American Evangelical and Pentecostal missionaries maintained from the struggle against apartheid and the oppressions heaped upon the

South African population. Another example was Evangelical and Pentecostal ideological complicity with massive economic and social inequalities in countries such as Nigeria, Liberia, Zaire, and Zambia. To the extent that these Protestant actors attempted to ignore rather than challenge the social framework within these contexts, they acquiesced to and, in some respects, enabled the problematic social arrangements and configurations prevailing within these African contexts.

Secondly, there were those who entered into conscious alignment and alliance with certain of these problematic social frameworks. Siding with power and privilege is by no means unique to the subset of Protestants this volume cast in that light—in fact, this association generally has been more the rule than the exception for church alignments. Still, one is left wondering why mid-twentieth century American Protestants—in the face of a swirl of early twentieth century "social gospel" critiques of social inequality—remained so prone to concessions toward white colonial rule in Africa through the 1950s (as described in the chapters by Hulsether, and Sarkela and Mazzeo). A partial explanation (though an unsatisfactory justification) has claimed that theological cautions emerging in the post-World War II context about political tyranny contributed to these concessions, which combined readily with a larger American Protestant suspicion of communism and a susceptibility to arguments about colonialism and white minority rule as antidotes to communist expansion (see Hulsether, especially p. 29)

American Protestants were not always able to transcend the Cold War logic defining the involvement of the United States with Africa during the mid- to late twentieth century; but mainline Protestants, at least, grew increasingly more sensitized from the 1960s through the1980s (likely as a result of the Civil Rights and Black Power movements in the United States) to the highly problematic nature of protracted white minority rule in southern Africa—which endured long after most of the Africa continent (and most of the rest of the world) had been decolonized. Nevertheless, the moral potency of black freedom struggles (as embodied in the successful decolonization movements across Africa from the 1950s to the 1970s, and in the American Civil Rights Movement and Black Power Movement in the 1950s and 1960s), still proved insufficient in convincing many American Evangelicals to emphasize black freedom rather than anticommunism as the basis for engagement with Africa. As chapters in this volume point out, certain American Evangelicals made what should have appeared as morally unconscionable and historically out-of-step concessions to racist regimes in southern Africa during the 1970s and 1980s (Smith, "Racial Politics") and to African dictators in contexts such as Zaire and Liberia during the 1990s (Smith, "Church-State Dilemmas"). Equally troubling is that even after the collapse of white minority rule throughout southern Africa and the fall of the dictators with whom American Evangelicals were allied in Zaire and Liberia, the Evangelical leaders who took up these mistaken causes still seem unrepentant about their choices. This lack of repentance raises concerns about the possibilities for similarly unfortunate political alignments by American churches in the future.

Thirdly, there were those who engaged in *direct* resistance to structures, policies, and ideologies that contributed to African oppression. Throughout at least the last two centuries within the United States, a strong activist cadre of American churchpersons has remained committed to social justice activism—including abolitionists during the 1800s, and activists promoting civil rights, human rights, women's rights, antipoverty concerns, and antiwar concerns during the 1900s. These activists have employed direct action protest, lobbying, electoral activism, and promotion of justice issues via sermons, speeches, popular media, and scholarship. American Protestants discussed in chapters within this volume employed each of these means on behalf of social justice in Africa—beginning with chapters recounting attempts in the 1950s to reform U.S. foreign policy toward Africa ("Introduction," Hulsether, Sarkela, and Mazzeo) and then continuing with chapters outlining anti-apartheid activism and efforts from the 1960s through the 1990s to shift theological and intellectual paradigms about the relationship between religion and justice and religion and race (Baldwin, Hopkins).

That no chapter in the volume deals with American Protestant activism related to social justice causes in Africa during the last ten years partly reflects the paucity of this activism. Few American churches made demands in the last ten years or so for justice or social transformation in the wake of genocidal conflicts in Rwanda, Sudan, Democratic Republic of Congo, Liberia, and Sierra Leone; U.S. church mobilization seldom targeted U.S. foreign policy responses to these situations (except with respect to Sudan, where the issue was couched mainly in terms of the need to prevent the persecution of Christians in southern Sudan). Few American Protestant efforts have attempted to engage the U.S. government, other western governments, or African governments on policies and practices contributing to increased African poverty or the growing AIDS pandemic across Africa. American Protestant scholars have made few efforts to build the kind of trans-Atlantic scholarly dialogue on black poverty and dwindling life expectancy that occurred during the 1960s through 1980s on matters related to racism. Certainly, engagement between American Protestants and Africa that takes the form of direct resistance to social injustice is desperately needed in the face of Africa's twenty-first century urgencies.[1]

Fourthly, a category capturing a great deal of American Protestant involvement with Africa is that of humanitarian and developmental assistance. In one sense, this involvement is a form of indirect resistance to social injustices and social misery within Africa—that is, it attempts to counter the effects without directly challenging the causes of social injustice and misery within the situation. U.S. churches have a long history of this largely social service approach (to persons in need within the United States and abroad). It is important to note that attention to faith-based social service delivery has dramatically increased in the last decade within policy-making circles, within the ranks of American Evangelicals, and as a function of collaborations between these two sectors. With American Evangelicals experiencing significant numerical growth, increased financial and institutional resources, and an expanding public interest and profile, they have provided momentum to a paradigmatic shift within the U.S. away from conceptualizing *social concern* in terms of justice and rights, defining it instead more along the lines of *private assistance*. ("Private" here alludes to both a more individuated approach and a greater emphasis on *economic* rather than *political* services and outcomes.)

American Evangelicals—and quite a few mainline Protestants as well—have carried this emphasis into their Africa involvements, as this volume's discussions of Pentecostal and Evangelical entrepreneurialism in Nigeria, South Africa, Zaire and Liberia make clear (Ojo, Smith). Contributors to the volume also pointed out additional forms this "development" emphasis by American Protestants has taken within Africa, including the educational activities of Mennonites in Angola (Pedro) and Quakers in Kenya (Angell), and even "church-planting" in many African contexts, (which takes into account the many social development by-products of church organizations, including leadership skill development and building facilities that can be put to multiple social development uses). One would hope, however, that entrepreneurial-oriented American Protestants will not completely lose sight of the need to respond to social problems and needs in general and systemically, given the large-scale, structural nature of social problems and needs in Africa. One outcome of the increased integration of Evangelical and Pentecostal Christians into public affairs perhaps encourages them to provide a fuller hearing to other perspectives about the required calculus between social need and social response

Nonetheless, despite the many failures and shortcomings in American Protestant involvements with Africa detailed within this volume, two things should not be missed. First, most of these involvements have been well intentioned and, more often than not, quite likely had mutually beneficial effects. Secondly, the various American Protestants discussed here were part of what has been historically a microscopically small number of American church persons who have made efforts to connect themselves to Africa, to African peoples, and to African affairs. In that respect, these American Protestants have been bridge builders between the U.S. and Africa, facilitating many levels of interaction that have contributed to the increasingly global nature of Christian ecclesiastical and social life (see especially Haney and Koopman on the latter point). In these global interactions, much has been learned but much more is still to be learned about how to build relationships premised on mutual respect and good will. Hopefully, the chapters in this volume provide further motivation in that direction.

Notes

Introduction

1 Stephen Neil, *A History of Christian Missions* (Middlesex, England: Penguin Books, 1964), 572.

2 Philip Jenkins, *The Next Christendom: The Coming of Global Christianity* (Oxford: Oxford University Press, 2003), 89–91.

3 One of the measures of Africa's increasing ecclesiastical importance is the number of Africans heading strategic global ecclesiastical bodies, including Sam Kobia from Kenya, the General Secretary of the World Council of Churches; Setri Nyomi from Ghana, the General Secretary of the World Alliance of Reformed Churches; Ishmael Noko from Angola, the General Secretary of the Lutheran World Federation; Musimbi Kanyoro from Kenya, the General Secretary of the World YWCA; and Ndaba Mazabane from South Africa, Chairman of the International Council of the World Evangelical Alliance.

4 Titus Presler, *Horizons of Mission* (Cambridge, Mass.: Cowley Publications, 2001), 91, 105.

5 Gerald H. Anderson, "A Moratorium on Missionaries?" *Christian Century*, January 16, 1974, 43–45.

6 Dana Robert, "Shifting Southward: Global Christianity Since 1945," *International Bulletin of Missionary Research* 24, no. 2 (2000): 50–58.

7 Elizabeth Isichei, *A History of Christianity in Africa* (Grand Rapids: Eerdmans, 1995), 325.

8 Timothy Yates, *Christian Mission in the Twentieth Century* (Cambridge: Cambridge University Press, 1994), 199; Anderson, "Moratorium," 43–45.

9 Isichei, *History of Christianity*, 326–27; Anderson, "Moratorium," 43–45.

10 All of the Pentecostal and Charismatic denominations listed under Barrett's Protestant and Independent categories were added together to reach these totals. It is important to note that the totals will not include Pentecostal and Charismatic practitioners affiliated with mainline denominations, i.e. Catholics, Methodists, Anglicans, etc. with Pentecostal and charismatic orientations. See David B. Barrett, George Kurian, and Todd Johnson, *World Christian Encyclopedia* (Oxford; Oxford University Press, 2001), 16–18.

11 With respect to the 1970s totals, more than 104,000,000 of the 147,000,000 were in Africa (70%). With respect to the 1995 totals, more than 379,000,000 of the 605,000,000 were in Africa (63%).

12 Harvey Cox, *Fire From Heaven: The Rise of Pentecostal Spirituality and the Reshaping of Religion in the Twenty-First Century* (Reading, Mass.: Addison-Wesley, 1995); M. P. Fisher, *Religion in the Twenty-First Century* (Upper Saddle River, NJ: Prentice Hall, 1999), 63–64.

13 Cox, *Fire From Heaven*, 63–64.

14 Steve Brouwer, Paul Gifford, and Susan D. Rose, *Exporting the American Gospel: Global Christian Fundamentalism* (New York: Routledge, 1996), 7.

15 Barrett, Kurian, and Johnson, *World Christian Encyclopedia*, 687, 689.

16 Professor Jesse Mugambi characterizes the phenomenon as an "invasion of Africa's living rooms and villages by the mass media from the affluent nations of Europe and North America." (Jesse N. K. Mugambi, "A Fresh Look at Evangelism in Africa," *International Review of Missions* 87 [1998]: 342). The subtext of Mugambi's comment and of most recent assessments of the impact of church mission outreach is that an increasingly unwelcome transmission of political (and cultural) values has accompanied European and American church involvements in Africa. Mugambi's critique also invokes concerns voiced by others about the problematic nature, in general, of foreign missionary activities aimed at converting and proselytizing persons in what have historically been the "receiving" countries (see Yates; and Abdullahi An-Naim, "Competing Claims to Religious Freedom and Communal Self-Determination in Africa," in *Proselytization and Communal Self-Determination in Africa*, ed. Abdullahi An-Naim [Maryknoll, NY: Orbis, 1999], 2–14). Not all scholars, however, are inclined to view mission relationships between the United States and Africa as having moved along this singular trajectory. For example, noted missiologist Lamin Sanneh points out that while western missionaries were complicit at many points with western efforts to undermine African self-determination, western missionaries also contributed in certain ways to the revitalization of African cultures through, among other ways, African cultural resistance to western cultural imposition as well as through missionary fortifications of African cultural forms as vehicles for transmitting the gospel (Lamin Sanneh, "The Yogi and the Commissar: Christian Missions and African Response," *International Bulletin of Missionary Research* [January 1991]: 2–11). Moreover, scholars have noted the new reality that no matter how the question of the cultural impact of western missions in Africa is settled, mission relations between Africa and the United States can no longer be understood through the paradigm of the United States (or other western nations) as *senders* and Africa as *receivers*. A two-way influence on American and African ecclesiastical life has resulted from American Protestant outreach to and in Africa—

including an Africanizing effect upon American Protestants within Africa and the United States and a growing reverse missionary outreach by African churches within the United States (Cox; and Philip Jenkins, *The Next Christendom: The Coming Global Christianity*. [New York: Oxford University Press, 2002]).

17 Important country studies of this phenomenon in Africa include Paul Gifford, *Ghana's New Christianity: Pentecostalism in a Globalizing African Economy* (Bloomington: Indiana University Press, 2004); Gifford, *The New Crusaders: Christianity and the New Right in Southern Africa* (LPC Group, 1991); and Brouwer, Gifford, and Rose, *Exporting the American Gospel*, 7.

18 Peter Schraeder, *United States Foreign Policy Toward Africa: Incrementalism, Crisis and Change* (Cambridge: Cambridge University Press, 1994); Herschelle Challenor, "The Influence of Black Americans on U.S. Foreign Policy Toward Africa," in *Ethnicity and U.S. Foreign Policy*, ed. Abdul Aziz Said (New York: Praeger, 1981), 143–76; Thomas Borstelmann, *The Cold War and the Color Line: American Race Relations in the Global Arena* (Cambridge: Harvard University Press, 2001); and L. R. Melvern, *A People Betrayed: The Role of the West in Rwanda Genocide* (London: Zed Books, 2000).

19 Lamin Sanneh, *Abolitionsits Abroad: American Blacks and the Making of Modern West Africa* (Cambridge: Harvard University Press, 1999), 182–237; John Walter Cason, *The Growth of Christianity in the Liberian Environment* (Ann Arbor: University of Michigan Press, 1962); and Philip Foner, *History of Black Americans: From Africa to the Emergence of the Cotton Kingdoms* (Westport, Conn.: Greenwood Press, 1975).

20 Paul Gifford, *Christianity and Politics in Doe's Liberia* (Cambridge: Cambridge University Press, 1993), 12–13.

21 E. U. Essien Udom, *Black Nationalism: A Search for Identity in America* (Chicago: University of Chicago Press, 1962), 19–23.

22 Udom, *Black Nationalism*, 37.

23 Peter Duignan and L. H. Gann, *The United States and Africa: A History* (Cambridge: Cambridge University Press, 1984), 288.

Chapter 1

1 "The Crisis of Commitment," *Rockland Record*, December 1, 1966, photocopy from *Christianity and Crisis* archives, page number illegible. The records of *Christianity and Crisis* are now generally sorted into boxes with folders, notebooks, and other materials at Archives of the Burke Library, Union Theological Seminary, New York; however, I began my research before the records were in this form. If I know the current box and folder for a document, my notes cite these; if I do not know (as in this case), I cite a photocopy that I obtained at an earlier stage of my research, using the formula "photocopy from *C&C* archives." All citations in these footnotes referring to *C&C* are from *Christianity and Crisis*.

2 Editors, "Toward Disengagement from South Africa," *C&C*, November 28, 1966, 261–63.

3 "Crisis of Commitment," *Rockland Record*; "Crisis Continues," *Time*, February 25, 1966, photocopy from *C&C* archives, page number illegible.

4 On *C&C*'s place in the world of U.S. religious journalism, see Martin E. Marty, "The Religious Press," in *Encyclopedia of the American Religious Experience*, ed. Peter Williams and Charles H. Lippy (New York: Scribners, 1988), 1697–709.

5 Leon Howell, "Ernest Lefever at the Edge of Power," *C&C*, March 2, 1981, 44. The Senate Foreign Relations Committee rejected Lefever's nomination in June 1981. Instead, he became an advisor to Secretary of State Alexander Haig on international terrorism and continued as the director of the neoconservative Ethics and Public Policy Center.

6 Reinhold Niebuhr, "Report on Germany," *C&C*, October 14, 1946, 6–7; variations of this argument appeared in *Life*, *Time*, and *Reader's Digest*; see Richard Wightman Fox, *Reinhold Niebuhr: A Biography* (New York: Pantheon, 1985), 228–29.

7 "Crisis of Commitment," *Rockland Record*.

8 "Christian Realism," *Newsweek*, February 28, 1966, 61. FBI surveillance of groups that Bennett helped lead is documented in Mitchell Hall, *Because of Their Faith: CALCAV and Religious Opposition to the Vietnam War* (New York: Columbia University Press, 1990) and James Findlay, *Church People in the Struggle: the National Council of Churches and the Black Freedom Movement, 1950–1970* (New York: Oxford University Press, 1993).

9 Richard John Neuhaus, "Desperately Pastoral," *First Things* (August/September 1991), 61.

10 Gayraud Wilmore, "What Seeds, What Flowers?" *C&C*, April 12, 1993, 86–87.

11 Henry Pitney Van Dusen, "First Glimpse of South Africa," *C&C*, February 16, 1953, 10–13; Lefever, "Africa: Tribalism Versus the State," *C&C*, December 27, 1965, 281, 279–80.

12 Mark Hulsether, *Building a Protestant Left:* Christianity and Crisis Magazine, *1941–1993* (Knoxville: University of Tennessee Press, 1999).

13 Angus Dun, et al., "Christian Conscience and Weapons of Mass Destruction," *C&C*, December 11, 1950, 165; Niebuhr, "Sex Standards in America," *C&C*, May 24, 1948, 65–66; S. Macon Cowles, "Can we Abolish Jim Crow in the Armed Services?" *C&C*, October 18, 1948, 134; Niebuhr, "The Moral and Political Judgments of Christians," *C&C*, July 6, 1959, 99.

14 Wayne Cowan and Vivian Lindermayer, "An Anniversary Statement," *C&C*, November 15, 1976, 258–61; John C. Bennett, "After Thirty Years," *C&C*, March 22, 1971, 38–40.

15 Some people use *social gospel* as a general term for liberal or modernist Protestantism at this time, but we will reserve it for the socially activist wing of liberal Protestantism. We can, thus, distinguish between social gospelers and liberal clergy who were less politicized, more individualistic, and more complacent about business, and/or quicker to offer justifications for social Darwinism.

16 Luce's widely reprinted essay is included in William Appleman Williams, et al., *America in Vietnam: A Documentary History* (New York: Anchor, 1985), 22–28.

17 Editorial, "The Crisis," *C&C*, February 10, 1941, 3; Niebuhr, "Imperialism and Irresponsibility," *C&C*, February 24, 1941, 6; Niebuhr, "Anglo-American Destiny and Responsibility," *C&C*, October 4, 1943, 2–4; reprinted in Conrad Cherry, ed. *God's New Israel: Religious Interpretations of American Destiny* (Englewood Cliffs, NJ: Prentice-Hall, 1971), 303, 304.

18 Niebuhr, "Imperialism and Irresponsibility," 6.

19 See Thomas J. McCormick, *America's Half-Century: United States Foreign Policy in the Cold War* (Baltimore: Johns Hopkins University Press, 1989), 78–79.

20 F. Ernest Johnson, "Our Date With Destiny," *C&C*, April 14, 1947, 1–2.

21 Walter LaFeber's influential *America, Russia, and the Cold War*, 2nd ed. (New York: Wiley, 1972) uses Niebuhr as its representative cold war liberal, presenting him moving (in Paul Merkley's words) in "lock-step conformity with official Cold War policy." For Merkley's commentary see his *Reinhold Niebuhr: A Political Account* (Montreal: McGill-Queens University Press, 1975), 207–8.

22 Cited in Bruce Cumings, ed., *Child of Conflict: The Korean-American Relationship, 1943–53* (Seattle: University of Washington Press, 1983), 49.

23 Liston Pope, "The Shift in American Policy," *C&C*, July 24, 1950, 98.

24 On *C&C*'s theological debates, see Hulsether, *Building a Protestant Left*, 11–19, 100–113, 181–184, and 195–201.

25 For example, Bennett, "'The Responsible Society' at Evanston," *C&C*, July 12, 1954, 90–92; M. Searle Bates, "World Council as Seen at Evanston," *C&C*, September 20, 1954, 115–18; Henry Pitney Van Dusen, "The Unity of Christendom," *C&C*, February 4, 1952, 2, 8.

26 Niebuhr, "Democracy, Secularism, and Christianity," *C&C*, March 2, 1953, 24.

27 Will Herberg, "Faith and Politics: Some Reflections on Whittaker Chamber's Witness," *C&C*, September 29, 1952, 124; Niebuhr, "False Defense of Christianity," *C&C*, June 12, 1950, 73.

28 Fox, *Reinhold Niebuhr*, 233–234, 201, 229.

29 F. E. Johnson, "Our Date With Destiny," 1–2.

30 Niebuhr, "Should We Be Consistent?" *C&C*, February 6, 1950, 1–2.

31 Bennett, "The Problem of Asiatic Communism," *C&C*, August 7, 1950, 109, 110.

32 Bennett, "Problem of Asiatic Communism," 111. Arguing on similar lines in "Positive Policy for Asia," *C&C*, November 14, 1949, 145–46, Van Dusen spoke of a broad-based Asian "revolution" in which "the deep motivation of the masses is . . . nationalist, [with] aspirations parallel[ing] those of our own Republic in the days of its birth."

33 Z. K. Matthews, "Crisis in South America" [sic., corrected to "South Africa" in the *C&C*, November 24, 1952 installment], *C&C*, November 10, 1952, 146–49 and November 24, 1952, 154–59. Liston Pope, "Communist Threat in South Africa," August 9, 1954, 105–6 worries that the more radical Congress of the Peopleare outflanking ANC moderates. *C&C* also followed the Algerian Revolution, trying to imagine a compromise that could satisfy both the French and the Algerians; see Kenneth Thompson, "Impressions of North Africa," October 27, 1958, 145–46 and Thompson, "Alternatives for Algeria," *C&C*, October 19, 1959, 146–47.

34 Melani McAlister, *Epic Encounters: Culture, Media, and U.S. Interests in the Middle East, 1945–2000* (Berkeley: University of California Press, 2001).

35 Niebuhr, "New Nations: Seeds, Buds, and Flowers," *C&C*, March 30, 1959, 34–35; Pope, "Communist Threat in South Africa," 106; Anonymous Missionary, "Crisis of Democracy in Latin America," *C&C*, May 14, 1951, 59, 60.

36 Niebuhr, "Our Latin Policy," *C&C*, April 2, 1961, 42–43; Niebuhr, "Laos and Cuba: Problems for Review," *C&C*, January 23, 1961, 209–10; Lefever, "Africa: Tribalism Versus the State," *C&C*, December 27, 1965, 279–80.

37 Niebuhr, "Moral and Political Judgments of Christians," *C&C*, July 6, 1959, 101; Niebuhr, "Editorial Notes," *C&C*, May 2, 1955, 51. See also J. G. Mees, "Dutch Church's Stand on Indonesia," *C&C*, May 2, 1949, 51–53.

On U.S. policy in the Philippines and Indonesia as imperialist, see Gabriel Kolko, *Confronting the Third World* (New York: Pantheon, 1988).

38 Board of Sponsors, "Program of Christianity and Crisis," *C&C*, February 16, 1948, 11–13; Will Scarlett, "Point Four," *C&C*, March 22, 1954, 25; WCC Division of Studies, "Common Christian Responsibility Toward Areas of Rapid Social Change," *C&C*, September 19, 1955, 115–17; Robert Good, "The Danger of Disillusionment with Africa," *C&C*, March 20, 1961, 33, 34.

39 Roy Blough, "Toward an International Economic Policy," *C&C*, April 29, 1963, 78.

40 Editorial Note," *C&C*, April 3, 1944, 2; Eugene Barnett, "Beirut, Palestine, and the Middle East," *C&C*, May 14, 1951, 114–17; Herman Reissig, "Another Look at the Arab-Israeli Problem," *C&C*, April 16, 1956, 44–46; Alan Geyer, "Christians and 'The Peace of Jerusalem,'" *C&C*, July 10, 1967, 160–64.

41 Van Dusen, "A First Glimpse of South Africa," *C&C*, February 16, 1953, 12. Niebuhr and Bennett probably disagreed with parts of Van Dusen's article and published it because he was president of Union Seminary; however, they did not dissociate themselves with it as they sometimes did with articles to which they objected strenuously.

42 David W. Noble, *The End of American History: Democracy, Capitalism, and the Metaphor of Two Worlds in Anglo-American Historical Writing, 1890–1980* (Minneapolis: University of Minnesota, 1985), 144.

43 In truth, conversations in the international ecumenical movement had informed many of *C&C*'s most forceful critiques of U.S. policy ever since the 1940s. These conversations were especially significant in the late 1940s, when *C&C* held out some hope for a neutralist alternative to the emerging Cold War. Later doubts about a North/South Cold War mentality built on these precedents. See, e.g., Bennett, "Some Impressions from Geneva," *C&C*, October 14, 1946, 5; Heinz-Horst Schrey, "German Church Between Russia and America," *C&C*, August 2, 1948, 108; Joseph Hromadka, "Voice From the Other Side," *C&C*, March 19, 1951, 27–29; and "Karl Barth's Letter on German Remilitarization," *C&C*, February 17, 1951; repr. in *Witness to a Generation: Significant Writings from Christianity and Crisis, 1941–1966*, ed. Wayne Cowan (Indianapolis: Bobbs-Merrill, 1966), 251–52.

44 Eugene Carson Blake, "The Church in the Next Decade," *C&C*, February 21, 1966, 17.

45 *C&C*'s strongest "pro-peace" position in a 1961 debate about nuclear weapons repudiated pacifism and explicitly (albeit grudgingly) endorsed Kennedy's policies. See Bennett, "Nuclear Dilemma," *C&C*, November 11, 1961, 200–203.

46 In an interview on November 18, 1989, Bennett recalled this debate as a key turning point in *C&C*'s history. See also Ronald H. Stone, *Reinhold Niebuhr: Prophet to Politicians* (Nashville, Abingdon, 1972), 180–91.

47 Editors' introduction to "Europe's Crisis and America's Dilemma," *C&C*, January 7, 1957, 181.

48 Kenneth Thompson, "Europe's Crisis and America's Dilemma," *C&C*, January 7, 1957, 182, 184–86.

49 Niebuhr, "Situation in the Mid-East," *C&C*, April 15, 1957, 42–43; Niebuhr, "The New International Situation," *C&C*, November 12, 1956, 151; Niebuhr, "Comments on 'Europe's Crisis and America's Dilemma,'" *C&C*, January 7, 1957, 186.

50 V. E. Devadutt, "Correspondence," *C&C*, June 10, 1957, 79–80; Bennett, "Comments on 'Europe's Crisis and America's Dilemma,'" *C&C*, January 7, 1957, 187, 188; Bennett, "Developments in the Middle East," *C&C*, March 18, 1957, 26.

51 Paul Scherer, "The Near East Kaleidoscope," *C&C*, September 21, 1953, 114–19.

52 Herbert Butterfield, "Western Policy and Colonialism," *C&C*, August 4, 1958, 112, 113; Butterfield, "Internationalism and the Defense of the Existing Status Quo," *C&C*, June 10, 1957, 76. *C&C*'s board later quoted Butterfield in a widely read statement, "We Protest the National Policy in Vietnam," *C&C*, March 7, 1966, 33–34.

53 George Shepherd, "The Challenge of Colonialism and Racialism," *C&C*, February 6, 1956, 3–6.

54 Niebuhr, "The Changing United Nations," *C&C*, October 3, 1960, 133–34; Thompson, "The Monroe Doctrine, 1823–1960," *C&C*, August 8, 1960, 118–19.

55 Elisha Greifer, "Needed: A Theory of Revolution," *C&C*, April 3, 1961, 49, citing Louis Hartz, *The Liberal Tradition in America* (New York: Harcourt Brace Jovanovich, 1955). Greifer noted that slavery was a "grand exception" to his argument about U.S. liberalism; however, he argued that this exception "ought to be explained away." He attempted to do so using Stanley Elkins's *Slavery: A Problem in American Institutional and Intellectual Life* (Chicago: University of Chicago Press, 1959), 50, which argued that African culture had been destroyed in the United States and replaced by a "Sambo" personality. According to Greifer, African Americans had either been absorbed into the mainstream and become liberals, or else they were so marginal that they were "not part of the society at all."

56 Greifer, "Needed: A Theory of Revolution," 51–52, citing Rostow, *The Stages of Economic Growth, a Non-Communist Manifesto* (Cambridge: Cambridge University Press, 1960).

57 Greifer, "Needed: A Theory of Revolution," 51.

58 In the Reagan era, conservatives justified their support for dictators like the Philippines' Ferdinand Marcos with a retooled version of this theory, sometimes invoking Niebuhr's authority. See Jeanne Kirkpatrick, "Dictatorships and Double Standards," *Commentary* 68 (1979): 34–45.

59 Lefever, "Africa: Tribalism Versus the State," *C&C*, December 27, 1965, 278.

60 Niebuhr, "Can Democracy Work?" *New Leader,* May 28, 1962, 9, cited in Stone, *Reinhold Niebuhr*, 193. On the Roosevelt quotation and Trujillo, see LaFeber, *America, Russia, and the Cold War*, 255. Niebuhr criticized the U.S. invasion of the Dominican Republic in "Caribbean Blunder," *C&C*, May 31, 1965, 113–14; he proposed U.S. policy toward Puerto Rico as a better model.

61 Bennett, "Senator Fulbright Speaks Out," *C&C*, April 13, 1964, 57–58. See also Bennett, "Cuba and the Monroe Doctrine," *C&C*, October 15, 1962, 173–74 and Wayne Cowan, "Premier Castro and Cuba," *C&C*, May 11, 1959, 62–63. The latter article appeared before Castro was driven into an alliance with the USSR; it portrayed Castro as a moderate and argued that U.S. policy should be "adapted to the realities" of Cuba.

62 WCC Division of Studies, "Common Christian Responsibility Toward Areas of Rapid Social Change," *C&C*, September 19, 1955, 116.

63 McLeod Bryan, "Whither African Nationalism?" *C&C*, May 2, 1960, 60, 59.

64 Bryan, "Whither African Nationalism?" 60, 61.

65 Anonymous African Christian, "Further Comment on Africa and the Church," *C&C*, June 27, 1960, 95.

66 Bola Ige, "Africa of the Sixties," *C&C*, March 20, 1961, 35–37.

67 Robert Good, "The Danger of Disillusionment with Africa," *C&C*, March 20, 1961, 30–34; Thompson, "Political Development in East Africa," *C&C*, March 20, 1961., 34–36; George Houser, "Our Faltering UN Strategy on Africa," *C&C*, March 20, 1961, 38–41; Arthur Moore, "The Sharpville Story," *C&C*, March 20, 1961, 42–43. For a perspective on Africa from Niebuhr at this time, see "The Church and the South African Tragedy," *C&C*, May 2, 1960, 53–54; it compares South Africa's regime to both slavery and Nazism and calls the WCC to expel the Dutch Reformed Church of South Africa from the WCC.

68 Bennett, "Epilogue: Issues for the Ecumenical Dialogue," in *Christian Social Ethics in a Changing World* (New York: Association, 1966), 379–80. See also Bennett, "The Geneva Conference 1966," *C&C*, July 11, 1966, 153–54 and Carl-Henric Grenholm, *Christian Ethics in a Revolutionary Age: An Analysis of the Social Ethics of John C. Bennett, Heinz-Dietrich Wendland and Richard Shaull* (Uppsala: Verbum, 1973).

69 Wayne Cowan, "Church and Society at Geneva," *C&C*, September 19, 1966, 202, 203. M. M. Thomas was a *C&C* contributing editor from 1958 to 1972. In his "Asian Security and Development," *C&C*, May 3, 1965, 98–99, he called for a Southeast Asian Marshall plan—that must be linked to "some pattern of socialism" since it will otherwise "take a neocolonial form," which would drive Asian nationalists into an alliance with communism.

70 For example, see Bennett, "A Critique of Paul Ramsey," *C&C*, October 30, 1967, 247–50; Ramsey, "Paul Ramsey Replies," *C&C*, November 27, 1967, 281; and Roger Shinn, "Paul Ramsey's Challenge to Ecumenical Ethics," *C&C*, October 30, 1967, 246. See also Garry Dorrien, *Soul in Society: the Making and Remaking of Social Christianity* (Minneapolis: Fortress, 1995), 173–78 and Jeffrey Hadden, *The Gathering Storm in the Churches* (New York: Doubleday, 1969).

71 Paul Devanandan, "Foreign Aid and the Social and Cultural Life of India," *C&C*, August 5, 1957, 108, 111.

72 Editorial note, *C&C*, February 7, 1792, 2.

73 Mary Dudziak, "Josephine Baker, Racial Protest, and the Cold War," *Journal of American History* 81 (1994): 544.

74 Dudziak, "Josephine Baker," 567. For *C&C*'s approach, see Frank Graham, "The Need for Wisdom: Two Suggestions for Carrying Out the Supreme Court's Decision Against Segregation," *C&C*, April 30, 1955, 66–72.

75 Andrew Young, "Thirtieth Anniversary Speech," *C&C*, May 3, 1971, 80–82; see also Adam Fairclough, "Martin Luther King, Jr., and the War in Vietnam," in *The African American Voice in U.S. Foreign Policy Since World War II, ed. Michael Krenn* (New York: Garland, 1998), 255–77.

76 For more on *C&C* and Vietnam, see Hulsether, *Building a Protestant Left*, 125–34. Almost all *C&C* writers were relatively moderate compared to the top leaders of the student antiwar movement.

77 Harvey Cox, "Gustavo's Grandchildren," *C&C*, June 12, 1989, 194–96 discusses allies in several countries. Articles on the Philippines include Paul Sherry, "Filipino Rewrites," *C&C*, June 12, 1989, 150–51; Gareth Porter, "Philippine Catholics: Hierarchy and Radicals," *C&C*, June 16, 1986,

203–6; John Dear, "Silencing an Aquino Critic," *C&C*, September 10, 1990, 264–65.

78 A good example of *C&C*'s writing on Latin America is its May 12, 1980, special issue on "Central America: A Season of Martyrs" with articles by Oscar Romero, Jorge Lara-Braud, William Wipfler, and others. For a more detailed discussion, see Hulsether, *Building a Protestant Left*, 140–44, 195–201. Christian Smith's *Resisting Reagan: The U.S. Central America Peace Movement* (Chicago: University of Chicago Press, 1996), 167–68, 110–15, treats the activist networks in which *C&C* participated.

79 Wayne Cowan, "South Africa and the Banks: a Progress Report," *C&C*, January 23, 1967, 321; Dorothee Sölle, "Faith, Theology, and Liberation," *C&C*, July 7, 1976, 139; Jim Cason and Mike Fleshman, "Profit Without Honor: Divesting from Apartheid," *C&C*, June 16, 1986, 212–17.

80 Beyers Naudé, "The Challenge of Political and Social Justice," *C&C*, January 20, 1975, 323–25; Charles Villa-Vicencio, "The Theology of Apartheid," *C&C*, March 13, 1978, 45-49; Allan Boesak, "To the Minister of Justice, Pretoria: We Cannot Obey God and You," *C&C*, November 26, 1979, 298; Desmond Tutu, "South Africa's Blacks: Aliens in Their Own Land," *C&C*, November 26, 1984, 440–44; Vernon Rose, "*Kairos* in South Africa," *C&C*, June 16, 1986, 208–9.

81 Leon Howell, "The Ecumenical Movement on Trial," *C&C*, March 6, 1967, 39–42; Albert Van Den Heuvel "A Letter to a White South African Friend," *C&C*, December 28, 1970, 284–286. For additional background, see Ernest Lefever, *Amsterdam to Nairobi: The World Council of Churches and the Third World* (Washington, DC: Ethics & Public Policy Center, 1979) and Paul Bock, *In Search of a Responsible World Society: The Social Teaching of the World Council of Churches* (Philadelphia: Westminster, 1974).

82 Alistair Kee, "Incident in Rhodesia," *C&C*, September 19, 1966, 203–5; Gail Hovey, "Soweto: Keeping Faith with the Children," *C&C*, June 16, 1986, 195–96; James Cason and Michael Fleshman, "Tensions Are Rising, Anger is Deepening: Allan Boesak on South Africa," *C&C*, November 26, 1984, 444–46; Jan Zita Grover, "Global AIDS: the Epidemic(s)," *C&C*, June 12, 1989, 197–99

83 Terry Swicegood, "Funeral at Cradock," *C&C*, September 16, 1985, 342–43.

84 Paul Abrecht, "The Revolution Implicit in Development," *C&C*, June 23, 1969, 178.

85 See Ronald Chilcote, ed., *Dependency and Marxism: Toward a Resolution of the Debate* (Boulder: Westview Press, 1982); Ronald Chilcote and Joel Edelstein, eds., *Latin America: The Struggle with Dependency and Beyond* (New York: Wiley, 1974), and McCormick, *America's Half-Century*. See also Walter Rodney, *How Europe Underdeveloped Africa* (Washington, DC: Howard University Press, 1982) and Harry Magdoff, *Imperialism from the Colonial Age to the Present* (New York: Monthly Review, 1978).

86 For *C&C*'s application to the politics of international debt, see Walden Bello and Claudio Saunt, "International Debt Crisis, Year Five," *C&C*, November 23, 1987, 403–10. For an analysis of international finance and the politics of international debt, see David Harvey, *The New Imperialism* (New York: Oxford University Press, 2005).

87 Without denying dependency, it remained true that markets had virtues in allocating resources, that supply and demand theory has important analytical uses, and that socialist economies sometimes have good reasons to seek access to international capital and trade. Useful discussions of these issues

include Dorrien, *Soul in Society*; Charles Lindblom, *Politics and Markets: the World's Political Economic Systems* (New York: Basic Books, 1977); and Carl Parrini, "Theories of Imperialism," in *Redefining the Past: Essays in Diplomatic History in Honor of William Appleman Williams*, ed. Lloyd Gardner (Corvallis: Oregon State University Press, 1986), 65–84. Arthur McGovern, *Liberation Theology and Its Critics* (Maryknoll, NY: Orbis, 1989), 156–76, assesses criticisms of dependency theory by Michael Novak and Paul Sigmund.

88 Alan Paton, "Africa, Christianity, and the West" (December 26, 1960), in Cowan, *Witness to a Generation*, 123.

89 Edward Norman, "A Politicized Christ," *C&C*, February 19, 1979, 18–25; Soelle, "Continuing the Discussion: 'A Politicized Christ,'" *C&C*, March 19, 1979, 50–52.

90 Soelle, "Faith, Theology, and Liberation," *C&C*, July 7, 1976, 138; Soelle, "Mysticism, Liberation, and the Names of God," *C&C*, June 22, 1981, 183.

91 Dom Helder Camara, "The Force of Right or the Right of Force?" *C&C*, August 5, 1974, 176.

92 Sharon Welch, A Feminist Ethic of Risk (Minneapolis: Fortress, 1990), 103–23.

93 William McGuire King, "The Reform Establishment and the Ambiguities of Influence" in *Between the Times: the Travail of the Protestant Establishment in America, 1900–1960*, ed. William Hutchison (New York: Cambridge University Press, 1989), 168–92.

94 Bennett, "Retrospect and Prospect," *C&C*, December 27, 1976, 312–13. To relate Niebuhrians to a larger group of cultural critics cited on the left today, see Hulsether, *Building a Protestant Left;* and Cornel West, *The American Evasion of Philosophy: A Genealogy of Pragmatism* (Madison: University of Wisconsin Press, 1989).

Chapter 2

1 State Department declarations such as, "Assist newly formed democracies in implementing democratic principles; Assist democracy advocates around the world to establish vibrant democracies in their own countries; and Identify and denounce regimes that deny their citizens the right to choose their leaders in elections that are free, fair, and transparent," would easily find support in Robinson's work. http://www.state.gov/g/drl/democ/ (accessed 3/1/2005).

2 Two exceptional individuals who have inspired renewed interest in the voice and achievements of James Robinson deserve special mention here. Ms. Laverne Brown, long-time administrative assistant to Dr. Robinson, who began her work in a windowless office in the Church of Master and who continued after his death as office manager for Operation Crossroads Africa, has begun to organize files and interviews for interested colleagues. Edward Dees, M.D., a former Crossroads group leader, wrote "Dr. James H. Robinson: The Impact of Personal Initiative upon International Affairs" (M.A. thesis, Tulane University, 2002). Along with a small group of New Orleans-based Crossroad's alumni, Dees has worked to create the James H. Robinson Foundation, dedicated to promoting the life work and achievements of Dr. Robinson and Operation Crossroads Africa. In addition, the web-based "Africana: Gateway to the Black World" does have a one-page introduction to Robinson that centers on the question "Who inspired the

Creation of the Peace Corps?" (2004). Also, Martha Biondi devotes several pages to James H. Robinson in *To Stand and Fight for Civil Rights in Post-War New York City* (Cambridge: Harvard University Press, 2003).

3 James H. Robinson, *Road Without Turning: The Story of Rev. James H. Robinson* (New York: Farrar, Straus, 1950), 18.

4 Robinson, *Road Without Turning*, 79–80.

5 Horace Mann Bond, "Forming African Youth: A Philosophy of Education," in *Africa Seen by American Negro Scholars*, ed. Alioune Diop and John A. Davis (New York: Presence Africaine; distributed by the American Society for African Culture, 1963), 253.

6 Robinson, *Road Without Turning*, 168.

7 Cited in John David Cato, "James Herman Robinson: Crossroads Africa and American Idealism, 1958–1972," *American Presbyterian* 68, no. 2 (1990): 102.

8 A detailed analysis of this episode is found in Dees, "Dr. James H. Robinson."

9 Cited in Harold R. Isaacs, *The Emergent Americans: a Report on Crossroads Africa* (New York: The John Day Co., 1963), 11.

10 "Canadian Crossroads International: Our History." http://www.cciorg.ca/history.html (accessed March 6, 2005).

11 James H. Robinson, "The Future Belongs to the Free," excerpts of a speech. Unpublished typescript with handwritten revisions. James H. Robinson Papers, Amistad Collection, Tulane University (April 14, 1953), 3–5.

12 James H. Robinson, "Africa—The Number One Challenge to the Next Generation," speech given at the summer session of Penn State University. Unpublished typescript. James H. Robinson Papers, Amistad Collection, Tulane University (July 23, 1957), 5.

13 Robinson, "Africa—The Number One Challenge," 8.

14 James H. Robinson, "The Aims and Purposes of Operation-Crossroads Africa," speech to the opening session of the Orientation Week for the participants in Operation-Crossroads Africa, Union Theological Seminary. Unpublished typescript. James H. Robinson Papers, Amistad Collection, Tulane University (June 14, 1960), 2.

15 James H. Robinson, "Declaration of Freedom," sermon preached at the Washington Cathedral. Unpublished typescript with handwritten revisions. James H. Robinson Papers, Amistad Collection, Tulane University (March 17, 1957), 4–5.

16 James H. Robinson, "The Crescent, Sickle and Cross over Africa," excerpts of a sermon at Smith College. Unpublished typescript. James H. Robinson Papers, Amistad Collection, Tulane University (1957), 2.

17 Cited in Adelaide Cromwell Hill and Martin Kilson, *Apropos of Africa* (New York: Frank Cass, 1969), 139.

18 James H. Robinson, *Africa at the Crossroads* (Philadelphia: Westminster Press, 1962), 66, cited in John David Cato, "James Herman Robinson: Crossroads Africa and American Idealism, 1958–1972," *American Presbyterian* (Summer 1990): 105.

19 A variety of sources report similar, if not identical, data. For example, see websites such as www.religioustolerance.org and www.gem-werc.org/mmrc.

20 Robinson, "The Crescent, Sickle and Cross over Africa," 3.

21 James H. Robinson, "Baccalaureate Service," sermon preached at Atlanta University, Morehouse College, Spelman College. Unpublished typescript. James H. Robinson Papers, Amistad Collection, Tulane University (June 2, 1957), 2.

22 Robinson, "The Crescent, Sickle and Cross over Africa," 4.
23 James H. Robinson, "The Nature and Roots of Christian Love," excerpts of a sermon. Unpublished typescript with handwritten revisions. James H. Robinson Papers, Amistad Collection, Tulane University (March 2, 1959), 2.
24 Robinson, "Baccalaureate Service," 2.
25 Edward C. Dees, "Interview of Laverne Brown, Administrative Assistant, Operation Crossroads Africa" (1996).
26 James H. Robinson, "Action for a Time of Promise and Despair," speech. Unpublished typescript with handwritten revisions. James H. Robinson Papers, Amistad Collection, Tulane University (1964), 7.
27 Ibid., 7–8.
28 James H. Robinson, "Keynote Address: American Negro Leadership Conference on Africa," unpublished typescript. James H. Robinson Papers, Amistad Collection, Tulane University (September 24, 1964), 3.
29 James H. Robinson, "Our Link to the Past, A Promise of the Future," sermon. Unpublished typescript with handwritten revisions. James H. Robinson Papers, Amistad Collection, Tulane University (June 3, 1956), 2.
30 See p. 34 above.

Chapter 3

1 Martin Luther King, Jr. used this term during the march from Selma to Montgomery in 1965, an event which included more than four hundred clergymen. See the film, "Martin Luther King, Jr.: An Amazing Grace," a videotape (Huntville, Tex.: Educational Video Network, Inc., n.d.).
2 See Martin Luther King, Jr., "Address at the Southern Association of Political scientists" (November 13, 1964), The Library and Archives of the Martin Luther King Jr. Center for Nonviolent Social Change, Inc., Atlanta, Georgia (hereafter referred to as The King Center Library and Archives), 2–3; Martin Luther King, Jr., "Remarks on Fear," Montgomery, Alabama (March 23, 1956), The King Center Library and Archives, 1; Martin Luther King, Jr., "Address at a Conference of Religious Leaders Under the Sponsorship of the President's Committee on Government Contracts," Washington, DC (May 11, 1959), The King Center Library and Archives, 1–4; Martin Luther King, Jr., "Address at a Public Meeting of the Southern Christian Ministers' Conference of Mississippi" (September 23, 1959), The King Center Library and Archives, 5; and Kenneth L. Smith and Ira G. Zepp Jr., *Search for the Beloved Community: The Thinking of Martin Luther King, Jr.* (Valley Forge, Penn.: Judson Press, 1974), 120–22.
3 Martin Luther King, Jr., *Where Do We Go from Here: Chaos or Community?* (NY: Harper & Row, 1967), 9; and Smith and Zepp, *Search for the Beloved Community*, 121–22.
4 For the most exhaustive study of these issues and concerns, see Lewis V. Baldwin, *Toward the Beloved Community: Martin Luther King, Jr. and South Africa* (Cleveland: Pilgrim Press, 1995), 1–185.
5 Coretta S. King, *My Life with Martin Luther King, Jr.*, rev. ed. (New York: Henry Holt, 1993), 142–43; Baldwin, *Toward the Beloved Community*, 8–10; Lewis V. Baldwin, *To Make the Wounded Whole: The Cultural Legacy of Martin Luther King, Jr.* (Minneapolis: Fortress, 1992), 165–67; and Walter and Albertina Sisulu, *In Our Lifetime* (Claremont 7700, South Africa: David Philip Publishers, 2002), 100–101.

6 Martin Luther King, Jr., "The Birth of a New Nation: Sermon Delivered at Dexter Avenue Baptist Church," in *Symbol of the Movement: The Papers of Martin Luther King, Jr., January 1957–December 1958*, ed. Clayborne Carson et al. (Berkeley: University of California Press, 2000), 4:155.

7 See "Conversation in Ghana," *The Christian Century* 74, no. 15 (April 10, 1957): 446–48; and Baldwin, *Toward the Beloved Community*, 10.

8 Sisulu and Sisulu, *In Our Lifetime*, 100–101; and Baldwin, *Toward the Beloved Community*, 8, 21–24.

9 Charles D. Lowery and John F. Marszalek, *Encyclopedia of African American Civil Rights: From Emancipation to the Present* (Westport, Conn.: Greenwood, 1992), 184–85.

10 George M. Houser, *No One Can Stop the Rain: Glimpses of Africa's Liberation Struggle* (New York: The Pilgrim Press, 1989), 12; and Baldwin, *Toward the Beloved Community*, 14.

11 Baldwin, *Toward the Beloved Community*, 14–15.

12 Houser, *No One Can Stop the Rain*, 123–24; Baldwin, *Toward the Beloved Community,* 15–19; and "Report on the Declaration of Conscience Campaign," an unpublished document circulated by the American Committee on Africa, New York, New York (1957–1958), The King Center Library and Archives, 1–3.

13 A draft of the entire "Declaration of Conscience" (1957) can be found in The King Center Library and Archives. Also see Eleanor Roosevelt, James A. Pike, and Martin Luther King, Jr., to the Members and Supporters of the American Committee on Africa (July 1957), The King Center Library and Archives, 1–2; Keith Spalding to Eleanor Roosevelt, James A. Pike, and Martin Luther King Jr. (August 21, 1957), The King Center Library and Archives, 1; Margaret Chase Smith to Eleanor Roosevelt, James A. Pike, and Martin Luther King, Jr. (August 23, 1957), The King Center Library and Archives, 1; Houser, *No One Can Stop the Rain*, 123–24; and Baldwin, *Toward the Beloved Community*, 15–19.

14 "Report on the Declaration of Conscience Campaign," 1–3; and Baldwin, *Toward the Beloved Community*, 17–18.

15 George M. Houser, "Report on South Africa's Treason Trials," unpublished document (February 11, 1958), The King Center Library and Archives, 1–2.

16 James A. Pike to Martin Luther King, Jr. (March 14, 1958), The King Center Library and Archives, 1; James A. Pike and Martin Luther King, Jr., to the Honorable Paul H. Douglas (November 4, 1957), The King Center Library and Archives, 1–2; "A Letter to the Religious Press," unpublished document (March 5, 1958), The King Center Library and Archives, 1–2; Baldwin, *Toward the Beloved Community*, 19; and James A. Pike and Martin Luther King Jr. to the Members and Supporters of the American Committee on Africa (February 25, 1958), The King Center Library and Archives, 1.

17 Michael Scott to Martin Luther King, Jr. (January 23, 1958), The King Center Library and Archives, 1; and Baldwin, *Toward the Beloved Community,* 10, 17–18, and 38.

18 Martin Luther King, Jr., "Introduction," in *Southwest Africa: The U.N.'s Stepchild* (New York: The American Committee on Africa, 1959), 1.

19 G. McLeod Bryan to Martin Luther King Jr. (October 10, 1959), The King Center Library and Archives, 1–2; G. McLeod Bryan, "South Africa," unpublished document (October 1959), The King Center Library and Archives, 1–7; G. McLeod Bryan, *Voices in the Wilderness: Twentieth Century Prophets Speak to the New Millennium* (Macon, Ga.: Mercer University Press,

1999), 22; Baldwin, *Toward the Beloved Community*, 20–21 and 197–98n72; and G. McLeod Bryan, "Two Birmingham Letters," Thirtieth Anniversary, Winston Salem, North Carolina (1993), Birmingham Civil Rights Institute Collection, 4.

20 Martin Luther King, Jr. to Albert J. Luthuli (December 8, 1959), The King Center Library and Archives, 1; and Baldwin, *Toward the Beloved Community*, 21 and 197–98 n. 72.

21 Donald Harrington to George M. Houser (March 4, 1958), The King Center Library and Archives, 1; Donald Harrington to Friends of the American Committee on Africa (September 24, 1958), The King Center Library and Archives, 1; Ann Morrissett to Martin Luther King, Jr. (December 10, 1959), The King Center Library and Archives, 1; Martin Luther King Jr. to Ann Morrissett (December 23, 1959), The King Center Library and Archives, 1; Martin Luther King, Jr. to the Friends of the American Committee on Africa (1959), The King Center library and Archives, 1; George M. Houser to Martin Luther King, Jr. (November 9, 1959), The King Center Library and Archives, 1; and Baldwin, *Toward the Beloved Community*, 19–20.

22 The names of these and other clergymen appeared on ACOA letterhead throughout the 1950s. For examples, see Roosevelt, Pike, and King to the Members and Supporters of the ACOA (July 1957), 1; Jim Gunther to the Friends of the American Committee on Africa (October 18, 1957), The King Center Library and Archives, 1; George M. Houser to Martin Luther King, Jr. (November 22, 1957), The King Center Library and Archives, 1–2; Jim Gunther to the American Committee on Africa (December 26, 1957), The King Center Library and Archives, 1; Eleanor Roosevelt to the Friends of the American Committee on Africa (January 24, 1958), The King Center Library and Archives, 1; Pike and King to the Members and Supporters of the ACOA (February 25, 1958), 1; Norman Thomas to Martin Luther King, Jr. (May 6, 1958), The King Center Library and Archives, 1; Harrington to Friends of the ACOA (September 24, 1958), 1; Morrissett to King (December 10, 1959), 1; and King to the Friends of the ACOA (1959), 1.

23 Milfred C. Fierce, "Selected Black American Leaders and Organizations and South Africa, 1900–1977: Some Notes," *Journal of Black Studies* 17, no. 3 (1987): 316–23.

24 Hope R. Stevens to the Friends of the American Committee on Africa (April 1960), The King Center Library and Archives, 1; "South Africa Emergency Committee Formed by Key Organization Leaders," a statement by the American Committee on Africa (April 23, 1960), The King Center Library and Archives, 1; George M. Houser to the Friends of the American Committee on Africa (April 23, 1960), The King Center Library and Archives, 1; and Baldwin, *Toward the Beloved Community*, 33.

25 "Liberals Urge Ambassador to South Africa Be Recalled for Consultation—Suspension of Gold Purchases," a Press Release by Americans for Democratic Action, Washington, D.C. (April 17, 1960), The King Center Library and Archives, 1–3; Paul W. Ward, "Liberals Bid U. S. Censure South Africa: A. D. A. Petition Urges Envoy Recalled, Halt in Gold-Buying," *The Baltimore Sun*, April 17, 1960; "A.D.A. Asks U. S. Protest on African Apartheid," *The Sunday Star* (Washington, DC), April 17, 1960; Hope R. Stevens to the Friends of the American Committee on Africa (April 1960), The King Center Library and Archives, 1; and Baldwin, *Toward the Beloved Community*, 33 and 202 n. 36. For other records of how American clergy responded to the

Sharpeville Massacre, see George M. Houser to the Friends of the American Committee on Africa (April 23, 1960), The King Center Library and Archives, 1; George M. Houser to the Friends of the American Committee on Africa (May 3, 1960), The King Center Library and Archives, 1; and Donald Harrington to the Friends of the American Committee on Africa (September 23, 1960), The King Center Library and Archives, 1.

26 George M. Houser to the Friends of the American Committee on Africa (March 1, 1961), The King Center Library and Archives, 1.

27 "A Consent Form to the American Committee on Africa," signed by Martin Luther King, Jr. (December 20, 1961), The King Center Library and Archives, 1; and Angier Biddle Duke to Martin Luther King, Jr. (January 20, 1961), The King Center Library and Archives, 1.

28 For important references to Luthuli's winning of the 1960 Nobel Peace Prize, see "Foe of Apartheid: Albert John Luthuli," *The New York Times*, October 24, 1961. The ACOA reprinted and circulated this article among its supporters; and "Luthuli Will Ask Visa to Accept Nobel Peace Prize," *The New York Times*, October 25, 1961.

29 "An Appeal for Action Against Apartheid," issued by the American Committee on Africa, New York, New York (1962), The King Center Library and Archives, 1–4.

30 George M. Houser to Roger Baldwin (July 26, 1962), The King Center Library and Archives, 1; George M. Houser to Lillian Smith (September 27, 1962), The King Center Library and Archives, 1; U. S. Senator Clifford P. Case to George M. Houser (October 4, 1962), The King Center Library and Archives, 1; George M. Houser to Adam C. Powell (October 9, 1962), The King Center Library and Archives, 1; George M. Houser to Martin Luther King, Jr. (November 26, 1962), The King Center Library and Archives, 1; Donald S. Harrington to the Friends of the American Committee on Africa (November 26, 1962), The King Center Library and Archives, 1–2; and "An Appeal for Action Against Apartheid," 1–2.

31 "An Appeal for Action Against Apartheid," 1–2.

32 "Call to the American Negro Leadership Conference on Africa," unpublished document (June 1962), The King Center Library and Archives, 1; George Houser to the American Negro Leadership Conference on Africa (June 27, 1962), The King Center Library and Archives, 1–2; Martin Luther King, Jr. to George Houser (July 2, 1962), The King Center Library and Archives, 1; M. S. Handler, "Negroes Ask Role in Foreign Policy: Leaders to Meet in Capital—White House Interested," *The New York Times*, July 9, 1964; Martin Luther King, Jr., "Statement at the American Negro Leadership Conference on Africa," Arden House, Harriman, New York," unpublished (November 24, 1962), The King Center Library and Archives, 1–2; "Resolutions of the American Negro Leadership Conference on Africa," New York, New York (November 23–25, 1962), The King Center Library and Archives, 1–6; The American Negro Leadership Conference on Africa to President John F. Kennedy (December 17, 1962), The King Center Library and Archives, 1–2; "Resolutions of the American Negro Leadership Conference on Africa," Washington, D.C. (September 24–27, 1964), The King Center Library and Archives, 1–7; Baldwin, *Toward the Beloved Community*, 32–63; and Houser, *No One Can Stop the Rain*, 266.

33 Martin Luther King, Jr., "On South African Independence," an unpublished speech, London, England (December 7, 1964), The King Center Library and Archives, 1–2; Martin Luther King, Jr., "The Negro Looks at Africa,"

unpublished speech (December 8, 1962), The King Center Library and Archives, 1; and Baldwin, Toward the Beloved Community, 30 and 41.

34 Martin Luther King, Jr., *Why We Can't Wait* (New York: The New American Library, Inc., 1964), 67 and 86–92 and "Powell Seeks Boycott of S. African Goods," *New York Amsterdam News*, April 16, 1960. Also see Martin Luther King, Jr., *Strength to Love* (Philadelphia: Fortress, 1981), 62–63.

35 See "South Africa Segregation Doomed, Graham Says," *Atlanta Constitution*, March 30, 1960; Edward Lee Moore, "Billy Graham and Martin Luther King, Jr.: An Inquiry into White and Black Revivalistic Traditions" (Ph.D. diss., Vanderbilt University, 1979), 453–68; Baldwin, *Toward the Beloved Community*, 83–84; and Lewis V. Baldwin et. al., *The Legacy of Martin Luther King, Jr.: The Boundaries of Law, Politics, and Religion* (Notre Dame: University of Notre Dame Press, 2002), 75 n. 201, 85, 87, 89, 91–93, 95–96, 98, 101–2, 116 n. 61, 118 n. 76, 120 n. 100, and 121 n. 110. Clearly, one source exaggerates Graham's significance for the struggles against Jim Crow and apartheid, and its saccharine depiction of King's response to Graham's ministry is misleading at best. See David L. Chappell, *A Stone of Hope: Prophetic Religion and the Death of Jim Crow* (Chapel Hill: The University of North Carolina Press, 2004), 96–97. For a very well-researched work with conclusions that offer a sharply-argued alternative to Chappell, see Jerry B. Hopkins, "Billy Graham and the Race Problem, 1949–1969" (Ph.D. diss., University of Kentucky, 1986).

36 See Bill J. Leonard, "A Theology for Racism: Southern Fundamentalists and the Civil Rights Movement," *Baptist History and Heritage* 34, no. 1 (1999): 49–68; and Andrew M. Manis, "'Dying from the Neck Up': Southern Baptist Resistance to the Civil Rights Movement," *Baptist History and Heritage* 34, no. 1 (1999): 33–48.

37 Martin Luther King, Jr. to William E. Newgent (October 20, 1959), The King Center Library and Archives, 1.

38 Martin Luther King, Jr., "A Knock at Midnight," an unpublished sermon delivered at All Saints Community Church, Los Angeles, California (June 25, 1967), The King Center Library and Archives, 8; and Baldwin, *Toward the Beloved Community*, 28.

39 King, "A Knock at Midnight," 7–8; and Baldwin, *Toward the Beloved Community*, 28.

40 Baldwin, *Toward the Beloved Community*, 42; and Martin Luther King, Jr. to Theodore E. Brown (April 1, 1963), The King Center Library and Archives, 1.

41 George M. Houser to Martin Luther King, Jr. (April 9, 1963), The King Center Library and Archives, 1.

42 E. S. Reddy to Martin Luther King, Jr. (28 June 1963), The King Center Library and Archives, 1. Reddy reports that "The U.N. Special Committee Against Apartheid (it had a long title at that time) was established in 1963 and had its first meeting on 2 April 1963. It was the first U.N. Committee boycotted by the Western powers, and there was a feeling that it would be a flop. I was appointed Principal Secretary." See Enuga S. Reddy to Lewis V. Baldwin (September 14, 1993), the author's personal collection, 1. Also see Martin Luther King, Jr. to Diallo Telli, Chairman of the Special Committee on the Policies of Apartheid of the Government of the Republic of South Africa (June 10, 1963), The King Center Library and Archives, 1.

43 George M. Houser to Martin Luther King, Jr. (September 6, 1963), the ACOA Collection, Amistad Center, Tulane University, New Orleans, Louisiana, 1.

44 Reddy to Baldwin (September 14, 1993), 1; and Baldwin, *Toward the Beloved Community*, 43 and 209 n. 74.

45 See "Religious Leaders Arrested in Albany, Georgia," an unpublished list (August 28, 1962), The King Center Library and Archives, 1–2; King, *Why We Can't Wait*, 51–58; and Andrew M. Manis, *A Fire You Can't Put Out: The Civil Rights Life of Birmingham's Reverend Fred Shuttlesworth* (Tuscaloosa: University of Alabama Press, 1999), 351.

46 Martin Luther King, Jr., "An Address to the American Jewish Congress," unpublished, New York, New York (May 20, 1965), The King Center Library and Archives, 6–7; and Lewis V. Baldwin and Amiri YaSin Al-Hadid, *Between Cross and Crescent: Christian and Muslim Perspectives on Malcolm and Martin* (Tallahassee: The University Press of Florida, 2002), 122 and 387 n. 112.

47 Eugene Carson Blake, "The Moral Responsibility of the Church in a Secular Society" (*The New York State Council Reporter*, June 1960; Syracuse: New York State Council of Churches, 1960), 1–4. Citations are to the earlier edition.

48 Martin Luther King, Jr., "Dreams of Brighter Tomorrows," *Ebony* 20 (1965): 34–35; and Baldwin, *To Make the Wounded Whole*, 249–50.

49 "Dr. King Given His Prize: Ceremony in Oslo," *The London Times* (London, England), December 11, 1964; and Martin Luther King, Jr., "Nobel Prize Acceptance Speech," in *Martin Luther King, Jr.: A Documentary . . . Montgomery to Memphis,* with an Introduction by Coretta Scott King, ed. Flip Schulke (New York: W. W. Norton, 1976), 219.

50 King, *Where Do We Go from Here?*, 167–91; Martin Luther King, Jr., *The Trumpet of Conscience* (San Francisco: Harper & Row, 1987), 21–34 and 53–78; Baldwin, *Toward the Beloved Community*, 245–85; Baldwin and Al-Hadid, *Between Cross and Crescent*, 313–58; and "A Statement Regarding SCLC's Participation in the National Conference on New Politics: Resolution on the Middle East," Chicago, Illinois (September 1967), unpublished document, The King Center Library and Archives, 1.

51 Martin Luther King, Jr., "Address on South African Independence," in *Four Decades of Concern: The Martin Luther King, Jr. Center for Nonviolent Social Change, Inc. and South Africa* (Atlanta: The Martin Luther King Jr. Center for Nonviolent Social Change, Inc., 1986), 18–19; and Baldwin, *Toward the Beloved Community,* 45–46.

52 King, "Address on South African Independence," 18–19; Martin Luther King, Jr., "Call for an International Boycott on Apartheid South Africa: A Benefit Speech," in *Four Decades of Concern*, 19–22; and Baldwin, *Toward the Beloved Community*, 31–32.

53 George M. Houser to Martin Luther King, Jr. (July 14, 1965), ACOA Collection, Amistad Center, Tulane University, 1.

54 Houser, *No One Can Stop the Rain*, 266; and Baldwin, *Toward the Beloved Community*, 47–50.

55 Chief Luthuli chose this title, which is also that of an African-American slave spiritual used during the Civil Rights Movement, for his own story of his life in 1962. See Albert Luthuli, *Let My People Go* (New York: McGraw-Hill, 1962).

56 King, "Call for an International Boycott on Apartheid South Africa," 19–21; Houser, *No One Can Stop the Rain*, 266; and Baldwin, *Toward the Beloved Community*, 47–50.

57 King, "Call for an International Boycott on Apartheid South Africa," 21–22; and Baldwin, *Toward the Beloved Community*, 49–50.

58 Martin Luther King, Jr. to the South African Embassy (February 9, 1966), The King Center Library and Archives, 1; N. M. Nel to Martin Luther King, Jr. (March 17, 1966), The King Center Library and Archives, 1; N. M. Nel to Martin Luther King, Jr. (February 11, 1966), The King Center Library and Archives, 1; and Baldwin, *Toward the Beloved Community*, 60–61.

59 See George M. Houser to Martin Luther King, Jr. (January 6, 1966), The King Center Library and Archives, 1; and Baldwin, *Toward the Beloved Community*, 50 and 211 n. 96.

60 Baldwin, *Toward the Beloved Community*, 51.

61 King, *Where Do We Go from Here?*, 173, 176; and King, *The Trumpet of Conscience*, 63.

62 T. Wendell Foster to Martin Luther King, Jr. (April 10, 1967), The King Center Library and Archives, 1; Jackie Robinson to Martin Luther King Jr. (April 10, 1967), The King Center Library and Archives, 1; Dennis Brutus to Martin Luther King Jr. (October 20, 1967), The King Center Library and Archives, 1; and Dennis Brutus to Lewis V. Baldwin (October 6, 1987), the author's personal collection, 1.

63 King, *Where Do We Go from Here?*, 57; King, *The Trumpet of Conscience*, 63; King, "Address on South African Independence," 18; and Baldwin, *Toward the Beloved Community*, 54–55 and 213 n. 117.

64 Baldwin, *Toward the Beloved Community*, 55, 213 n. 117.

65 "A Press Statement," issued by the Delegates at the Annual General Conference of the International Defence and Aid Fund, London, England (April 19–21, 1968), ACOA Collection, Amistad Center, Tulane University, 1.

66 Houser, *No One Can Stop the Rain*, 357.

67 "SCLC V.P. Demands U.N. Peace Force in South Africa," *Jet*, September 16, 1976, 18; and Baldwin, *Toward the Beloved Community*, 79–80.

68 See Jim Galloway, "King's Passive Philosophy Faces Hard Sell in Africa," *St. Paul Pioneer Press Dispatch* (St. Paul, Minnesota), January 18, 1987; *Contending Ideologies in South Africa*, ed. James Leatt et. al. (Grand Rapids: Eerdmans, 1986), 59, 83–119; Mokgethi Motlhabi, *Challenge to Apartheid: Toward a Moral National Resistance* (Grand Rapids: Eerdmans, 1988), 27–28, 33, 37, 67–68, 82, and 143–56; David Woods, *Biko* (New York: Vintage Books, 1978), 45–46; Roger Omond, *The Apartheid Handbook: A Guide to South Africa's Everyday Racial Policies* (New York: Penguin Books, 1986), 20, 206, 216, 226, and 236; Aelred Stubbs, ed., *Steve Biko—I Write What I Like: A Selection of His Writings Edited with a Personal Memoir and a New Preface* (San Francisco: Harper & Row, 1978), 20–21, 42–43, 121, 139, and 146–47; Basil Moore, ed., *The Challenge of Black Theology in South Africa* (Atlanta: John Knox, 1974), 40; and Baldwin, *Toward the Beloved Community*, 66–73.

69 Galloway, "King's Passive Philosophy."

70 Ranganath Murthy, "Good Intentions Aren't Enough: A Critique of the Sullivan Principles," unpublished paper (April 24, 1986), 1–6, on file with author; Fierce, "Selected Black American Leaders," 318, 322–23; and Baldwin, *Toward the Beloved Community*, 81–82.

71 Tutu treats black theology in both contexts as emerging out of the black Christian experience, an experience from which he most certainly would not have excluded King. See Desmond Tutu, "Black Theology/African Theology: Soul Mates or Antagonists?," *Journal of Religious Thought* 32, no. 2

(1975): 25–33; Allan Boesak, *Coming Out of the Wilderness: A Comparative Interpretation of the Ethics of Martin Luther King, Jr. and Malcolm X* (Kampen, Holland: J. H. Kok, 1976), 1–48; and Baldwin, *Toward the Beloved Community*, 73–79.

72 Desmond Tutu, "The South African Struggle," an unpublished speech, delivered at the Partners in Ecumenism Conference of the National Council of Churches, Washington, D.C. (September 26, 1984), 1; Allan A. Boesak, *Farewell to Innocence: A Socio-Ethical Study on Black Theology and Black Power* (Maryknoll, NY: Orbis Books, 1977), 15; Naomi Tutu, Comp., *The Words of Desmond Tutu* (New York: Newmarket Press, 1989), 26–91, 101; Desmond Tutu, *Crying in the Wilderness: The Struggle for Justice in South Africa*, ed. John Webster (Grand Rapids: Eerdmans, 1982), 113; Desmond Tutu, *Hope and Suffering: Sermons and Speeches*, ed. John Webster (Grand Rapids: Eerdmans, 1983), 48–56, 69; John W. de Gruchy, *The Church Struggle in South Africa* (Grand Rapids: Eerdmans, 1988), 232–33; and Boesak, *Coming Out of the Wilderness*, 1–48.

73 Boesak disagrees with the contention that King rejected black power, noting that for the civil rights leader, it "was not the concept of power, or even black power; it was how this concept was understood that caused the problem." In other words, King reacted against the idea of black power as a call to racial separatism and violence. See Boesak, *Farewell to Innocence*, 6–7, 39–149; and Baldwin, *Toward the Beloved Community,* 76–79.

74 Boesak, *Farewell to Innocence*, 66–67.

75 de Gruchy, *The Church Struggle in South Africa*, 232–33.

76 *International Tribute to Martin Luther King, Jr.* (New York: United Nations Centre Against Apartheid, Department of Political and Security Council Affairs, 1979), 37–38.

77 "A. M. E. Bishop's Council to Seek Kissinger Meeting," *Jet*, September 25, 1975, 31; and "Black Churches Tell Banks to Halt South African Loans," *Jet*, March 30, 1978, 31.

78 King had actually praised both the NCC and the WCC for condemning racism during his lifetime, but at the same time, he knew that they were capable of doing much more than they actually did. See John J. Ansbro, *Martin Luther King, Jr.: The Making of a Mind* (Maryknoll, NY: Orbis Books, 1982), 180.

79 "We All Need a New Heart: Rev. Graham to South Africa," *Jet*, April 5, 1973, 13; "South Africa Segregation Doomed, Graham Says," 3; and Moore, "Billy Graham and Martin Luther King, Jr.," 454, 457.

80 Galloway, "King's Passive Philosophy"; Beyers Naude, "Where is South Africa Going?," *Africa Report* 30 (1985): 4–9; *Apartheid in Crisis*, ed. Mark A. Uhlig (New York: Vintage Books, 1986), 1–12; *Theology and Violence: The South African Debate*, ed. Charles Villa-Vicencio (Grand Rapids: Eerdmans, 1987), 1–308; and Baldwin, *Toward the Beloved Community*, 93–94.

81 *Contending Ideologies in South Africa*, ed. Leatt et al., 102–3; Motlhabi, *Challenge to Apartheid*, 143–56; Galloway, "King's Passive Philosophy"; and "South Africa Discussed This Week," *Vanderbilt Register*, Vanderbilt University (Nashville, Tenn.), January 24, 1986.

82 Galloway, "King's Passive Philosophy"; and Baldwin, *Toward the Beloved Community*, 96.

83 Galloway, "King's Passive Philosophy"; and Baldwin, *Toward the Beloved Community*, 96–97.

84 Galloway, "King's Passive Philosophy."

85 Carole Collins, "Chronology of South Africa: A History of Black Struggle," *National Catholic Reporter*, March 22, 1985, 16; Naude, "Where is South Africa Going?," 4; *Apartheid in Crisis*, ed. Uhlig, 7; and Baldwin, *Toward the Beloved Community*, 94–96.

86 Motlhabi, *Challenge to Apartheid*, 151.

87 Quoted in Jim Wallis and Joyce Hollyday, eds., *Crucible of Fire: The Church Confronts Apartheid* (Maryknoll, NY: Orbis Books, 1989), 99.

88 Walter Wink, *Violence and Nonviolence in South Africa: Jesus' Third Way* (Philadelphia: New Society, 1987), 7.

89 *Theology and Violence*, ed. Villa-Vicencio, 71–78; *Apartheid in Crisis*, ed. Uhlig, 25; "'We Will Be Free' Says Bishop Tutu: Seeks International Community Aid," *Update on the Black Church* (Summer, 1981), 1; Tutu, *Crying in the Wilderness*, 53; Tutu, *Hope and Suffering*, 130; and Baldwin, *Toward the Beloved Community,* 102–5. King's and Tutu's approaches to nonviolence were compared in many circles in the 1980s, especially after the latter received the Nobel Peace Prize in 1984. See Sheila Briggs, "Church Theology," in *The Kairos Covenant: Standing with South African Christians*, ed. Willis H. Logan (New York: Friendship Press, 1988), 91; and Shirley Du Boulay, *Tutu: Voice of the Voiceless* (Grand Rapids: Eerdmans, 1988), 198.

90 Allan Boesak, *Black and Reformed: Apartheid, Liberation and the Calvinist Tradition* (Maryknoll, NY: Orbis Books, 1984), 26, 48–49.

91 *Crucible of Fire*, ed. Wallis and Hollyday, 8, 15–16.

92 Frank Chikane, *No Life of My Own: An Autobiography* (Maryknoll, NY: Orbis Books, 1988), 55–56.

93 "South Africa Discussed This Week," 1; and Baldwin, *Toward the Beloved Community,* 106–7.

94 See *The Kairos Document—Challenge to the Church: A Theological Comment on the Political Crisis in South Africa* (Grand Rapids: Eerdmans, 1986), 13–15; Logan, *The Kairos Covenant*, 2–178; "South African Theologians: Taking a Stand," *Christianity and Crisis*, November 11, 1985, 435–37; and Baldwin, *Toward the Beloved Community*, 100, 106.

95 Official Records of the United Nations General Assembly, Thirty-Seventh Session, 56th Plenary Meeting, New York, New York (November 5, 1982), 971–72; and Baldwin, *Toward the Beloved Community,* 116–18.

96 "Congressmen Blast Reagan Executive Order Applying Sanctions to South Africa," *Jet*, September 23, 1985, 5; William H. Gray, III, to Friends of the Free South Africa Movement (April 1988), 1; and Baldwin, *Toward the Beloved Community*, 119, 128–29.

97 Baldwin, *Toward the Beloved Community*, 118–36; and "King Family Arrested and Jailed for Embassy Protest," *Jet*, July 15, 1985, 5.

98 Michele N. K. Collision, "Colleges See Pressure on South African Investments Following Sullivan's Call for U. S. Withdrawal," *Chronicle of Higher Education* 33, no. 39 (1987): 2.

99 Joseph E. Lowery, "An Appeal to Eliminate Apartheid on Human Rights Day," a speech printed under the auspices of the SCLC (December 10, 1983), 1–3.

100 "Lowery Suggests Reagan Show Concern for S. Africa," *Jet*, June 27, 1988, 38.

101 Reverend Jesse L. Jackson: *Straight from the Heart*, ed. Roger D. Hatch and Frank E. Watkins (Philadelphia: Fortress, 1987), 232–45.

102 D. Michael Cheers, "Jackson Tours Europe and Joins Marches against South Africa," *Jet*, June 3, 1985, 30–33; and Baldwin, *Toward the Beloved Community*, 120–22.

103 D. Michael Cheers makes these conclusions in his three articles: "Jesse Jackson: Rebuilding Bridges to Africa—PUSH Founder Renews Spiritual Bond Between U.S. Blacks and Africa," *Ebony* 42, no. 2 (1986): 132–33, 136, 138; D. Michael Cheers, "After Visit to African Nations, Jesse Jackson Urges Joint Partnership," *Jet*, January 30, 1989, 12–16; and "What Black Americans and Africans Can Do for Each Other," *Ebony* 41, no. 6 (1986), 156.

104 "National Baptist Confab Raps South African Racism: Gears for Economic Growth," *Jet*, September 30, 1985, 24–25; and *National Baptist Union-Review* 89, no. 20 (1985): 2.

105 "Final Statement of the Black Church Summit on Southern Africa," *A.M.E. Church Review* 104, no. 333 (1989): 53–54.

106 "A Resolution of the National Council of the Churches of Christ in the U.S.A.: Current Developments in Southern Africa," Chicago, Illinois (November 5–7, 1986), 1–2; "Religious Leaders Call for New South Africa Policy," *Report to Presbyterians from Washington* 6, no. 6 (1985), 1–4; and Baldwin, *Toward the Beloved Community*, 130–31.

107 "70,000 Greet Released Leaders in South Africa," *The Tennessean* (Nashville, Tenn.), October 30, 1989; Charles Villa-Vicencio, "South Africa: Options for the Future," *Africa Report*, 35, no. 2 (1990): 29; Sebastian Mallaby, *After Apartheid: The Future of South Africa* (New York: Times Books, 1992), 3, 6, 11, 15–16, 27, 100–101, 103, and 252; "Churches Seen Continuing as Reconcilers," *United Methodist Reporter of the Tennessee Conference* 140, no. 3 (1993): 3; and Baldwin, *Toward the Beloved Community*, 137–64.

108 Nelson Mandela, *Long Walk to Freedom: The Autobiography of Nelson Mandela* (Boston: Little, Brown, 1994), 544.

109 Anthony DeLuca, *Gandhi, Mao, Mandela, and Gorbachev: Studies in Personality, Power, and Politics* (Westport, Conn.: Praeger, 2000), 89.

110 "South Africa Hails President Mandela: First Black Leader Pledges Racial Unity," *The New York Times*, May 11, 1994; and Baldwin, *Toward the Beloved Community,* 137–70.

111 Desmond M. Tutu, *No Future Without Forgiveness* (New York: Doubleday, 1999), 3–287.

112 "South Africa to Pay $3,900 in Reparations to Families of Each Apartheid Victim," *Jet*, May 5, 2003, 19; and "South Africa Celebrates 10th Year of Democracy; Inaugurates Mbeki as President," *Jet*, May 17, 2004, 10–13.

113 See Martin Luther King, Jr., *Stride Toward Freedom: The Montgomery Story* (New York: Harper & Row, 1958), 33–34.

114 Baldwin, *Toward the Beloved Community*, 165, 170–85.

Chapter 4

1 Gayraud S. Wilmore, "Appendix, The Theological Commission Project of the National Committee of Negro Churchmen, Fall 1968," in *Christian Faith in Black and White*, ed. Warner R. Traynham, 84 (Wakefield, Mass.: Parameter Press, 1973).

2 The following are useful references for the origin and concerns of NCNC-NCBC: James H. Cone, *For My People: Black Theology and the Black Church, Where Have We Been and Where Are We Going?* (Maryknoll, NY: Orbis Books, 1984); Alex Poinsett, "The Black Revolt in White Churches," *Ebony* 23, September 1968, 63–68; and Leon W. Watts II, "The National Committee of Black Churchmen," *Christianity and Crisis*, November 2, 1970 and November 16, 1970, 237–43.

3 Quotations in the text come from the author's interviews with Rev. Dr. Calvin B. Marshall, March 17, 1987, and Rev. Leon W. Watts, March 23, 1987.

4 Nathan Wright, Jr., *Black Power and Urban Unrest* (New York: Hawthorn Books, 1967), 153.

5 *Time*, November 15, 1968, 78.

6 See Cone's first book length manifesto. James H. Cone, *Black Theology and Black Power* (New York: Seabury Press, 1969; repr., Maryknoll, NY: Orbis, 1997).

7 For more analysis on this period, see Stubbs, *Steve Biko*.

8 *SASO Newsletter* (Natal, South Africa: SASO, August 1971), 11.

9 Stubbs, *Steve Biko*, 144, 151.

10 Unless otherwise cited, references to Dr. Bonganjalo Goba are from the author's interview with him on March 2, 1987.

11 Basil Moore, ed., *The Challenge of Black Theology in South Africa* (Atlanta: John Knox, 1973), 35. This book was originally edited by M. Motlhabi and was titled *Essays on Black Theology* (Johannesburg, South Africa: Black Theology Project of the University Christian Movement, 1972). The book was banned immediately by the apartheid government.

12 See Stubbs, *Steve Biko*, 31.

13 The quotes and conclusions from this paragraph come from my interview with M. Motlhabi on March 20, 1987.

14 On the Freedom Charter, see *30 Years of the Freedom Charter*, ed. Raymond Suttner and Jeremy Cronin (Johannesburg, South Africa: Raven Press, 1986).

15 "Prophetic" Christians, black and white, began the process of writing the Kairos Document in June of 1985. South Africa was under a state of emergency and the country, particularly evidenced by military occupation of the townships, was in a civil war. See *The Kairos Document*, 2d ed. (Johannesburg, South Africa: Skotaville Publishers, 1986).

16 See James H. Cone, *My Soul Looks Back* (Nashville: Abingdon, 1982), 41–63.

17 James H. Cone, "Black Power, Black Theology, and the Study of Theology and Ethics," *Theological Education* 6 (1970): 209.

18 From my March, 31, 1987, interview with Dr. Cone.

19 James H. Cone, *Black Theology and Black Power* (New York: Seabury Press, 1969), 32, 38; idem, *My Soul Looks Back*, 53.

20 Regarding the "non-person" comment, see Cone, *Black Theology and Black Power*, 11. See pp. 40–41 for Cone's view on "white structure of this American society."

21 See James H. Cone, "Freedom, History and Hope," *The Journal of the Interdenominational Theological Center* 1, no. 1 (1973): 56.

22 See James H. Cone, "Black Theology and Black Liberation," *The Christian Century*, September 16, 1970, 1086–87.

23 Cone, *Black Theology and Black Power*, 35, 38, 120.

24 In 1974 Roberts stated: "For blacks, Jesus is understood in a psychocultural sense. He leads us to a new self-understanding. He helps us to overcome the identity crisis triggered by white oppression of blacks" (*A Black Political Theology* [Philadelphia: Westminster, 1974], 137). Cone responds in his *God of the Oppressed* (New York: Seabury Press, 1975), 136.

25 Cone, *God of the Oppressed*, 135–37.

26 See James H. Cone, *A Black Theology of Liberation*, 2d ed. (Maryknoll, NY: Orbis Books, 1986), 110–24.

27 Cone, *Black Theology and Black Power*, 36, 42–43

28 See Cone, "Introduction," *Black Theology and Black Power*, 1–4.

29 See James H. Cone, "Toward a Black Theology," *Ebony* 25, no. 10 (1970): 114.

30 See James H. Cone, "Theological Reflections on Reconciliation," *Christianity and Crisis*, January 22, 1973, 307–8.

31 See Charles Villa-Vicencio, "An All-Pervading Heresy: Racism and the English-speaking Churches,' in *Apartheid Is a Heresy*, ed. John W. de Gruchy and Charles Villa-Vicencio, 59 (Grand Rapids: Eerdmans, 1983).

32 Allan A. Boesak, "Theology for Justice" speech presented at Stony Point, NY, March 2, 1987.

33 See Allan A. Boesak, "Wholeness Through Liberation," *Church and Society*, May/June 1981, 36; and idem "The Black Church and the Future," *South African Outlook*, July 1979, 102.

34 Allan A. Boesak, "Civil Religion and the Black Community," *Journal of Theology for Southern Africa* (June 1977): 36.

35 Allan A. Boesak, *Black and Reformed* (Maryknoll, NY: Orbis Books, 1984), 87.

36 See Boesak, *Farewell to Innocence*, 143; and idem, *The Finger of God* (Maryknoll, NY: Orbis Books, 1982), 1–3, 16–17, 27–30.

37 Boesak, *Farewell to Innocence*, 9.

38 Allan A. Boesak, "Holding on to the Vision," *All African Council of Churches Magazine*, December 1983, 20.

39 Boesak, *Farewell to Innocence*, 148–49.

40 Boesak, *Black and Reformed*, 118; and idem, *If This Is Treason, I Am Guilty* (Grand Rapids: Eerdmans, 1987), 36.

41 Allan A. Boesak, "The Black Church and the Future," *South African Outlook*, July 1979, 103.

42 Allan A. Boesak, "Courage to Be Black, Part 1," *South African Outlook*, October 1975, 152.

43 On the tasks of blacks in reconciliation, see Allan A. Boesak, "Courage to Be Black, Part 2," *South African Outlook*, November 1975, 168

44 On the task of whites, see Allan A. Boesak, "The Black Church and the Future," 101; and idem, *EcuNews Bulletin*, August 3, 1979.

45 Allan A. Boesak, "The Relationship Between Text and Situation, Reconciliation and Liberation in Black Theology," *Voices of the Third World* 2, no. 1 (1979): 36.

46 Allan A. Boesak, "Coming Out of the Wilderness," in *The Emergent Gospel*, ed. Sergio Torres and Virgina Fabella (London: Geoffrey Champion, 1976), 87.

47 Boesak, "The Black Church and the Future," 103.

48 The two representatives were Dr. J. Metz Rollins, then executive director of NCNC, and Prof. Gayraud S. Wilmore, then the first chair of NCNC's theological commission. For the history of black theology's relation to African theology, see Gayraud S. Wilmore's "The Role of Afro-America in the Rise of Third World Theology: A Historical Reappraisal," in *African Theology En Route*, ed. Kofi Appiah-Kubi and Sergio Torres (Maryknoll, NY: Orbis Books, 1979), 196–208.

49 Papers from this meeting are found in Priscilla Massie, ed., *Black Faith and Black Solidarity: Pan-Africanism and Faith in Christ* (New York: Friendship Press, 1973). For relevant commentary and analyses, also see Cornish Rogers, "Pan-Africanism and the Black Church: A Search for Solidarity,"

Christian Century, November 17, 1971; E. E. Mshana, "The Challenge of Black Theology and African Theology," *Africa Theological Journal* 5 (1975): 19–30.

50 For the papers from this gathering, see the *Journal of Religious Thought* 32, no. 2 (1975). For important commentary, see James Cone's "Black and African Theologies: A Consultation," in *Christianity and Crisis* 35, no. 3 (1975), 50–52; and Gayraud S. Wilmore, "To Speak With One Voice?: The Ghana Consultation on African and Black Theology," *Christian Century*, February 19, 1975, 167–69.

51 Papers from the December Accra meeting are found in *African Theology En Route*. Also see Gayraud S. Wilmore "Theological Ferment in the Third World," in *Christian Century*, February 15, 1978, 164–68.

52 Papers were published in Simon S. Maimela and Dwight N. Hopkins, eds., *We Are One Voice: Black Theology in the USA and South Africa* (Johannesburg, South Africa: Skotaville Press, 1989).

53 Some of the South African presenters were Simon S. Maimela and Itumeleng J. Mosala, and some of the American lecturers were Jacquelyn Grant, Dwight N. Hopkins, and Randy Bailey.

54 For primary documents and extended analyses of African theology and black theology, see *African Theology En Route*; Josiah U. Young, *Black and African Theologies: Siblings or Distant Cousins?* (Maryknoll, NY: Orbis Books, 1986); Dwight N. Hopkins, *Black Theology U.S.A. and South Africa: Politics, Culture, and Liberation* (Maryknoll NY: Orbis Books, 1989); and Emmanuel Martey, *African Theology: Inculturation and Liberation* (Maryknoll, NY: Orbis Books, 1993).

55 James Cone's *Black Theology and Black Power* was part of the international intellectual trends that went into the political and cultural formation of the Black Consciousness Movement and black theology in South Africa. See Stubbs, *Steve Biko*; Gail Gerhart, *Black Power in South Africa: The Evolution of an Ideology* (Berkeley: University of California Press, 1979); Robert Fatton, Jr., *Black Consciousness in South Africa* (Albany: State University of New York Press, 1986); and Ernest Harsch, *South Africa: White Rule Black Revolt* (New York: Monad Press, 1983).

56 See his *African Theology: An Introduction* (Johannesburg: Skotaville Press, 1986). For fuller interpretations of how black theology developed in relation to African theology, see James H. Cone, "The Future and . . . African Theology," *Pro Veritate*, January 15, 1972, and February 15, 1972; the following articles in in *Black Theology: A Documentary History*, Volume 1: *1966–1979*, ed. James H. Cone and Gayraud S. Wilmore, 393–403 (Maryknoll, NY: Orbis Books, 1993): John Mbiti, "An African Views American Black Theology," 477–82; Desmond M. Tutu, "Black Theology/African Theology—Soul Mates Or Antagonists?" 483–91; James H. Cone, "A Black American Perspective On The Future Of African Theology," 393–403. See also J. Deotis Roberts, "An Afro-American/African Theological Dialogue," in *Black Theology in Dialogue*, ed. J. Deotis Roberts, 28–42 (Philadelphia: Westminster, 1987).

57 For French-speaking Africans and those outside of South Africa working with the idea of liberation, see Englebert Mveng, *African Cry* (Maryknoll, NY: Orbis Books, 1986) and Jean-Marc Ela, *My Faith as an African* (Maryknoll, NY: Orbis Books, 1986).

Chapter 5

1 Jeremiah I. Mogufu, *Silent Look: Friends in Kenya* (Shinyalu, Kenya: privately published, 1988), 9.

2 Elisha M. Wakube, "History of Friends Church in Kenya" (D. Min. Thesis, Bethany Theological Seminary, 1990), 89.

3 Hugh Barbour and J. William Frost, *The Quakers* (Richmond, Ind.: Friends United Press, 1994), 43.

4 H. Larry Ingle, *First among Friends: George Fox and the Creation of Quakerism* (New York: Oxford University Press, 1994), 258. Superb and informative works on early Quaker women include Mary Garman et al., *Hidden in Plain Sight: Quaker Women's Writings, 1650–1700* (Wallingford, Penn. Pendle Hill Books, 1996); Phyllis Mack, *Visionary Women: Ecstatic Prophecy in Seventeenth-Century Women* (Berkeley: University of California Press, 1992); Christine Trevett, *Women and Quakerism in the Seventeenth Century* (York, England: Sessions Book Trust, 1995); and Rebecca Larson, *Daughters of Light: Quaker Women Preaching and Prophesying in the Colonies and Abroad, 1700–1775* (Chapel Hill: University of North Carolina Press, 1999).

5 Ingle, *First among Friends*, 234–36.

6 David Sox, *John Woolman, 1720–1772: Quintessential Quaker* (York, England: Sessions Book Trust in association with Friends United Press, 1999), 56–58.

7 Barbour and Frost, *The Quakers*, 147–49.

8 Henry J. Cadbury, "Negro Membership in the Society of Friends," *Journal of Negro History* 21 (1936): 151–213.

9 Barbour and Frost, *The Quakers*, 266.

10 Margaret Hope Bacon, *Mothers of Feminism: The Story of Quaker Women in America* (San Francisco: Harper & Row, 1986), 1, 117.

11 John Oliver, "Emma Brown Malone: A Mother of Feminism?" *Quaker History* 88 (1999): 4–21; Carole D. Spencer, "Evangelism, Feminism and Social Reform: The Quaker Woman Minister and the Holiness Revival," *Quaker History* 80 (1991): 24–48.

12 This theological contention is drawn most directly from John 1:9.

13 These figures are drawn from the Website of the Friends World Committee for Consultation: http://fwcc.quaker.org/totals.html (accessed September 5, 2003).

14 Levinus K. Painter, *The Hill of Vision: The Story of the Quaker Movement in East Africa, 1902–1965* (Nairobi, Kenya: East Africa Yearly Meeting, 1966), 19–24; Ane Marie Bak Rasmussen, *A History of the Quaker Movement in Africa* (London: I. B. Tauris, 1995), 40–43.

15 Willis R. Hotchkiss, *Sketches from the Dark Continent* (Cleveland: Friends Bible Institute and Training School, 1901), 107–8.

16 Clifford Wesley Gilpin, "The Church and the Community: Quakers in Western Kenya, 1902–1963" (PhD diss., Columbia University, 1976), 7.

17 Painter, *Hill of Vision*, 30–31, 45–48; quotation, 30.

18 Painter, *Hill of Vision*, 35, 38; Rasmussen, *History of the Quaker Movement*, 94.

19 Gilpin, "The Church and the Community," 81, 121.

20 Esther Mombo, "Haramisi and Jumaa: The Story of the Women's Meetings in East Africa Yearly Meeting, 1902–1979," *Woodbrooke Journal*, Issue 5, page 19. A World Health Organization report for 1996 estimates the prevalence of female genital cutting in Kenya at 50 percent. A 1992 survey

conducted in four regions of Kenya found a prevalence of 89.6 percent, but the lower national estimate is based on the fact that several large ethnic groups that do not practice female genital cutting were excluded from the 1992 survey. Some Kenyan girls underwent female genital cutting during the years 1956 to 1959 as a means of defiance against laws set down by British colonial rulers; it is not known whether Kenyan Quaker women participated in this means of rebellion. Bettina Shell-Duncan and Ylva Hernlund, Female "Circumcision" in *Africa: Culture, Controversy and Change* (Boulder: Lynne Rienner Publishers, 2000), 11, 174.

21 Gilpin, "The Church and the Community," 114, 122.

22 Mombo, "Haramisi and Jumaa," 17–18.

23 Mogufu, *Silent Look*, 9.

24 Gilpin, "The Church and the Community," 30, 88.

25 Chuck Fager, *A Friendly Letter*, 32:3.

26 Harold Smuck, *Friends in East Africa* (Richmond, Ind.: Friends United Press, 1987), 75; Rasmussen, *History of the Quaker Movement*, 70–75; Wakube, "History of Friends Church," 230.

27 See, e.g., Smuck, *Friends in East Africa*, 7.

28 Mombo, "Haramisi and Jumaa," 6.

29 Rasmussen, *History of the Quaker Movement*, 55; Gilpin, "The Church and the Community," 65; Mombo, "Haramisi and Jumaa," 5–6.

30 *Advocate*, March 1980, 9.

31 Rasmussen, *History of the Quaker Movement*, 55.

32 *The American Friend*, December 29, 1927.

33 Wakube, "History of Friends Church," 94.

34 Mombo, "Haramisi and Jumaa," 7–8. See also Samuel Thomas, "Gender and Religion on the Mission Station: Roxie Reeves and the Friends Africa Mission," *Quaker History* 88 (1999): 24–46.

35 Painter, *Hill of Vision*, 51.

36 Rasoa Matua may not have known her age precisely, and the estimates that she gave to her interviewers differed greatly. In general, the older she got, the earlier she implied that her birth date was. In 1942 she claimed a birth date in 1908 or 1909 (*Friends Missionary Advocate*, January 1942, 5); in 1983, she implied she was born in 1901 (*Quaker Life*, June 1983, 20); and reminiscences given to her son-in-law in the late 1980s seem to imply an 1895 birth date (Wakube, "History of Friends Church," 318).

37 Wakube, "History of Friends Church," 320.

38 Painter, *Hill of Vision*, 57; Rasmussen, *History of the Quaker Movement*, 56.

39 Dorothy Pitman, *Four Score and Ten Years* (Hagerstown, Ind.: Exponent Publishers, 1992), 63–65.

40 *Faith in Action: Encounters with Friends. Report from the Fifth World Conference of Friends (Quakers), 1991* (London: Friends World Committee for Consultation in association with the Sessions of York, 1992), 177.

41 Pitman, *Four Score and Ten Years*, 90.

42 *Friends Missionary Advocate*, July–August 1950, 9.

43 Thomas, "Gender and Religion," 26–27.

44 Mombo, "Haramisi and Jumaa," 12–13.

45 Thomas, "Gender and Religion," 29.

46 *Friends Missionary Advocate*, July–August 1948, 12.

47 *Friends Missionary Advocate*, July–August 1950, 9.

48 *Friends Missionary Advocate*, February 1959, 24.

49 *Friends Missionary Advocate*, February 1963, 28.

50 *Friends Missionary Advocate*, January 1942, 6.
51 *Quaker Life*, June 1983, 20; November 1996.
52 Wakube, "History of Friends Church," 322.
53 Wakube, "History of Friends Church," 319.
54 Wakube, "History of Friends Church," 209–11.
55 Conversation with Patrick Nugent, July 2003.
56 *Friends World News*, 1996/2, 12.
57 *First International Theological Conference of Quaker Women, Held at Woodbrooke, England, July 24–31, 1990* (Richmond, Ind.: Earlham School of Religion, 1991), 46.
58 Painter, *Hill of Vision*, 68.
59 Smuck, *Friends*, 21.
60 Mombo, "Haramisi and Jumaa," 13–14.
61 *Friends Missionary Advocate*, July–August 1971, 22.
62 http://www.kenyaweb.com/history/heroes/#mekatilili (accessed September 5, 2003).
63 Rasmussen, *History of the Quaker Movement,* 70; Wakube, "History of Friends Church," 232–33.
64 Quoted in Wakube, "History of Friends Church," 233.
65 Quotation in *Friends Missionary Advocate*, January 1955, 26; see also *Friends Missionary Advocate*, November 1954, 8; and February 1959, 10.
66 Simeon Shitemi, *You Are Your Brother's Keeper—The Divine Imperative* (Philadelphia: The Wider Quaker Fellowship, a program of the Friends World Committee for Consultation, 1984), 8.
67 Anne W. Webster, "East Africa Yearly Meeting of Friends: An Evaluation of its Growth" (M.A. thesis, Earlham College, 1963), 63.
68 Herbert Kimball and Beatrice Kimball, *Go into All the World: A Centennial Celebration of Friends in East Africa* (Richmond, Ind.: Friends United Press, 2002), 44.
69 *Friends Missionary Advocate*, February 1963, 28. http://www.kenyaconstitution.org/docs/09cd002.htm (accessed July 23, 2003).
70 Maria Nzomo, "Engendering Governance through the Constitutional Review Process." http://www.kenyaconstitution.org/docs/09cd002.htm (accessed July 23, 2003).
71 *Faith in Action*, 177.
72 Webster, "East Africa Yearly Meeting," 91.
73 Kimball and Kimball, *Go into All the World*, 78–103.
74 *Quaker Action*, March 1957, 6, qtd. in Kimball and Kimball, *Go into All the World*, 44–45.
75 *Friends Missionary Advocate*, October 1961, 28.
76 Rose Adede, "Let Our Lives Speak: Reflections on the Quaker Testimony of Simplicity," keynote address at the 1985 World Gathering of Young Friends held at Greensboro, North Carolina, (Philadelphia: Wider Quaker Fellowship, a program of the Friends World Committee for Consultation, 1987), 6.
77 Adede, "Let Our Lives Speak," 4.
78 Shitemi, *You Are Your Brother's Keeper*, 8–9.
79 Adede, "Let Our Lives Speak," 6–7.
80 *Friends Missionary Advocate*, February 1968, 10.
81 *Friends Missionary Advocate*, October 1968, 22–23.
82 *Friends Missionary Advocate*, May 1961, 10.

83 Maria Nzomo, "Engendering Governance," http://www.kenyaconstitution.org/ docs/09cd002.htm (accessed July 23, 2003).
84 *Friends World News*, 1996/2, 7.
85 *Faith in Action*, 177.
86 Janet Minshall, Letter, included in "Reader Responses to Letter No. 15 on Kenya," in Jack Powelson, *The Classic Liberal Quaker,* Letter No. 16, June 25, 2001. http://tqe.quaker.org/letter-16.html (accessed July 21, 2003).
87 Kenyan National Archives, qtd. in Mombo, "Haramisi and Jumaa," 13.
88 Mombo, "Haramisi and Jumaa," 20–25; quotation on 25.
89 Conversation with Roland Kreager and Cindi Goslee, July 2003. See also http://www.rswr.org.
90 *Friends Missionary Advocate*, June 1969, 10.
91 *Faith in Action*, 177.
92 *Friends Missionary Advocate*, October 1971, 26.
93 *Friends Missionary Advocate*, May–June 1986, 5; March–April 1987, 21.
94 Gwendolyn Mikell, *African Feminism: The Politics of Survival in Sub-Saharan Africa* (Philadelphia: University of Pennsylvania Press, 1997), 4.

Chapter 6

1 Denny J. Weaver, *Becoming Anabaptist: The Origin and Significance of Sixteenth Century Anabaptism* (Scottdale, Penn.: Kitchener, 1987), 120.
2 John Redekop, *Anabaptism: The Basic Beliefs* (Mennonite Brethren Faith & Life Pamphlets Series), 1993.
3 Henry A. Hubert and John H. Redekop, *Christians and War: A Call To A Biblical Counter-Culture* (Mennonite Brethren Faith & Life Pamphlets Series, 1993).
4 John Mbiti, foreword to *Justice, Reconciliation and Peace in Africa*, David Shenk (Nairobi: Uzima Press, 1997), vii.
5 Shenk, *Justice, Reconciliation, and Peace*, 10–21
6 Brendan Salisbury, "Angola: Inside Africa's Forgotten Country," *New Africa* 438 (2005): 48.
7 E. M. Braekman, *Histoire du Protestantisme au Congo* (Bruxelles: Librairie des Eclaireurs Unionistes, 1961), 242.
8 Peter Falk, *La Croissance de l'Eglise en Afriqu* (Kinshasa: Institut Supérieur Théologique de Kinshana, 1985), 350.
9 Fimbo Ganvunze, *Impact du Christianisme au Zaire a Travers l'oeuvre de la Communaute Mennonite (1911–1987)* (Kinshasa: Faculté de Théologie Evangélique de Bangui, 1989), 41–42.
10 J.B. Toews, *The Mennonite Brethren Church in Zaire* (Fresno, Calif.: Board of Christian Literature, 1978), 45–48.
11 See John A. Lapp and C. Arnold Snyder, eds., *A Global Mennonite History,* Volume 1: *Africa* (Scottsdale, Penn.: Herald Press, 2003).
12 Cornelius J, Dyke, *An Introduction To Mennonite History* (Scottsdale, Penn.: Herald Press, 1993, 1976), 269.
13 Mennonite World Conference, *Global Gift Sharing (Progress Report To The General Council)* (Kitchner, Ontario: Mennonite World Conference, 2003), 23.
14 Dyke, *An Introduction to Mennonite History*, 50–280.
15 See Edwin Weaver, *From Kuku Hill: Among Indigenous Churches in West Africa* (Elkhart, Ind.: Mennonite Board of Missions, 1970).
16 Weaver, *From Kuku Hill.*

17 Mennonite Brethren Mission and Service International (MBMSI), *People Reach Out and Touch Your Missionaries 2002–2003* (Abbotsford, British Columbia: MBMSI, 2003), 14.

18 *Global Gift Sharing,* 30–32.

19 Brethren in Christ World Missions Website: http://www.bic-church.org/wm/countries.soafrica.htm.

20 Dialogue with Pastor Ernesto Campira Magudelia in Zimbabwe 2003; dialogue in Zimbabwe between Portuguese Speaking Countries, Mennonite World Conference.

21 Pedro Lutiniko L.M, "Une Interpellation Missiologique de l'Anabaptisme Africaine, Memoire de Licence en Missiologie," in *Structures Redemptives dans Actes* 13:1-3 (CUM 1996), 32.

22 Lutiniko, "Une Interpellation," 18.

23 Lutiniko, "Une Interpellation," 18.

24 Salisbury, "Inside Africa's Forgotten Country," 48.

25 Abebe Zegeye et al., "Images: The Seesaw Haunting Keeps Killing the Living," *Social Identities* 5, no. 4 (1999): 11.

26 Interview with Father Simon in Luanda, Angola, February 4, 2004.

27 Zegeye et al., "Images: The Seesaw Haunting," 19.

28 Zegeye et al., "Images: The Seesaw Haunting," 14.

29 Jose Eduardo dos Santos, Angola, *O Futuro Comeca Agora* (Luanda, 2003), 1.

30 Daniel Ntoni Nzinga, speech given at the Angolan Leadership Conference, Luanda (2001).

31 David J. Bosch, *Transforming Mission Paradigm Shifts in Theology of Mission* (Maryknoll, NY: Orbis Books, 1991), 3.

32 "Peace I leave with you; my peace I give to you; I do not give to you as the world gives" (John 14:27).

Chapter 7

1 For more on these incidents see: "Falwell Says Foreign Minister Calls Apartheid Wrong," *Associated Press,* August 18, 1985; "Fundamentalist Sees Racial Progress in South Africa," *Associated Press*, August 19, 1985; Luix Overbea, "Two Ministers' Polar Views on South Africa," *Christian Science Monitor*, August 22, 1985; Anthony Lewis, "Abroad at Home; Black is Red," *The New York Times*, September 20, 1987; Pamela Schaeffer, "Falwell Urges Baptists to be Wary of Mandela," *St. Louis Post-Dispatch*, June 30, 1990.

2 James Adams, "Top TV Evangelist Trumpets a Tyrant," *The New York Times,* August 20, 1995; Jonathon Randal, "Robertson Aids Zaire, Its Leader," *Washington Post*, May 18 1995; Bill Sizemore, "Evangelist Lost Millions in Mines," *Seattle Times*, March 17, 1997.

3 Daniel Roth, "Pat Robertson's Quest for Eternal Life," *Fortune*, June 10, 2002.

4 700 Club, July 7, 2003; and Alan Cooperman, "Robertson Defends Liberia's President," *Washington Post*, July 10, 2003.

5 Cooperman, "Robertson Defends Liberia's President."

6 Robert Boston, for example, charges that latter-twentieth century Religious Right activists were among the leading proponents of "anti-separationism," promoting as they did a problematic reading of history that argued for the idea that the United States was founded upon Christian principles (Rob Boston, *Why the Religious Right is Wrong About Separation of Church and State* [Buffalo, NY: Prometheus Books, 1993], 67–74). Pat Robertson has been quite vocal in arguing for initial and contemporary Christian designs within

American government. He points to an "incredible reservoir of Christian beliefs and customs . . . we have inherited from the precepts of our founding fathers and the framers of the Constitution" and claims that "the Constitution, rightly interpreted, was clearly a document based on Christian concepts of sin and justice." He goes on to call for "concerned Christians in the West to support the growth and development of Christian principles in these emerging governments [in other parts of the world]" (Robertson, *The New Millennium: 10 Trends That Will Impact You and Your Family by the Year 2000* [Nashville: W. Publishing Group, 1990], 42, 44). On African-American churches, see R. Drew Smith, "African American Protestants, Political Activism, and 'Liberal' Redemptive Hopes," *Theology Today* 53, no. 2 (1996): 191–200; and David Howard-Pitney, "'To Form a More Perfect Union': African Americans and American Civil Religion," in *New Day Begun: African American Churches and Civic Culture in Post-Civil Rights America*, ed. R. Drew Smith (Durham: Duke University Press, 2003), 89–112.

7 Peter Schraeder, *United States Foreign Policy Toward Africa: Incrementalism, Crisis and Change* (Cambridge: Cambridge University Press, 1994), 248.

8 Much of this data comes from David Barrett et al., *World Christian Encyclopedia* (Oxford: Oxford University Press, 2001) and from Paul Gifford, *Christianity and Politics in Doe's Liberia* (Cambridge: Cambridge University Press, 1993). See also Vinson Synan, "The Origins of the Pentecostal Movement" (unpublished paper on file with author); and Albert Wardin, "Who Are the Baptists: Africa" (Baptist World Alliance, Heritage and Identity Commission; http://www.bwa-baptist-heritage.org/hst-afr.htm).

9 Robert E. Smith, "Historical Perspective of Zaire," in *Mission in Mid-Continent: Zaire*, ed. Dean Kirkwood (Valley Forge, Penn.: American Baptist Church, International Ministries, 1982), 46, 48, and 63.

10 John Walter Cason, "The Growth of Christianity in the Liberian Environment" (Ph.D. diss., Columbia University, 1962), 87, 105.

11 Gifford, *Christianity and Politics*, 12–13.

12 Gifford, *Christianity and Politics*, 57.

13 Gifford, *Christianity and Politics*, 65.

14 Walton Johnson, *Worship and Freedom: a Black American Church in Zambia* (New York: Africana Publishing 1977), 2–3.

15 Peter Duignan and L. H. Gann, *The United States and Africa: A History* (Cambridge: Cambridge University Press, 1984), 165.

16 David J. Cook, "Church and State in Zambia: the case of the African Methodist Episcopal Church," in *Christianity in Independent Africa*, ed. Edward Fashole-Luke, et al. (London: R. Collings, 1978), 287.

17 See Duignan and Gann, *The United States and Africa*, 248–49.

18 Duignan and Gann, *The United States and Africa*, 288–98.

19 Adrian Hastings, *A History of African Christianity, 1950–1975* (Cambridge: Cambridge University Press, 1979), 135–36.

20 Hastings, *A History of African Christianity*, 148.

21 Richard Pierard, "Religion and the New Right in the 1980s," in *Religion and State: Essays in Honor of Leo Pfeffer*, ed. James E. Wood Jr. (Waco, Tex.: Baylor University Press, 1985), 401.

22 Bill McCloskey, "Fundamentalist and Liberal Differ on South Africa," *Associated Press*, February 5, 1985.

23 Mary McGrory, "Sinking to New Lows," *Washington Post*, August 27, 1985.

24 Paul Gifford, "Prosperity: A New Foreign Element in African Christianity," *Religion* 20 (1990): 374; idem, *The New Crusaders: Christianity and the New Right in Southern Africa* (London: Pluto Press, 1991), 50.

25 All of the Pentecostal and Charismatic denominations listed under Barrett's Protestant and Independent categories were added together to reach these totals. It is important to note that the totals will not include Pentecostal and Charismatic practitioners affiliated with mainline denominations, i.e., Catholics, Methodists, Anglicans, etc. with Pentecostal and charismatic orientations. See Barrett et al., *World Christian Encyclopedia*, 16–18.

26 With respect to the 1970s totals, more than 104,000,000 of the 147,000,000 were in Africa (70%). With respect to the 1995 totals, more than 379,000,000 of the 605,000,000 were in Africa (63%).

27 Patrick Johnstone, *Operation World* (Grand Rapids: Zondervan, 1993), 36.

28 R. Drew Smith, "Missionaries, Church Movements, and the Shifting Religious Significance of the State in Zambia," *Journal of Church and State* 41 (1999): 548–50.

29 William Reno, "Sovereignty and Personal Rule in Zaire," *African Studies Quarterly* 1, no. 3 (1997). http://www.africa.ufl.edu (accessed December 12, 2005).

30 John Dennis, "Landmark Crusade Successfully Ends in Monrovia," http://www.AllAboutLiberia.com (accessed February 25, 2002).

31 "Televangelist's Pal Charles Taylor Again Linked to Al Qaeda Money Laundering," http://www.americanatheists.com (accessed January 2, 2003).

32 "Benin: Building a Message of Hope for Africa," cbnworldreach.org (March 26, 1999), clipping is on file with the author.

33 Ted Olsen, "TBN's Paul Crouch Gets Involved in Politics—Zambian Politics, That Is," *Christianity Today* 45 (April 2001).

34 "Zambian President Takes Action After Churches Criticize Him," *Christianity Today* (online posting, August 8, 2002). http://www.christianitytoday.com.

35 David Barstow, et al., "Nigeria Sent Cash to Lyons Fund," *St. Petersburg Times*, November 25, 1997.

36 Banjo Odutola, "Devaluing a President's Office," *The Village Square,* November 30, 2003.

37 James Adams, "Top TV Evangelist Trumpets a Tyrant," *The New York Times,* August 20, 1995.

38 For example, Jesse Jackson, serving as President Clinton's special liaison to Liberia, was dispatched to Sierra Leone to attempt to soften Sierra Leone's opposition to Taylor's rule (although Sierra Leonian leaders shouted him down and drummed him out of the country for promoting this unpopular position).

Chapter 8

1 Paul Gifford, "Prosperity: A New and Foreign Element in African Christianity," *Religion* 20 (1990): 382–400.

2 Paul Gifford, "Ghana's Charismatic Churches," *Journal of Religion in Africa* 24, no. 3 (1994): 241–65; Paul Gifford, "Some Recent Developments in African Christianity," *African Affairs* 93 (1994): 513–33.

3 Richard Van Dijk, "From Camp to Encompassment: Discourses of Transsubjectivity in the Ghanaian Pentecostal Diaspora," *Journal of Religion in Africa* 27 (1997): 135–60; Rosalind J.Hackett, "Charismatic/Pentecostal Appropriation of Media Technologies in Nigeria and Ghana," *Journal of Religion in Africa* 28, no. 3 (1998): 258–277; Ruth Marshall, "Power in the Name of Jesus," *Review of African Political Economy* 52 (1991): 21–38; and Ruth Marshall, "Pentecostalism in Southern Nigeria: An Overview," in *New*

Dimensions in African Christianity, ed. Paul Gifford (Nairobi: All-African Conference of Churches, 1992), 8–39.

4 Allan Anderson and Gerald J. Pillay, "The Segregated Spirit: The Pentecostals" in *Christianity in South Africa: A Political, Social and Cultural History*, ed. Richard Elphick and Rodney Davenport (Cape Town: David Philip, 1997), 229.

5 Ogbu U. Kalu, *Power, Poverty and Prayer: The Challenges of Poverty and Pluralism in African Christianity, 1960–1996* (Frankfurt am Main: Peter Lang, 2000).

6 Matthews A. Ojo, "The Charismatic Movements in Nigeria Today," *International Bulletin of Missionary Research* 19 no. 3 (1995): 114–18.

7 Karla Poewe, ed., *Charismtic Christianity as a Global Culture* (Columbia: University of South Carolina Press, 1994), xii, 17, 58–66.

8 S. G. Adegboyega, *Short History of the Apostolic Church in Nigeria* (Ibadan: Rosprint Press, 1978); J. D. Y. Peel, *Aladura: A Religious Movement Among the Yoruba* (London: Oxford University Press, 1968); T. N. Turnbull, *What God Hath Wrought* (Leeds: Puritan Press, 1959); H. W. Turner, *History of an African Independent Church* (Oxford: Clarendon, 1967).

9 For more details of this religious awakening, see G. O. M. Tasie, *Christianity in the Niger Delta 1864–1918* (Leiden, E. J. Brill, 1978).

10 Adegboyega, *Short History*, 10–14.

11 Turnbull, *What God Hath Wrought*, 72.

12 J. O. Durojaiye, *Morris Joshua and the Holy Spirit in Nigeria* (Ibadan, n.d.), 14–16, 20–21.

13 Interview with Kola Ejiwumi, Lagos, August 31, 1985.

14 Durojaiye, *Morris Joshua*, 15.

15 Interview with Wilson Badej, Lagos, October 2, 1985. Confirmed by others outside WATC.

16 Franklin Hall, *The Body-Felt Salvation* (Phoenix: Franklin Hall Ministries, 1968), 11–12.

17 Hall, *The Body-Felt Salvation*, 6.

18 Hall, *The Body-Felt Salvation*, 36.

19 Franklin Hall, *Atomic Power with God* (Phoenix: Franklin Hall Deliverance Foundation, 1975), 29–31. See also Franklin Hall, *The Fasting Prayer* (Phoenix: Franklin Hall Ministries, 1976), 94–97.

20 "The Bonfire," tract (Phoenix: Franklin Hall Ministries, n.d.). See also Franklin Hall, "80 Reasons Why We Should Fast," tract (Phoenix: Franklin Hall Ministries, n.d.), 6–7.

21 The healing activities and doctrinal position of William Branham can be found in W. J. Hollenweger, *The Pentecostals* (London: Hendrickson, 1972), 354–57.

22 Bola Akande, "An Issue Paper on False Teachings," paper read at a Scripture Union Training Course in Benin City (July 1977).

23 *Today's Choice*, March 10, 1998, 4–7.

24 *Today's Choice*, March 10, 1998, 4–7. See also Ruthanne Garlock, *Fire in His Bones: The Story of Benson Idahosa* (South Plainfield, NJ: Bridge Publishing, 1981), 103–15.

25 *Today's Choice*, March 10, 1998, 4–7.

26 *Redemption Faith Magazine* 4, no. 23 (1988): 8.

27 Paul Gifford, "Ghana's Charismatic Churches," *Journal of Religion in Africa* 24, no. 3 (1994): 241–65.

28 Interview with Pastor Suleiman Umar, Niamey, Niger Republic, March 1997.

29 *Full Gospel Business Men's Advance* 1, no. 4 (1991): 1–8.

Chapter 9

1 Allan Anderson, "Pentecostals and Apartheid in South Africa During Ninety Years, 1908–1998," Article on file with author, 1998.

2 Charles Villa-Vicencio, *Trapped in Apartheid: A Socio-Theological History of the English-Speaking Churches* (Maryknoll, NY: Orbis Books, 1988), 77.

3 Gustav Gous, "From the Church Struggle to a Struggling Church: A Tale of Three Conferences; Cottesloe, Rustenburg and Cape Town," *Missionalia* 21, no. 3 (1993): 255.

4 Villa-Vicencio, *Trapped in Apartheid*, 19.

5 Other historically English-speaking churches, such as the Anglicans, maintained a largely paternalistic and gradual approach to racial reform through the mid-1970s, despite prodding by black Anglicans and progressive white Anglican clergy. The latter included Michael Scott, who organized a Campaign for Rights and Justice in 1944 that challenged racist practices in both church and society, and Trevor Huddleston who, among other things, published an article condemning the political gradualism of churches on race issues.

6 Gous, "From the Church Struggle," 258.

7 Gous, "From the Church Struggle," 260, 263.

8 Rehana Rossouw, "Adventists Vote for Segregation," *Weekly Mail & Guardian*, October 25, 1996.

9 "NGK Denounced Apartheid at Last," *Electronic Mail and Guardian*, October 14, 1998.

10 John De Gruchy, *The Church Struggle in South Africa* (Grand Rapids: Eerdmans, 1979, 1986), 100.

11 Peter Lodberg, "Apartheid as a Church-Dividing Ethical Issue," *The Ecumenical Review* 48 (1996): 73.

12 Nico Horn, "Crossing Racial Borders in Southern Africa: A Lesson From History," *Cyberjournal for Pentecostal Research*, June 1991, 4 (copy on file).

13 Horn, "Crossing Racial Borders," 4.

14 Peter Watt, *From Africa's Soil: The Story of the Assembles of God in Southern Africa* (Cape Town: Struik Christian Books, 1992), 20–21; Vinson Synan, The Origins of the Pentecostal Movement" 1996. http://www.oru.edu/university/library/holyspirit/pentorg.1.html#origins, (accessed December 12, 2005); and Malcolm Harris, "Coastal Assemblies of God . . . Our Roots," http://www.caog.org.za/hist.asp.

15 Watt, *From Africa's Soil*, 23, 27.

16 "Apartheid Divisions to be Buried as Church Becomes One," *Pretoria News*, October 6, 1997, 5.

17 Allan Anderson and Gerald Pillay, "The Segregated Spirit: The Pentecostals," in *Christianity in South Africa*, ed. Elphick and Davenport, 235.

18 Watt, *From Africa's Soil*, 199.

19 Leroy Fitts, *Lott Carey: First Black Missionary to Africa* (Valley Forge: Judson Press, 1978), 130–31.

20 Terry Rae, "Reconciliation Between Baptists in South Africa," paper presented at the Baptist World Alliance meeting, Seoul, Korea, 2004.

21 Rae, "Reconciliation Between Baptists."
22 "It Takes Courage to Apologise," *Pretoria News,* October 7, 1997, 13.
23 J. Nico Horn, "After Apartheid: Reflections on Church Mission in the Changing Social and Political Context of South Africa," *Transformation* 11, no. 1 (1994): 25.
24 Moss Ntlha, Evangelical Alliance of South Africa, Testimony Before the Truth and Reconciliation Commission, East London, South Africa, November 18, 1999.
25 Ntlha, Evangelical Alliance, 1999.
26 Ray McCauley, Rhema Ministries, Testimony Before the Truth and Reconciliation Commission, East London, South Africa, November 18, 1999.
27 Isak Burger, *Apostolic Faith Mission*, Testimony Before the Truth and Reconciliation Commission, East London, South Africa, November 19, 1999.
28 Dirkie J. Smit, "The Truth and Reconcialition Commission: Tentative Religious and Theological Perspectives," *Journal of Theology for Southern Africa* 90 (1995): 13.
29 Khela Shubane and Colin Reddy, "BEE is changing SA's business environment," *Business Report* (South Africa: Business Map Foundation, 2005), 3–4. (The exchange rate between the South African rand and the U.S. dollar is approximately six rand to the dollar, as of mid-2005).
30 Burger, *Apostolic Faith Mission*, Testimony.
31 Allan Anderson, "Pentecostals and Apartheid in South Africa during Ninety Years 1908–1998," paper on file with author, 1998, 4.
32 Noel Bruyns, "South African Church Fails to Bridge Racial Divide," *Presbyterian News Service*, November 20, 1996. http://www.pcusa.org/pcnews/oldnews/1996/96471.htm, (accessed December 12, 2005).
33 "Tears Prevail as Two Churches Reconcile," *Pretoria News*, October 10, 1997, 2.
34 "Church to Unite After Split during Apartheid," *The Citizen*, October 7, 1997, 11.
35 Rae, "Reconciliation Between Baptists."
36 Rae, "Reconciliation Between Baptists."
37 "Church to Unite After Split During Apartheid," *The Citizen*, October 7, 1997, 11.
38 Nico Horn, "Crossing Racial Borders in Southern Africa: A Lesson from History," paper on file with author, 1991, 15–16.
39 This has been the case with the Dutch Reformed Church as well, which has still not reunited with the various black and colored Reformed churches that comprise the Uniting Reformed Church.
40 Anthony O. Balcomb, "Left, Right and Centre: Evangelicals and the Struggle for Liberation in South Africa," *Journal of Theology for Southern Africa* 118 (2004): 153.
41 Penny Sukrhaj, "Fracture in the Rapture at Giant Fast-Food Church," *Sowetan*, October 1, 2001, 17; and Vusi Mona, "Rainbow Religion of Rhema," *City Press*, March 14, 1999, 13.
42 McCauley, Rhema Ministries, Testimony.
43 "South Africa: Truth-Telling on Trial," *Christianity Today*, February 9, 1998, 18.
44 Southern African Catholic Bishops Conference, March 21, 2003.
45 South African Council of Churches, Triennial National Conference at the Liban Conference Centre, Woodmead, Johannesburg, August 14–17, 2001.

46 Quoted in Phiroshaw Camay and Anne J. Gordon, *Land Restitution and Redistribution: Providing Opportunities for Broad-based Rural Development South Africa*, Civil Society and Governance Case Study No. 2, The Cooperative for Research and Education, 2000, 6.

47 Quoted in Werner Vogt, "Hart erkämpften Frieden nicht stören," *St. Galler Tagblatt*, November 12, 2002.

48 SAPA and Christelle Terreblanche, "State Not Backing Tutu Support for Lawsuits," *Cape Times*, February 2, 2004, 1; and press release, *Jubilee South Africa*, February 2, 2004.

49 Anthony Balcomb, "Evangelicals and Democracy in South Africa," *Journal of Theology for Southern Africa* (March 2001): 10.

50 Allan Anderson, "Pentecostals and Apartheid in South Africa During Ninety Years, 1908–1998," paper on file with author, 12

51 Pat Sidley, "The Silent Majority Raises its Voice," *Weekly Mail and Guardian*, June 9, 1995.

52 "Christians Who Have Not Changed Yet," *Challenge Magazine* (Johannesburg: Contextual Publications, October/November 1996), 9.

53 "Christians Who Have Not Changed Yet," 9.

54 Mike Atkins, "New Equity Bill Contradicts God's Law," *Weekly Mail and Guardian,* November 5, 1999.

55 Moss Ntlha, meeting with author, Khotso House, Johannesburg, May 24, 2005.

56 Research Institute on Christianity in South Africa, *Faith Communities and Apartheid: A Report Prepared for the Truth and Reconciliation Commission*, March 1998, 3 (parentheses mine).

Chapter 10

1 Gayraud S. Wilmore has accurately observed that

> Any system of Christian theology or missiology that sincerely seeks to understand and appreciate the insights and sensibilities of black people, who have persevered and flourished despite centuries of institutional racism as the hands of their white brothers and sisters, must be helped, by a fundamental redirection of content and methodology, to tap into a surprising funds of common sense knowledge, pragmatic spiritual, and "street smarts" related to an indigenous religion that will enlighten and enhance the mainline of Euro-American Christianity and the theological academy on both sides of the Atlantic.

See the foreword (xii) in *Mission is Crossing Frontiers: Essays in Honour of Bongani A. Maziuiko* (South Africa: Cluster Publications, 2003).

2 See Jonathan J. Bonk, "Ecclesiastical Cartography and the Invisible Continent," *International Bulletin of Missionary Research* 28, no. 4 (2004): 158.

3 David Bosch in *Transforming Mission: Paradigm Shifts in Theology of Mission* (Maryknoll, NY: Orbis, 1995) has noted that from the perspective of mission, issues such as the official attitude of the church related to complicity of the church in colonialism, the subjugation and exploitation of other races, the enslavement of non-Christians, the paternalism and imperialism endemic in Western Christians, the elitism of the official church over against marginalized persons, and other issues seem to raise questions about the ability of U.S. churches to respond faithfully to the challenge of mutual respect and equality toward churches in Africa.

4 "That All May Have Life in Fullness" was the theme of the recent 24th General Council of the World Alliance of Reformed Churches in Accra, Ghana,

August 2004. The gathering of Reformed church leaders from around the world in Ghana and the deliberate selection of this theme were intended to draw attention not only to the challenges facing churches in Africa, but also to the process of covenanting for justice.

5 The term *missio Dei*, which first became popular following the Willingen Conference of the International Missionary Council (1952), has since then absorbed several meanings held together by the central belief of God's concern and activity for the whole world. As African Methodist Episcopalians, Lutherans, Presbyterians, Methodists, and most mainline Christian denominations have declared in their faith statements, "Mission has its origin in the heart of God." This affirmation recognizes that mission belongs to God and thus distinguishes this current mission paradigm from that of previous periods.

6 Bosch, *Transforming Mission*, 274.

7 Bosch, *Transforming Mission*, 279.

8 Bosch, *Transforming Mission*, 299.

9 It is worth noting that as more African historians, missiologists, theologians, and others engage in the life and works of the western academy, their writings are broadening and deepening existing knowledge related to the influence and impact of Christian missions. As expected, the literature is diverse, overall summations of the positive influence and impact of western mission on Africa is mixed, and critique is present in the various forms of Christianity—(1) Christianity as transplanted from Europe and North America, (2) Christianity as indigenous to Africa, and (3) independent Christian churches. Illustrative representatives of this diversity include Basile Akiele and Lamin Sanneh. While Akiele has written about the attributes of Simon Kimbangu, founder of the Kimbanguist Church, and how the precedents of this indigenous church were spurred by missionaries who burned at the stake the African prophetess Kimpa Vita and her son, Lamin Sanneh has suggested that the missionary movement contributed not only the communications of the Christian gospel that has transformed lives, but also the very process of western education that has enabled Africa to participate in global conversations on many levels. The writings of Kwame Bediako have particularly called attention to Africa playing a significant role in the resurgence of the Christian faith worldwide.

10 A great deal of available data and commentary discusses the meaning and purpose of this act initiated by the Presbyterian Church of East Africa. The church declared a moratorium to allow member churches to pause and reassess the value and nature of its relationship with churches overseas. The Board of Social Responsibility, one of the most positive outcomes, represents the church's commitment to ministering to the needy throughout East Africa in a variety of ways including the following: community education for sustainable development and progress; relief, rehabilitation, and resettlement for displaced persons; food production; water conservation; improved health care; care for the environment; small scale enterprises, and special concern programs for youth, women, and health education. Although Africans (sometimes in collaboration with missionaries sponsored by U.S. ecclesiological bodies) established and developed new congregations and ministries, the use of Euro-American Protestant liturgies, unfortunately, often prevails.

11 The dangers of this narrow perspective include the preoccupation of the church with its own well-being and the failure to recognize that the church,

wherever it exists, does so only that it might be God's instrument for the salvation of the world.

12 Interesting and worth noting are the writings of womanist theologians in both Africa and the United States that articulate the need to be concerned with not only surviving but flourishing.

13 The following resources provide invaluable insight into the nature of this challenge: Marthinus L. Daneel, ed., *African Christian Outreach: African Initiated Churches,* vol. 1 (South Africa: Southern African Missiological Society, 2001); Audrey R. Chapman and Bernard Spong, eds., *Religion and Reconciliation in South Africa: Voices of Religious Leaders* (South Africa: Cluster Publications, 2003); Clarence Lusane, *Race in the Global Era: African Americans at the Millennium* (Boston: South End Press, 1997); and Edward Blyden, *Christianity, Islam, and the Negro Race* (Baltimore: Black Classic Press, 1994). The latter, scholar Edward Wilmot Blyden (1832–1912), who served as a U.S. missionary for many years in Africa, published the second edition of this book in 1888 as a direct response to the global race problem.

14 Particularly in the metropolitan urban areas of the United States, an increasingly large number of African Christian refugee and immigrants communities, such as the Sudanese, Sierre Leonians, and Liberians, are very much affected by the concepts of sending and receiving related to Christian mission as they seek to respond to the overwhelming needs facing children, youth, adults, and families. For insight into how Sudanese in the Dallas area have impacted diverse congregations of that city, see Nita Thomason, "Beauty from Ashes," *Prism: America's Alternative Evangelical Voice* 5, no. 5 (2002): 18–21.

15 Scott M. Thomas is correct in his acknowledgment of development as an important aspect of the global resurgence of religion since 2001 and of the way that culture, religion and spirituality have become part of the policy discourse on the meaning of development. "However it be defined," writes Thomas quoting Denis Goulet," development is a normative experience; it involves, for those who propose it as for those to whom it is proposed, central value choices about the meaning of life." See "Faith and Foreign Aid: How the World Bank Got Religion, and Why it Matters," *The Brandywine Review of Faith and International Affairs* 2, no. 2 (2004): 21.

16 See Jehu J. Hanciles, "Missionaries and Revolutionaries: Elements of Transformation in the Emergence of Modern African Christianity," *International Bulletin of Missionary Research* 28, no. 4 (2004): 150. While he refers to a British missionary, ample evidence suggests that a number of U.S. missionaries were involved in the true transformation of Africa, such as Edward Wilmot Blyden, Henry McNeil Turner, and Maria Fearing and that the William Shepherd family also exemplified the same missional outcomes in terms of engaging in Christian mission in Africa's liberation.

17 Lamin Sanneh, in *Whose Religion is Christianity? The Gospel Beyond the West* (Grand Rapids: Eerdmans, 2003) observes that African Christianity offers fresh insight for theological reflection, but for U.S. Christians to posture themselves to receive these new insights, they must get over western colonial guilt.

18 Utilizing spiritual discernment, "There were missionaries who were racial bigots and colonial bullies, but there were also others who were excellent pastors, counselors and teachers," writes J. N. K. Mugambi in *Christian Theology and Social Reconstruction* (Nairobi: Acton Publishers, 2003), 86.

19 Walter Williams, *Black Americans and the Evangelization of Africa, 1877–1900* (Madison: University of Wisconsin Press, 1982) provides an excellent historical critique of key missionaries and mission advocates their engagement in Christian missions during the most active historical involvement of Black churches in Africa.

20 For instance, when serving as a missionary in the Sudan (North Africa, 1979–1981), I did so as a Christian seconded to the Sudan Council of Churches. Four years later, my husband and I were seconded to work three years with the Presbyterian Church of the Cameroon. In both cases, our assignments, discipline, and program support came from the church in Africa. The home church (denomination) was responsible for housing, transportation, language study, furlough and medical support.

21 In "A Christian Response to the Situation in the Sudan," Caroline Cox of the Lutheran Church, who has served in the Sudan, describes her work as such: "CSI had adopted a twofold strategy in response to slavery: documenting and reporting the evidence in order to try to prevail on the international community to make the NIF regime open all areas to human rights monitors, to identify and free slaves; and, in the meantime, helping the African communities to redeem their people who are enslaved. We have helped to make possible the redemption of over 400 slaves; but we estimate that there are tens of thousands of Africans still in slavery" (undated document, shared in June 1997). In response to the excuses that come from churches in the West who speak of "donor fatigue" and "compassion fatigue," with a sense of righteous indignation, she continues, "First, we in the West owe a debt of gratitude to the people of Sudan, who are holding a front-line against the spread of a brand of fundamentalist totalitarian and terrorist Islam for the rest of us. They are also holding a front-line of Christianity for those of us who are Christians. They are paying the highest price in holding this front-line: over 1.5 million died and over 5 million driven from their homes. We should be profoundly grateful and massively supportive; the concept of 'donor fatigue' is a travesty, an insult and shameful."

22 As a result of a Ford foundation grant (1997) awarded to the Interdenominational Theological Center, under the leadership of Dr. Ndugu T'Ofori-Atta, founder and director of the Religious Heritage of the African World (RHAW), a detailed research-action-advocacy program and report was developed entitled, "The African American Church Presence in Africa," which stands as a model of mission advocacy and education. During 1998, RHAW worked in collaboration with other organizations and agencies to produce the National Summit on Africa, an unprecedented nationwide effort to create a shared policy agenda to guide U.S. relations with the countries of Africa, educate the American public about Africa, and broaden and strengthen the network of Africa's supporters in the United States.

23 Numerous African scholars and writers have assisted us in understanding that for Christian mission to be communicated effectively in the various contexts of Africa, it cannot be viewed as generically shaped and formulated; more attention must be given to the context of mission as well as the role and function of the contextualizers. For this contextualization, see Mercy Amba Oduyoye, *Hearing and Knowing: Theological Reflections on Christian in Africa* (Maryknoll, NY: Orbis Books, 1986); Kwame Bediako, *Christianity in Africa: The Renewal of a Non-Western Religion* (Maryknoll, NY: Orbis Books, 1995); Michael C. Kirwen, *The Missionary and the Diviner* (Maryknoll, NY: Orbis Books, 1987); Robert J. Schreiter, ed., *Mission in the*

Third Millennium (Maryknoll, NY: Orbis Books, 2001); William Dyrness, *Learning About Theology From the Third World* (Grand Rapids: Zondervan, 1990); Priscilla Pope-Levison and John R. Levison, *Jesus in Global Contexts* (Louisville: Westminster/John Knox, 1992); Gerald West, *Biblical Hermeneutics of Liberation: Modes of Reading the Bible in the South African Context* (Pietermaritzberg, South Africa: Cluster, 1991); Jean-Marc Ela, *My Faith as an African* (Maryknoll, NY: Orbis Books, 1988); Mercy Amba Oduyoye, *Daughters of Anowa: African Women and Patriarchy* (Maryknoll, NY: Orbis Books, 1995), Peter Paris, *The Spirituality of African Peoples* (Minneapolis: Fortress, 1995); and Boesak, *Farewell to Innocence*.

24 Although Sanneh's *Whose Religion is Christianity*, Philip Jenkins's *The Next Christendom: The Coming of Global Christianity* (New York: Oxford University Press, 2002), and Bediako's *Christianity in Africa* are helpful in understanding this reality from a macro perspective, the following provide significant insights from various contextual perspectives: Mercy Amba Oduyoye, "Three Cardinal Issues of Mission in Africa," in *Mission in the Third Millennium*, ed. Robert J. Schreiter (Maryknoll, NY: Orbis Books, 2000); and Lamin Sanneh, *Translating the Message: The Missionary Impact on Culture* (Maryknoll, NY: Orbis Books, 1989).

25 The Acholi Religious Leaders Peace Initiative (1999), sponsored by the Episcopal church, consist of Muslims and Christians in northern Uganda who have come together in the face of a thirteen year crisis that has resulted in the death, injury, rape, and mutilation of children by the Lord Resistance Army (LRA). As Christians and Muslims, they have made a threefold commitment to peace-building and reconciliation relevant to this essay: (1) an appeal to partners in mission to come to the assistance of the suffering people of Uganda by active participation in peace building, rehabilitation, resettlement, and post-war reconstruction programs; (2) an appeal to the government of the United States to use its offices to bring pressure to bear on the government of the Sudan in order to facilitate the immediate and unconditional release of the abducted children; and (3) an appeal to the U.S. government to exert pressure on the governments of Uganda and Sudan to resolve their conflicts through dialogue and diplomatic means.

26 The Rev. Dr. Samuel Kobia, the first African appointed as General Secretary of the World Council of Churches, is offered as an example. The World Council of Churches, according to the *Ecumenical Courier* 64, no. 1 (2004): 1, has recently engaged in a process of re-visioning and reorganizing its presence in the United States, accompanied by the U.S. Conference for the WCC. The United States is the focus of the 2004 "Decade to Overcome Violence," and at the October 5–6, 2004, meeting in Atlanta, Ga., Dr. Kobia encouraged churches worldwide to use spiritual discernment in ending violence and to remember the membership of churches worldwide as a global Christian fellowship.

27 Persons in leadership positions who can help foster a new paradigm of mission partnership must function well cross-culturally and value intercultural studies. The role that theological education has made in encouraging such partnerships in the life of the Interdenominational Theological Center (Atlanta, GA) for more than forty years is chronicled in several volumes of the *Journal of the Interdenominational Theological Center* (*JITC*). The African-centered orientation of the *JITC* and other publications of the ITC community is reflected in issues of the *JITC* such as *Stories About Ethiopia: An African Holy Land* (1998); *Reflections on the All African Conference of Church*

(1998); and the book *African Roots: Toward An Afrocentric Christian Witness* (1994). The emphasis continues through the life and work of members of the faculty who are African-centered missiologists, such as Josephus Cone, Ndugu G.B. T'Ofori-Atta, Darius L. Swann, Tumani Mutassa Nyajeka, Burgess Carr, and the author. The advocacy and promotion of projects involving seminarians and church leaders in global mission travel seminars throughout Africa, the African Diaspora (especially in the Caribbean, Brazil, and India), and the emphasis on African scholars as valued members of the faculty help emphasize the importance of global partnerships and collaborations and help pass this priority on to a new generation of scholars, pastors, mission leaders, and Christian educators.

28 See the *Journal of the Reformed World: Mission, Justice Covenant* 54, no. 1 (2004) for a more indepth discussion and critique on what it means for the various regions of Africa to unite in mission. The theme of the 24th General Council of the World Alliance of Reformed Churches that met in Ghana in an effort to focus on the contexts, concerns and challenges of the churches in Africa was derived from the verse, "That All May Have Life In Fullness."

Chapter 11

1 Allister Sparks, *Beyond the Miracle: Inside the New South Africa* (Johannesburg and Cape Town: Jonathan Ball Publishers, 2003), 3–4.

2 Sampie Terrèblanche, *A History of Inequality in South Africa* (Pietermaritzburg: University of Natal Press, 2002), 374, 383, 412.

3 Data from Statistics South Africa, *1999 Bulletin of Statistics* cited in Hein Marais, *South Africa Limits to Change: the Political Economy of Transition* (Cape Town: University of Cape Town Press, 2001), 175.

4 Cornel West, "Black Theology and Human Identity," in *Black Faith and Public Talk*, ed. Dwight Hopkins (New York: Orbis Books, 1999), 18.

5 Max Stackhouse, "Public Theology and Ethical Judgment," in *Theology Today* 54 (1996): 165, 167.

6 Linell Cady, "The Task of Public Theology," in *The Legacy of HR Niebuhr* (Minneapolis: Fortress Press, 1991), 119.

7 Robert Benne, *The Paradoxical Vision: A Public Theology for the Twenty-First Century* (Minneapolis: Fortress Press 1995), 4.

8 John DeGruchy, "From Political to Public Theologies: the Role of Theology in Public Life in South Africa," in *Public Theology for the 21st Century: Essays in Honour of Duncan B. Forrester*, ed. W. F. Storrar and A. R. Morton (London: T&T Clark, 2004), 45–46.

9 Ernst Conradie, "How Should a Public Way of Doing Theology Be Approached?" *Scriptura* 46 (1997): 32–38.

10 David Tracy, *The Analogical Imagination: Christian Theology and the Culture of Pluralism* (London: SCM Press, 1981), 3, 5. For examples of this engagement of South African theologians with David Tracy, see amongst others, B. Lategan, "Taking the Third Public Seriously," in *Religion and the Reconstruction of Society. Papers from the founding congress of the South African Academy of Religion*, ed. John DeGruchy et al. (Pretoria: University of Pretoria Press, 1995), 217–30; and Nico Koopman, "Theology and the Fulfillment of Social and Economic Rights: Some Theoretical Considerations," in *Enforcement of Social and Economic Rights*, ed. Andre van der Watt (Stellenbosch: Sunmedia, 2005).

11 Tracy, *Analogical Imagination*, 21.

12 Dirkie Smit, "Oor die unieke openbare rol van die kerk" [On the unique public role of the church]. *Tydskrif vir Geesteswetenskappe* 36, no. 3 (1996): 190–98.

13 For South African engagements with Gustafson's discourses, see, amongst others, D. E. De Villiers and D. J. Smit, "Met watter gesag sê U hierdie dinge?" *Opmerkings oor kerklike dokumente oor die openbare lewe, Skrif en Kerk* 16, no. 1 (1995): 39–56; and Nico Koopman, "Freedom of Religion and the Prophetic Role of the Church," *NGTT*, 43, no. 1, 2 (2002): 237–47.

14 James Gustafson, "An Analysis of Church and Society: Social Ethical Writings," *Ecumenical Review* (1988), 267–78; idem, *Varieties of Moral Discourse: Prophetic, Narrative, Ethical and Policy* (Grand Rapids: The Stob Lectures of Calvin College and Seminary, 1988).

15 For an extensive discussion of the notion that God is in a special way the God of the poor, see Nico Koopman, ". . . In a Special Way the God of the Poor, the Destitute and the Wronged: A Basic and Neglected Conviction of (Reformed) Theology?" in *350 Years Reformed: 1652–2002*, ed. P. Coertzen (Bloemfontein: CLF, 2002), 252–60.

16 James Cone, "Looking Back, Going Forward, Black Theology as Public Theology," in *Public Faith and Black Talk: Critical Essays on James H. Cone's Black Theology and Black Power*, ed. Dwight N. Hopkins (Maryknoll, NY: Orbis, 1999), 252, 255, 257.

17 Qtd. in C. Rowland, "Epilogue: the Future of Liberation Theology," in *The Cambridge Companion to Liberation Theology*, ed. C. Rowland (Cambridge: Cambridge University Press, 1999), 250–51.

18 Cornel West, *Prophesy Deliverance! An Afro-American Revolutionary Christianity* (Louisville: Westminster/John Knox, 1982; rpt. 2002), 111–13.

19 Tracy, *Analogical Imagination*, 56–59.

20 For an extensive discussion of two opposing views regarding the contribution of religion and theology to ethical challenges, see Nico Koopman, "The Role of Tradition in Moral Decisionmaking and Moral Consensus," *NGTT* 45 (2004): 838–48. In this article I discuss the so-called liberal position of Dutch scholar Harry Kuitert who reckons that religion and theology do not contribute to the contents of morality but that it merely serves as protector, feeder, and sustainer of morality and as motivator for morally good living. I bring this position in dialogue with the so-called post-liberal position of Stanley Hauerwas, who reckons that religion and theology fulfill a crucial role with regard to the contents of morality since morality is in essence agent, narrative, and community-dependent.

21 In my doctoral dissertation on the post-liberal ethics of Hauerwas and the liberal approach to ethics of the Dutch theologian Harry Kuitert, I identified the various central features in Hauerwas's ethics. In his earlier works he focused on the moral agent who is constituted by rationality, emotions, tendencies, inclinations, vision, virtues, and character. In a next phase of his work, he is able to describe the moral agent in less philosophical and technical language through the emphasis on the notion of narrative. It is the Christian narrative of God's work in Israel, Jesus Christ, and the church that form people into people of virtue, character, and integrity. The next phase is that of the Christian community, namely, the church in which this formation and transformation takes place. Nigel Biggar reckons that we might have to use the latest development in Hauerwas's thinking, specifically with regard to the public role of churches, namely, that he now, in accordance

with Oliver O'Donovan, leaves more room for the positive potential of the idea of a Christendom. See Nigel Biggar, "Is Stanley Hauerwas Sectarian?" in *Faithfulness and Fortitude. In Conversation with the Theological Ethics of Stanley Hauerwas*, ed. T. Nation and S. Wells (Edinburgh: T&T Clark, 2000), 160.

22 Stanley Hauerwas, *The Peaceable Kingdom* (Notre Dame: University of Notre Dame Press, 1983), 99.

23 Hauerwas, *Peaceable Kingdom*, 99.

24 James Gustafson argues that Hauerwas's work "ensures a clear identity which frees persons from ambiguity and uncertainty, but it isolates Christianity from taking seriously the wider world of science and culture and limits the participation of Christians in the ambiguities of moral and social life in the patterns of interdependence in the world" ("The Sectarian Temptation: Reflections on Theology, the Church and the University," *Catholic Theological Society* 40, [1985]: 93). The South African theologian Neville Richardson also reckons that Hauerwas runs the risk of emphasizing the argument in favour of the unique nature of the church to such an extent that an inadequate response to issues of social justice is given ("Community in Christian Ethics and African Culture," *Scriptura* 62 [1997]: 373–85).

25 The question for Hauerwas is not whether the church has a public role, but rather how it should fulfill this role (Stanley Hauerwas, "Will the Real Sectarian Theology Stand Up?" *Theology Today* 44, no. 1 [1987]: 87).

26 Biggar, "Is Stanely Hauerwas Sectarian?" 144.

27 See in this regard H. Hendriks, "The Future of the Church, the Church of the Future," unpublished inaugural lecture, University of Stellenbosch, 2004. This trend of growth in religiosity is not limited to South Africa. Peter Berger has replaced his secularization thesis with a desecularization thesis. After arguing since the sixties of the previous century that secularization will spread all over the world and that religion will be increasingly marginalized, he now observes growth of religiosity in all parts of the world, especially in South America, Africa, and Asia. Although Western Europe is highly secularized, he thinks that religion survives in non-institutional forms in some of the Western European regions. See P. Berger, ed., *The Desecularization of the World: Resurgent Religion and World Politics* (Grand Rapids: Eerdmans, 1999), 1–18.

28 Dirkie Smit, "Oor die kerk as unieke samelewingsverband [On the Church as Unique Social Institution]," *Tydskrif vir Geesteswetenskappe* 36, no. 2 (1996): 119–29.

29 It should be noted that Hauerwas does not offer a completed ecclesiology or sacramentology. In fact, many commentators on his work, like Robert Jenson, appeal for a more systematic theological outline of his position. Hauerwas recognizes the importance of dogma, but is cautious about the danger that an overarching system might become more important to theology than the dogma itself. See Stanley Hauerwas, *Wilderness Wanderings* (Boulder: Westview, 1997), 188–99. D. Stephen Long states that although Hauerwas has not offered sustained reflection on the dogmatic tradition, all of his works presuppose such dogma. See D. Stephen Long, *The Goodness of God: Theology, the Church and Social Order* (Grand Rapids: Brazos Press, 2001), 101. My purpose in this paper is not to enter this debate but to investigate Hauerwas's identification of the public nature of these church practices.

30 Stanley Hauerwas, *Christian Existence Today: Essays on Church, World and Living in Between* (Durham: Labyrinth Press, 1988), 124.

31 Stanley Hauerwas and William Willimon, *Resident Aliens: Life in the Christian Colony* (Nashville, Abingdon, 1989), 46

32 Hauerwas, *Peaceable Kingdom*, 108.

33 Hauerwas, *Christian Existence Today*, 121. This emphasis on the presence of God is central in Hauerwas's thinking. It is God who is redeeming the world (cf. *After Christendom. How the Church is to Behave if Freedom, Justice and a Christian Nation are Bad Ideas* [Nashville: Abingdon, 1991], 31, 166 n.2); also Stanley Hauerwas and William Willimon, "Embarrassed by God's Presence," *Christian Century* 102, no. 4 (1985): 98–100.

34 Hauerwas, *Peaceable Kingdom*, 108.

35 Hauerwas, *Christian Existence Today*, 185.

36 Hauerwas, *Peaceable Kingdom*, 109.

37 Stanley Hauerwas, *A Community of Character: Toward a Constructive Christian Social Ethic* (Notre Dame: University of Notre Dame Press, 1981), 190–91.

38 Stanley Hauerwas and William Willimon, *The Truth About God: The Ten Commandments in Christian Life* (Nashville: Abingdon, 1998), 19–20.

39 See Allen Boesak and Charles Villa-Vicencio, *When Prayer Makes News: Call for an End to Unjust Rule* (Philadelphia: Westminster, 1986) for a theological discussion on the call for prayer for the fall of the apartheid government.

40 L. Mudge, *The Church as Moral Community: Ecclesiology and Ethics in Ecumenical Debate* (Geneva: WCC Publications, 1998), 151.

41 U.S. theologian Peter Paris, who also explores the potential of moral categories like virtues and character for public life, articulates these lessons as follows: "In my judgment, one of the principal achievements of the black theology movement was its systematic explication of the theology of the black churches and is success in gaining legitimation for it in the curricula of theological education . . . its most decisive impact on the practical life of the churches occurred not in this country, but in South Africa . . . black theology enabled black and so-called colored South African theologians to construct a contextual theology with which to proclaim a prophetic message of liberation within the context of Christian devotion, biblical exegesis, and courageous action to overthrow a racist constitution" ("Comparing the Public Theologies of James H Cone and Martin Luther King, Jr.," in *Black Faith and Public Talk*, ed. Hopkins, 229).

Conclusion

1 Certainly, Sudan and its situation has received one of the broader American church responses in the last decade, with black and white Evangelicals and mainline Protestants engaging in activism, sometimes separately, sometimes jointly. On the matter of AIDS in Africa, a cadre of African American churches have grown more vocal, especially churches connected with a largely black church based advocacy group called "Balm in Gilead." On the matter of trans-Atlantic theological dialogue, initiatives that facilitated dialogue on social urgencies within the current African context include a Ford Foundation funded initiative headed by Peter Paris at Princeton Theological Seminary that has convened scholars in the United States, Africa, and the Caribbean for scholarly research and dialogue on black poverty in the three contexts.

About the Contributors

STEPHEN W. ANGELL is the Geraldine C. Leatherock Professor of Quaker Studies at the Earlham School of Religion. He has coedited *Social Protest Thought in the AME Church* (2000) with Anthony B. Pinn, and he is author of *Bishop Henry McNeal Turner and African-American Religion in the South* (1992).

LEWIS V. BALDWIN is a professor in the department of religious studies at Vanderbilt University, Nashville, Tennessee. He is the author of numerous articles on various aspects of African and African-American experiences. His books include *There is a Balm in Gilead: The Cultural Roots of Martin Luther King, Jr.* (1991) and *Toward the Beloved Community: Martin Luther King, Jr. and South Africa* (1995).

MARSHA SNULLIGAN HANEY is associate professor of missiology and religions of the world at the Interdenominational Theological Center, Atlanta, Georgia and director of the Urban Theological Institute. She has traveled the world extensively and is the author of various writings including *Islam and Protestant African-American Churches: Responses and Challenges to Religious Pluralism* (1999).

DWIGHT N. HOPKINS is professor of theology at the University of Chicago Divinity School. His publications include *Being Human: Race, Culture, and Religion* (2005); *Heart and Head: Black Theology Past, Present, and Future* (2003); *Down, Up & Over: Slave Religion and Black Theology* (1999); *Introducing Black Theology of Liberation* (1999); and *Shoes That Fit Our Feet: Sources for a Constructive Black Theology* (1993). He edited *Black Faith & Public Talk: Critical Essays on James H. Cone's Black Theology & Black Power* (1999) and coedited *Global Voices for Gender Justice* (2001).

MARK HULSETHER is associate professor of religious studies and American studies at the University of Tennessee. Recent publications include "Religion and Culture," in *Routledge Companion to the Study of Religion*, ed. John Hinnells (NY: Routledge, 2005) and "Religion and Radical Democracy Since the 1960s," *American Quarterly* (March 2005).

NICO KOOPMAN is associate professor and chair of the department of systematic theology and ecclesiology, as well as director of the Beyers Naude Centre for Public Theology, at the University of Stellenbosch in South Africa. He has authored various articles and chapters in books and is a regular speaker at national and international conferences. A book that he coauthored with Robert Vosloo, titled *Die ligtheid van die lig: Morele orientasie in 'n postmoderne tyd* [*The Lightness of the Light: Moral Orientation in a Postmodern Time*], has won the Andrew Murray Prize for theological literature.

PATRICK MAZZEO was a group leader and staff member at Operation Crossroads Africa from 1980 to 1987. His work involved both the volunteer Africa program and the reverse exchange short term visitor programs for African professionals. He has M.A. degrees in sociology and anthropology from the University of Oregon.

MATTHEWS A. OJO earned his Ph.D. in theology from the University of London, England in 1986. His specialization is in church history, and his research interest centers on the dynamics of the Pentecostal and Charismatic movements in contemporary Africa. He is presently a professor and head of the department of religious studies, Obafemi Awolowo University, Ile-Ife, Nigeria. His most recent publication is *The End-Time Army: Charismatic Movements In Modern Nigeria* (Laurenceville, NJ: Africa World Press, forthcoming).

LUTINIKO LANDU MIGUEL PEDRO is a Ph.D. student in missiology at the University of Pretoria, South Africa, having received an M.A. in missiology from the Centre Universitaire de Missiologie in Kinshasa. He is from Angola and is an ordained Mennonite pastor who served as general secretary of the Inter-Mennonite Conference in Angola (2003–2004).

SANDRA J. SARKELA is associate professor and interim director of Graduate Studies in the Communication Department at the University of Memphis. Her research and teaching interests focus on the rhetoric of American social movements. She has a Ph.D. in communication studies from the University of Massachusetts.

R. DREW SMITH is scholar-in-residence at the Leadership Center at Morehouse College where he directs a number of projects on religion and public life. He edited *New Day Begun: African-American Churches and Civic Culture in Post-Civil Rights America* (2003); *Long March Ahead: African-American Churches and Public Policy in Post-Civil Rights America* (2004); and coedited with Fredrick C. Harris, *Black Churches and Local Politics: Clergy Influence, Organizational Partnerships, and Civic Empowerment* (2005).

Index